# Emergency in Transit

CRITICAL REFUGEE STUDIES

Edited by the Critical Refugee Studies Collective

1. *In Camps: Vietnamese Refugees, Asylum Seekers, and Repatriates*, by Jana K. Lipman

2. *Networked Refugees: Palestinian Reciprocity and Remittances in the Digital Age*, by Nadya Hajj

3. *Departures: An Introduction to Critical Refugee Studies*, by Yến Lê Espiritu, Lan Duong, Ma Vang, Victor Bascara, Khatharya Um, Lila Sharif, and Nigel Hatton

4. *Suspended Lives: Navigating Everyday Violence in the US Asylum System*, by Bridget M. Haas

5. *Lived Refuge: Gratitude, Resentment, Resilience*, by Vinh Nguyen

6. *Almost Futures: Time, Dispossession, and the Haunting of Vietnamese Refugees*, by Nguyễn-võ Thu-hương

7. *Emergency in Transit: Witnessing Migration in the Colonial Present*, by Eleanor Paynter

8. *The Cleaving: Vietnamese Writers in the Diaspora*, edited by Isabelle Thuy Pelaud, Lan P. Duong, and Viet Thanh Nguyen

# Emergency in Transit

*Witnessing Migration in the Colonial Present*

———

Eleanor Paynter

UNIVERSITY OF CALIFORNIA PRESS

University of California Press
Oakland, California



Suggested citation: Paynter, E. *Emergency in Transit: Witnessing Migration in the Colonial Present*. Oakland: University of California Press, 2024.
DOI: https://doi.org/10.1525/luminos.210

Library of Congress Cataloging-in-Publication Data

Names: Paynter, Eleanor, author.
Title: Emergency in transit : witnessing migration in the colonial present/ Eleanor Paynter.
Other titles: Critical refugee studies ; 7.
Description: Oakland, California : University of California Press, [2024] | Series: Critical refugee studies ; 7 | Includes bibliographical references and index.
Identifiers: LCCN 2024026596 (print) | LCCN 2024026597 (ebook) | ISBN 9780520402904 (paperback) | ISBN 9780520402928 (ebook)
Subjects: LCSH: Refugees—Italy. | Colonies. | Italy—Migration—Personal narratives. | Italy—Emigration and immigration—Personal narratives. | Mediterranean Region—Emigration and immigration.
Classification: LCC JV8131 .P368 2024  (print) | LCC JV8131 (ebook) | DDC 305.9/069140945—dc23/eng/20240724

LC record available at https://lccn.loc.gov/2024026596
LC ebook record available at https://lccn.loc.gov/2024026597

34   33   32   31   30   29   28   27   26   25
10   9   8   7   6   5   4   3   2   1

The publisher and the University of California Press Foundation gratefully acknowledge the generous support of the Anne G. Lipow Endowment Fund in Social Justice and Human Rights.

Le frontiere cambiano, non rimangono mai fisse. . . . Le frontiere cambiano, ho ripetuto ad Elena. Basta ascoltare le storie di chi viaggia, per accorgersene.

*Borders change; they never stay the same. . . . Borders change, I said to Elena. You just have to listen to the stories of those who travel, to realize it.*

—ALESSANDRO LEOGRANDE, *LA FRONTIERA*

Non si può parlare per anni di emergenza.

*You can't talk for years about emergency.*

—ISABELLA, *SOCIAL WORKER IN CALABRIA*

*My memory stammers: but my soul is a witness.*

—JAMES BALDWIN, *THE EVIDENCE OF THINGS NOT SEEN*

# CONTENTS


*List of Illustrations*     *xi*

*Acknowledgments*     *xiii*

*A Note on Language*     *xvii*

Introduction: Emergency Imaginaries     *1*

PART I: ARRIVALS

1. Strange Grief and Elegiac Possibilities in the Black Mediterranean     *31*

2. Hospitality as Emergency Response     *58*

3. Emergent Practices of Hospitality in the Camp     *84*

PART II: THE RIGHT TO REMAIN

4. Street Vendor as Witness     *115*

5. Seen and Unseen in the City     *140*

6. Oranges and Riot Gear     *167*

Epilogue: Mobility in an Age of Emergency, or, A Small and Stubborn Possibility     *191*

*Appendix*     *199*

*Notes*     *207*

*Bibliography*     *231*

*Index*     *255*

# ILLUSTRATIONS

## FIGURES


1. Still from *A chiunque possa interessare*  32
2. Still from *Asmat*  45
3. Postcard from the campaign Fatal Policies of Fortress Europe  47
4. Barca Nostra as seen from a bar at the 2019 Venice Biennale  55
5. The *Katër i Radës* at the Port of Otranto, 2019  56
6. Rescue scene on a mural by a reception center in Africo, 2018  57
7. Campobasso industrial zone  65
8. Strollers for communal use at a CAS  69
9. CAS cafeteria where language classes were held  75
10. Piazzale Maslax entrance after authorities added barricades, 2017  87
11. Piazzale Maslax, 2018  88
12. Tea at Piazzale Maslax, 2018  97
13. Signs at Piazzale Maslax about the regular camp assembly, 2018  102
14. *"La vie des immigration"* ("Immigration Life")  105
15. Piazzale Maslax entrance after its final closure, 2019  111
16. Cover of *Il mio viaggio della speranza*, by Bay Mademba  118
17. "Uno a caso" ("One at random"), by Mauro Biani  135
18. Memorial display for Idy Diene on the Ponte Vespucci, July 2018  136
19. Demonstration in Rome following the murder of Soumaila Sacko, 2018  138
20. Flyer for the Invisible Guides soundwalks  147
21. Rocket on the mural outside of MAAM  158
22. *Rane infinite* ("infinite frogs")  159
23. Inside MAAM, artworks including the boat by Sara Bernabucci  160

24. Abas harvesting oranges. Still from *Mediterranea*, by Jonas Carpignano    *180*
25. Widely circulated photograph of the January 2010 riots    *184*
26. Still from *Mediterranea*    *184*
27. George Floyd mural and BarConi entrance    *196*

## MAPS

1. Primary field sites    *5*
2. Mediterranean crossing zones    *9*
3. Piazzale Maslax in relation to Rome's Centro Storico    *86*

## TABLES

1. Precarious Mediterranean migration to Europe: Arrivals and deaths, 2013–2023    *201*
2. Emergency measures: Major asylum, immigration, and rescue policies affecting migrants in Italy, 1986–2024    *202*
3. Main reception categories and center types    *205*

This story and the stories within it found their way to these pages through more conversations, collaborations, friendships, writing group sessions, and encounters than I can name. Here I will do my best to thank those who most immediately made this book possible.

First and foremost, thanks to the people who shared their stories and lives with me and trusted me to do them justice.

Many people made my research in Italy possible, including the staff and residents of the centers and camps I visited. Though I can't share everyone's name, I want to acknowledge their generosity. Those I can thank directly include the Baobab Experience community, Simonetta Bonadies, Andrea Costa, Marida D'Andrea, Francesca Del Giudice, Concetta Fornaro, Jungi Mundu, Giulio Picchi, Alberto Polito, and the Benedetti family. A walk I took with Khaled Karri was more important than he may know.

Many of the people who have read this book at various stages have also been incredible colleagues and mentors. I am especially grateful to Stephanie Malia Hom, Dana Renga, Rachel Beatty Riedl, and Amy Shuman.

The research at the heart of this book started as my dissertation at Ohio State University, where I studied, taught, and collaborated with a number of people across departments whose work has impacted my own. Interdisciplinary work like this is possible because a department like Comparative Studies exists. I am deeply thankful for faculty and graduate school comrades in Comparative Studies and French and Italian, everyone who was part of the Migration Studies Working Group, and teaching mentors Philip Armstrong, Janice Aski, and David Horn. Dissertation committee members Ashley Hope Pérez and Julia Watson, and advisors

Dana Renga and Amy Shuman were wonderful interlocutors and championed the project in numerous ways. Dana Renga's generous mentorship and insightful feedback have been invaluable. Amy Shuman has forever shaped how I think about narrative, ethics, rights, and teaching, and I quite simply would not be where I am without her wisdom and support.

Writing with Melissa Curley and Miranda Martinez has given rhythm to my routine. Our Zooms got me through the pandemic and have often seemed like the one consistent thing—I am grateful for this friendship.

Thanks to readers who have engaged with this book at various stages of its becoming. Feedback from a manuscript workshop with Donald Carter, Mary Jane Dempsey, Stephanie Malia Hom, Shahram Khosravi, Katrina Powell, and Rachel Beatty Riedl encouraged me to, among other things, return to language and think across borders. Amadou Diallo and Khaled Karri shared insightful comments. Dan DiPiero read and reread and asked me about empathy. Nicole Miller read and called and sent me *The Blue Clerk*. Editor Meghan Drury made excellent suggestions on the introduction. Victoria Baker produced the index with care. Laura Portwood-Stacer's advice on the publication process was so important. Joel Pruce was on the International Studies Association committee that recognized my dissertation with the Lynne Rienner Publishers Award for Best Dissertation in Human Rights, and his work in human rights research and pedagogy has inspired my own. My summer writing group saw much of this project in process, and their fine-tuned eyes made it a better book: Abby Wheatley, Gabriella Soto, and Oren Kroll-Zeldin. Collaborations with journalist Annalisa Camilli informed my approach to these topics. Many thanks also to Ubah Cristina Ali Farah, Monamie Bhadra Haines, Virginia Carlsten, Sarah Craycraft, Michele De Gregorio, Giovanni Fontana and Second Tree comrades, Seth Gaiters, Leighla Khansari, Hana Maruyama, Emilia Morelli, Carolin Mueller, Sara Riva, Tristana Rorandelli, Johanna Sellman, Yumna Siddiqi, Amrita Wassan, and Enrico Zammarchi, whose friendship, writing, and work have fed this book. So much nourishment from #Dunkle and the likes of Dan DiPiero, Hannah Segrave, and Gennaro Di Tosto.

Conversations with a number of people at Cornell University and the Mario Einaudi Center for International Studies informed my thinking and buoyed me while writing during my postdoc. Thanks to Migrations initiative colleagues Shannon Gleeson, Eric Tagliacozzo, Steve Yale-Loehr, Gunisha Kaur, Wendy Wolford, Rachel Beatty Riedl, Ángel Escamilla García, and Megan DeMint. Chiara Galli offered wisdom and camaraderie. It was wonderful to be in conversation about these ideas at different points with Tim Campbell, Deb Castillo, Saida Hodžić, Tristan Ivory, Molly O'Toole, Natasha Raheja, Peter Rich, the fabulous undergrad Migration Scholars, and—what luck—Columbus-then-Ithaca colleagues and friends Jon Branfman, Juno Salazar Parreñas, and Noah Tamarkin.

It was a joy to move forward with this project while on a postdoc at Brown University, and to think with colleagues in Italian Studies and the Cogut Institute for the Humanities. Thanks to Peter Szendy and Cogut fellows and staff. Thanks to my students, whose care for the world and for each other holds me to account. In Italian Studies, thanks to Cristina Abbona-Sneider, Caroline Castiglione, Bailey Killian, and Evelyn Lincoln, and to the graduate students whose own work and insights are absolutely inspiring. A profuse thanks to Suzanne Stewart-Steinberg and Massimo Riva for their support and dialogue, and for believing in this book. What a privilege to have shared this time with you all.

This project benefitted from funding support thanks to a Fellowship with the American Council for Learned Societies, the Oral History Association's Emerging Crises Fund, and the Qualitative and Interpretive Research Institute at Cornell. While at Ohio State, my research was supported by a Presidential Fellowship and through the Global Arts and Humanities Discovery Theme, the Mershon Center for International Security Studies, the Global Mobility Project, the Office of International Affairs, the Critical Difference program, and the Graduate School. Research was conducted under IRB ethics protocols at Ohio State and Cornell, including particular attention to protecting the identities of interlocutors with uncertain legal status.

The seeds for chapter 4 appear in the article "The Transits and Transactions of Migritude in Bay Mademba's *Il mio viaggio della speranza (My Voyage of Hope)*," which appeared in the 2020 *minnesota review* special issue on migritude edited by the wonderful Ashna Ali, Christopher Ian Foster, and Supriya M. Nair.

At the University of California Press, thanks to Naomi Schneider, Aline Dolinh, and the editorial board for supporting this book and advocating for the open-access format. Thanks also to Emily Park, Theresa Winchell, and the broader editorial team who moved it through the publication process. A huge thanks to reviewers. I am thrilled that this book is part of the Critical Refugee Studies series, and I thank Yến Lê Espiritu and the Critical Refugee Studies Collective for welcoming *Emergency in Transit* into the series.

It is an honor to have on the cover the work of Dawit Petros, whose art poignantly and provocatively engages colonial memory.

What an absolute thrill to have this book meet the world as I settle into life in the Pacific Northwest. Many thanks to my University of Oregon colleagues in Romance Languages and the School of Global Studies and Languages for the warm welcome and for your engagement with this work.

Finally, I would like to thank my family for the many ways they have supported the writing of this book. Thanks to Maria Emilia, Andrea, Paolo, Marco, and Adriana. Thanks to my mom, Peggy, and to Jon, Julie, and the niblings. To Gennaro, for all of it.

Transit and translation go hand in hand, and the work you are about to read emerged through multiple languages, especially Italian and English. Throughout the book, translations are mine unless otherwise indicated. This includes interviews I conducted in Italian, as well as literary, filmic, journalistic, and scholarly work I quote in English that was originally produced in Italian.

As you will notice, I also invoke Italian terms that bear a specific set of meanings—*accoglienza*, or hospitality/reception, being one such example. I both define and highlight terms like this and also move fluidly between English and Italian iterations to gesture to these multilayered meanings. Across chapters, I have worked to weave in terms that people I spoke with used to describe their movements, spaces, and relationships. We cannot change current systems without new language, and I hope my own attention to the limits and possibilities of language contributes in some small way to that much-needed critical and imaginative work.

# Introduction

*Emergency Imaginaries*

On October 11, 2016, at the height of what was then globally recognized as Europe's "refugee crisis," a group of men from Eritrea, Somalia, and Ethiopia stood on the steps of the Campidoglio, Rome's municipal square, and unfurled a banner that read *We are not dangerous . . . we are in danger!*

The men weren't talking about their long and perilous journeys across the Sahara, their imprisonment and exploitation in Libya, or the unseaworthy vessels on which they eventually crossed the Mediterranean. Instead, they were calling attention to the danger they confronted after reaching Europe and making their way to the heart of the Italian capital. Holding the sign across the Campidoglio steps with a crowd of supporters behind them, the men—a few of them donning the orange life vests that had come to symbolize the plight of Mediterranean migrants—chanted: "We are homeless! We need protection!"

More specifically, they were protesting their eviction from the street they had occupied outside a former migrant reception center in Rome's San Lorenzo neighborhood. When local authorities closed the center months earlier, volunteers and center residents moved to the street outside, forming a collective they called Baobab Experience. For more than eight months, Baobab coordinated meals and legal and medical aid there in Via Cupa for thousands of people who had recently reached Italy, mostly men in their teens and twenties, many originally from West Africa, the Sahel, and the Horn of Africa. Despite repeated Italian state declarations of emergency that had released aid funds and facilitated the rapid opening of centers to accommodate people seeking protection in Europe, these newcomers found themselves unhoused and without access to official assistance. Now police had cleared Via Cupa, too, removing the mattresses and tents and blocking the administration of aid.

At the Campidoglio, the men's invocation of the language of danger called public attention to their struggles and to the implications of what they recognized as a broad misframing of their movements: popular discourses surrounding African arrivals to Europe suggest that border crossers are themselves the source of crisis and pose a threat to European and Italian security and culture. Yet these men feared for their own safety and well-being *within* Italy where, rather than obtaining protection, they were being held in limbo. City authorities refused to accommodate these newcomers, claiming to have reached capacity. In turn, while attempting to apply for asylum, the men could not access the meals, housing, or legal, linguistic, and medical aid available through such centers. They remained *in transit*: living in the liminality, or in-betweenness, of uncertain legal and social status, and effectively still on the move, despite having reached Europe, and despite their eagerness to build stable lives and plan for the future. At the October 2016 demonstration and in subsequent protests, social media campaigns, and public events, the group advocated for migrant rights not only through broad appeals for justice, but through testimony—in this case, through an embodied act of protest that centered migrants' understanding of the challenges they faced.

This book responds to the pervasive framing of migration from global south to global north as an "emergency" or "crisis"—or in Italy, an *emergenza immigrazione* (immigration emergency). Declarations of emergency dominate political and public responses to precarious migration—that is, mobilities sometimes called "irregular" or "undocumented" that, regardless of migrants' legal status, occur "under highly constrained conditions."[1] From the US-Mexico borderlands, to oceanic crossings to Australia, to the Mediterranean, today's dominant narratives frame migration as a problem. The sense of crisis as a constant threat becomes rapidly clear in a quick scan of media. At one extreme, sensationalizing, fearmongering stories depict migrants as criminals or drug dealers. Yet more broadly, political and media discourse abounds that treats crisis and emergency as inherent facts, including headlines like "'Naïve and Dangerous': Australia Urged to Do More as Refugee Crisis, and Boats, Return" (*Sydney Morning Herald*, 2023); "Chaos, Fury, Mistakes: 600 Days Inside New York's Migrant Crisis" (*New York Times*, 2023); and "Is the Migration Emergency Back?" (*Il Sole 24 Ore*, 2023).

Emergency and crisis labels correspond to actual situations of urgency, as people undertake incredibly risky voyages to seek legal protection and better lives. Yet, critically, they also cultivate what historian Michele Colucci has called "an obsession with the present," suggesting that arrivals to southern borders are sudden, unforeseeable, and unprecedented.[2] Yet, while displacement from one's home country can happen abruptly, the migration "emergencies" so prevalent at global north borders often mark not sudden change but continuity. Precarious migration to Italy has been described as an emergency not since the mid-2010s, but since at least the early 1990s, when Albanians fleeing regime collapse crossed the Adriatic to the southern Puglia region.[3] Broad legal and discursive treatments of migration in emergency terms perpetuate a pervasive focus on precarious migration, and on border crossers themselves, as existing within an endless, ahistorical "now," and as defined by their perceived unbelonging. Focusing on the Italian case, *Emergency in Transit* asks: In light of a more than thirty-year *emergenza*, what does "emergency" mean? What work do this label and related policies perform, and how do they influence cultural imaginaries? How do people in transit navigate the "crisis" their movements supposedly represent, if that "crisis" is both urgent and endless?

Through the testimonies of Africans who bear witness to their experiences reaching Europe via Italy and navigating Italian spaces and institutions, this book shows how emergency responses to Mediterranean migration reproduce colonial logics and racialize those crossing borders, and how people on the move expose and challenge this violence. I conceptualize "emergency" as an apparatus (via Foucault): what we might think of as a singular border emergency, or what gets framed in media as a migration crisis with clear temporal parameters, in fact reflects a set of shifting and often contradictory discourses, policies, practices, and material experiences that together shape people's lives. The emergency apparatus operates at multiple scales and across geographies, from national borderzones to the living and working spaces where locals and newcomers negotiate new futures. It is powered by a pervasive *emergency imaginary of foreignness* that perceives certain bodies and lives as perpetual outsiders who embody threat, rupture, and risk.

The emergency apparatus is a crucial mechanism of the colonial present, or the ways that historical colonial campaigns and power relations repeat, echo, and continue to structure border regimes and notions of national identity and otherness today.[4] In Italy, the emergency apparatus shapes migration realities by perpetuating power differentials, refusals of memory, and related racial logics. As a consequence, emergency responses often perpetuate circumstances of urgency and uncertainty, rather than resolve them, and the treatment of arrivals as a "crisis" at external borders in fact significantly impacts migrants and local communities throughout the country. The men at the Campidoglio faced an uphill battle not simply because of their legal limbo as asylum seekers awaiting a decision, but because of how their movements figure within the colonial present. As foreigners from former European colonies in the heart of a former colonizing power, these migrants were racially and socially excluded from a society that has yet to reckon with its own violent colonial history and how the racial hierarchies it reified continue to inform dominant ideas about who can be Italian. Like so many of the testimonies I heard, read, or viewed in research across Italian migrant reception sites and migration-centered cultural production, this witnessing reveals that what dominant media narratives portray as a crisis spurred by increased arrivals to Europe's southern borders in fact involves a much more complex set of dynamics related to who is welcomed into Italian and European spaces, and through what legal and social processes.

Shaped by a politics of in/exclusion and (in)visibility, sites of "emergency" are sites of contested witnessing: emergency functions by relying on *some* witnessing accounts—by government officials and NGOs, for example—while severely limiting the possibilities for people in transit to bear witness to their experiences on their own terms. Indeed, as Janet Roitman writes of crisis, emergency "raises the dilemma of the very possibility of bearing witness, or of representation."[5] At the Campidoglio protest, most demonstrators did not yet have visas and could not risk returning to their home countries. Yet they viewed their struggles in Italy as extreme enough to merit the risks of hypervisibility, and they bore public witness to their presence and struggles in hopes of provoking change. Their witnessing aligns with other testimonies that point to the constructed nature of borders we often think of as fixed and clarify how borders change in geographical, political, and social terms, as Alessandro Leogrande observes in one of this book's epigraphs.[6] This is one illustration of how testimonies that emerge from within these constraints challenge emergency framings of migration and invoke alternative visions of mobility and belonging.

In conceptualizing the emergency apparatus and its relationship to witnessing, *Emergency in Transit* bridges critical refugee studies, postcolonial studies, and transnational Italian studies through the methods of narrative analysis, oral history, and ethnography. With this interdisciplinary approach, I adopt what I call "testimony as method" to document how the emergency apparatus shapes the lives of people on the move and, simultaneously, to challenge how emergency responses to migration often obscure migrant-centered, migrant-authored narratives.[7] In doing so, I center how border crossers narrate, mediate, and navigate their experiences through testimonies including interviews, writing, film, and visual art. Ranging from the fleeting to the monumental, these testimonies document life well beyond the national borders where media and scholarly attention often focuses.[8] Drawing extensively on ethnographic research I carried out at migrant reception centers, camps, and public spaces in four Italian regions (map 1), this book itself bears witness to the operations of emergency that shape contemporary Mediterranean migration.

Italy offers a significant case for the study of migration "crises," as a country historically shaped by internal migration and emigration abroad that is now a main port of entry for people hoping to obtain asylum in Europe. Focusing on Italy, I elaborate the emergency apparatus through the framework of the Black Mediterranean, which understands the Afro-European borderzone as a site of colonial relations and racialized anti-immigrant violence, as well as migrant agency.[9] Black Mediterranean mobilities and politics shape the lives of people in the African diaspora living in and beyond the Mediterranean region; critically, they also shape Mediterranean spaces and communities as they posit a reengagement of colonial history, collective memory, and notions of belonging, and as migrants' movements and words "defy Fortress Europe" and represent, as Harsha Walia observes, "a

MAP 1. Primary field sites. Made by the author with Datawrapper.

form of decolonial reparations."[10] Through this perspective, I address how migration "emergencies" are both lived and imagined, and how the ways the emergency apparatus holds migrants in precarity are directly related to the limits it imposes on conceptualizations of mobility.

We live amid multiple global "crises" of public health, climate change, racial and social injustice, conflict and terror, and economic hardship, and movements within and across borders are inextricable from these issues and are often upheld as a "crisis" or "emergency" in their own right. Declarations of emergency—whether legal or discursive—sound an alarm, the nature of which depends on distinguishing threatening subjects from citizens who uphold the normal order of the law: Who or what is threatening? Who is outside the normal order? The prevalence of emergency rhetoric reminds us that, indeed, to invoke Walter Benjamin, "the state of exception has become the rule."[11] Discourses and experiences of emergency are at the center of global debates about asylum, human rights, citizenship, and border regimes, and asylum seekers, refugees, and people in transit without papers are often understood to represent the state of exception, not considered full political subjects.[12] Refugees are simultaneously seen to represent both humanitarian concern and "a crisis to world order."[13] As Yến Lê Espiritu has discussed, nations "externalize" refugees legally, socially, and ideologically.[14] What rights and social and political capital newcomers can exercise changes radically depending on the racial politics and constructions of foreignness in the countries where they arrive.

The critical refugee studies focus on the *production* of the refugee in material and figurative terms prompts an interrogation of the current emphasis on "crisis" in global debates about migration. Rather than conceptualize refugees as harbingers of emergency, humanitarian subjects, or a singular figure of vulnerability or threat, a critical refugee studies approach recognizes those making precarious crossings as bearers and makers of knowledge and as people "who possess and enact their *own* politics."[15] In Saida Hodžić's words, "the refugee" is not simply the "shallow figure" or "test case" of Agamben's *homo sacer* but "a rich tapestry of complex human experience."[16] This perspective is fundamental for questioning the prevalence of crisis and emergency labels to describe precarious mobilities. In recognizing how those labels construct an *emergency imaginary of foreignness*, my approach is aligned with Craig Calhoun's discussion of the emergency imaginary that shapes humanitarianism through a fixation on seeming suddenness and unforeseeability; in considering how such ideas are invoked more broadly in relation to foreignness, I focus on how they perpetuate racialized ideas of belonging.[17]

A growing body of migration scholarship critiques politicized invocations of crisis in North America, Australia, and Europe.[18] Yet the often default use of such terms by politicians, journalists, humanitarian workers, activists, and scholars risks reifying the association between precarious mobilities and notions of threat, vulnerability, and unknowable outsiderness. Debates about these labels often argue for one kind of crisis or another—refugee, border, humanitarian, institutional—revealing emergency to be a concept deployed in multiple overlapping, sometimes contradictory, and often problematic senses. In migrant advocacy, migrant-centered scholarship, and xenophobic campaigns alike, "crisis" and "emergency" get treated as inherent attributes of mobility or borders, or fixed points of reference.

Instead, these labels refer to what are in fact shifting dynamics produced by an apparatus itself in flux, and they rarely account for how migrants themselves describe their experiences. Likewise, the harms they pose to people on the move emerge through the constant production of "emergency" via a changing set of discourses, policies, and practices. These consequences exceed temporal bounds and cross political administrations. Increasingly, they unfold in a context in which asylum itself is threatened, as countries around the world rely on prison-like camps and detention centers, or build walls to keep out people who would seek protection within their borders, or attempt to ship asylum seekers elsewhere for processing.[19]

Rather than presume crisis or emergency to be inherent qualities or conditions of migration, this book adopts a critical refugee studies approach to show how the emergency apparatus itself reshapes asylum and reception regimes, how a disregard for colonial histories enables these precarious realities, and how migrant testimonies invite audiences to witness precarious mobilities beyond the emergency imaginary that often defines them. In bringing this lens to bear on Mediterranean migration, and guided by the testimonies of people whose transit holds them at the margins of Europe, I posit the Mediterranean as a key site where global questions of refugeeness are being negotiated in relation to race and collective memory. In doing so, I also expand the transnational Italian studies focus on the place of migration in formations of Italian identity to encompass this reckoning with race, precarity, and refugeeness. Invocations of emergency in the Afro-European borderzone, I argue, recall and reproduce the colonial emergency, or what Frantz Fanon describes as a world "cut in two" along the lines created by the "rule of oppression."[20] In tracing the operations of the emergency apparatus as imperial formations that enable Europe to continue to control African movements and futures, this book situates Mediterranean migrations in relation to Black Europe and border imperialism to advance recognition of migrant justice and racial justice as inextricably linked.

## EUROPE'S "REFUGEE CRISIS"

The year 2015 is widely recognized as a watershed year for migration to Europe, marked by the April 18 shipwreck near the Italian island of Lampedusa in which as many as eleven hundred people died, and by the September 2 death of Syrian toddler Alan Kurdi on a Turkish beach. But in Italy, 2014 had already made its mark as a year of *emergenza*. When arrivals by sea from Libya and Tunisia increased fourfold between 2013 and 2014, Italian leaders and publics invoked "emergenza" to question the capacity of Italian systems to accommodate so many people, as well as how the presence of so many newcomers might impact Italian society. Following the now infamous October 3, 2013, wreck near Lampedusa in which at least 368 people lost their lives, Italy implemented the military-humanitarian mission Mare Nostrum ("Our Sea") that prioritized rescue at sea through most of 2014. Authorities regulated non-European foreigners' movements in new ways, with increased biometric surveillance and by modifying the reception system that houses people while their asylum claims are processed.[21]

European Union (EU) leaders formally recognized a migration "crisis" through multiple emergency measures from 2014 until March 6, 2019, when they declared the crisis over.[22] Yet in the years since, as arrivals by boat and by foot have continued, and given a backlog of asylum cases, emergency policies and rhetoric have remained at the fore. Mediterranean crossings have a long history, and it's now well established that people undertake precarious journeys only when safer legal routes are closed to them.[23] As Italy has increasingly limited visas and policed mobility, dangerous sea crossings have become a primary means of reaching Europe. Authorities insist, however, that precarious migration is itself the problem and frequently frame the post-2014 period as a crisis of numbers: between 2014 and 2019, more than three million people reached Europe's borders by boat or on foot. During those same years, more than nineteen thousand people died or went missing at sea—a conservative underestimate (table 1, appendix).[24] These losses, which have only continued, underscore how crisis discourses are bolstered by the failures of empathy—of imagination, as Susan Sontag put it—to prompt lasting, substantive change for people on the move.[25] Border deaths also raise the question of the (im)possibility of complete witnessing in the context of these crossings, if the true witnesses who could speak to this violence to the fullest extent, to invoke Primo Levi, are those who do not survive it.[26]

The people behind these tallies include asylum seekers, refugees, and people with and without papers. While dominant crisis discourses in 2015 focused especially on Syrians fleeing conflict and heading to Germany, people undertake lengthy, precarious journeys to Europe from multiple world regions, often in hopes of obtaining asylum, the international protection that would grant them refugee status and legal residency in Europe. They leave Afghanistan, Bangladesh, the Congo, Eritrea, the Gambia, Mali, Nigeria, Pakistan, Palestine, Syria, Tunisia, and a host of other countries and reach Europe's borders by crossing in one of three zones: the Eastern Mediterranean, via Türkiye, Greece, and the Balkan countries; the Western Mediterranean route to Spain, including via the "autonomous communities" of Ceuta, Melilla, and the Canary Islands; or by crossing the Sahara and then the Mediterranean Sea, leaving Libya or Tunisia for Italy or Malta (map 2). This Central Mediterranean borderzone is notoriously treacherous; wrecks near Lampedusa and Southern Italian coasts regularly make the news. This route has been rendered more dangerous by political turmoil in North Africa, Libya in particular, and by Europe's abandonment of migrants in transit.[27]

The spectacle of wrecks maintains emergency imaginaries because it repeats and repeats yet fails to wield real structural or systemic transformation. By repetition I mean, for instance: in February 2023, a boat carrying approximately 180 people hit a shoal near Cutro, on Italy's Calabrian coast. It splintered, sending passengers flailing into the water. The wreck made global headlines, but the ensuing public outcry quieted quickly. Just two months later, another boat carrying more than seven hundred people entered Greek waters, where it was observed by Frontex surveillance and commercial vessels and cited by activists, only to be pulled further out to sea by the Greek coast guard, where it capsized.

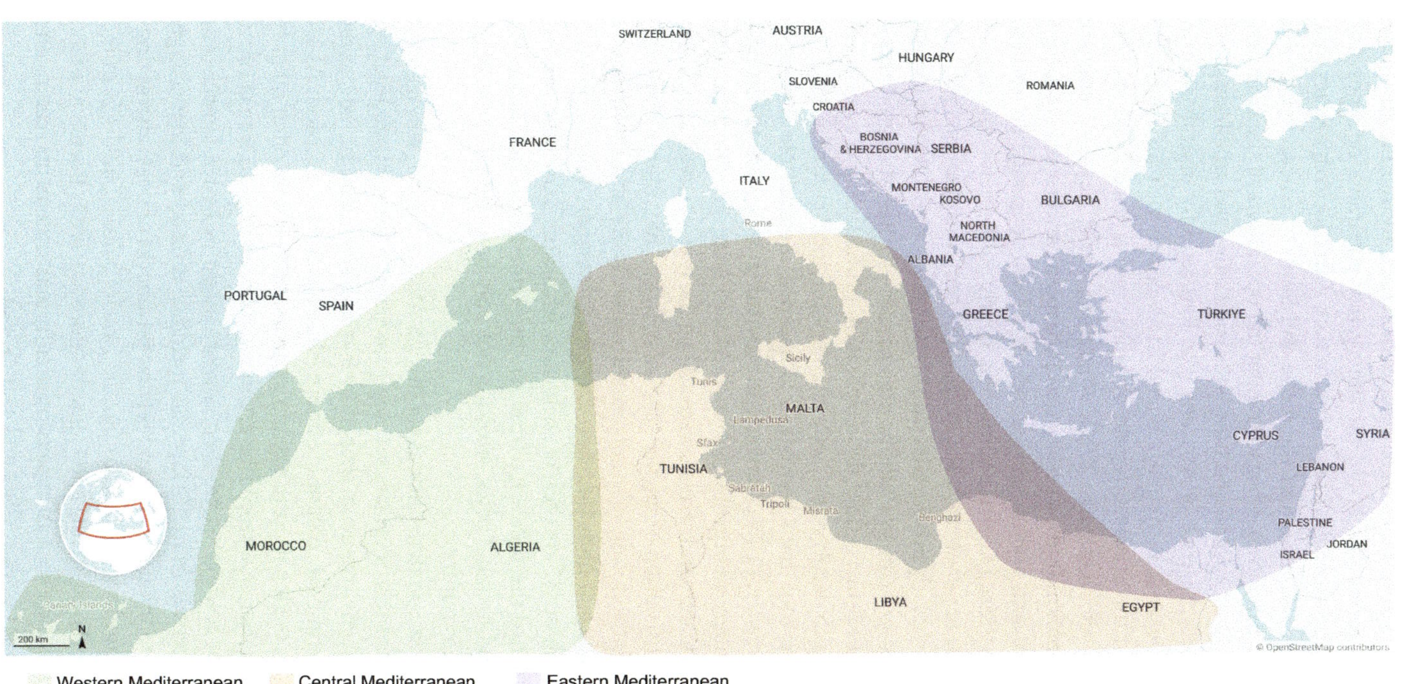


Western Mediterranean    Central Mediterranean    Eastern Mediterranean

MAP 2. Mediterranean crossing zones (approximate). Made by the author with Datawrapper.

These wrecks and the charged politics of rescue are significant. Yet, as I demonstrate throughout this book, the emergency apparatus operates not only at national borders but well within them. In fact, it was local dynamics that initially raised questions for me about the scope and limits of emergency as a frame for understanding migration. I began tracing the operations of the emergency apparatus in late 2015 as I witnessed how both large cities and small towns responded to the increased presence of Africans who had recently disembarked on Italian shores. That December, my partner and I traveled to visit his family in Campobasso, a city in the southern region of Molise and a place I had grown to know over a decade of such visits. While migration wasn't new in Campobasso, the recent arrival of hundreds of newcomers prompted concern among locals. I visited a large tent housing asylum seekers outside a local soup kitchen—an emergency response to increased arrivals. Until then, nearly all the news coverage I had seen showed images of people in boats, at crowded centers in Lampedusa, or on Greek islands, and scholarly work reflected this emphasis on sites of initial contact or arrival. At this tent run by Catholic organization Caritas, though, I was struck by the scope of the "emergency," the desperation of the Italian response, and how it seemed bound to deeply affect both migrants and local communities.

It was there, too, that I first began to question the multiple and vague uses of the term *emergency*, or *emergenza*. The provisional tent with its cots and generators was absolutely an urgent situation, but locals were quick to critique the set-up. It wasn't sustainable, and arrivals were still on the rise – arrivals seen, in general, as a rupture or disruption of normal, everyday Italian life. Rumors circulated about the trouble that loitering migrants might cause. There and throughout Italy, the growing presence of nonwhite, non-European foreigners revealed familiar places to be "borderscapes," or sites of inclusion, exclusion, possibility, and friction.[28] When I returned the following summer, the "emergenza immigrazione" dominated local and national news, marking not only boat arrivals but circumstances throughout the country.

In EU border countries, like along the US-Mexico border, emergency management has meant that migrants seeking protection must navigate legal systems in flux and social environments shaped by fear and suspicion. In Italy, asylum seekers bide their time in reception centers while awaiting a decision. As is increasingly true across global north asylum systems, this process often takes two years or longer. Alternatively, would-be asylum seekers attempt to transit on and reach another city or country where their chances might be better. Greece's emergency response to arrivals from Türkiye has included isolated and increasingly militarized island and inland camps and regular pushbacks of boats attempting to reach safety. Spain continues to police migration via its colonial holdings in the Canary Islands and enclaves Melilla and Ceuta in Morocco. From Bosnia to France, European countries have seen an expansion of informal settlements (camps and squats) as people transit between cities and as they wait.

*Emergency* produces precarity, with Europe as both destination and site of extreme uncertainty. Foreigners in legal and social limbo remain a key source of labor for European economies, including women in domestic positions or people working the harvest, as well as people in a larger set of temporary, uncontracted jobs ("There is no capitalism without migration," Sandro Mezzadra reminds us).[29] In addition to precarious labor, migration "emergencies" position newcomers in social and political vulnerability that, to invoke Judith Butler, leaves people "differentially exposed to injury, violence and death"[30] and holds newcomers in transit, in positions from which they are largely unable to advocate for themselves.

*Emergency* is also a term thick with meanings, and it bears emphasizing early on that the precarity prompted and maintained by the emergency apparatus intersects with circumstances and conditions that people have long recognized on their own terms as emergency or the related notion of catastrophe. As Black studies scholars and writers have elaborated, Black life unfolds in the emergency conditions wrought by colonialism, enslavement, and ongoing oppression. "I am washed in this emergency," writes Dionne Brand in *The Blue Clerk*, meditating on the constant state of risk she occupies as a Black woman living within the operations of racial capitalism: "I wake up in emergency."[31] Fred Moten describes this state as one of fugitivity—of constant flight, instability, desire, including the desire to be free.[32] James Baldwin reflects on how this "terror" radically shapes what it means, for him, to bear witness as a Black man writing about racialized violence. In *Evidence of Things Not Seen* (from which I quote in one of this book's epigraphs), he states, "My memory stammers: but my soul is a witness." In this "stammering," he grapples with the impossibility of remembering the terror of the past—"one blots it out." At the same time, he sees confronting the terror of always-impending violence, of erasure, "not the terror of death . . . but of being destroyed," as a crucial way to locate hope for change.[33] He bears witness to how this emergency shapes Black life in the US—a recognition, I want to suggest, that we must also bring to bear in understanding how race and refugeeness intersect today in Europe. In my focus on Africa-Europe migrations, this emergency is central. It speaks to how the emergency apparatus of migration exploits conditions already understood as perpetual crises, and how it renders some lives especially precarious, especially disposable. I trace the contours of the emergency apparatus in ways shaped by my implication in and struggles with structures of racial capitalism as a white US citizen,[34] and I engage the work of Black studies scholars who address emergency from both lived and studied experience.[35]

These perspectives illuminate the emergency apparatus—from the securitization of borders to the broader treatment of "irregular" migration as a threat—as a set of racializing processes that structure the colonial present. With "colonial present," I have in mind in particular Derek Gregory's use of this phrase to signal "the constellations of power, knowledge, and geography that . . . continue to colonize lives all over the world"[36] and his insistence that the colonial present is built not only through geopolitics and economics but via "mundane cultural forms and cultural practices that mark other people as irredeemably 'Other.'"[37] Gregory developed this concept in the context of post-9/11 Western imperialism in Afghanistan, Palestine, and Iraq, all countries from which people continue to flee and make their way to Europe. Coloniality operates in distinct ways across all these contexts; at the same time, by focusing on how coloniality shapes the present, we can recognize how, across these places and communities, questions of rights and belonging, and even the borders of the human, are articulated not only through historical echoes, but through an ongoing policing of mobilities that reproduces longstanding power differentials. Examining Italy's colonial present via the Black Mediterranean reveals how the emergency apparatus relies on the racial logics that built Europe through anti-Black violence and the exclusion and subjugation of people deemed "other."

That is, emergency framings of migration enact racial hierarchies and delineate Europe's borders as racial borders.[38] In the Italian popular imaginary, Black migrants are presumed to be "economic migrants" attempting to steal places that belong to those more deserving of humanitarian protection and Italian residency. These ideas of crisis, deservingness, and refugeeness reflect a white European gaze, recalling Fanon on the violence of colonial projection in *Black Skin, White Masks*: "I am given no chance. I am overdetermined from without . . . I am being dissected under white eyes, the only real eyes. I am *fixed*. Having adjusted their microtomes, they objectively cut away slices of my reality. I am laid bare."[39] In contemporary Italy, images of risk, danger, and crisis are projected onto the bodies and lives of migrants who are "laid bare" and overdetermined as an anonymous mass of strangers yet are in fact a heterogeneous group of people with no established platform for bearing witness to their experiences on their own terms.

MOBILITY AND MEMORY IN ITALY
AND THE BLACK MEDITERRANEAN

As emergency imaginaries orient public and political attention around an endless present, they obscure how multiple mobilities have shaped Italian society, including historical movements within, out of, and to the country, and the notions of race that accompany them.[40] These movements are often presented in linear terms, including Italy's shift in status from a country of emigration to a net destination country, with more arrivals than departures beginning in the late 1970s. While narratives that emphasize this shift recognize significant trends, they tend to elide the extent to which mobility and ideas of race have long shaped modern Italy.[41] For instance, beginning in the late nineteenth century and expanded under Fascism, the country's colonial campaigns sent thousands of Italians to the Horn of Africa and Libya, displaced indigenous populations there, and eventually prompted the arrival in Italy of students and political appointees from the colonies. Romani and Sinti communities in Italy have dealt with exclusion and discrimination since before the country's 1861 Unification. The 1938 Racial Laws institutionalized antisemitism and restricted interracial marriage.[42] The postwar period saw ongoing internal and international movements, including as Italians went abroad or returned; as Southerners moved north for jobs in a growing industrial sector, confronting racial stereotypes as they moved; and during decolonization, as the residents of former colonies moved to Europe.[43] Today, internal rural-to-urban migration continues, as do high rates of emigration of young Italians abroad for employment.

At the same time, compared to Northern Europe, Italy's status as an immigrant destination and the racial and religious diversity that brings are still relatively new phenomena, and this affects the reception of those crossing the Mediterranean today. In many smaller Italian towns, 2014 marked the arrival of the first Black residents. (Note that I am using "resident" to indicate someone who lives in a place, regardless of legal status.) Newcomers represent a diversity of backgrounds, as well as a range of needs and expectations. They navigate systems and communities that are grappling with the changes migration brings within a society that treats it as a novelty and that has largely not reckoned with longer histories of colonialism and mobility entangled in today's border crossings.

To elucidate the coloniality of the emergency apparatus and how it shapes and is shaped by acts of witnessing, this book engages the Black Mediterranean as both analytical framework and political praxis.[44] The Black Mediterranean builds on the Black radical tradition to center colonialism and racial politics in the histories, cultures, and mobilities of the Mediterranean region. Contemporary precarious migration marks the centrality of the Black Mediterranean—and its erasure from official histories—to the continual formation of Europe and its borderscapes.[45]

Contexts deemed "border crises" may seem to represent the key "contact zones" of the twenty-first century. Yet a Black Mediterranean analytic reveals that the contemporary Afro-European borderzone only *appears* to fit Mary Louise Pratt's description of historical contact zones as "spaces where disparate cultures meet, grapple with each other." The emergency apparatus enables the circulation of this myth of the "disparate" and of migration as constituting an encounter between "peoples geographically and historically separated."[46] In fact, Mediterranean studies scholars have long defined the region not by how it separates different communities and cultures but as a space of ongoing trade, encounter, conflict, exchange, and imagination.[47] And as I show throughout this book, those occupying Italy's legal and social margins often express a keen sense of familiarity with Europe and with Italian culture. Instead, migrants and Italians of African descent are widely perceived as strangers who could never possibly be or become Italian, and who have no connection to Italian history or culture—an idea that emergency imaginaries of foreignness uphold. Discourses of emergency obscure how, in fact, contemporary mobilities extend longer histories of diaspora and relations between African and European communities.

Black Mediterranean perspectives also underscore Italy's fraught relationship with Southernness, via its own South and its position as a Southern European nation. As Gramsci's Southern Question (*questione meridionale*) articulates, debates about how to unify the country relied on racist stereotypes of Southerners as backward and behind, and Northerners as more industrial and advanced. Perceived differences between North and South concerned not only territorial Italy, but its position "between" Africa and Europe in terms of both geography and (perceived) development.[48] Italy's birth as a nation coincided with the expansion of European colonialism, and the newly unified country sought to assert its position through campaigns that could shift balances of power toward the Mediterranean—in particular in the Horn of Africa and North Africa (Libya).[49] Emergency rule was implemented repeatedly, both within the nation—for instance, in Sicily to quell unrest among workers known as the Fasci Siciliani in the 1890s—and in the colonies, including when Italian forces consolidated powers in Cyrenaica (Libya) by imprisoning people from rural and nomadic communities in concentration camps and cutting off key supply routes.[50] This in turn shaped public perceptions of those governed—Southern Italians or African colonial subjects—as disorderly and threatening. Notions of race and foreignness were reified in mainstream Italian culture through dehumanizing colonial propaganda, including music, film, and advertising that shaped dominant narratives about Africa, Italy, and Italy's "others."[51]

A Black Mediterranean analytic thus sheds light on the emergency management of borders and belonging as a historical practice applied in new ways in the post–Cold War securitization of migration.[52] Indeed, since the 1980s, as Italy has grappled with its position as a gatekeeper for Fortress Europe, the country has largely handled fluctuating arrivals through emergency governance (table 2, appendix). The year 1990 saw a paradigm shift in Italy's approach to migration, including the country's first comprehensive immigration legislation, the Martelli Law, and Italy's signing of the EU's Schengen agreement. Schengen guarantees freedom of movement between EU member states for European citizens and legal residents; at the same time, it marks the tightening and securitizing of external borders.[53] The Martelli Law expanded the geographical scope of Italy's asylum adjudication so that non-Europeans could seek protection there, while also regulating the movements of non-Europeans more broadly through a series of visa stipulations. Like other major immigration legislation that followed, Martelli was instituted "under emergency conditions."[54] In 1991, thousands of people fleeing persecution in Somalia and the former Yugoslavia made their way to Italy. The August 8, 1991, arrival by boat of twenty thousand Albanians fleeing regime collapse affirmed widespread fears that equated precarious migration with invasion. Images of people leaping off the crowded *Vlora* ship as it reached the port of Bari still circulate in media as representative of so-called emergenze immigrazione.[55]

In line with trends across the global north, the post-1990 period is marked by the conflation of migration, security, and "crisis." As Mezzadra and Neilson put it, "'migration management' has become a kind of synonym for 'crisis management.'"[56] Since the 1990s, lawmakers have on the one hand attempted to manage legalized migration "flows" through country-based quotas and periodic amnesty for undocumented migrants. On the other hand, they have repeatedly addressed "irregular" migration through emergency declarations that change how arriving migrants are processed and limit their options for accessing aid and claiming asylum.[57] In fact, from 2013 to 2024, the country saw seven different governments, including left- and right-wing leadership, each of which implemented emergency legislation and relied on emergency discourse to govern migration.

Emergency declarations open access to funding and aid and enable swift action, but they also serve as political tools. In Italy, policies issued under a state of emergency or *in via d'urgenza* ("urgently") procure immediate funding for reception and asylum procedures, but they do not offer a long-term vision for migrant or community well-being—let alone an idea that "Italian communities" might be understood as including migrants and their children. Newcomers consistently represent a diverse and changing set of countries of origin[58] and include parents, children, cousins, manual laborers, artists, political organizers, veterans, teachers, university students, ambulant vendors, farmers, and tradespeople. A majority are men in their teens and twenties, and in light of the regular arrivals of people from West Africa, the Horn of Africa, and the Sahel, the image of the young Black male migrant dominates Italian media coverage of migration.[59]

This is the case because emergency imaginaries are shaped by a pervasive "forgetting" of the violent realities of Italian colonial campaigns, in particular those in Libya and the Horn of Africa. This "colonial aphasia," as Ann Stoler terms these forms of displaced colonial memory, manifests in the widely held belief that Italian colonialism was a brief and finite endeavor, encapsulated in the common phrase *italiani brava gente*, or "good Italians."[60] This phrase suggests that Italian colonizers weren't as bad as, say, the British or the French. This idea stems in part from what is seen as an anticlimactic ending to colonial rule with World War II, when Italy lost its colonies to Allied forces, and from associations of colonialism with the twenty-year Fascist period only.[61] "Italiani brava gente" discourse downplays the actual length and violence of colonial campaigns, and how they molded and furthered discourses of nationalism and "the other."[62] This phrase continues to circulate, even among younger generations, despite movements to correct the narrative. Media coverage of migrants as constituting an emergenza perpetuates this aphasia, with little acknowledgment of the histories linking Italians to migrants from former colonies in the Horn of Africa and to the role of Libya, also a former colony, as a key point of departure, detention, and struggle for those who cross the sea.

Processes of racialization in Italy are part of larger "racializing assemblages"[63] that exceed a single nation: they were applied across Europe to justify territorial expansion and exclusionary citizenship, and they manifest today in violent bordering practices and racist anti-immigrant sentiment that positions African migrants and people of color to feel they are "in but not of Europe," to borrow from Stuart Hall.[64] Precarious Mediterranean migration and related testimonies inscribe Italian spaces not with the forgotten past but with these ongoing entanglements, that is, history as life unfolding, in the sense Baldwin describes: "History, I contend, is the present—*we*, with every breath we take, every move we make, *are* History."[65]

Emergency imaginaries also rely on gender stereotypes, with African men often presumed by European publics—and by border and asylum officials—to be economic migrants, and women presumed to be sex workers or the victims of sex trafficking. Although women consistently comprise less than 15 percent of people crossing the Central Mediterranean, their representation in or erasure from media coverage of precarious migration influences public notions of deservingness, or who is seen as meriting legal protection or social belonging.[66] A number of organizations and activists work to challenge these stereotypes, but sexualized language about black bodies still appears in mainstream cinema and television and can be traced back to the colonial racial logics that marked the bodies of colonized women as "dangerous."[67] These discourses mark the Black Mediterranean as a site where colonialism's longue durée shapes lives through widespread disregard for its influence.

Emergency imaginaries of foreignness construct "imagined communities" through an ahistorical view of belonging that enables the emergency apparatus to displace the already displaced.[68] The normalization of Italy's emergency imaginary means that debates about immigration policy and border governance unfold almost exclusively within the parameters dictated by emergency thinking.[69] In turn, the repeated, seemingly endless emergenze immigrazione directly concern understandings of who deserves to move to and through Italian spaces or to have the chance to become Italian, and by extension, who can be European.

## THE EMERGENCY APPARATUS: A CRITICAL REFUGEE STUDIES APPROACH TO "CRISIS"

As the Italian case shows, the emergency apparatus of migration is a definitive twenty-first century network of relations, an "ensemble" that, via Foucault's notion of *dispositif*, "consist[s] of discourses, institutions, architectural forms, regulatory decisions, laws, administrative measures, scientific statements, philosophical, moral and philanthropic propositions—in short, the said as much as the unsaid."[70]

Emergency reception policies and border surveillance practices, crisis discourses, media representations of suffering and vulnerability, detention and reception centers and improvised camps, and the routines and challenges of daily life in borderzones operate in relation to one another to produce what is recognized as a migration crisis. These "emergencies" are mediated at multiple scales. The United Nations High Commissioner for Refugees (UNHCR) maintains a web portal explicitly called "emergencies" which, during the writing of this book, has consistently included from eight to fifteen situations around the globe, including in Europe—situations of extreme urgency where emergency response mechanisms offer some relief but also risk decontextualizing and spectacularizing people's suffering.[71] Dynamics in Europe are echoed in Australia's island detention system and at the US-Mexico border, which media and politicians alternately portray as a humanitarian emergency, a drug trafficking crisis, an immigrant invasion, and a crisis of institutions.[72] In migration contexts, as in emergency-oriented governance concerning climate change or economic collapse, emergency policies and discourses radically alter collective imaginations about past, present, and future.[73] The "crises" that emerge through these ensembles shift and morph in relation to particular sites and subjects, "appear[ing] at the intersection of power relations and relations of knowledge."[74] That is, the emergency apparatus of migration is a "system of relations" that shapes how we conceptualize mobility and people on the move.

The crisis discourses that dominate Western imaginaries focus on transit from global south to global north. These regional designations are problematic; I use them here to indicate movements between former colonies and colonizing powers, and to trouble the homogenizing force of north/south terms. Epitomizing these problematics, emergency and crisis framings of migration in Europe, Australia, and the United States entirely disregard the fact that a significant majority of the world's displaced people in fact reside in the global south and either remain within a country or move to a neighboring nation. Nor are walls and violent bordering only the purview of the West. Yet the border crossings that have come to define debates about immigration policy and migrant rights in the twenty-first century overwhelmingly concern the movement of people between former colonies and former colonizing powers.

At this broad level, then, the emergency apparatus reifies Eurocentric notions of development and belonging, and the racial hierarchies those notions affirm. In turn, as *emergency* has become the standard mode of response for these mobilities, it has defined the challenges that asylum seekers confront in the twenty-first century. In addition to putting border crossers' lives at greater risk and bolstering xenophobia, the emergency apparatus furthers discourses that purport to support refugees yet in fact consistently undermine notions and practices of protection, calling into question the legitimacy of the refugee in legal and cultural terms, and upending how rights and protections are recognized.

Operating as an apparatus, emergency is anything but static, and I refer to it as "in transit" to indicate multiple kinds of movement. First, Europe's "crisis" is a site of transit migration. Not only do migrants often reach Europe after crossing multiple borders, but Southern European nations then often function as transit countries that people hope to pass through en route to a country where they already speak the language or have heard reception conditions are better.[75] EU policy renders this transit especially difficult. Through 2024, the Dublin Regulation ("Dublin III") required migrants to apply for asylum in the country where they first enter the EU (and the new EU Pact on Migration and Asylum, adopted in April 2024, does not afford migrants any additional autonomy).[76] In practice, this has meant that Italy, Greece, Malta, and Spain have faced what media and politicians highlight as a particular burden to process a majority of applications. This is one reason that the phrase "refugee crisis" calls to mind images of lines of migrants disembarking in Lampedusa, or overcrowded Greek camps; Southern, external borders are seen as *the* sites of emergency.

For these border crossers, arrival means ongoing transit that involves both enforced precarity and strategic decision-making. This is akin to how Jodi Byrd defines transit in the context of settler colonialism and indigenous genocide: "to exist liminally in the ungrievable spaces of suspicion and unintelligibility" and also, importantly, as "active presence in a world of relational movements and countermovements."[77] In this sense, transit is a crucial mode within the colonial present, and a focus on transit recognizes the agency expressed by people on the move and in solidarity efforts.

At the same time, *transit* here can also be understood as a form of fugitivity—of flight, escape, the search for refuge, and movement toward an uncertain future. Semantically, fugitivity and refugeeness are linked as concepts that center flight—links Moten also highlights in describing fugitivity as an "essential" force of Black life,[78] naming fugitivity as a state of "stolen breath, stolen life" and as revealing a world of possibilities: "What if being-fugitive bears the possibility of a recalibration of the human, a reopening of, rather than an opening to, the not open?" Testimonies in transit, as forms of fugitive witnessing, create and signal some of these possibilities.[79]

Emergency is also in transit across differing and oppositional rhetorics. As I emphasize above, invocations of crisis and emergency describe migration alternately as a problem of sovereignty, solidarity, security, or in Europe, as Vicki Squire has discussed, "European values."[80] This is especially salient in visual media, which perform distinct forms of "image operations" that shape ideas about migration as they circulate, as Krista Lynes, Tyler Morgenstern, and Ian Alan Paul posit.[81] Fear-mongering discourses that treat migration as a threat have oriented European public and political debate not around improving reception and protection systems, but around the gendered, racialized suspicion that most of those crossing must not be "real refugees" but are in fact "economic migrants." Per Article 14 of the Universal Declaration of Human Rights, those crossing have a right to claim asylum. Yet in practice, they are othered and adjudicated—informally and now also formally—before they have a chance to testify before officials.

While governments regularly declare states of emergency in response to shifts in border crossing, not all such declarations function equally. A case in point: just over five years after the Campidoglio protest, Italy declared a state of emergency for Ukrainians fleeing Russia's early 2022 invasion of their country. While in principle the declaration tapped the same mechanisms and institutions used to manage Mediterranean crossing, the rhetoric surrounding Ukrainian flight had a wholly distinct tenor, including in decrees that recognized Italy's already large Ukrainian community and emphasized that Italian reception structures would expand to accommodate Ukrainians "regardless of whether they had filed a claim for international protection"—a stipulation unheard of for those arriving by sea.[82] The welcome and necessary protections extended to Ukrainians thus also signaled a different kind of hospitality and set of expectations about those approaching Italy from Eastern Europe, rather than Africa.

In yet another kind of transit, these emergency imaginaries feed political shifts. Over the last decade, they have bolstered the election of populist leaders running on anti-immigration platforms. They also legitimize the militarization of Fortress Europe, which polices mobilities in the Mediterranean, within Europe, and beyond it.[83] These measures include border walls (more than doubled in number since 2015), pushbacks at sea, and agreements with third countries including Türkiye, Libya, and Albania to detain people attempting to reach Europe. Italian authorities have criminalized migration and rescue, including, since 2018, by periodically preventing NGO-operated vessels from disembarking rescued migrants at Italian ports—a practice that violates international agreements and effectively holds migrants captive at sea.[84] The emergency apparatus thus operates on people in transit to Europe and through externalization measures that move in the opposite direction, carrying Europe's borders into other countries. As I discuss in chapters 2 and 3, it also shapes the possibilities and limits of *accoglienza*, or reception, within a country.

Contemporary precarious migration to Europe has spurred a large body of research on violent border policies, racialized responses to migrant arrivals, the (post)coloniality of Mediterranean migrations, and the mediation of these issues across multiple outlets and platforms.[85] This work sheds light on the necropolitical, gendered, racialized, and Islamophobic realities of migration in Europe. In the Italian context, a growing body of interdisciplinary scholarship engages postcolonial perspectives, positing questions of migration, race, and racial capitalism as central to Italian history and culture, and recognizing the constancy of Italian discourses of *emergenza*.[86] Collectively, this scholarship underscores the urgency of "undoing border imperialism," as Walia contends, by recognizing, challenging, and dismantling the material and imagined borders that "keep us separated from one another."[87]

This work requires that we interrogate dominant narratives and discursive framings that enable violence to continue. Yet it remains challenging to talk about contemporary migration without invoking "crisis," a convenient and widely used point of reference and one that many scholars adopt, even in scare quotes as I have done here, to signal a particular period of migration or conditions of extreme urgency. If we are to move beyond the ready othering of people in transit and the violence that borders provoke, then scholars, journalists, activists, politicians, and humanitarian workers must find ways to articulate migration beyond terms that reify spectacle and uphold emergency imaginaries of foreignness. In conceptualizing the emergency apparatus, this book attempts to move us forward in responding to this challenge.

A critical refugee studies approach to the emergency apparatus of migration builds on the premise that people on the move are knowledge producers who make meaning and write history through and despite circumstances of risk, uncertainty, fleetingness, and fugitivity. Refugees, undocumented migrants, and displaced people more broadly both risk and require anonymity, and their movements trace the limits and violence of the nation-state.[88] As "a paradigmatic figure of geopolitical critique,"[89] the refugee "illuminates the interconnections of colonization, war, and global social change."[90] People undertaking precarious journeys are fleeing a series of "crises," including war, climate change, and economic hardship, only to be treated as if they are the source of disaster. In testimonies, and in creative work that utilizes testimony, they reclaim and resignify their positions in Italy.

This approach also embraces the tensions of terminology as a source of insight. As a term, *emergency* operates within the seemingly contradictory categories of urgency and permanence, describing situations whose initial urgency transforms into a longer-term state of unresolve, as well as circumstances of extreme urgency and unpredictability. Emergency refers to the biopolitics of sovereignty; it is also, following Calhoun, "the primary term for referring to catastrophes, conflicts, and settings for human suffering." Colloquially, public discourse moves relatively fluidly between the term emergency and these cognates, including crisis.[91] All these terms describe significant large-scale problems of significant consequence. In theory, calling these circumstances a crisis recognizes them as a turning point, via the Greek *krisis*. Emergency, from the Latin *emergere* or *emergens*, instead connotes a bringing to light, or an arising. In its associations with urgency and its shared origins with the emergent, I understand *emergency* to suggest a disruption of what is perceived as normal and, in line with Hall, as marking "a moment of profound rupture . . . an accumulation of contradictions."[92] I'm interested in how these emergent properties are revealed through a range of witnessing forms, themselves also emergent. While I refer to *crisis* throughout this book, my specific focus on *emergency* centers emergency response approaches to migration and the related situations that unfold at multiple scales across political, legal, humanitarian, and quotidian contexts.

While etymologically related to *emergency*, *emergenza* does not invoke the same association with "emergence" ("emergence" in Italian is more readily translated as *emersione* or even *nascita* or *apparizione*, depending on the context). In Italian, *emergenza* frequently refers to institutional failure, and more generally to the simultaneous urgency and interminability of a crisis or disaster situation.[93] *Emergenza* has particular associations with polemics about government response to, and responsibility for, the aftermath of a range of crises, circulating in recent memory in connection with *emergenze rifiuti* (garbage crises) in Naples and Rome,[94] and with the *emergenze* that marked the long aftermath of the 2009 earthquake in L'Aquila and the 2023 flooding in Emilia Romagna.[95] Italy's *emergenza immigrazione* intersects with numerous other issues in a neoliberal "crisis Italy" and, like its other emergencies, disregards the histories bound up in these multiple and entangled issues.[96] The cultural and historical specificity of *emergenza* informs my understanding of emergency as itself a concept constantly in transit and in translation.

The word *refugee* is especially contentious in the Afro-European borderzone, where public discourses of crisis reinforce a problematic binary between "real refugees" and "undeserving economic migrants." While some scholars and activists understandably use "refugee" for anyone who has fled their home country, here I adopt the broader umbrella term "migrant" in order to address mobility both within and outside of legal frameworks.[97] The protagonists of *Emergency in Transit* are border crossers, newcomers, people in transit, activists, demonstrators, camp residents, workers, authors, and narrators. Throughout the book, I use the terms with which they described their movements, spaces, and relationships, and when relevant to a specific situation, I refer to legal status—for example, "asylum seeker" or "refugee."

## TESTIMONY AS METHOD

In this book I move between multiple witnessing accounts, including my own, to elaborate the emergency apparatus and new or alternative understandings of mobility and belonging that emerge in relation to it. Recalling Mezzadra and Neilson's "border as method" approach to the border "not only as a research 'object' but also as an 'epistemic' angle,"[98] I engage published life narratives and also participate in the production of testimony through what I term "testimony as method," through oral history and ethnographic research in which I bore witness as interviewer, listener, and observer. As I elaborate here, this approach encompasses an understanding of witnessing as a genre of encounter—one bears witness before a real or imagined audience—and testimony as the "text" that emerges from that encounter. My discussion is significantly informed by research I conducted in 2017–2019, years that saw critical shifts in policy and discourse, including the expansion of the Italy-Libya Memorandum of Understanding, the rise of right-wing populist leaders and their emphasis on "emergenza," and the criminalization of migration and humanitarian aid. In subsequent research, I have seen the corresponding dynamics of transit and precarity become only further exacerbated.

*Emergency in Transit* moves from the premise that our colonial present is shaped in part by the failures of empathy. That is, my focus on witnessing acts is not an appeal to empathy; the seemingly endless deaths in global north borderzones are themselves a stark lesson in the limits of empathy. In this context, some kinds of witnessing power the emergency apparatus, for instance when the state memorializes deaths to control broader narratives of migration, as I discuss in chapter 1. Other kinds of witnessing, including the migrant-centered literary and multimedia works I discuss throughout the book, imagine beyond emergency. In focusing especially on migrant testimonials, I consider how narrators transact with (potential) audiences. While trauma is absolutely relevant, in line with narrative scholars Sybille Krämer and Sigrid Weigel, I do not limit my engagement to representations of trauma.[99] Here I understand testimony as an account that bears witness to lived or observed experiences of struggle, suffering, or transformation.

Testimony is critical to the operations of emergency for at least two reasons: First, testimony is *the* critical genre for asylum seekers, whose potential legal recognition as refugees hinges on the account they give of why they had to flee their home country. In other words, refugee status determination is largely a narrative problem, dependent on establishing a "well-founded fear" of persecution, per UNHCR protocols. The burden of proof, though, generally rests with the asylum seeker: to furnish evidence and, crucially, to tell the story of their fear, persecution, and escape in ways that are recognizable to asylum officials.[100] How asylum seekers tell their story—what they include or omit, what they name or emphasize—influences asylum officials' assessment of whether someone's fear is well founded. This notion of deservingness operates outside of asylum courts as well, as discourses of emergency center the economic migrant, widely viewed as "undeserving" of protection or legal residency. Carried out amid the absence of individual testimony, this public adjudication is a vehicle for the "overdetermination"[101] that racializes people in transit and protection processes.

Second, emergency itself depends on acts of witnessing. Emergency, like crisis, is in one sense "an observation that produces meaning."[102] How circumstances come to be marked as emergency, and the questions we can ask about them, depend on that initial observation, or witnessing moment. Emergency responses depend on witnessing as a real possibility: to make known what is happening in circumstances of flux requires ongoing transactions of testifying and listening, or bearing and becoming witness. Witnessing is neither inherently "good" nor always possible. Witnessing can reveal or obscure particular experiences, spotlighting or censoring details. States of emergency and related discourses simultaneously prompt acts of witnessing and raise questions about the "tellability" of certain experiences, where tellability refers to the possibilities and limits for representing those experiences in narrative form.[103] Through acts of witnessing and the narrative and discursive questions to which they call attention, *emergency*, initially an observation, becomes a narrative frame that enables and engages testimonial narratives. Processes of witnessing are linked to the politics of visibility: whose testimony emerges and how it circulates are crucial for eliciting public and political responses to actual need, for the writing of history, and for imagining alternative futures.

The designation of emergency is managed through a range of testimonial forms, including direct witnessing acts, as in eye-witness journalistic accounts or migrant-authored memoirs; and secondary witnessing such as news coverage with interview clips, works of literature where narrators report the testimony of others, or scholarship that reproduces witnessing texts, as I do here. Testimony is also crucial for humanitarian workers who assess risk. For example, UNHCR trains responders on specific interview processes for crisis situations. NGOs regularly feature migrant testimony in reports and press releases about border violence or detention. Bureaucratic records constitute yet another form of witnessing texts. Italian reception center managers submit monthly reports documenting life in the center; in this sense, they regularly testify to the functioning of emergency response. These texts represent distinct and critical encounters through which the emergency apparatus takes shape, including both acts of witnessing that support emergency imaginaries, as well as testimonies that reveal their limits and omissions.

Instances of witnessing abound, but these "texts" are often excerpted without extensive engagement[104] or are used in ways that reify crisis framings. In cultural texts, media coverage, and political debate, uses of testimony often align with "available narratives" of migration—those already dominant in discourse—and reproduce border spectacle or underscore suffering and vulnerability.[105] The globally celebrated film *Fire at Sea* (*Fuocoammare*, dir. Gianfranco Rosi, 2016), for instance, incorporates the witnessing of a Sicilian child, of Nigerian migrants, and of surveillance technology. While the account of Lampedusa is moving, the film ultimately positions viewers to see migration via the lenses of surveillance and anonymized migrant suffering. Likewise, in media and political discourse, spectacle abounds. Meanwhile, in general, migrants' own witnessing possibilities are limited because of the legal and social structures that hold them in limbo, and because the narratives that do circulate overwhelmingly treat migration as an immediate, unforeseen problem. Yet testimony is critical for countering violence and its subsequent erasure from public memory, as we know from the testimony of Holocaust survivors.[106] Narrators bearing witness from within contexts of limbo and extreme uncertainty may struggle to find "adequate witnesses" who receive testimony on its own terms, and they often have to find new forms for their stories—a shift in form, practice, and even language in order to hold the world to account.[107]

As a genre of encounter, testimony is an emergent form, taking shape through the transactions of bearing and becoming witness. As such, testimonies are evidentiary and relational: they represent material circumstances, and they do so through the actual or potential exchange of an account produced for an audience, be it media consumers, readers and viewers, or an individual interviewer. That audience, whether real or imagined, necessarily shapes the testimony itself, in form and content. This witnessing transaction can be understood in rhetorical and ethical terms as an exchange that enlists witnesses in both "an appeal and an oath."[108] In this sense, testimony is also a political form, one that "*emerges* out of a political context, in response to a particular set of political circumstances and rhetorical conditions."[109]

Testimony's emergent property inscribes it as a form bound to the state of emergency, recalling Homi Bhabha's oft-cited statement that "states of emergency are also always sites of *emergence*"—which he observes through a reading of Fanon's work on resistance from within the colonial state of emergency.[110] At the same time, witnessing is also a process for imagining beyond "crisis." In this sense, in engaging testimonies in transit, I draw on Baldwin's work on witnessing and Black life, which bridges struggles across the Atlantic, and in which he recognizes witnessing as truth telling and as a gesture toward the future, a practice of being "witness to what I've seen and the possibilities that I think I see"[111] and a site of hope or possibility, however small. As he wrote in a piece protesting the US war in Vietnam and arguing for global racial justice, "I think that mankind can do better than that, and I wish to be a witness to this small and stubborn possibility."[112] To witness beyond crisis logics, then, is to create and communicate modes for understanding movement outside dominant framings, and also to make possible the "small and stubborn possibility" of change.

This is not to suggest that testimony is necessarily on the side of the oppressed. Testimonies can be deployed by those in power to maintain dominant narratives and are fraught, even in humanitarian contexts where individual testimonies are used to "mak[e] individuals 'save-able' or 'rescue-able' by those with the power to do so."[113] Critically, they are also potentially "mobilized as potent political weapons to wield against agents of a state, political factions, and the threat of national forgetting."[114] Like the Latin American practice of *testimonio*, which has itself been described as "an 'emergency' narrative," testimony can challenge dominant narratives by reorienting narrators and audiences in relation to one another, and to a particular set of dynamics.[115]

Testimonies produced by those whose voices are most often disregarded in political debate and media coverage constitute an alternative archive and are also processes of seeing and making visible that might unsettle dominant narratives about refugees, rights, and national belonging, including by potentially "troubling" the distance between various groups.[116] I focus on testimonies that document underrepresented experiences and that emerge through an impulse not to cultivate empathy across difference but to shift how audiences understand their own position. I see these testimonies as enacting what Baldwin proposes as a key function of witnessing: to prompt a new way of seeing among audiences and to challenge the ways one is seen by contesting what others accept as normal. "The black man insists, by whatever means he finds at his disposal," writes Baldwin about his experience in a Swiss village, "that the white man cease to regard him as an exotic rarity and recognize him as a human being."[117]

The testimonies I consider represent the voices of border crossers, Black Italians, and staff and volunteers working with migrants at reception sites in Italy (not mutually exclusive categories). They include memoir and film that center migrant experiences and "(re)inscrib[e] the presence of racialized communities onto the European landscape,"[118] oral history interviews I conducted during ethnographic research, and a set of encounters in urban spaces. To be clear, literary and filmic witnessing and oral history interviews produce distinct kinds of testimony. As Johanna Sellman contends, "literary narratives of migration are often powerful precisely because they operate in a very different kind of truth economy . . . [and engage in] intertextual dialogue with various other *kinds* of narratives about migration, literary and otherwise."[119] In conceptualizing testimony as method, I acknowledge and respond to these differences while also recognizing various testimonial forms in relation, within an expanding "testimonial network."[120] In discussing published literature and film together with locally circulating narratives and oral histories, I build on Gillian Whitlock's discussion of literature and recognize cultural texts as having a particular capacity "to 'bear' testimony—not just to duplicate or record events, but to make history available to imaginative acts."[121] My discussion of multiple textual forms draws extensively on the time I spent with refugees, asylum seekers, undocumented migrants, and Italian volunteers and staff in Italian cities, reception centers, and camps, during ethnographic research in 2017, 2018, and 2019 in the regions of Lazio, Tuscany, Molise, and Calabria, in follow-up correspondence, and in post-pandemic field visits in 2022.

To that end, oral history shaped this project in significant ways, as a method that reckons explicitly with witnessing as a layered, relational, and interpretive act.[122] In narrativizing individual and collective memories, oral history can attend to the consequences that nations and nationalisms bear on bodies and communities, especially in its application as "a postcolonial enterprise [that] pays special attention to nationalism's excesses: the violation of borders, forced migrations, global wars and internal political conflicts that disturb the social order."[123] The Italians I interviewed were, in general, locals who worked or volunteered with migrants in their own hometowns. Reflecting general trends in migration to Italy, the migrants I interviewed had fled situations of conflict, persecution, and extreme precarity in countries throughout the Middle East and Africa. Given my focus on (post) coloniality and the convergence of anti-immigrant and anti-Black sentiment in the last decade, the interviews and exchanges I draw on here are primarily with people who left their home countries in West Africa, the Sahel, and the Horn of Africa, traversed the Sahara, and spent time in Libya before crossing the sea. Conscious of the ease with which portrayals of suffering can perpetuate the power dynamics they criticize, I take care to honor their stories and experiences as critical sites of meaning making while also protecting their identities. To this end, I offer different degrees of detail, depending on individual situations. This means I often use pseudonyms, especially for interlocutors who were still in transit when we spoke. These priorities apply to the images I share as well.

Working across multiple languages requires attention to the pressures, risks, possibilities, and inadequacies of translation. In the case of oral histories, I conducted interviews in Italian or English, and though I offered to include an interpreter, few people opted for this. Many of the migrants I interviewed were still awaiting papers yet had lived in Italy long enough to have learned the language and feel confident discussing their experiences in Italian. Transcribing and translating multilingual or second language interviews raises important ethical questions. Here, following oral history principles, I have edited for clarity without imposing my own "corrections" on anyone's speech. Ethnographers approach this process in multiple ways; here I view staying close to the language people themselves chose to use as a matter of respect and honesty.

This book is of course also my testimony, one that emerged in conversation with the myriad people, spaces, and texts that I discuss in its pages, through my perspective as someone who has come to know Italy and the Italian language through my own foreignness. The difference between the ways my whiteness, my US citizenship, or my marriage to an Italian citizen facilitates my movement across borders and within Italian spaces becomes starkly apparent in encounters with people whose every movement toward and within Europe is treated as suspect. My interrogation of Italian colonial memory as a transnational problem began more than two decades ago, when my initial encounters with literary and artistic work by Italians of African descent prompted me to reconsider what I knew about Italian history and how I experienced Italian spaces. Reading Somali Italian authors Ubah Cristina Ali Farah and Igiaba Scego on the erasures of history in a place so weighted with historical layers, I also grappled anew with US history and racial politics—with Baldwin observing the civil rights movement from France, with Toni Morrison on how a "real or fabricated Africanist presence was crucial to [white writers'] sense of Americanness"[124]—recognizing how the specificity of underdiscussed Italian histories not only mirrors but is entangled in broader structures of racial capitalism. My motivation to challenge the pervasive public and political fixation on "crisis" became clearest to me in moments like a conversation I had in 2018 with Yousef (pseudonym), who had reached Italy to seek political asylum after fleeing the Gambia. As we shared mint tea at an improvised camp in Rome, he talked about migration as a creative act, one that is both necessary for reaching safety and that remains full of possibility. "Even if in Italy they ban migration," he said, "that will not stop migration. Because the world is big. [Migration is] something with you—it must *have* to be in my life and I have to travel in life. . . . No one is useless on this earth."[125]

In drawing oral history and written, visual, and filmic testimonies into conversation, I move between multiple kinds of borders, recognizing them as virtually ubiquitous "complex social institutions"[126] and "structures of the imagination."[127] In this way, the book transits across multiple sites in which the emergency apparatus operates, via multimedia and ethnographic testimonies that reveal the coloniality of emergency while also proclaiming the emergence of new subjectivities, networks, and mobilities. They point to how, from amid widespread injustice and the failures of empathy, we might reclaim rights and come to see the world—and our own place in it—differently.

## ORGANIZATION OF THE BOOK

The following chapters trace a temporal and geographic arc, following migrants' paths from sea crossing to longer-term living in Italy. Each main chapter centers a key site of encounter along this journey and presents witnessing texts that emerge at these sites through meetings between migrants and a range of actors and institutions. The appendix contains tables representing arrival and death data, Italy's emergency-driven migration policies, and types of reception centers.

Part 1, Arrivals, focuses on the production of crisis and the machinery of the emergency apparatus as it immediately affects people crossing the Mediterranean, turning to the sea, the reception center, and the camp. Chapter 1, "Strange Grief and Elegiac Possibilities in the Black Mediterranean," addresses the centrality of death to the emergency apparatus, and the relationship between emergency, border violence, and grievability. I put state commemorations that use migrant deaths to bolster crisis narratives in conversation with migrant-led elegies that document peril and death at sea. Unlike what I describe as the *strange grief* of the Italian state, these elegies honor lost lives in ways that challenge necropolitical bordering practices. Chapter 2, "Hospitality as Emergency Response," focuses on Italy's official accoglienza (reception) system. I turn to oral history interviews with reception center residents to show how structural responses to emergency hold recently arrived migrants in *paradoxes of proximity* in which they are encouraged to "integrate" into Italian society and yet are held, geographically and socially, just outside those communities. Following frustrations with official reception or rejected claims, migrants may exit the formal system and make their way to one of the country's numerous informal settlements. In chapter 3, "Emergent Practices of Hospitality in the Camp," I draw on observations, interviews, and writing produced at an encampment in Rome to argue that, rather than spaces of exception, these camps should be understood as sites critical to the government's emergency response strategies, as well as sites of struggle and collective agency, and spaces constructed through multiple acts of witnessing.

In part 2, The Right to Remain, I consider witnessing practices that challenge the sense of an interminable present imposed by crisis framings. These chapters explore the complex social and historical entanglements that emergency labels obscure, how those entanglements affect migrant realities today, and how border crossers stake a claim in Italian spaces, challenging their exclusion and imagining alternative futures. This second part moves away from immediate contexts of arrival to consider how emergency framings of migration shape lives well beyond those spaces and temporalities. In chapters 4 and 5, I consider these social and historical entanglements in cities. Senegalese street vendors are central figures in Italian imaginaries of foreignness and blackness and in the material history of irregular migration and migrant labor in Italy. Chapter 4, "Street Vendor as Witness," considers how ambulant vendors' witnessing reveals the high stakes of their labor and the ways it enacts possibilities for social change. Chapter 5, "Seen and Unseen in the City," discusses how emergency imaginaries and emergency responses to migration obscure the ways colonialism's longue durée visibly shapes urban spaces within the former colonizing power, taking Italy's capital city as a key site of encounter. Within contexts deemed "crisis," I argue, urban space prompts creative acts of witnessing that remap relations between migrants, white Italians, and Italians of African descent. Chapter 6, "Oranges and Riot Gear," addresses the relationship between precarious mobility and precarious labor, recognizing exploitative agricultural labor in particular as a product of the nexus of globalization, border control, the criminalization of migration, and organized crime. By invisibilizing migrants' key role in these economies, emergency approaches to bordering fail to disrupt this racialized violence and support an exploitative system that produces further precarity.

The epilogue, "Mobility in an Age of Emergency, or, A Small and Stubborn Possibility," reflects on how the emergency apparatus of migration thrives on the failures of empathy and intersects with multiple other global issues including climate change, pandemics, racial and social injustice, economic precarity, and conflict—circumstances that necessitate mobility even as they restrict it. As I argue throughout the book, critical and creative uses of witnessing not only address these challenges but invoke alternative modes of encounter, imagination, and action that recognize migration beyond the restrictive bounds of *crisis*.

# PART I

# Arrivals

*Foreigners who, in their own country, are denied the actual exercise of the democratic freedoms guaranteed by the Italian Constitution shall have the right of asylum in the territory of the Italian Republic, in accordance with the conditions set forth by law.*
—ARTICLE 10 OF THE ITALIAN CONSTITUTION

1

# Strange Grief and Elegiac Possibilities in the Black Mediterranean

At the end of the 2012 documentary short *A chiunque possa interessare* (*To Whom It May Concern*), Somali filmmaker and narrator Zakaria Mohamed Ali stands before the boat cemetery in Lampedusa, the small island via which he entered Italy in 2008, which has become an EU migration "hotspot" in the years since, and which he's come to revisit and record. "When I see the boats," he says, "I have the feeling of remembering and of not forgetting my migration journey, from when I arrived at Lampedusa." As he speaks, the camera pans across the remains of rickety wooden vessels brought or washed to shore after carrying migrants from Libyan, Tunisian, or even Egyptian coasts, into international waters and toward this southernmost Italian island (figure 1). "You risk your life, and so many names are still unknown," Ali continues. "They died at sea and we don't even know how many they were, whom they left, who was waiting for them in their countries. What were their dreams?" The boats are small, their metal rails rusting, hulls piled atop one another; it's hard to imagine them upright in the water, filled with dozens of men, women, and children—yet here is a small collection of evidence testifying to the tens of thousands of migrants who attempt this crossing each year. In calling to mind the journeys themselves, the boats speak to both survival and death.

To write about Mediterranean crossing is to write into the spaces of incomplete records, a kind of impossible archive: of risk, of near death, of loss. Counts of lives lost at sea are rough underestimates (table 1, appendix). There is no standardized process for whether or when to recover bodies or vessels, or for determining whose responsibility that should be. Since 2014, of the more than 1.9 million people who have attempted to cross the Mediterranean Sea to Europe, more than thirty thousand have disappeared in a watery grave. We do not know most of their names.

31

FIGURE 1. Still from *A chiunque possa interessare*. Reproduced with permission from Zakaria Mohamed Ali, Archive of Migrant Memories.

All who cross confront the risk of death, and of anonymous death. Records that cite these migrants and their disappearance as mere numbers write them into "the farce . . . of counting people without being accountable to them."[1] Ali's documentary calls attention to the nature of this archive—built of wreckage and of absence, and caught between processes of memory and erasure. The boats on shore suggest survivors; countless vessels lie instead at the bottom of the sea.

The risk of death is central to the emergency apparatus that shapes the lives of people attempting to reach Europe and obtain asylum there. This risk permeates the discourses, policies, and material and imagined experiences of urgency that arise as European authorities regulate the movements and futures of Africans on the move, and in dominant cultural narratives of migration that portray today's Mediterranean crossings to Europe as an encounter between disparate, unknown strangers with whom Europeans have no cultural or historical ties. In Europe's crisis narratives, the sea often figures as *the* site of migration, ignoring that these journeys begin thousands of miles south or east of the sea and continue long after survivors reach Italian coasts. Coverage of shipwrecks and rescue operations dominates migration news, and images of packed rubber dinghies and of survivors wrapped in gold thermal blankets often accompany such stories, no matter their specific focus. The migrant boat features prominently, as a vehicle of criminality on the one hand, or a sign of migrant vulnerability on the other—regardless of the multiple other meanings it holds for those on board. Recognizing the real urgency of these crossings is essential, and visibilizing this violence can prompt humanitarian responses. Yet prevalent and repeated media representations of people suffering at Europe's external borders, via images of Black African men in particular, feeds a "spectacle of enforcement at 'the' border, whereby migrant 'illegality' is rendered spectacularly visible."[2] This racialized, gendered border spectacle sustains perceptions of migrant arrivals as sudden and unanticipated, feeding an emergency imaginary of migration that is constructed around the erasure of migrants' own individual and collective experiences and the heterogeneous set of uncertainties, fears, decisions, and desires that shape them.

This chapter focuses on the sea as a significant but by no means singular site of "emergency" in both material and narrative terms. Death and the risk of death set the emergency apparatus in motion, creating situations of urgent need, prompting emergency response policies, and perpetuating an emergency imaginary that perceives death at sea as either a natural tragedy or evidence of individual migrant criminality. *How* border deaths get written into or withheld from public memory is critical in a climate that necessitates precarious journeys while also criminalizing them, especially in contexts defined by historical erasure, or aphasia. Dominant European media and political discourse makes it all too easy to disregard border deaths as if they have nothing to do with Europe and European communities, as if the shores of Italy delimit a boundary of concern.

But spectacle-laden narratives are not the only ones in circulation. The sea is a site of contested witnessing where narratives of crisis and practices of mourning emerge simultaneously. That is, the risk of death at sea is a fulcrum for narrative negotiations between state actors who preserve dominant discourses of national cohesion and of migration itself as a threat or problem, humanitarian groups who cite shipwrecks as evidence of the state's complicity in migrant deaths, and migrants and allies who offer representations of these dangerous crossings that move beyond dominant emergency frames. What limits do dominant representations of precarious migration establish, to invoke Saidiya Hartman, "on what can be known, whose perspective matters, and who is endowed with the gravity and authority of the historical actor"?[3] When are these losses inscribed into a collective conscious, rather than glossed in passing—through whose perspectives, and through what transactions of testifying and listening? Engaging these questions in the Afro-European borderzone requires recognizing the Mediterranean not simply as a geopolitical border, a site of tragedy, or an in-between space, but as what Iain Chambers terms a "liquid archive" where histories are produced, alliances made and broken, and journeys continued and interrupted.[4]

Recognizing the sea as a site where transit is a matter of life and death, this chapter examines commemorative and elegiac witnessing acts that negotiate dominant narratives of migration, memories of sea crossing, and material and symbolic understandings of the migrant boat. I begin by elaborating the centrality of risk in emergency responses to migration, recognizing risk as a product of necropolitical border governance. The chapter then discusses Italian state commemorations at which authorities bear witness to migrant deaths through an erasure of individual experience and entangled histories.

These witnessing events are performances of what I call *strange grief,* a term I posit to describe a display of mourning that affirms the presumed unknowability of the deceased.[5] In contrast to *strange grief* and its erasures, the migrant-centered elegiac writing and film I then discuss instead inscribe shipwrecks into a larger narrative of colonial violence, contemporary border regimes, and collective mourning. The figure of the boat recurs throughout this chapter, and the final sections take up its significance in elegiac and scholarly work that bears witness to migration beyond the spectacle of "crisis."

## MATERIAL AND MEDIATED RISK

The Mediterranean is a rough sea, with pockets of fierce currents and powerful storms. But it's not simply the challenges of navigating in inclement weather that make crossing dangerous. The risk exists first and foremost because boarding a rickety boat or rubber dinghy to claim asylum in Europe is the only route many people can access.[6] Then, there are the risks of the voyage itself: an unseaworthy vessel, a motor that breaks, no navigation tools, and too often, little hope of rescue. The dynamics of risk underscore how, as a site of emergency, the Mediterranean is also a site of production of race: the funneling of people in transit along more dangerous routes, and the treatment of their lives as disposable, perpetuates hierarchies of belonging that position Brown and Black migrants as Europe's "undesirables." In other words, death and the risk of death in crossing reveal the racial borders of Fortress Europe.

While emergency discourses may paint precarious crossings as a problem of the current moment, deadly journeys are not new. On the sea's southern shores, Tunisian fishermen in Zarzis have regularly rescued migrants at sea and buried the dead since the early 2000s.[7] Likewise, on northern coasts, Sicilian fishermen have testified to their ongoing work of rescue and to the risks they themselves face as a consequence of EU border policies, including their capture by Libyan forces.[8] In the 2010s, the three-hundred-mile trek between Libya and Italy became the world's deadliest border crossing. In the infamous 2011 case of the so-called left-to-die boat, seventy-two people departed Libya only to find themselves stranded at sea for fourteen days, while multiple ships and helicopters observed their predicament and did not intervene, during which time all but nine of the passengers died.[9] This form of knowing abandonment has since repeated, for instance in April 2023, when a boat carrying four hundred people was left adrift near Malta for more than two days. As these incidents exemplify, the risks migrants confront are manufactured by border control methods that "bridg[e] humanitarianism and crime fighting."[10]

Understood within a Black Mediterranean framework, today's precarious migrations are not sudden or isolated crises, but part of the ongoing construction of Europe and a longer history of precarious mobilities and forced labor in the region. Long before the Scramble for Africa, the Mediterranean was a site of enslavement and slave trade that supported expanding economies. As Cedric Robinson outlines in *Black Marxism*, these earnings powered Spanish and Portuguese colonial expeditions; they also profited Venetian and Genovese financiers from the thirteenth to fifteenth centuries.[11] These practices echo in the colonial present, as Europe's deadly border policies maintain a precarious labor force that sustains European economies, along with notions of blackness as an undesirable, unknowable foreignness.

The emergency apparatus relies on seemingly contradictory discourses of migration. For instance, crossings are described as threatening and unwanted, but shipwrecks are treated as tragedies, with headlines announcing "Migrant Tragedy," "New Mediterranean Boat Tragedy," "Tragedia al largo di Lampedusa," or "More Tragedy at Sea"—framings that appear to acknowledge loss. Yet, together with practices of border patrol and enforcement, these "tragedies" also construct the border spectacle, inscribing death at sea into public consciousness as a set of natural accidents that cause the death of "clandestine" or "irregular" migrants who should not have been traveling in the first place. While migrant deaths can certainly be understood in tragic terms, these deaths are not natural tragedies but consequences of violent bordering practices through which the Italian state, along with EU authorities, ensures that to reach Europe, African migrants must risk—and lose—their lives.

These bordering practices are necropolitical; that is, to apply Achille Mbembe's framing, they govern through death rather than support migrant survival, ensuring that people confront great peril while crossing borders.[12] As such, and as scholars and activists have emphasized, they enact what Judith Butler describes as "the division of the globe into grievable and ungrievable lives."[13] In the Mediterranean, necropolitical bordering includes both direct acts of violence—as when the Libyan coast guard fires at migrant vessels from boats it was given by Italy—and the closing off or policing of safer routes.[14] These practices, along with limited visa options and immigration quotas, effectively abandon migrants to the forces of nature and weaponize land- and seascapes. Those fleeing violence and precarity in their home countries are effectively routed through terrains where they are more likely to die.

Weaponization of the environment and the policing and externalization of borders have defined Fortress Europe since the 1990s and the early days of Schengen, and are paralleled by similar shifts in policy and practice across the global north.[15] From US strategies that knowingly pushed border crossers to travel through what agents acknowledged as "more hostile terrain" (e.g., Operation Blockade in 1993), to Australia's island detention centers that incarcerate asylum seekers far from Australian shores, these policies render asylum an arduous process and treat asylum seekers like criminal suspects or anonymous pawns rather than people seeking protection. In recent years, these approaches have gained ground. In a 2016 deal with Türkiye, the EU agreed to trade "irregular" migrants arriving to Greece by boat with Syrian refugees in Türkiye—an agreement that reified the notion of some migrants as more deserving of asylum than others. Türkiye has used the agreement as political leverage, threatening to "release" migrants across the Greek border.[16] Between 2018 and 2022, the United States implemented "Remain in Mexico" protocols that held Mexican and Central American asylum seekers on the Mexican side of the border, unable to file their claims. Beginning in 2022, a post–Brexit United Kingdom repeatedly attempted to send asylum seekers to Rwanda and has housed them in offshore barges. These instances of externalization paralleled Italian policies that kept migrants at bay, including efforts to close Italian ports to rescue ships.

Authorities claim that such measures discourage would-be migrants from attempting to cross, but this logic presumes that migration involves a binary choice between two equivalent options, staying or leaving. "Deterrence" policies do not alter people's needs or desires to move. They simply leave people with no options except the dangerous journey. This is evident along Europe's borders. For instance, beginning in 2015, the near-closing of the eastern Balkan route via heightened surveillance and new "smart" fences did not stop movement toward EU nations but held migrants in limbo in EU border states, including Bosnia, where they live in makeshift camps along the border.[17]

In the Central Mediterranean we see all too clearly how these policies enact a brutal disregard for Brown and Black migrants and reproduce colonial violence. The rate of death at sea has remained high even as stricter policies were followed by a decrease in arrivals; in the summer of 2019, nearly one in ten migrants crossing between Libya and Italy died (tables 2 and 3, appendix). The Italy-Libya Memorandum of Understanding (MOU), signed in 2017 and subsequently renewed, formalizes Italian support for Libyan border control, enlisting the Libyan Coast Guard to apprehend migrants at sea and detain them in Libya, where centers are so reprehensible that the United Nations and Amnesty International have cited the country for human rights violations. This MOU recalls the 2008 agreement between Silvio Berlusconi and Muammar al-Qaddafi, when Italy promised Libya €5 billion if Libyan authorities would stem sea departures to Italy. Framed as reparations for colonialism, the agreement in fact reinforced Italian control over the movement of Africans there. By design, these policies mobilize risk to control people's movements.[18] In a deadly circular logic, these risks are central in what leaders then term a crisis in need of a solution.

This violence persists in part because necropolitical bordering practices render witnessing a fraught process. Border deaths mark one of the emergency apparatus's fundamental paradoxes: that the primary subjects of *emergency* cannot speak out against its effects. In a 2016 speech at the Centro Primo Levi, author Maaza Mengiste connected today's deaths in the Mediterranean with Levi's discussion of witnessing the Holocaust and the impossibility of understanding atrocity from outside—the idea, Mengiste says, that to impart understanding, we simplify things, using ready symbols and "set[ting] aside the lingering questions." The true witnesses, those who could testify the fullest to this violence, are those who do not survive it, who experience additional violence as they are anonymized in death:

> If your body cannot be named then it is just a corpse. It is a corpse that is less than human, it is a thing. . . . There is no ritual for mourning the unclaimed. There is no paying of respects for unmarked graves. . . . You will become one of the disappeared, *gli scomparsi*. You were here and now you are not.[19]

The ultimate victims of state abandonment, those who die in transit, are unable to bear witness to these final experiences of suffering. How border deaths are recognized and recorded is essential to tracing the operations of the emergency apparatus and accounting for the histories and experiences that emergency imaginaries obscure from view.

## STATE AS WITNESS: STRANGE GRIEF

The state is a primary witness of Mediterranean migration, including in its role surveilling the sea. Yet officials often opt for silence, acknowledging neither the thousands of annual deaths and disappearances, nor the struggles of survivors. Very occasionally, the government has held a memorial for migrants who drowned near the Italian coast. By my count, in the last two-plus decades, despite often daily deaths and disappearances at sea, the Italian government held state funerals three times: on November 17, 2017, for twenty-six Nigerian women and girls whose bodies were recovered near Salerno; on October 21, 2013, for 368 migrants from the Horn of Africa whose vessel wrecked near Lampedusa in a moment often seen as marking the start of the "crisis"; and on October 25, 2003, for thirteen Somalis who drowned near Lampedusa. In these rare commemorative occasions, the state positions itself as witness and mourner. Via government ministers and mayors who officiate, the state controls the narratives that Italian publics consume about border deaths—or at least indicates which narratives are sanctioned—by inscribing deaths at sea into a larger narrative of emergency that removes state culpability, framing losses instead as "tragedies at sea" or deaths "at the hand of nature." These rare events serve as critical sites of negotiation over cultural narratives of migration, race, rights, and, sometimes, over policy.[20]

The idea of natural tragedy fosters a sense that Mediterranean crossings are unmoored from history and don't represent connections between communities. For example, in the 2003 state funeral held in Rome's Campidoglio Square for the thirteen Somalis who lost their lives, then-Mayor Walter Veltroni spoke of Somalia only as a distant place, "a forgotten land . . . destroyed for too long by civil war."[21] This statement disregards Italy's colonization of Somalia beginning in the late nineteenth century and the decades of migration between the two countries since. It rhetorically displaces Somali-Italians from the Italian national body and disregards these shared histories, including for exiles who fled Siad Barre's regime in the 1970s, those who escaped civil war in the 1990s, and those who arrive today.

Veltroni's statements represent what I term *strange grief*, a performance of mourning that reifies the unknowability of the deceased. Strange grief reminds us that emergency responses to migration amplify some of the ways in which race has long operated in Europe, exacerbating what Cristina Lombardi-Diop calls the "moral imperative of whiteness" that excludes Black subjects from Italian communities or marginalizes representations of blackness as Italianness.[22] "Strangerness," which Sara Ahmed defines as the migrant's seemingly inherent and permanent otherness, is central to these processes.[23] Strange grief carries the production of strangerness into death. It pretends empathy while upholding emergency imaginaries of foreignness by obscuring both historical and ongoing ties between communities, and state culpability in border deaths.

Perhaps the most prominent state commemoration in public memory is the memorial service held for victims of the 2013 shipwreck that is often recalled in debates about deadly border policies. On October 3, an overcrowded, repurposed fishing vessel—a *peschereccio*—carrying more than five hundred people from Libya to Italy caught fire and capsized near the island of Lampedusa. Only 155 people survived. Most of the passengers were Eritreans and Ethiopians traveling to Europe to seek asylum. While immediately condemned as a tragedy, the wreck also prompted a moment of hope: the number of victims garnered global attention and returned Mediterranean migration to the public eye with conversations about migrant rights and policy reform. European politicians responded by calling for the immediate convening of EU leaders. Italian president Giorgio Napolitano called this wreck and one that followed a few days later "a succession of true slaughters of innocents," gesturing to the deaths as violent but emphasizing the sea as culprit.[24] Pope Francis called October 3 a "day of tears." Soon after, the Italian government launched Operation Mare Nostrum, the state-sponsored military and humanitarian operation that prioritized rescue and ran until November 2014—also launching the period EU leaders would soon term a crisis.[25]

Amid this global attention, the question of whether and how the Italian government should honor those who died at its doorstep remained fraught. Visiting Lampedusa with EU leaders, Prime Minister Enrico Letta promised a state funeral for victims. Lampedusa mayor Giusi Nicolini requested that the funeral be held on the island, where locals had assisted in rescue and recovery, and where victims' relatives now arrived daily from elsewhere in Italy and Europe. But to the dismay of Nicolini and other advocates, days went by, then weeks, without a service. Local authorities proceeded with burial, laying the bodies to rest in some 15 municipal cemeteries throughout Sicily, following Christian and Muslim rites. When possible, graves were marked with victims' names; most plots were simply numbered.

Questions of testimony pervade these negotiations: Who will bear witness to these lost lives? What would survivors say? Yet when a state-sponsored commemoration finally did take place, nearly three weeks after the wreck, neither victims nor survivors were included. On October 4, Prime Minister Letta granted the victims honorary Italian citizenship, proclaiming, "The hundreds who lost their lives off Lampedusa yesterday are Italian citizens as of today."[26] Instead, survivors remained in Italy's reception system, waiting to learn whether they would be granted protection and allowed to remain in Italy.

Like the Campidoglio funeral held a decade earlier, the state-sponsored service for the October 3, 2013, shipwreck victims also furthered a narrative of tragedy at sea, failing to acknowledge how Italian colonialism and historical ties between Italy and the Horn of Africa have shaped both notions of Italian identity and belonging, and communities in diaspora. Held not on Lampedusa but at "the touristic port of San Leone" in Agrigento, on mainland Sicily, the event featured the sea as backdrop at a site notably *not* associated with migrant arrivals. Members of Eritrean and Ethiopian communities in Italy attended, as did some locals, though the service was not especially large. Speakers included Italian Minister for Integration Cecile Kyenge; Interior Minister Angelino Alfano; and Zemede Tekle, Eritrean ambassador to Italy, an especially contentious figure for Eritrean survivors of the wreck and others in the diaspora who had fled the regime that Tekle represented.[27]

This, too, was *strange grief*, a commemorative performance defined by its own delays and erasures and an event orchestrated in ways that affirmed migrants' exclusion. Framing these deaths not as a political problem but as a tragic loss of life, the memorial displaced concerns about the state's role in border deaths, relying on the faulty logic that demonstrating grief or empathy eliminates complicity. Indeed, journalists and demonstrators alike criticized the absence of victims and survivors, calling the service a farce and a political ploy. In these performances of strange grief, the state works to control the narrative around border deaths. Like other formalized "memory activities," state funerals "are always mediated by relations of power and accompanied by elements of repression."[28] Through discursive and material omissions, they circulate a narrative of border deaths as the tragic loss of unknown and perhaps criminal "others," illustrating how acts of witnessing that claim to honor the dead can in fact perform additional erasures, recognizing some deaths while also marginalizing both survivors and the deceased. In this way, these memorials perpetuate emergency imaginaries that figure those crossing the sea as detached from Italian society and as a source of "crisis." As a result, these rare funerals exceptionalize deaths that should be understood as *un*exceptional—as all too common—inscribing them as a consequence of sudden natural tragedies. The infrequency of such events serves as a reminder that where precarious migration, asylum, and racial politics intersect, victims are doubly abandoned—left to die in transit, then left to the elements.

The first official migrant funeral in contemporary Italy was held not for shipwreck victims but for a refugee shot to death by four white Italian men in the camp where he lived while working the tomato harvest. Jerry Essan Masslo, a South

African national, had reached Rome in 1988 and applied for asylum. At the time, Italy only granted political asylum to Eastern Europeans, so Masslo was denied refugee status by Italy but granted it through UNHCR. His funeral was held in Caserta at the request of national labor union CGIL, broadcast live on state television network RAI2, and attended by officials including Deputy Prime Minister Claudio Martelli. Masslo's murder was among multiple acts of racist violence that year that together prompted a state response and broader conversations about racism and rights.[29] A month following the funeral, "the first huge anti-racist demonstration was held in Rome," with more than 150,000 people in attendance.[30] In early 1990, the Martelli Law expanded asylum recognition beyond Eastern Europe and regulated immigration through country-based quotas for the first time in Italian history. Later that year, Masslo's attackers were sentenced to a total of sixty-one years in prison.

Yet Masslo's death didn't prompt a radical shift in racial politics; since the 1990s, emergency imaginaries of foreignness have prevailed. In Fortress Europe, the choice to occasionally host funerals for the drowned victims of "tragedies at sea," and no longer for the victims of racist violence within Italian spaces, mirrors the reliance on framing immigration as a crisis that can be managed by securitizing and externalizing European borders. But controlling and criminalizing mobility in the name of safety upends notions of rights and calls international law into question. "No society," Baldwin writes, "can smash the social contract and be exempt from the consequences, and the consequences are chaos for everybody in the society."[31] If dominant narratives and state witnessing are essentially constructed to "reassure" publics, then these are circumstances that beg for another kind of witnessing.[32]

## LITERARY RESPONSES TO STATE NARRATIVES

State performances of strange grief serve, simultaneously, as a platform for protest and for the emergence of multiple counternarratives that challenge the abandonment of migrants in detention and in death. For instance, two literary accounts of the 2003 funeral in Rome by Somali Italian authors bear witness beyond the narrative offered by the state, narrating the scene at the Campidoglio from the perspective of diasporic communities who saw it as crucial, long-awaited recognition, while also temporary and symbolic. In her 2010 memoir *La mia casa è dove sono* (*My Home Is Where I Am*), Igiaba Scego recalls that when she arrived to the square and saw the coffins, she realized just how close to home this incident actually was: "It was full of Somalis, that little sunken vessel, here is reality! . . . That paper boat was full of people with my same nose, my same mouth, my same elbows. The day we heard that news, those of us in the Somali diaspora no longer knew what to do with our bodies."[33] Seeing herself in the bodies of the deceased, the narrator recognizes the inextricability of this twenty-first-century story from her own. Her comment calls attention to the corporeality of displacement and the ways in which "narratives told by and about the body, even if they contradict, are inscribed on the body."[34]

Scego's parents, Somali political exiles, flew to Italy in the early 1970s, and Scego was born in Rome and now has Italian citizenship (a point I discuss at more length in chapter 5). As a member of Italy's *seconde generazioni* ("second generations," or "G2"), her Somali heritage directly links her to these thirteen victims, as does public debate about migration that reinforces the idea that blackness exists only outside of *italianità*. This exclusion is what Caterina Romeo observes as "racial evaporation," or the invisibilizing of race to obscure, as well, the longer histories of colonialism so crucial to the building of the Italian nation, along with other European nations.[35] Literary works like *La mia casa* instead visibilize race and the colonial past together. As a memoir, *La mia casa* narrates an individual life while speaking also to collective experience.[36] Personally moved by the 2003 funeral, the narrator also describes how it had the potential to make these cultural and historical connections apparent. That said, narrator-Scego argues, the event took place at the wrong site: it should have been held not below an equestrian statue of Marcus Aurelius in the Renaissance-era municipal square, but in Termini train station, a gathering place for Rome's Somali residents.

The 2003 funeral also appears in works of fiction. Early in Ubah Cristina Ali Farah's 2007 novel *Madre piccola* (*Little Mother*), the character Barni speaks to a journalist documenting Somali experiences. In describing Somali life in Rome, Barni begins with the funeral:

> One story in particular that I think would be suitable for your project. Forgive me if I start in a roundabout way, but do you remember the shipwreck that happened a month ago? The bodies of those nine [*sic*] Somalis that were taken to Rome? The funeral that took place in the famous Campidoglio Square? I think that funeral struck a chord in the hearts of people. I don't think that I'm overstating your role, the role of the press. But all week long newspapers and TV stations spoke of nothing else but that shipwreck.[37]

Ali Farah's use of a journalistic exchange to incorporate the actual event into her novel signals this as an important witnessing moment. Barni emphasizes the importance of the funeral and of media coverage for bringing visibility to border deaths.

At the same time, she recalls the funeral as an event marked by incongruities. Through this nested testimony, we hear how her physical experience of that day reflects her reckoning with these realities and erasures, beginning with her own dizzying arrival up the "crooked" steps—"they seem to slant the wrong way"—to the square. Upon seeing the coffins, she feels "as if I couldn't breathe." The space feels wrong, but the event, once she arrives, appears inviting: "Everyone was clapping . . . [as if] this would mark the beginning of future cooperation between

Somalia and Italy." Barni contrasts the funeral with the ways in which migrants' bodies are usually seen, as part of the "garbage" that washes to shore: "tomato cans, shards of green glass, small tubes of medicine, clumps of tar, and plastic bags. . . . And, carried by the sea, lifeless bodies, wearing tattered clothes, their purplish skin blotched with white salt."[38] In commemorating the dead migrants, the funeral potentially counters their representation as marine detritus.

But even if the funeral attempts to humanize the deceased and strikes a chord with the public, it still fails to acknowledge deadly border regimes. Barni remains skeptical of real change: "The boatloads of illegal immigrants did not stop coming, even after that solemn funeral. And what about the living?"[39]

Addressing the journalist and implicitly raising questions for readers, she calls attention to the limits of this performance of national mourning. She also leaves open the question of "the living," especially as she recalls not only the official state ceremony but the Muslim burial that followed. It's not at the Campidoglio but taking the bus with other Somalis from there to the mosque that Barni describes hearing "not a lullaby, rather the wail of a prayer." As she describes watching the coffins carried in—"tears and salt"—she notes ongoing migrations as obviously, inextricably linked with established diasporic communities, and with their exclusion from discourses of national belonging. "You'll see," she recalls another woman saying, looking toward the coffins, "We, too, will end up like that, beneath wet earth that is not our own."[40]

Amid strange grief and a pervasive lack of recognition of migrant deaths beyond sheer numbers, these literary accounts are critical records, inscribing grief not for a count or incident, but for lived and lost lives, generations connected through survival and grief. I mean to underscore how personal accounts of these deaths and their commemoration can bring the intimacy of mourning to the fore both for readers in the diaspora and for broader (white) Italian audiences and readers like myself, prompted to grapple with our own various connections to or distance from these losses and the structures that enable them. This is crucial to the kinds of witnessing that might recognize migration beyond crisis framings—not by cultivating empathy for an "other" but by prompting audiences to see their own position differently. Through memoir, fiction, and other forms, and inspired by oral histories and actual events, Ali Farah, Scego, and other writers and artists circulate an archive of experiences of migration and citizenship among and beyond Italian publics. They ask us to hold space for elegy while repeatedly asking, as Barni does, "And what about the living?" As Alessandro Portelli puts it in a reflection on the growing body of literature by Italians of African descent, "These books and these tales *are* us. Italy makes no sense if we don't feel them to be ours. The most exciting new development of recent times . . . is that the very idea of what it means to be Italian is changing in our hands."[41] In interviews, Scego has described creative work as "an incredible tool, because it has the potential to arrive at places closed off to politics, places that a slogan may touch upon but not really explore."[42] This is witnessing as both documentary and imaginative act, and a critical means for writing diasporic memory into national memory, while also interrogating the limits of the latter.

## NAMES AND ELEGY IN *ASMAT*

A decade later, the 2013 memorial in Agrigento was itself a site of protest. Mayor Nicolini refused to attend, traveling instead to Rome to meet with President Napolitano and present a humanitarian plan for Lampedusa. Italian citizens and migrants alike stood just outside cordoned off areas of the pier, calling out the negligent laws that allow such wrecks to take place, shouting, "Leggi di assassini!" *Assassins' laws!* and calling for the infamously restrictive Bossi-Fini immigration law to be overturned. A number of local advocacy groups including Jodit Abraha, representing Palermo's Eritrean-Ethiopian community, and Noureddine Adnane, which combats race-based discrimination, released a statement citing the deaths as "sangue nostrum e non mare nostrum"—our blood, not our sea (an implicit reference to the new SAR operation too). "We vocalize our pain, but also our indignation at the restrictive and xenophobic politics that have already killed more than 20,000 people and have transformed the Mediterranean Sea into an immense liquid cemetery."[43] They protested the presence of the Eritrean ambassador and the exclusion of survivors from the event.

Survivors also protested. Still being processed into the Italian reception system and not allowed to travel to the ceremony, they left their center to hold a sit-in at the Lampedusa city hall and their own ceremony on a cliff overlooking the sea.[44] To be barred from the official memorial was to be excluded from public commemoration of the family members and fellow travelers whose deaths they would continue to mourn while awaiting documents and decisions in the local detention center. By preventing those who had survived the crossing from participating in public, state-sanctioned mourning, the state effectively sought to manage not only death but also the processes of grief. Survivors' fugitive witnessing in the marginal space where their detention site joined the waters that had swallowed their boat exemplifies practices ongoing around the Mediterranean that construct and make visible the liquid archive.

Why continue to talk about the October 3 wreck, so many years after? As activist Amadou Diallo put it in a conversation we had nearly a decade later when at least ninety-four people died in a wreck near Cutro, Calabria, October 3 has become a clear marker for migrants and solidarity groups as a day of remembrance and of action, and an incident that echoes and haunts in the many wrecks that have followed. In annual demonstrations, organizers have remembered those who lost their lives and have also demanded structural change. It is an exercise, in part, in rupturing the temporalities imposed by emergency framings, which, as Miriam Ticktin argues, keep people "reeling from crisis to crisis" rather than "look[ing] to the future, and not simply in hope but in mourning."[45] Even at the height of the COVID-19 pandemic, on October 3, 2020, groups demonstrated across Europe. In Rome, Diallo said, they rallied in protective masks to commemorate the dead, denounce ongoing violence, and demand change, using the hashtag #NonSiamoPesci (We're Not Fish).

The October 3, 2013, wreck is also significant because, for the first time, and thanks to survivors' assistance, officials were able to assemble a list of many of the victims' names. Identifying the deceased is rarely a priority for authorities in the Mediterranean; wrecks and bodies are rarely recovered from the seafloor.[46] When it does happen, identification is challenging: migrants may travel without documents or with falsified papers to protect their identities, and the Mediterranean's salty waters can rapidly make them unrecognizable. For film director Dagmawi Yimer, having the names necessitated another kind of commemoration that would make them present for multiple audiences. Yimer's 2014 short film *Asmat (Names)* is an elegy to the 368 Eritrean and Ethiopian victims. Shot mostly looking up from underneath the water, and shifting without explication between the sea, artistic renderings of the journey, and a reading of the names, the seventeen-minute film commemorates outside the terms dictated by dominant discourses and state authorities. *Asmat* bears witness to loss through necropolitical violence, enabling public mourning for viewers while countering the Italian state's strange grief. In important contrast to the 2013 funeral, *Asmat* counteracts the anonymous, disembodied modes of state commemoration, inscribing the wreck and each life lost within the Black Mediterranean.

This dreamlike elegy moves between watercolors of a migrant's journey, by Luca Serasini, and underwater shots of the legs and torsos of dancers threaded together by a giant swath of white cloth. These scenes foreground the physicality of crossing and of loss by centering dancers' legs and torsos, and by giving physical space on the screen to each name. Given trauma's bodily impact, corporeal experience remains "one of the most singular and effective dimensions of testimony."[47] The pain of trauma can split the body from language—that is, can separate a person's corporeal experience from their ability to articulate that experience with words. Given the impossibility of representing the actual bodies of the deceased, now drowned or buried, the film's lyric visuals return the body to the center of the moment from which it has been erased.[48] One of the early watercolors shows a man with enormous hands—emphasizing the body and the graspability and ingraspability (or problematic ungrievability) of these drownings and their afterlives (figure 2). Near the beginning, the hull of a boat shot from below resembles a whale, breathing, swelling, and shrinking in the water. A voiceover hums a soft melody, then reads a kind of invocation—I hear it as a poem—before reciting the names.

The poem, read by Eritrean human rights worker Eden Getachew Zerihun, creates "virtual witnesses"[49] by describing the context of the wreck, and of the broader crises of which it is part, by addressing the multiple audiences engaged in this

FIGURE 2. Still from *Asmat.*

emergency—survivors and relatives of the deceased, whose experience viewing the film I cannot pretend to know, as well as African and European audiences who could challenge the violence causing these deaths. Read in Tigrigna with English or Italian subtitles, the poem invokes European publics who are "condemned to listen to these screams . . . because our cry is loud and strong." It calls out African politicians who "make people flee . . . you make laws you would not enforce on your children." To European politicians, the speaker says, "we are here, we came here to observe your actions, the civilization you boast of." Meanwhile, the sound of waves gives way to the periodic strum of a guitar, and to silence. The camera cuts to underwater shots of people standing and swaying beneath the sea. The speaker also acknowledges the parents of the deceased who "live without know-ing what happened to your children," says the speaker, "Call them / if they can hear you / tell them the meaning of their names / Speak their endless names." Then Zerihun reads the names, from Adhanom to Yohannes, pronouncing each name together with its meaning, read in English. Typed names crowd the screen. It takes ten minutes to read the list.

Yimer has described the urgency of this project in interviews, saying, "In *Asmat* I wanted to force my spectators to listen to all of [the names], from first to last."[50] *Asmat* is a form of fugitive witnessing and an example of what Christina Sharpe terms "wake work," responding to movements between former colonies and colonizers that occur "in the wake" of the violences of historical displace-ment and enslavement.[51] For Sharpe, wake work "troubles mourning" by refusing the seeming finality of a memorial—refusing, that is, to pretend that the violence has ended.[52] The film as wake work addresses historical and ongoing violence, in part by enacting elegy as a testimonial form that creates an intimate space for mourning while demanding witnessing from a broader public. It is both elegy that emerges from a state of overwhelm, to invoke Brand—"[Elegy] is the great complaint . . . the complaint is 'what's happening to me overwhelms me.' Not simply that I am in pain but what has taken away my power of action overwhelms me. And why do I see these things why do I know these things why must I endure seeing and knowing."[53] And it is elegy that asks viewers to see the single wreck within a history of systemic violence.

Testimony is a critical act of visibility for those bearing witness to necropolitical violence and to the losses it enacts. Here, testimony is collective elegy, heard in the "we" of the voiceover. This "we," a diasporic collective defined in part through the crossing of borders, expresses communal agency and counters the "we" of the state and its construction through borders and ideas of cultural homogeneity. In this sense, the film embodies the abolitionist and emancipatory possibilities that are a crucial part of a Black Mediterranean political praxis.[54] *Asmat's* "we" speaks from the wake, from the grave—the seafloor. In contrast to the formal, procedural rituals of government officiants and clergy at the state funeral, the "we" that narrates *Asmat* is a grieving and grievable subject that bears witness to the suffering of the drowned, who can no longer speak for themselves, and recognizes that suffering as a form of historical trauma that has long affected this "we," directly related to what Hall describes as "the traumatic character of 'the colonial experience.'"[55]

Naming and elegizing are not inherently subversive, but in *Asmat* they serve this function in that they disrupt the border spectacle, "working on the gaps and fissures that are opened up as instabilities in such constructions."[56] The film creates an encounter between narrators, performers, images, and viewers that functions as both archive and call to action. In line with other testimonial films, *Asmat* is "designed to summon politically, morally, and socially engaged publics."[57] These witnessing texts frame precarious Mediterranean mobilities within an imaginary that refutes the erasures and displacements of emergency discourses, even as it calls attention to the extreme urgency of these circumstances.

Within Italian cinema, *Asmat* is part of a body of films that portray the risky boat journey and its afterlives with particular care to center the voices, bodies, and experiences of border crossers, including work ranging from Zakaria Mohamed Ali's short film, to the widely released *Terraferma* by Emanuele Crialese (2011), to Jonas Carpignano's *Mediterranea* (2015), which I discuss in chapter 6, and the Oscar-nominated *Io Capitano* by Matteo Garrone (2023).[58] While these films don't all focus on a shipwreck, they integrate scenes of precarious voyages to push for a reckoning both within Italy—to situate these losses within Italian history and culture—and beyond it.

As an elegy that calls out the violence behind border deaths, *Asmat* is also part of a transnational archive of texts and practices that honor the dead across and beyond the Mediterranean region. The work of recovering bodies and burying the dead transpires at the edges of emergency and often goes unnoticed in mainstream

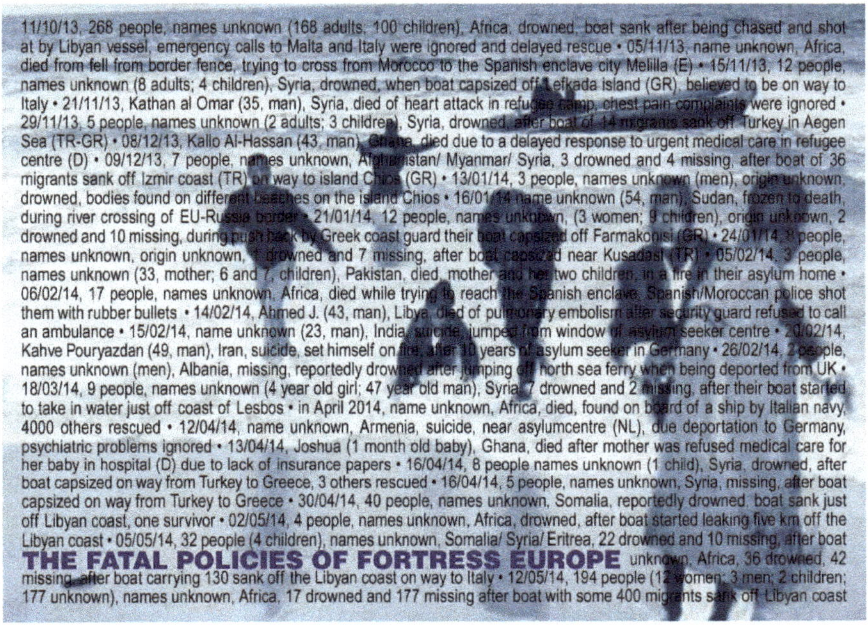

11/10/13, 268 people, names unknown (168 adults, 100 children), Africa, drowned, boat sank after being chased and shot at by Libyan vessel, emergency calls to Malta and Italy were ignored and delayed rescue • 05/11/13, name unknown, Africa, died from fell from border fence, trying to cross from Morocco to the Spanish enclave city Melilla (E) • 15/11/13, 12 people, names unknown (8 adults; 4 children), Syria, drowned, when boat capsized off Lefkada island (GR), believed to be on way to Italy • 21/11/13, Kathan al Omar (35, man), Syria, died of heart attack in refugee camp, chest pain complaints were ignored • 29/11/13, 5 people, names unknown (2 adults; 3 children), Syria, drowned, after boat of 14 migrants sank off Turkey in Aegen Sea (TR-GR) • 08/12/13, Kallo Al-Hassan (43, man), Ghana, died due to a delayed response to urgent medical care in refugee centre (D) • 09/12/13, 7 people, names unknown, Afghanistan/ Myanmar/ Syria, 3 drowned and 4 missing, after boat of 36 migrants sank off Izmir coast (TR) on way to island Chios (GR) • 13/01/14, 3 people, names unknown (men), origin unknown, drowned, bodies found on different beaches on the island Chios • 16/01/14 name unknown (54, man), Sudan, frozen to death, during river crossing of EU-Russia border • 21/01/14, 12 people, names unknown, (3 women; 9 children), origin unknown, 2 drowned and 10 missing, during push back by Greek coast guard their boat capsized off Farmakonisi (GR) • 24/01/14, 8 people, names unknown, origin unknown, 1 drowned and 7 missing, after boat capsized near Kusadasi (TR) • 05/02/14, 3 people, names unknown (33, mother; 6 and 7, children), Pakistan, died, mother and her two children, in a fire in their asylum home • 06/02/14, 17 people, names unknown, Africa, died while trying to reach the Spanish enclave, Spanish/Moroccan police shot them with rubber bullets • 14/02/14, Ahmed J. (43, man), Libya, died of pulmonary embolism after security guard refused to call an ambulance • 15/02/14, name unknown (23, man), India, suicide, jumped from window of asylum seeker centre • 20/02/14, Kahve Pouryazdan (49, man), Iran, suicide, set himself on fire, after 10 years of asylum seeker in Germany • 26/02/14, 2 people, names unknown (men), Albania, missing, reportedly drowned after jumping off north sea ferry when being deported from UK • 18/03/14, 9 people, names unknown (4 year old girl; 47 year old man), Syria, 7 drowned and 2 missing, after their boat started to take in water just off coast of Lesbos • in April 2014, name unknown, Africa, died, found on board of a ship by Italian navy, 4000 others rescued • 12/04/14, name unknown, Armenia, suicide, near asylumcentre (NL), due deportation to Germany, psychiatric problems ignored • 13/04/14, Joshua (1 month old baby), Ghana, died after mother was refused medical care for her baby in hospital (D) due to lack of insurance papers • 16/04/14, 8 people names unknown (1 child), Syria, drowned, after boat capsized on way from Turkey to Greece, 3 others rescued • 16/04/14, 5 people, names unknown, Syria, missing, after boat capsized on way from Turkey to Greece • 30/04/14, 40 people, names unknown, Somalia, reportedly drowned, boat sank just off Libyan coast, one survivor • 02/05/14, 4 people, names unknown, Africa, drowned, after boat started leaking five km off the Libyan coast • 05/05/14, 32 people (4 children), names unknown, Somalia/ Syria/ Eritrea, 22 drowned and 10 missing, after boat

**THE FATAL POLICIES OF FORTRESS EUROPE** unknown, Africa, 36 drowned, 42 missing, after boat carrying 130 sank off the Libyan coast on way to Italy • 12/05/14, 194 people (12 women; 3 men; 2 children; 177 unknown), names unknown, Africa, 17 drowned and 177 missing after boat with some 400 migrants sank off Libyan coast

FIGURE 3. Postcard from the campaign Fatal Policies of Fortress Europe, listing a selection of deaths from 2013 to 2014. Reproduced with permission from Amsterdam-based United Against Refugee Deaths (https://unitedagainstrefugeedeaths.eu/).

media coverage. But in what Maurice Stierl terms "grief activism," these practices of elegy and care are also used to draw attention to state negligence.[59] Some more explicitly link death at Europe's geopolitical borders with violence within European territories, like campaigns by the Dutch group United Against Refugee Deaths (figure 3). The list of the dead they maintain is one such example: initially produced through a collaboration with Istanbul-based artist Banu Cennetoğlu, the list is a catalogue of migrant deaths, with and without names, from 1993 through the present. Posted in public spaces and repeatedly published in *The Guardian*, the list is an attempt to record, aggregate, and publicize deaths and to connect drownings with migrant deaths throughout Europe. I first encountered it in 2017 in printed spreadsheet form at a museum in Milan, where it stretched the length of a gallery room, at that point containing more than thirty-three thousand deaths.

Now, nearly doubled, it would require a larger room.

Literature and visual media play an especially powerful role in documenting and reflecting on violence and loss. As anthropologist Michael Jackson observes,

as long as we think of refugees solely as victims, we do a grave injustice to the facts of refugee experience, for loss is always countermanded by actions—albeit imaginative, magical, and illusory—to regain some sense of balance between the world within and the world without.[60]

These elegiac modes are critical for revising Italian collective memory, and these uses of testimony expand Italy's literary and artistic canonical boundaries. At the same time, they resonate across global contexts. Naming the victims of racist violence and police/state brutality has united people in the Movement for Black Lives and situates work in Italy within transnational justice movements around the globe, including by reciting the names of victims in lists that are always incomplete.[61] These recitations are part of a web of counternarrative practices, protest, and meaning making that work to do what Hartman describes as "recover[ing] the insurgent ground of these lives."[62]

Testimonies that perform wake work in the context of Africa–Europe migration make the Black Mediterranean present for their audiences as a site of the colonial present whose future can still be liberated from today's "oppressive regimes."[63] As the speaker says: "We are more visible dead than alive . . . We existed even before October the Third / We have been sailing for years / We've been traveling for years / We've been drowning for years." These lines and the repetition of "for years" are one example of how the film speaks against forgetting.[64] Like *A chiunque possa interessare*, the short film with which I opened this chapter, *Asmat* is the product of an interrogation of loss and displaced histories, and one that challenges the violence of borders. Both films wrestle with the problem of making visible the journeys and deaths of those who can no longer speak. They also center the figure of the boat, which is itself a key site of emergency and an icon that has generated a multitude of memorials and elegies.

## TITANICS IN THE BLACK MEDITERRANEAN

Today's migrant vessels are a means of escape for people from countries throughout Africa, the Middle East, and South Asia, even as they reflect the (neo)colonial forces that create the situations from which people need to escape—and even as they deliver migrants to European countries where they are not free. I close this chapter on death, strange grief, and elegy by reflecting on the migrant boat as both material vessel and symbol. These boats—rubber dinghies or rickety pescherecci taken from Tunisian fishermen and repurposed by Libyan smugglers—are vessels of memory, sites of death, hope, trauma, and survival.

For some survivors, the sea crossing becomes evidence of flight, of arrival, of survival. "Google my arrival date," a Liberian man told me at an Italian reception center, "my rescue is on YouTube."

For others, the crossing continues to haunt. A Gambian man I'd interviewed and stayed in touch with, who would eventually be granted a humanitarian visa, once texted me photographs of dead bodies washed to shore—he didn't say whether in Libya or Tunisia—their flesh swollen and scarred with salt. "Today is my birthday," he wrote.

Redeem (pseudonym), a Nigerian woman I met in Calabria, said the boat journey was so harrowing, "I couldn't remember things again. It took me time before I would be myself."[65]

For many, to cross is to survive *and* to be haunted—to leave "the abyss" of the sea and of the boat, as Eduoard Glissant writes of the slave ship, and to carry the knowledge and experience of that abyss into the limbo of life in Europe. Ferrying people between former colonies and former colonizers, today's Mediterranean boats are inextricably tied to slave ships that transported "human cargo" across the Atlantic, linking the Black Mediterranean and the Black Atlantic, "pregnant with as many dead as living under sentence of death."[66] Understanding today's Mediterranean mobilities within the wake of history means recognizing the boats as material and symbolic structures within the "crisis of capital," as Sharpe elaborates, "in the forms of migrants fleeing lives made unlivable."[67] That is, migrant boats move within a colonial present shaped by the longue durée of history, by the ongoing extraction of resources in Africa, by the reliance of European economies on exploited laborers, and by white supremacy and the refusal to see those crossing as people with whole lives and with rights.

Journalistic and popular media accounts sometimes gesture to this comparison but often remain problematically superficial or reify the crisis-spectacle of black bodies in a crowded boat. A *New York Times* article about an October 2016 rescue operation described the situation in this way: "The wooden vessel's cargo hold contained two-thirds of the roughly 1,000 people found aboard, Ms. Lanuza said, calling the conditions 'just like a slavery boat—the same.'" Another aid worker quoted in the same article calls the analogy "exactly right—except that it's not hundreds of years ago.'"[68] Here the slave ship is most immediately a point of reference for the *spectacle* of today's boats: crowded, tragic nonspaces, their passengers absent of agency.

Comparisons that suggest these vessels as analogous rather than entangled figures risk affirming the idea that precarious crossings deserve periodic attention only because they happen at Europe's gates, without interrogating migrant shipwrecks as part of a broader set of violent structures and practices. These boats bound to sink move in the same wake as young men of North African descent killed by police in France, as Black US citizens shot by police while driving to work or playing in a park, and as migrants abused in borderzones while seeking safety—think of the Haitians beaten and whipped by US Customs and Border Patrol agents on horseback while attempting to cross the Rio Grande into Texas in 2021, or more recently, the Central and West African men captured by Tunisian police and abandoned at the border, left to die in the desert. Collectively, these incidents reveal the violence "emergency" enables as it transits across contexts and times—evidence of the "colonial structures" that render some groups as unwanted, disposable, deportable.[69] Such violence is foundational to "the emergency" that

Brand describes, one in which, she says, "I leave my house and immediately my body is ripped from me to enact some colonial idyll."[70]

As the *Asmat* voiceover reminds us, authorities on all sides of the sea are complicit in enabling what Yimer has elsewhere called "essentially a twenty-first century slave trade"[71]—not a descriptive metaphor but a fact of material reality. Within the "afterlife of slavery," today's migrants transit between oppressive conditions, sometimes including their enslavement in Libya and the exploitation of their labor in Italy, their lives "still imperiled and devalued by a racial calculus and a political arithmetic that were entrenched centuries ago."[72] Recognizing today's precarious mobilities within this afterlife, rather than as merely analogous to historical images of Black victimhood, is critical for understanding how the emergency apparatus reproduces colonial relations in the present.

Amid oppressive violence, as postcolonial and Black feminist scholars and artists have argued, the slave ship is not a singular monolith of victimhood. Katherine McKittrick describes it as a site of "struggle for freedom *in place*."[73] Donald M. Carter emphasizes the "translocal, transcultural" communities disrupted and (re)shaped through these experiences and posits the slave ship not as a singular, definitive icon for African diaspora, but as a site to understand in relational terms, both among those "held together in this extraordinary voyage" and in terms of the multiple journeys, vessels, histories, and lives that the slave ship might point us to interrogate. Responding to Gilroy's notion that Black lives move "from slave ship to citizenship," Carter also cautions against writing the slave ship into a narrative that reifies the nation-state as the primary frame for conceptualizing belonging – one that forecloses other possible configurations of belonging, past and future.[74]

As a heterotopia, in Foucault's words, the boat exemplifies relationality and the significance of space and spatial relations to modern life, and it speaks to a range of experiences.[75] Mediterranean crossings might also make us think of the stories of "boat refugees" fleeing Europe during World War II, Cuba beginning in the 1960s, or Vietnam in the late 1970s. As Evyn Lê Espiritu Gandhi observes in the case of Vietnam, "images of the boat refugees circulated prominently in the international media, prompting the United Nations High Commission for Refugees (UNHCR) to declare a global crisis. In response, countries around the world . . . offered to resettle the boat refugees."[76] In the contemporary Mediterranean, images of boats also prompt talk of crisis, but their circulation often sparks only short-lived sympathy and stokes anti-immigrant sentiment. The boats' abstraction through surveillance technologies that visualize them as dots on a map literally dehumanizes these crossings, as Ruben Andersson notes, making it easy for authorities to "fram[e] migrants and facilitators as sources of risk."[77] As iterations of the hold that "repeats and repeats in and into the present,"[78] migrant boats in the Mediterranean signal the wake in which contemporary migrations unfold and speak to this complex web of meanings.

One set of associations within this web comes in the form of testimonial narratives that use the migrant boat to push the discursive boundaries of the colonial present by moving the vessel between multiple symbolic grammars. We might think, for instance, of the Wolof phrase "Barça wala barsakh" (Barcelona or death) used by Senegalese migrants as they embark on pirogues to cross the Atlantic toward the Canary Islands, knowing and claiming the risks.[79] For Zakaria Mohamed Ali, the boats are an archive, a record he hopes reaches broader publics. As he stands at the Lampedusa boat cemetery near the end of his short film, these words appear on screen:

> These boats which have been abandoned here
> They are monuments to those who seek freedom
> To remember all the people who arrived, and make our story known,
> to whom it may concern.

They are their own commemoration, a memorial statement meant to make new witnesses.

Another set of texts invokes the *Titanic* and its place as a tragic voyage in collective memory. In Abu Bakr Khaal's 2008 novella *African Titanics*, the title itself highlights the severity of these dangers and victims' anonymity, qualifying African deaths in the Mediterranean through reference to the famous ship that sank while transporting mostly European passengers across the Atlantic. The novella is a tale of fugitivity. Focusing on the fictional account of Abdar, who leaves Eritrea and crosses Sudan and Libya in hopes of reaching Italy, it offers a story of characters who dream of boarding "Titanics" on Libyan shores and yet never set foot in Europe. They die or turn back; imprisoned in Libya, they speculate on the experiences of their travel companions and those who have passed through these spaces before them. The risks of crossing and the possibility of survival arguably comprise the novella's main subject, though mobility is a way of being in the story, and unromanticized. Eritrean author Khaal wrote the novella in Arabic while living in Libya and published it serially in the Libyan newspaper *Oya*. Following the 2011 Arab Spring, he fled Libya, eventually reaching Denmark. The book was translated into English in 2014.[80]

In the novella, the suitability of the term "Titanic" comes up directly when an Egyptian migrant waiting with others in a holding space near Tripoli challenges Abdar and his companions for referring to boats as "Titanics":

[He] contemplated the group of Eritreans huddled around the TV. "Isn't it you lot that called the boats 'Titanikaat'"? he continued, mimicking our Arabic, "As in *al-Titanik?*"

"*Yes*, that's us."

"Damn you all! Who gave you the right to pluralize it as Titanikaat anyway? Are you experts in Arabic grammar these days—or is the great grammarian Sibawayh travelling with you and personally advising you on new words?"

> "What else should we call them?"
>
> "Something optimistic. Noah's Ark perhaps. Or any other ship that never sank. Well? What d'you have to say for yourselves?"
>
> "What can we say? The matter's closed. You are the all-knowing one."
>
> "Whatever! Just so long as you know that around seventy percent of your Titanikaat sank—only around thirty out of a hundred survive! So I guess Titanic is an appropriate name for them after all. *Tita . . . niiiiik*," he said with force, heavily emphasizing the second syllable, transforming it into the Arabic word for "fuck."[81]

Titanic, acknowledged as an "appropriate name," alludes to the hope of the original ship, pre-iceberg, while acknowledging the risk. In this spirit, death in the novella is not a tragedy but a moment of heroism and celebration. The characters sing about figures like Abdar's friend Malouk, a Liberian man whose drowning transforms him into a legendary figure. A woman tells Abdar of Malouk's death, "He was apparently walking on the crest of a wave as calmly as people walk on land."[82] These descriptions figure mobility itself not along a scale of tragedy but as a matter of both fate and choice, underscoring the agency border crossers exercise despite that Titanics are their only option.

Among some Somali diasporic communities, "Titanic" also refers to survivors. In Ali Farah's *Madre piccola*, after describing the 2003 funeral, Barni links experiences of death, survival, and diaspora through a brief reference to "Titanic." As she mourns the dead and questions the possibility of real change, she refers to "all those who wash up on these shores in the boats or who have escaped the shipwrecks, nicknamed Titanic by their fellow countrymen."[83] Both a gesture of solidarity and an acknowledgment of great risk, this naming also suggests a degree of irony in the notion of survival or arrival. In interviews, Scego has described Titanic as one turn in a name game played between older Somali women who came in the 1970s and the younger migrants, mostly men, arriving now. Younger men dubbed "Titanic" by older women refer, in turn, to these women as "vecchia lira," or "old money":

> Naturally one can't be disparaged and not respond. Since, in Somalia, verbal exchange becomes theater or poetry, it happened that the young asylum seekers, tired of being called Titanic, started calling women of the diaspora old money. As if to say, "Fine, we're Titanic, but you're coins that are no longer in use." A lot of cruelty, mutual distancing, misunderstandings. I wanted to use it in [*Adua*] because for the media, Italians and migrants are like two giant football teams. But who are the Italians? The Friulians? The Campanians? The Venetians? What is their social class? Their sexual orientation? And the migrants, who are they? Albanian? American? Somali? Eritrean? Syrian? Brazilian? WHO?[84]

If dominant narratives posit "Italians" and "migrants" as singular, fixed categories in opposition, uses of Titanic within diasporic communities instead highlight migration and identity as broader, historical, and complex phenomena. Scego herself invokes Titanic in her 2015 novel *Adua*. The protagonist, a Somali woman named Adua who moves to Rome in the 1970s, vents in the present-day about her marital troubles with Ahmed, a younger man she calls "Titanic," who arrived more recently by sea. Adua feels she has rescued Ahmed through marriage, saving him from a life on the street. She confesses, "It's not nice to call a guy who risked his life at sea by the name of a sunken ship. . . . Once my husband even said, 'I know that Titanic is a film where everyone dies. But you have to remember that I didn't die.'"[85] The name "Titanic" is the site of Ahmed's plea for recognition in the book's present day.

The seeming incongruity of the *Titanic* and the slave ship is part of their rupture within Black Mediterranean discourse, which calls into question what we view as tragic and how we locate agency in violent borderzones. They also link the Black Atlantic and Black Mediterranean as sites of racialized transit. More than a century ago, the *Titanic* transported ticket-paying citizens between Western Europe and New York. The 1912 wreck has since entered global popular culture, becoming "something of a currency in tragedy." Those who drowned with the ship were "uncomplaining heroes rather than terrified captives." They were victims in part of institutional hubris, given the lack of sufficient lifeboats on board.[86] In cultural mythology, the original *Titanic* is recalled as "a floating microcosm of society," part of "one of the great human migrations," and a famous disaster.[87] That we can scroll its passenger lists in online archives contrasts with the anonymity of those who have lost their lives in the Mediterranean. It was in fact the sinking of the *Titanic* that prompted the first International Convention for the Safety of Life at Sea, at which participants established international agreements on search and rescue.[88] The US government formally protects the site of this wreck as "perhaps the most important historic shipwreck in history."[89] In June 2023, when five self-dubbed explorers died attempting to visit its ruins underwater, multiple governments spent millions to recover their bodies and the wreckage of their submersible. Migrant Titanics wrecked in international waters are generally left where they fall.[90]

Whether they are referring to the historical event or its representation in James Cameron's 1997 blockbuster production, migrant narrators' use of this symbol calls attention to the very different currency that today's migrant boats have. Narrators who reinscribe Mediterranean migration with this complex icon call attention to the dynamics of hope and fate, and to the power of nature in shipwrecks, but also to the role of institutions. Rupturing emergency logics might begin with such shifts in perspective. The various Titanics here, from a derelict boat to a young migrant moving north, suggest multiple means through which narratives of Mediterranean migration participate in the project of decentering Europe. These narrators claim Titanic as an African story, refuting accounts that use migrant deaths to reify national borders or that abandon migrants at the bottom of the sea, as if unknown, as if nameless.

## CONCLUSION: ON ART AND EDEN

A fraught and powerful symbol, the boat also returns our attention to the materiality of migration. Most wrecks remain on the seafloor, but very occasionally, a boat is recovered. Some of those vessels have been made into memorials. Setting the wrecks before European and global publics has not stopped ongoing violence and erasure—but could it point us to another ethics of witnessing?

In 2019, I visited two boats recovered more than twenty years apart. In Venice, Swiss-Icelandic artist Christoph Büchel's team had installed a migrant boat as part of the Venice Biennale global art exhibition (figure 4). The boat, which sank on April 18, 2015, remains the largest known migrant shipwreck in recent years: only twenty-eight of its estimated eleven hundred passengers survived. The wreck and its continued transit in Italy highlight some of the challenges of transforming emergency imaginaries without relying on empathy. Forensic investigator Cristina Cattaneo, whose team led the recovery of human remains from the wreck, has called for a "human rights science," or rights work based in materiality rather than moralism. The boat's inclusion at the Biennale, in Venice's historic Arsenale (fortress) site, made it publicly visible—through media coverage and for ticket-holding visitors—rather than locked from view in the NATO dock near the Sicilian town of Augusta, where it had sat for the previous two years. At the same time, its installation as a memorial artwork called *Barca Nostra (Our Boat)* prompted more debate about artistic provocation than attention to migrant deaths at sea.[91] With no label or explanation, the boat appeared to unknowing visitors as part of the Arsenale architecture. When I asked a couple sipping Peroni at the bar in front of the boat if they knew it had carried hundreds of migrants to their death, they were shocked. Already knowing the boat's story can instead enable witnessing. As Rinaldo Walcott writes, "*Barca Nostra* allows Black subjects (like myself) to bear witness to our dead in the contemporary era in a way that we were not able to do in the era of transatlantic slavery"—linking Mediterranean and Atlantic through processes of erasure and of witnessing.[92] The boat has since returned to Augusta, a key disembarkation point for migrants. Local groups have proposed a memorial garden, but for now the boat sits at the military port there, closed to the public, its witnessing role uncertain.

There isn't much precedent for such memorials.[93] A second boat sits in Otranto, at the southern tip of Italy's heel. This boat marks the initial period of contemporary mass migration into Italy, with the post–Cold War mobilities of the 1990s. It now also marks Italy's aphasic relationship with migration histories. The Albanian *Katër i Radës* sank on March 28, 1997, when an Italian coast guard boat rammed its hull. Only eighty-five of at least 142 passengers survived. Recovered for the trial

FIGURE 4. Barca Nostra as seen from a bar at the 2019 Venice Biennale. Photo by the author.

against the captains of the two ships, the boat initially served as criminal evidence. It then stayed in Brindisi for years, cordoned off and left to decay at the port. Since 2011, the boat has stood at the port of Otranto, which offered to give it a permanent home (figure 5). Apparently because no funding source emerged to send the boat back to Albania, it has stayed in Otranto, geographically and symbolically far from victims' relatives. There, the vessel was rendered a memorial artwork by Greek sculptor Costas Varotsos, who added horizontal sheets of glass to the relic. In its memorial form, the boat's structure, largely intact, appears cut by waves, or perhaps held together by them. Yet the memorial's title—*The Landing: Work Dedicated to a Migrant Humanity* (*L'approdo: Opera all'umanità migrante*)—renders it a generic monument to those who die at sea rather than enabling people to recall "the actual story of the sinking" or to recognize the victims as grievable subjects.[94]

A material trace of migrants' precarious crossings and their hopes to reach safety, the boat is also a trace of the systemic violence that compelled them to incur such risks. These memorials and installations may respond to the practical and ethical question of what to do with the relics of these wrecks. But do they make those traces apparent to visitors—and for which visitors are they intended—or do they transform the boats into objects of strange grief? *And what about the living?*

When I first visited these vessels, I was struck by how small they seemed—impossibly small for the number of people who died in their hulls. In Venice,

FIGURE 5. The *Katër i Radës* at the Port of Otranto, 2019. Photo by the author.

then in Otranto, I was both upset and profoundly moved. But then, I had traveled the length of the Italian boot to reach these vessels: I recognized what I had come to see, the histories and events bound up in these metal and wooden hulls. Objects can represent, trigger, or suggest particular memories, but they rely on their human witnesses to complete the memory work they initiate. As Leogrande wrote about his own encounter with the *Katër i Radës*, "Monuments . . . remain whitewashed coffins, empty containers, if they are not sprinkled with stories and memories, of anger and redemption. They remain as empty structures if memory does not intervene, rendering them living sites."[95]

Enabling witnessing is a crucial part of enabling a reckoning with past and present, and positioning people to see a different future. Walcott's meditation before *Barca Nostra* takes up this future as an ethical gesture that might move us "toward a planetary resolution where a possibility for full life/lives becomes conceivable as a necessary reinvention of the planet."[96]

When I think about what that "necessary reinvention" might entail, another boat comes to mind. This one appears in a mural painted by the residents of a reception center in Africo, a small town on the Ionian coast in Calabria. Outside the center, a kind of graphic narrative of sea crossing runs along a concrete wall (figure 6). Across the bottom half is a turbulent black and blue sea. Above the water at one end stands a horned devil, holding out a device shaped like an "L"—Libya?—then we see a boat crowded with silhouettes who hold up their arms as a storm rains down. To the right of the migrant boat, a rescue scene unfolds, with two figures observing from the deck of a large ship as others in smaller vessels reach out to people on board a boat. Then: Eden. The mural turns the corner of the wall and shifts from a scene of rescue to a lush garden with animals and fruit-bearing trees.

FIGURE 6. Rescue scene on a mural by a reception center in Africo, 2018. Photo by the author.

The mural is a reminder that those who reach Italy are survivors. Eden appears as a gesture toward the future. But in the meantime, their arrival in Europe often marks less an arrival in Eden than the beginning of an extended period of uncertainty, including, sometimes, of uncertain hospitality.

2

———

# Hospitality as Emergency Response

Outside the migrant reception center in Campobasso, there was a sense of anticipation. It was dark out, the June heat finally relenting a bit, and staff and residents stood on the patio of this repurposed hotel in the city's periphery, waiting for the buses—two buses, to be precise, transporting just over one hundred people who had disembarked five hundred kilometers away in the Calabrian coastal city of Crotone. Following their identification and initial processing by border officials, these asylum seekers were now being brought to live in the Molise region while awaiting a decision on their claims for protection. Staff from several area reception centers told me they had spent the afternoon figuring out room arrangements based on each center's available beds and which structures could accommodate families, women, or unaccompanied minors. Now they waited, eager to get everyone sorted. Current residents waited outside, too, hoping to see someone from their country among the new arrivals.

Having the buses arrive after dark was intentional: less visible, fewer local witnesses. In 2017, buses bringing newcomers to town weren't an anomaly, a fact that continued to alarm locals. Arrivals by sea remained high. While other major arrival countries like Greece built large camps on islands and remote areas, starting in 2014 Italy had instead opted to "distribute" migrants (the official word) throughout the country utilizing a new kind of structure for "extraordinary reception," abbreviated in Italian as CAS (*Centro di accoglienza straordinaria*).[1] Newcomers thus entered a reception system transformed through emergency response approaches to migration, including these structures. Intended to house asylum seekers temporarily, for two to three months, CAS instead became a main accommodation, at times housing more than 80 percent of asylum seekers, often for two years or more.[2] This meant that several of the people I interviewed in 2017 were still at the CAS when I returned the following year—waiting. In Molise, a region on the southeastern side of Italy's boot, CAS like this one remained at capacity, and new centers regularly opened. What was often framed in national media as an *emergenza immigrazione* at the nation's external borders had become the subject of everyday local concern and fraught debate. Meanwhile, these "extraordinary" structures became the norm.

That June evening, the buses were an hour or so late, and while the passengers might not have known the schedule or destination, surely they felt the hours. More than six hours in the bus from Crotone—after traversing the Sahara, after fleeing Libya, after crossing the sea, after being fingerprinted and filing their request for asylum in Italy. Men, women, and children stepped off the bus slowly, each person wearing flip flops they'd received upon disembarkation and carrying a plastic bag containing a plastic water bottle and whatever few belongings had survived the journey with them. They filed into the building, into a large room where they sat in rows of chairs while waiting to be summoned. One by one, as staff called out countries, people rose and walked to the front, where they were paired with the CAS where they would reside throughout the asylum process. It was the end of a long day and an even longer voyage. For these newcomers it was also, in one sense, just the beginning.

Italy's reception system is framed by the language of hospitality. The Italian word for reception, *accoglienza*, means both welcoming and hospitality. *Accogliere* is to welcome, to receive a guest. In the context of immigration, *accoglienza* refers to the system of migrant reception established throughout the country, indicating both official, bureaucratic reception procedures and the structures themselves: *centri di accoglienza* (reception centers). In addition, *accoglienza* also refers to the formal and informal practices of hospitality and welcoming that take place alongside official processes, from activities organized with local communities, to certificate programs that prepare migrants for future employment, to conversations that help newcomers orient to the reception center or city. These multiple meanings blur structures, systems, and social practices, creating ambiguity that feeds the emergency apparatus, which thrives on confusion.

As a site of emergency, Italy's reception system is a site of contested witnessing. Testimony is a crucial part of accoglienza: in witnessing acts that transpire within reception centers, and in broader terms because an individual's testimony at their *commissione* (asylum hearing) itself looms over the reception period, effectively a testimonial transaction stretched across time until officials issue a decision on the person's claim. Potential witnessing between newcomers and local communities also shapes these realities: the centers on which I focus here (CAS) are not meant to be widely witnessed by publics, yet they are ubiquitous, present in every Italian region and virtually every city. Developed as temporary holding spaces, not permanent structures, for many locals the CAS are just as visible as they are unknowable.

This chapter argues that Italy's reception system is a key site of emergency where the limits of witnessing reveal *paradoxes of proximity* that hold migrants in limbo and shape life in these emergency structures. I identify and elaborate these paradoxes as a way of describing migrants' positions in relation to Italian communities and institutions, and to their own stories. In doing so, I reframe accoglienza as an emergency response strategy that establishes the expectation that asylum seekers should prepare for life in Italy yet holds them at the legal, social, and geographical margins of Italian society. Purportedly concerned with welcoming and hospitality, accoglienza reifies difference. Through testimony as method, including interviews I conducted with center residents and observations of Italian language classes in CAS, I describe how "hospitality" as an emergency response strategy perpetuates migrant precarity. I show how practices of witnessing within accoglienza reveal the paradoxical logics at the heart of the emergency apparatus. By recognizing reception structures as themselves a product of the decades-long public and political framing of migrants in emergency terms, this chapter redefines reception not as a space or process for "welcoming" newcomers but as a site where foreignness is constantly being negotiated.

Reception centers and related spaces of detention and deportation are key sites of emergency throughout the global north, reflecting emergency imaginaries of foreignness as a structuring mechanism of border and migration governance. These logics cross political administrations, though they are also exacerbated by political shifts. In Italy, their paradoxical operations within the emergency apparatus were especially salient in CAS in 2017–2019, during key shifts in migratory and political trends. CAS operated at or over capacity despite fluctuating sea crossings; right-wing leaders rose to power on anti-immigrant platforms; and anti-Black racism gained political legitimacy through exclusionary policies, including as Italian border management shifted from facilitating rescue to blocking arrivals from Africa—trends that have continued.

I am driven to look at paradoxes of proximity by comments made in interviews with people who articulated a particular challenge in their experiences in the Italian reception system: that they do not feel welcome and yet are expected to "integrate." In other words, they confront the impossibility of genuine accoglienza. They navigate *conditional* welcome, or what Derrida calls "hostipitality," blending hospitality and hostility to suggest that, for "hosts" to maintain their sovereign role in the home (or in a country), any welcoming of guests (foreigners) is necessarily conditional, or selective.[3] In the context of migrant reception, encounters between migrants and locals, whether actual or anticipated, embody the conditional welcome in stark ways: these encounters are almost inevitably "strange encounters," to use Sara Ahmed's term, or meetings that affirm the migrant as an outsider.[4] For many reception center residents, marginalization and racialization are salient, everyday aspects of accoglienza.[5] Pervasive crisis and emergency framings of migration amplify a dissonance between the concerns of the Italian public at large, which generally expects the government to handle and process arriving migrants with minimal disruption to daily life, and the possibilities available to recently arrived migrants, who look to establish lives in Italy or other European countries yet are held in an ongoing state of transit, or nonarrival.[6] Likewise, scholarship on integration often glosses the role that the reception period itself plays in shaping relations between migrants and locals, and in perpetuating emergency imaginaries of migration.

Like the films, writings, and other cultural texts I discuss throughout this book, the oral histories produced through my interviews with asylum seekers offer a critical and underrepresented perspective on how "emergency" affects people's lives. These testimonies in and of transit "mediat[e] between personal memory and the social world" in contexts of extreme uncertainty.[7] Here I first offer an overview of Italy's emergency-response approach to reception, and of the Campobasso context. I then describe life in the CAS via the limits of witnessing, turning to a series of testimonies by asylum seekers. I close the chapter by reflecting on how reception relies on problematic ideas of integration. While I use "migrant" as an umbrella term to avoid legal status connotations, it is important to recognize that the stories I share in this chapter come from people who were seeking asylum at the time.

## ITALY'S EMERGENCY-RESPONSE RECEPTION SYSTEM

Some people enter Italy with refugee status; others avoid registering in the country in hopes of seeking asylum elsewhere; still others are funneled immediately into deportation centers (CIE or CPR; see table 3, appendix), despite that this violates the right to claim asylum. But most people who arrive by sea claim asylum upon entry, testifying in written or oral form to their need for protection, and entering the formal reception system. There they await the commissione, where they present their claims about their fear of violence or persecution in their country of origin and their need for asylum or another form of humanitarian protection. Then they wait for officials' assessment of their claim or to appeal a rejection.

EU member states govern migration both collectively, through EU-level policies and international agreements, and also at a national level, especially when it comes to reception. Broadly speaking, Italy's reception system operates through two scopes. In *prima accoglienza*, or primary reception, migrants are identified, fingerprinted, and registered, and their applications for asylum or other forms of humanitarian protection are filed. *Seconda accoglienza*, or secondary reception, initiates integration processes through extended stays in centers where staff support legal and cultural aspects of integration into life in Italy (table 3, appendix).[8] Both prima and seconda accoglienza occur in government-funded centers throughout the country, with locally hired staff responsible for providing room and board and ensuring that residents can access legal and medical aid.[9] This system was nationalized in 2002 through the Bossi-Fini Law and implemented during yet another state of emergency for immigration declared that year. It has been regularly adapted since, including multiple changes since 2014. For migrants, this means navigating a system in flux.

While the paradoxes and limits of reception are significant, I want to underscore that the accoglienza system represents a range of experiences. Forms of seconda accoglienza like the SPRAR (*Sistema di protezione per richiedenti asilo e rifugiati*, or System of Protection for Asylum Seekers and Refugees), and its subsequent iterations SIPROIMI (*Sistema di protezione per titolari di protezione internazionale e per minori stranieri non accompagnati*, or System of Protection for Beneficiaries of International Protection and for Unaccompanied Foreign Minors) and SAI (*Sistema di accoglienza e integrazione*, or Reception and Integration System) sometimes utilize local apartments to house their residents, offering more independence via apartment housing alongside Italian neighbors and support in transitioning to independent living. Despite their establishment via the controversial and otherwise restrictive Bossi-Fini Law, the SPRAR was celebrated as a promising model. In some small towns, SPRAR made a significant difference in the local economy, employing young people who would otherwise have left for larger cities. Locals I spoke with in towns in Molise and Calabria often commented that having a SPRAR meant that schools reopened, thanks to the presence of young Italian and foreign parents.

At a SPRAR I visited in the Calabrian village of Acquaformosa, tucked into the slopes of the mountainous Pollino National Park, locals celebrated accoglienza practices as part of a long tradition. This town and several neighboring villages were founded by Albanian migrants some five hundred years ago, a heritage story that remains vivid in the town's celebrations and traditional costume, as well as in the Arbëresche language spoken by many locals. At the pizzeria where I had dinner with my Italian bed and breakfast hosts, a local family originally from Nigeria dined at the next table and caught up with my hosts after we ordered. This scene should not have struck me as anything but normal, but it gave me pause because it was, in my experience, quite rare. In town, I met migrant parents who had come through the SPRAR, learned Italian, and now left their kids with *le nonne* (grandmothers), older Italian women who looked after the children while their parents went to sell wares in nearby Cosenza or work in the SPRAR offices. A young man who had crossed from Libya spoke with me about his experience living in the local center for unaccompanied minors, obtaining papers, turning eighteen, and being hired as a cultural mediator. SPRAR staff foregrounded the village's immigrant founding as shaping their commitment to helping newcomers integrate into Italian life while holding onto their own cultural traditions.

Of course, Acquaformosa is no paradise: it is a relatively remote village in one of Italy's poorest regions, and many migrants move elsewhere to find work once they obtain their documents. Racism and resentment live alongside experiences of harmony. Reception staff feel the pressures of constant "crisis" invocations. As Isabella, a social worker there, told me, "You can't talk for years about emergency."[10] Still, as I encountered it, the town was, in general, committed to remaining a positive example of reception, and to a large extent, what I witnessed in this mountain village is the way migrant reception in Italy is supposed to work.

Most migrants arriving after 2014, however, would never see a SPRAR but would remain in a CAS, which functions somewhere between prima and seconda accoglienza, and which many migrants refer to not as a centro di accoglienza, but simply as *il campo*. Calling the CAS a camp reflects migrants' understanding of accoglienza as part of a longer trajectory, linking their time in official and unofficial camps in Africa and in Libyan detention centers with their experience of European reception. It also links these official centers to the informal settlements I discuss in the next chapter, and to the official and unofficial reception spaces that opened throughout Europe in response to increased arrivals in the last decade. As emergency structures, and as *campi*, the CAS perform what Shahram Khosravi has described as the "spatial stretching of waiting," postponing arrival itself through an undefined limbo.[11] While they ostensibly enable people to initiate processes of "integration" into Italian society, residents' deportability—the possibility of being denied protection and sent away or left undocumented—imbues the space with collective and very personally felt anxiety.

The CAS was itself a revision of past forms that, together, show how Italian reception has developed in relation to the country's role as a gatekeeper for Fortress Europe, and has long functioned through emergency logics. While a limited number of "assistance centers" existed in the 1970s and 1980s, the government established reception procedures and centers in the early 1990s as the country received people fleeing conflicts and turmoil in Albania, the Balkans, and Somalia.[12] What were initially labeled *interventi straordinari* (extraordinary interventions) became established modes of housing, processing, and responding to the needs of refugees and asylum seekers. Reception structures have been consistently funded and regulated under declarations and repeated extensions of a *stato di emergenza immigrazione*, and it is no surprise that they differentiate and marginalize those seeking protection and legal residency. While it can support people's adjustment to life in Italy, accoglienza is inextricable from emergency as a primary strategy through which the Italian government manages migration from Africa, the Middle East, and South Asia.

Emergency modifications and the regular revamping of Italy's accoglienza system also affect relations between migrants and local communities and point to how the emergency apparatus reinvents forms of control without laying groundwork for longer-term community well-being. During the period of my fieldwork, while locals managed both CAS and SPRAR, the SPRAR sites were opened at the request of the local community, with local cooperatives proposing a budget and applying for government funds to run these programs. Instead, opening a CAS was a top-down decision, determined at a national level and (through 2018) based on a formula designed to balance the ratio of locals to migrants throughout the country, and funded with a nation-wide budget based on €35 per migrant, per day, representing all operating expenses and including €2.50 in daily "pocket money" per migrant.[13] Following state requirements, the local prefect would solicit applications for a team that would provide the site and staff the center, which often meant that local property owners collaborated with cultural organizations on proposals.[14]

At the CAS, extreme uncertainty about the future is metered out in the mundane routine of each day: meals, class, a trip to the store to recharge a cell phone or send money home. In standard set-ups, residents can choose to join daily Italian lessons; they have access to three basic meals per day, offered at set times; and they are free to come and go as they please, so long as they sign in each day in person. It is nearly impossible for migrants to obtain legal employment while awaiting documents, and reception includes a significant amount of downtime, which residents at the Campobasso CAS spent largely in their shared rooms, watching films or football matches or chatting with friends and family back home. In the city center, they might be accused of loitering, presumed to be begging, or, at a minimum, viewed with suspicion. As the site in which migrants confronted so many unknowns, the CAS fostered a mood of collective boredom and anxiety.

Formal, or official, reception embodies the paradoxical relationship between local and foreigner, host and guest, hospitality and hostility, welcome and control. This is a particularly vexed limbo for those housed in CAS. Salvatore, a CAS director in Campobasso, explained to me that when a migrant arrives to a SPRAR (or other seconda accoglienza), they sign a contract with management that stipulates the planned length of stay and outlines the requirements to which they must adhere—for example, attending language classes:

> In the SPRAR, the reception contract has a start date and an end date. At the CAS we can only write the start date, because we don't know the end date. . . . If you send me a migrant and you have me put only the start date, but I don't know when the person will leave the CAS, you give me no possibilities to use, so to speak, reward and punishment.[15]

In other words, there are no incentives, no ways to plan an individual trajectory, and no sense of consequences, positive or negative. Instead, time in the CAS is left undefined and, with few exceptions, unaccounted for.

## PARADOXES OF PROXIMITY IN CAMPOBASSO

From 2014 to 2019, most asylum seekers in the city of Campobasso were housed in CAS located in the *zona industriale* (industrial zone), just over three kilometers from the center of town (figure 7). While the city center is filled with parks, shops, and pedestrian-only areas, the industrial zone is home to a pasta factory, warehouses, corporate offices, a small shopping mall, and a multiplex

FIGURE 7. Campobasso industrial zone, near RAI offices and multilplex cinema, 2017. Photo by the author.

cinema, and is navigable via wide roads and parking lots. Living on the edge of town with restricted options for legal work, migrants' interactions with campobassani are limited. These realities became more apparent to me through interviews with CAS residents, and as I myself witnessed the frictions or the absence of such interactions.

One afternoon, on a walk I took in the city center with Sulayman, from Guinea, and Bakary, from Côte d'Ivoire (pseudonyms), both of whom were living at a CAS in the zona industriale, the men recounted multiple incidents that had made them feel generally unwelcome in Campobasso, despite their efforts to learn the language and meet locals. In fact, we held many of these interviews in Italian, as many migrants had lived in the country long enough to feel comfortable describing their experiences in the language. They expressed a sense that CAS staff are an exception; other Italians did not like foreigners and did not want Africans in the city. When Bakary went to ask for a job at a local shop, he was told, "Vai nel tuo paese!" *Go back to your country!* They said that if only migrants were waiting at the bus stop, the bus driver often passed on by. They recounted a range of incidents, from microaggressions to overt hostility.

At a certain point, Sulayman said, essentially, look, they see us as foreigners, and they see the presence of foreigners as a problem. So we try to get closer to them and to their culture, but they refuse us. I asked him to say more: "Dite che vi trattano cosí male, ma dite anche che ci volete rimanere." *How is it that if you get treated badly, you want to stay here?* And Sulayman responded, "Ma mi hanno anche salvato la vita." *But they also saved my life.*

He was describing a kind of *proximal distance* that both links and separates migrants and local communities, fostering a nearness without extended interaction and without mutual belonging. In this case, it facilitates not integration but racialization and the reification of the migrant as stranger, including through the presumption that Black subjects in the city center are out of place. When migrants are associated with crisis, terrorism, and fear of drastic cultural change, that recognition produces "the migrant" as a fetishized figure, an abstraction onto which desires and fears are projected. As Ahmed explains, "the stranger only comes to be recognised as such by coming *too close* to home."[16] The figure of the stranger is, for Baldwin, produced through the "luxury" of such projection, a kind of white or colonial seeing that merely reinforces dominant racial logics.[17] In turn, there is violence in expecting people to integrate into a society that continues to exclude nonwhite subjects. "You are asking me to be an accomplice to my own murder," Baldwin says about the idea that Black Americans should be "integrated" into US society.[18] In Italy, the dynamics of proximal distance differ between cities with larger diasporic communities and small-to-mid-size towns, but in general, the rapid expansion of emergency structures in response to "crisis" segregated populations and perpetuated the racist presumption that Black Africans are undeserving economic migrants. In this culture of suspicion, those awaiting protection—who may or may not want to stay in Italy—are then expected to integrate, to live Italian lives.[19]

The culture of suspicion regarding migrants and the limited interactions around which it grew were palpable upon my own first encounters with asylum seekers in Campobasso. For me, since I first visited the city in 2005, it has always been the place where my in-laws live and where my partner grew up. Campobasso is the small regional capital of Molise, which has a largely agricultural economy built through a long tradition of small farms. It is a region rich in culinary and musical traditions, with three principal cities: Isernia and Campobasso, the two provincial capitals, and Termoli on the Adriatic coast. Joined with neighboring Abruzzo until the two regions were split in 1970, it is now Italy's second smallest region and among its poorest.[20] Like other southern regions, Molise saw postwar out-migration to northern Italy and abroad. Several local towns have monuments to the emigrant—the one who left. My partner and many of his childhood friends, too, have left. In recent years, as younger generations have moved elsewhere to study or find work, Molise's numerous mountain villages have become home to aging populations; community life there often centers around holiday festivals that draw home those who have moved away. And so Molise is, in one sense, a place all too familiar with departures.

Immigration into the region did not begin in 2014: Campobasso has been home to a small Chinese community since the early 2000s, and a Romani community has lived for decades in a neighborhood west of the old city center. Molise has been a destination for Albanian and Romanian immigrants who have worked in domestic care or construction since the 1990s. Yet until 2014, immigration there was only sporadically addressed by media and politicians. When national authorities began bussing hundreds of migrants into Molise's main cities in 2014, the difference was of both scale and spectacle. Discourses of a migration crisis or a Mediterranean emergency no longer only referred to Greek islands, Sicilian coasts, or politics in Rome but suddenly seemed to describe situations in Molise as well.

This scenario may sound familiar to readers elsewhere, including in the United States where, in recent years, hotels housing asylum seekers have become an increasingly familiar sight. These situations are, however, notably distinct in ways that reflect how the politicization of migration management is tied to dynamics of (in)visibility. In the United States, this emergency response tactic is not a nationwide plan but a political stunt initiated in 2022 as Republican governors in southern border states began bussing migrants to "liberal" states like New York and Massachusetts. While in places like Molise, arrivals were arranged to be noticed as little as possible, in the United States, transporting migrants across state lines is intended to be hypervisible.[21] Still, in both cases, migrants themselves have little to no say in their actual destination.

As is common, emergency migrant reception structures in Molise largely occupy repurposed buildings, in particular former hotels. Like other small and family-owned businesses, hotels in rural and more remote areas of the country have struggled to survive given the rise of remote work and online commerce and following the 2008 global financial crisis. As Campobasso-based cultural mediator Concetta Fornaro explained to me, these shifts meant that hotels outside major cities no longer saw the traffic of traveling businesspeople. The government call for CAS appeared as an opportunity: staying open or reopening for migrant reception let hotel owners retain their property and allowed many employees to retain their positions. As local *prefetture* (judicial districts) solicited proposals, teams applying to open a CAS needed to prove that they could use government funds to support a certain number of staff and beds (given a predetermined ratio of staff to migrants) and connect migrants with legal and health-related services. While some management teams came to CAS work out of interest and experience, in general, staff were not trained in migration, displacement, or trauma-related care (this is still the case). Spaces were transformed into dormitory-like facilities, despite rumors circulating among right-wing groups that migrants were being put up in four-star hotels with VIP treatment. With minor remodeling and new collaborations, the transition could happen relatively quickly.

In the first such transformation in Campobasso, a former three-star hotel whose restaurant had, until recently, hosted birthday parties and formal events, was made to accommodate just over one hundred asylum seekers at a time in shared rooms. It was regularly at capacity, and by 2018, management had opened an additional five structures, including in a former gym and a former office space, all in the zona industriale. These peripheral locations positioned CAS residents in proximal distance with locals, a fact that might have mattered less had CAS remained sites of rapid transition, quickly sending people on to SPRAR.

In Campobasso, locals would tell you that reaching the industrial zone requires a car, maybe a bus ride. Virtually the only people regularly walking the route between there and the city center are migrants, most of them young Black men. The physical locations of the CAS thus position migrants to be seen as walking through spaces where locals avoid going by foot, meeting stereotypes of migrants as wandering aimlessly or as likely up to no good. For many locals, the CAS are a rupture of the local map, disturbing "the purified space of the community [and] the purified life of the good citizen."[22] For Bakary, Sulayman, and others I spoke with at the daily Italian language classes, their paradoxical proximity to the local community contributed to their anxiety. They felt they were stagnating in this campo.

In recorded interviews, while they addressed their frustration with the waiting period, most of the residents I talked with spoke positively about their experiences in reception and their interactions with locals. Things are generally okay, they said, though they wished it were easier to speak with Italians. Outside of recorded interviews, more concerns rose to the surface: they wanted to get to know the locals, but when they approached people in Italian, locals responded in English. When migrants spoke in English, locals responded in Italian, a move the migrants read as intentionally marking their outsiderness. They felt excluded and observed with suspicion, as if existing outside of "national time."[23]

Rather than marginal spaces or the aftermath of "border crises," the CAS are part of a long history of "black spaces of social control and institutionalized violence"[24] and are critical to the production of unknowable strangers and of "Europe." As migration shapes Europe politically, socially, and demographically, newcomers' experiences of limbo necessarily influence how they later make their way within Italy or elsewhere, with implications for future generations. Yet dependence works both ways: citizens depend on foreigners to define their collective bodies.[25] Emergency discourses heighten this dependence as they underscore homogenized notions of national identity and foreign "otherness." In practical terms, too, communities come to depend on the presence of migrants and on continued arrivals. A CAS for one hundred migrants might employ six to fifteen locals, from administrators to cooks. In town, cell phone vendors and Western Union outlets count migrants among their regular customers. Their fate also comes to depend on the politics of emergency.

CAS test the limits of witnessing, on the one hand by making it difficult to have genuine interactions with locals, and on the other hand by prompting some migrants to try to remain invisible—nearly unwitnessable, unengageable. Partly because of their peripheral location, some migrants rarely leave the CAS and so are hardly seen at all outside the campo. This seemed to be the case for

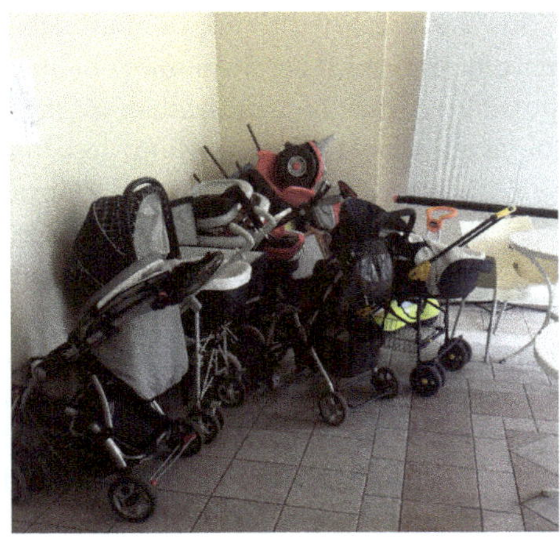

FIGURE 8. Strollers for communal use at a CAS (Centro di accoglienza straordinaria, or Center for Extraordinary Reception), Molise, 2017. Photo by the author.

women in particular, pointing to gender as a significant factor not only in asylum proceedings[26] but also in reception (figure 8). Women, who comprise a minority of asylum seekers in Italy, navigate a set of invisible obstacles, in and outside of reception centers, related to gendered stereotypes.[27] While Bakary and Sulayman were often assumed to be economic migrants (despite their asylum seeker status), women like Samanta (pseudonym), a Nigerian woman I met in 2018, were treated as either victims or criminals in connection with sex trafficking and sex work.[28] Pregnant when we met, Samanta preferred to stay in her room rather than attend language lessons or hang out in common spaces. When she did venture to the city center, she told me, she only visited a municipal park:

> *Samanta:* If I leave [the CAS] . . . I'm playing in the *villa comunale*. You know the garden? . . . I would just sit down there, be looking at those Italian children playing. After that I will leave there, I'll come back [to the reception center]. . . . I don't know any place other than that.

Samanta, like other Nigerian women I spoke with there, took refuge in invisibility, spending time in communal CAS spaces and outside the CAS only occasionally, to protect her reputation. Their choice to be less seen reflects, on the one hand, the right to opacity (via Glissant). On the other hand, it speaks to invisibility as a kind of "social erasure . . . that shapes the contours of social imagination and relegates the newcomer to the margins."[29] Despite these challenges, beginning in fall 2017, many CAS residents, including several women, undertook the commute from the zona industriale to the city center more regularly to attend courses offered by a local school for adult education.

Invisibility emerges in other forms as well. For those who don't live or work in the CAS, accoglienza remains obscured from view in ways that make global, national, and even local Italian publics only ever partial witnesses to the realities of hospitality as emergency response. This is exacerbated by a lack of available data. As CAS operators confirmed to me, official records list the number of open CAS and SPRAR, but it's virtually impossible to track how individual migrants move between centers, or to know the average wait for an asylum decision, average length of stay in a CAS or SPRAR, or staffing information for accoglienza structures. An example of what Ulrike Krause terms "nonknowledge," this set of unknowns renders it difficult to address uncertainties yet "still facilitates the governance of refugees" and others on the move.[30] This vagueness is a strategic facet of the emergency apparatus. It limits what the public can know or understand about the reception of migrants and the heterogeneity of migrant experiences, implicitly restricting what forms of witnessing are possible, and limiting available narratives of reception to those circulated in media and political discourse.

## RECKONING WITH TEMPORALITIES IN THE CAS

Caught up in these paradoxes are questions of temporality, both the undefined limbo of reception itself and the ways a person's past becomes present during that limbo. After all, reception is marked by extreme uncertainty, but it is not empty time. So much happens between the filing of the claim and official status determination: people come and go. Laws change. Other asylum seekers are granted or denied protection. Short-term jobs appear and disappear. Public opinion on immigration shifts. Connections at home, memories of the voyage, and desires for the future all shape how a person experiences reception and the decisions they make while waiting. Rather than a strictly legal limbo, or simply an in-between time, reception is a space in which people's "'capacity to act' is differentially and relationally shaped."[31]

Reception exemplifies the impossibility of inscribing migration within clear temporal markers, and waiting as, paradoxically, a key element of the urgency of "crisis."[32] In its aims to support migrant integration, accoglienza appears forward looking, but for many, its enforced waiting suspends normal time and constrains individual agency, holding hostage the chronologies of those in transit. Yet it is also a period of imminent encounter: the asylum hearing could be announced at any moment. The reception of African migrants in Italy also calls attention to what Mbembe describes as the "multiplicity of times" that coexist and interact in postcolonial contexts.[33] The control of migrants' time reproduces the colonial-era control of bodies and subjectivities. As Khosravi says in *Waiting*, the 2020 short film he made with Dagmawi Yimer, one of these temporalities is a constant belatedness that is also racialized:

> We migrants, we refugees, we foreigners, we are always seen as delayed people. We arrive to the right time and it is always too late. We arrive to a pre-existing world of meanings. A world already shaped in which a nonwhite person is not a subject with a

history and agency, but only an object fixed as a category and imagined in a different temporality.[34]

Migrants' own perceptions and refusals of the temporalities imposed upon them during this period offer an important critique of accoglienza itself. The residents I spoke with saw CAS as spaces of frustration that oscillate between practices of accoglienza and of *abbandono*—abandonment, as one person termed the denial of asylum claims. Time is not linear during reception: while this limbo holds asylum seekers in transit months and even years after they disembark on Italian shores, uncertain futures weigh on their waiting, and the past remains present both in the testimonies they give for asylum and as they (may) reflect on their journeys.

Witnessing haunts the limbo of accoglienza. This suspended time can become a constant encounter with the past, and with the self—or an avoidance of such confrontations. Center residents may revisit the narrative they presented upon arrival, or question how an interpreter translated their account into Italian. Or they may avoid thinking about their testimony, not ready to confront the trauma it recalls. I bring up trauma not to fetishize suffering in the campo, but to reflect on how residents exercise agency and navigate limbo despite these amorphous challenges.[35] For many, going over their initial testimony involves actively questioning the protocols, definitions, and parameters of refugee status determination; these processes are, like any autobiographical act, part of "investigations into and processes of self-knowing."[36] Whether vocalized or internal, it is part of what makes this waiting an active time, and it shapes how people situate their past in relation to their possible futures in Europe.[37]

Revisiting their initial testimonies or preparing for the commissione also often means confronting the disconnect between what people know as their most urgent needs and what asylum officials are likely to recognize as a legitimate asylum claim. In oral history interviews, I told people I was interested in hearing about their time in Italy and asked where they would like to begin their stories. Many chose to retell their story of leaving home and eventually (sometimes after years) reaching Italy, and transit through Libya was a common focus. Most of the people I interviewed were men in their twenties who had left West Africa and reached Libya after months of travel. There, many were imprisoned and tortured prior to crossing the sea. They consistently opted to emphasize their time in Libya, often suggesting that those experiences represented their most pressing need for protection.

Aman (pseudonym) had left the Gambia and, like many, gone to Libya looking for work. Threatened and robbed at gunpoint multiple times, he decided to return to his home country.[38]

> *Aman:* To go to work [in Libya] is a big problem. I am kidnapped three times
> in Libya . . . I want to return back to, . . . but because—there's no money.
> There's no money. And the boss, this Arab man, used to give us work—

> his name is [X]. His name is [X]. He used to give us work. So this Arab man is the one who helped me. He said to me, [Aman], you want to go back? I say I want to go back, let me go back. And he tells me, no, you cannot go back. The road is not safe. There's many criminals in the way. So I can help you to go to a place where you are safe. But I didn't think about this Europe here because I didn't think about coming here for a fear of water—I didn't want to go on the water. Only one night the commander takes me and says let's go. I say where are we going? He says let's go. And they take me along, they put me on this boat. They take me to Sabratha [a Libyan port city], they take me on this boat.
>
> *Eleanor:*  They wanted you to pay them?
>
> *Aman:*  No, I didn't pay nothing. I was not thinking to come to Europe.

For many in Aman's position, Libya was a turning point—not a step in a plan, but a point at which plans changed. It wasn't easy to find work. They were robbed, held hostage, tortured, or enslaved. Many wanted to leave Libya and return to their home countries but were unable, for safety or financial reasons. Instead, the only way out was a boat.

I am not repeating the details of Aman's torture here, or the ways that captors demanded ransom, held him at gunpoint, or sold him for labor. Accounts like Aman's are well documented, but despite reporting, humanitarian campaigns, exposés, and testimonials by survivors on social media and in news coverage, EU policies have only further restricted people's safe passage.[39] In this telling, I have tried to honor people's stories while also resisting the ways in which my own reporting of these accounts might produce voyeurs rather than witnesses.[40] Know this: people arrive on the northern shores of the Mediterranean bearing physical and emotional scars that are the traces of only some of what they have experienced. For the purposes of this discussion of emergency and witnessing, it is important to understand that these experiences en route are themselves transformative, revealing transit as not simply movement from departure to destination but a series of encounters that (re)shape a person's journey and how they think about the future.

Aman's account of how he ended up on a boat illustrates how asylum seekers' understandings of their own need for protection are not fixed but are shaped by the changing circumstances in which they live and move. However, this fluctuating understanding, inflected with memory, emotion, and uncertainty about the future, may or may not correspond with the criteria asylum officials use in case adjudication. Official status determination focuses on conditions in a person's country of origin. But in telling their journey outside the context of the court, Aman and others foregrounded these experiences in Libya as central. They were frustrated that more attention wasn't being paid to injustices in Libya, and this appeal for more and different witnessing added to the sense of urgency during the accoglienza period.

Aman's description of his arrival in Italy is a statement of extreme fear; he cites fear of water as the very reason it would not have occurred to him to come to Europe. In his account, this fear proves that he did not intend to come to Italy. It also describes his first months following rescue at sea. Aman described his initial time in Italy as fearful and anxious; he said he did not know much about the country and was not certain he was safe:

> I was thinking maybe they will come and sell me, or they will come and do me something, or—you understand. . . . Because in Libya you always see these people with big guns . . . every time problems. Bombs in your area. Many people run away, but because you are migrants you don't know where to go.

He feared that in Italy he would have to confront a repetition of what he endured in Libya. This fear—this reckoning with the past—haunted his time in reception. He stayed mostly in his shared room at the CAS until he realized that, as he put it, "We are where the pope is. When I know that, I know that this is safe. Because as a Christian place, it's not a problem." And he continued talking about Italy as the home of Christians and of the pope, reiterating that he is Muslim but recognizes Christianity as a peaceful religion and Christian spaces as safe spaces. Aman emphasized danger and suggested that because Italy itself did not initially hold specific meanings for him, he didn't trust his surroundings. In telling his story, he positioned himself as someone who now understands the culture of the host country, and notes that this culture will, in turn, protect him.

For asylum judges, the question is, protect him from what? In one sense, accounts like Aman's push back at established criteria for determining asylum cases that adjudicate based on conditions in one's country of origin and the tendency of officials to listen for prescribed narratives of violence and persecution.[41] Incredible pressure falls on the act of witnessing—on official testimony and on other instances of relating the past—because asylum seekers must decide what part of their story, and of their sense of need, will be recognizable to officials.[42]

Migrants' understandings of the past and their hopes for the future are transformed by their experiences in transit. Their stories of flight remind us that crisis narratives often fetishize Europe's external borders as *the* site of migration, a border spectacle that disregards that for many migrants, crossing the sea to Italy was not their plan when they first left home. Having fled violence, conflict, or extreme precarity in one country, they also have to reckon with what happens to them along the way. This, too, is a paradox of proximity: that a person's immediate experiences might shape them profoundly and must be set aside in the context of asylum, where only some of the past matters.[43]

It is paradoxical, too, to be on the move and to have lost control over time, to have arrived in Europe and find oneself constantly at its margins. Amid this uncertainty, to borrow from Ma Vang's discussion of Hmong refugees, the fugitivity of Mediterranean migrants "unsettles the nation-state, democracy, and liberal empire"—including asylum regimes—"as well as knowledge formation."[44] Accounts like Aman's illustrate how the emergency apparatus operates at the level of the individual and of memory, as limbo becomes, potentially, a site of narrative crisis—processing recent trauma, reflecting on one's official testimony, and watching the political climate shift.

## DESERVING HOSPITALITY

In the spring of 2018, anxiety was high at the campo. CAS residents told me that, following a period of few asylum decisions, multiple people had learned that their applications had been rejected. For the men I met in Italian classes, this was not only a rejection of their initial claims but of the commitment they had made to integrating: they had followed the rules, taken initiative, even studied extra, perhaps to no avail. The asylum system seemed increasingly arbitrary. They knew that their cases depended on their accounts of persecution in their countries of origin, but they hoped their efforts to integrate might somehow help their claims be decided more quickly, and favorably. They were also concerned by recent national elections that had brought right-wing parties to power promising harsher migration policies.

Forms of witnessing were a regular feature of language classes, held in the CAS cafeteria (figure 9). Introductory language learning often first orients around self-presentation, enabling a person to describe who they are and where they're from. While these exercises were relatively brief, simple, and of course distinct from official asylum testimony, some residents felt the weight of performing their stories repeatedly and chose not to attend; sitting in class brought up past trauma. For others, learning Italian was a practical choice and a way to pass the time. In general, residents were protective of their actual asylum testimonies; while they speculated together on how their cases would go, they told me they rarely discussed the details of their stories with each other. Likewise, oral and written testimonies produced in the context of a class understandably exemplified a selective and often limited sharing before fellow residents, center staff, and privileged visitors like me. These testimonies seemed at times to be as much exercises in hope as in grammar.

Given my presence as a foreigner now fluent in Italian, students often wanted to talk about how I had learned the language. Some wanted to practice English with me, which they recognized as useful across Europe. Louis (pseudonym), a man in his mid-twenties from Mali, asked me to help him write out the story of another reception center he'd lived in, which officials had recently closed. He had been happy in the previous center and was "afraid of not finding other places like that."[45] Louis described reaching the Campobasso CAS and being encouraged by Salvatore, the manager, that he would be okay. He concluded the piece: "And in these few months, I discovered that it was true. The people . . . are kind and helpful,

FIGURE 9. CAS (Centro di accoglienza straordinaria, or Center for Extraordinary Reception) cafeteria where language classes were held, Molise, 2017. Photo by the author.

and I am doing well here. If you try hard, people will help you find your way." He wrote hope onto his own story, reassuring himself, as much as any reader.

In a short writing assignment in Italian, Sulayman referred to conversations with me and with the Italian instructor: "While [Eleanor and I] were talking, Maestro Luca wrote the title of the day's lesson on the board. Then we spoke with Prof. Luca. I told him how my asylum hearing had gone. Then Prof. Luca began to explain the title of the day's lesson."[46] Sulayman chose to record the fact that they discussed his hearing but not what it involved. In fact, he would remain incredibly anxious about that hearing for the coming months, unsure he had been treated fairly.

While produced for the small audience of the language class, autobiographical texts like these constitute another critical witnessing act. They represent a kind of rehearsal, as their authors practice defining themselves in new languages. They also illustrate the work the residents put into learning languages they hope will help them in Europe. Importantly, they are also performances of deservingness, testimonies produced for audiences—teachers, guests like me, perhaps asylum officials—whom these authors see as potential judges of their merits for remaining in Europe outside the bounds of asylum adjudication. In this sense, such texts also testify to what migrants think is expected of them.

The fraught relationship between precarity, protection, and notions of deservingness emerged in another exchange with Sulayman and Bakary.[47] The two men asked to record an interview and insisted on speaking with me away from the

CAS, saying they wanted me to understand what the wait was like for them. Here deservingness arose as both legal and social entitlement, exceeding the bounds of the asylum court.[48] At a café in the city center, they described their deservingness of visas in terms of their desire to stay in Italy and their efforts to "integrate." Sulayman also justified their deservingness in terms of risk: "In Africa it was too difficult and we took the risk of coming here." We spoke in Italian, which both men had made remarkable efforts to master while living at the CAS.

Sulayman and Bakary did not want to discuss their reasons for leaving their home countries with one another (and therefore also not with me there in the café), but they both addressed the difficulty of adjusting to life in the CAS and presenting a case for asylum while finding ways to deal with their past experiences. We spoke about how their stress regarding visas was mixed with other concerns and psychological issues related to their lives before Italy. I asked Bakary, "What strategies do you have for dealing with the anxieties of this waiting period?" "I try to forget what happened," he replied. But with the undefined wait between arrival, hearing, and potential appeal, forgetting is never a real option.

Sulayman said he was upset at how his recent hearing had gone. His case was based on the account he had given a year earlier, shortly after reaching Italy, a narrative he says he "was not yet ready to tell" at the time. Compounding the problem, he said, the interpreter, from a different region and ethnic group, had not sufficiently translated his story.[49] Afterward, feeling helpless, he turned to the CAS staff, who I know held him in high regard. "[I told them] 'This is my life. And my life . . . without you [CAS staff] I don't know what I'd do.' And they made me believe that 'you have to trust them' [CAS staff]." Staff members had reassured Sulayman that "they would do everything possible" for him.[50] He saw these interactions as a promise of empathy and action.

We also spoke at length about both men's efforts to integrate, which they framed as a testament to their sincerity and as a matter of fairness: they frequented the language class at the CAS; other residents did not.

> *Sulayman:* In any case it's a disaster. Because someone who . . . whoever wanted to stay with you all [Italians], you don't have a vision for him. He must leave your territory. Unfortunately, unfortunately . . . it's difficult.
>
> *Eleanor:* You're both saying that you want to remain in Italy.
>
> *Bakary:* Yes, but it's their decision, not mine.

Sulayman addressed Italians as a collective "you." In his remarks about "your territory," he does not distinguish authorities who decide cases from the general public. In the logic of this conflation, a decision in favor of one's claims suggests not simply a legal recognition but acceptance by the population. Denial, on the other hand, is read as broad rejection.

> *Sulayman:* If our friends who arrive in Italy, if it doesn't work out for them, they head out to go to France or Germany. But we've decided to stay here, to be

> here. Because we waited for the commission, we studied their language.
> . . . What's [happening now], it's too dangerous for us, too difficult.
>
> *Eleanor:*  You're also attending the CPIA [school for adults].
>
> *Sulayman:*  I go to school every day, Monday to Friday.

Both men divided their time between language classes at the CAS and subject courses at the CPIA, where they were earning an Italian middle school diploma. Their roommates teased them: "Why do you go to school? What's the point?" The general perception among center residents was that fewer asylum seekers were being granted protection and more were receiving *negativi*, the word with which they referred to rejected claims. In our interview, in light of the recent set of negativi for fellow residents, Bakary and Sulayman questioned the commitments they had made to studying.

Language courses exemplify how different ideas of deservingness influence the reception period and migrants' anticipation of post-accoglienza life but not necessarily the outcomes of asylum applications.[51] In multiple CAS I visited, staff lamented the low attendance rate in the Italian classes, which were offered six days per week and were frequented by around 10–15 percent of residents. Some of my visits coincided with Ramadan, during which attendance was notably diminished, as people preferred to rest more while fasting. But outside of Ramadan, too, only a minority of residents ever attended. In my experience, migrants were praised for attending and gently teased or reprimanded for skipping (attendance is not required). In Sulayman's view, his commitment to language learning should have counted in the judgment of his case, perhaps offsetting any problems caused by the interpreter of his original testimony. Instead, he worried his time studying rendered his situation more difficult:

> *Sulayman:*  When you're in school you can't have the opportunity to arrange things for yourself better.
>
> *Eleanor:*  Why? Instead, if you didn't go to school you'd have this opportunity?
>
> *Sulayman:*  There are a lot of people who don't come to school, who work. The people who don't come to school have more opportunities and they have power . . . what's the point, anymore? Now when I think about all this, I get very discouraged. I'm more educated, surely. But the life that we live isn't easy.

I imagine it is difficult not to compare behavior and intent, as Sulayman does here. Living in close quarters, with limited contact with locals or communities in diaspora in larger Italian cities, migrants in Campobasso seemed to hang their hopes on the outcomes of fellow residents. One migrant obtaining papers made others optimistic; a rejection augmented collective anxiety.

Was it worth demonstrating other forms of deservingness? While rare, it's true that migrants are sometimes rewarded with legal residency for their expressions of good character. In May 2018, Mamoudou Gassama, a Malian young man living in France, scaled the exterior of a building to save a child who was dangling from a balcony rail.[52] This nimble feat garnered the attention of both global media, which dubbed Gassama "Spiderman," and of the French government. Although Gassama had entered France without papers, he was rewarded with a job with the Paris Fire Brigade, as well as the possibility of not only legal residency but French citizenship. In Venice a year later, a Malian migrant was granted residency for being "well integrated" despite not meeting the criteria for political asylum. According to an article in *la Repubblica*, the Venetian court determined that he "had proven optimal familiarity with the Italian language and, thanks to this, a capacity to seriously integrate."[53] The judge cited the man's efforts to work in multiple sectors and his participation in an education program. Wide circulation of such stories illustrates how notions of deservingness travel outside the purview of the asylum court and are ushered into public discourse on migration and brought to the awareness of migrants looking toward their own future.

## GUESTS OF EMERGENCY

As a set of emergency structures and practices, the accoglienza system is subject to regular scrutiny and manipulation. In recent years, along with the growing criminalization of migration and humanitarian aid, some celebrated reception models have come under threat. In 2018, Interior Minister Matteo Salvini centered the SPRAR in Riace, on Calabria's Ionian coast, in a campaign to criminalize humanitarian assistance and some forms of accoglienza. Riace was widely recognized as having created a reception program that supported both migrants and local communities. Two years earlier, long-time mayor Domenico "Mimmo" Lucano was named one of the "world's greatest leaders" by *Fortune* magazine for his efforts to rebuild the dying village through job training programs for recently arrived migrants, including by training them in the traditional masonry methods—a literal rebuilding.[54] In late 2018, at Salvini's urging, Lucano was put under house arrest, then exiled from Riace, while authorities investigated him on charges of abuses of power and aiding in illegal immigration by arranging "marriages of convenience."[55] Although charges were eventually dismissed, the process effectively dismantled the Riace SPRAR, and in 2019 Lucano lost his mayoral seat to a candidate from Salvini's Lega party. The undoing of the Riace system shows that even model reception sites do not represent "*the* law of hospitality"[56] but remain susceptible to the fluctuations of emergency politics. (And in yet another turn, in 2024 Lucano was elected mayor once again and became an EU parliamentarian.)

While attacks on the Riace model were clearly political, reception is sometimes also a site of corruption. While many centers are run by employees passionate about migrant rights and well-being (I think of the bike repair area that staff at a Campobasso CAS set up for residents), CAS management teams work as fairly autonomous entities, their day-to-day operations and use of funds largely unchecked by government authorities. As I heard regularly in interviews, teams sometimes run centers with a minimum of staff, offering a minimum of resources. Some CAS management have been cited or arrested for enabling dangerous and unsanitary conditions, including cases like the 2017 situation in Ostuni of "unpotable water, which is causing skin irritations and allergies, [putting migrants] at risk for salmonella infection."[57] In addition, criminal organizations are known to operate in accoglienza to profit from migrants' presence. This corruption, most noted through the Mafia Capitale investigation in Rome, situates accoglienza as one of many systems in "crisis Italy"[58] implemented without a long-term vision and therefore ripe for exploitation and profiteering.

But even when centers operate as planned—and again, many people do make it through accoglienza and obtain protection—still it is not enough to presume integration as an outcome of reception or, more broadly, as a solution to the "problem" of migration. On the one hand, a migrant's possibilities for participating in and shaping life in Italy change radically depending on whether and how the accoglienza system receives them. On the other hand, accoglienza is only the beginning. Whatever adjustments "integration" stands for require public and long-term dialogue on race, racism, citizenship, communities, workplaces, and schools.

Accoglienza racializes migrants not only in cases of dehumanizing neglect[59] but, more generally, in its dependence on the recognition of the stranger. These processes are exacerbated during so-called crises, as Étienne Balibar observed more than three decades ago in his discussion of crisis racism.[60] The terms used to refer to migrants and to reception processes reflect these problematics. I take up the question of labels at the close of this chapter on accoglienza, paradoxes of proximity, and the limits of witnessing because these terms correspond to available narratives about migration. That is, dominant ideas about reception and integration shape what kinds of stories are tellable about how migrants live and adapt to life in Europe—and therefore what kinds of witnessing are possible in mainstream Italian and European contexts.[61]

Within crisis racism, the common framing of migrants as *ospiti* (guests) enables their continued marginalization instead of facilitating their genuine welcome into contexts of belonging or—still harder to imagine—into processes of collective transformation. Guest language fits the notion of reception centers as "welcome centers" (centri di accoglienza), but in many cases, "the space for guests is cold and inhospitable."[62] Italians working in reception have referred to migrants as "ospiti" since reception structures were expanded in the 1990s.[63] This "humanitarian euphemism" suggests that accoglienza is a relationship of generosity on the part of Italian communities and institutions and implies that migrants stay in centers by choice. It's paternalistic, even if well intended, suggesting that migrants are indebted to Italian benefactors and should be grateful. These terms also mask or disregard migrants' own perspectives. Across CAS, SPRAR, and informal settlements, I never heard asylum seekers refer to themselves as guests. Moreover, their reference to the centers as "campi" suggests that they see centers as more directly linked to refugee camps than to guest hostels.

Just as "guest worker" suggests the temporary nature of a migrant's stay in a "host" country, so, too, does labeling Mediterranean migrants as guests suggest that they will not make Italy their home.[64] "Ospite/guest" normalizes the transient, temporary aspects of a migrant's presence, affirming their strangerness and erasing their agency. On the contrary, as Stephanie Malia Hom observed in a large deportation center in Rome, "*ospiti* believed in the emancipatory potentials of mobility and they acted on those hopes."[65] Other terms, such as the frequently used *ragazzi* (guys, youth), instead infantilize CAS residents, another kind of racializing practice that recalls white savior paradigms. The common humanitarian category of *beneficiari* or beneficiaries, emphasizes a more transactional relationship between migrants and the state or local organizations and aligns migrants with beneficiari in other social welfare contexts.

It is no surprise that a system developed through emergency response conceives the guest/host relationship within the emergency imaginary and its obsession with the present, positing migrants' arrival as a meeting between strangers who do not share a history—as if displacement between Africa and Europe had no connection to European histories, laws, or practices. These connections are evident in the reception system's configuration as a set of imperial formations, inextricably linked with Italy's historical attempts to control the movements of those deemed outside the national body. As Hom has discussed, contemporary reception and detention sites are among the "messy constellations" of structures, practices, and erasures that link past and present. For instance, in serving the state's policing of *some* mobilities, today's deportation centers are "haunting reminders" of colonial-era concentration camps such as those Italy constructed in Libya.[66]

Although integration is a contentious term, European governments use it, SPRAR managers use it, many migration scholars use it, and migrants use it—but with what assumptions about collective identity and belonging?[67] Migration and critical race scholars in the US context have critiqued how discourses of integration reiterate fixed, generally white, notions of the citizen. Common uses of integration imply that migrants should conform to dominant cultural norms. In the United States, notions of people's "unassimilability" were repeatedly used to justify laws that excluded immigrants based on nationality and ethnicity.[68] In Europe, too, integration is often a racialized term, weaponized against forms of racial and religious otherness that do not fit dominant notions of European bodies as white. Yet because of the challenges of naming race/racism as an issue in Europe, the racialization of migrant strangers is disguised as a matter of foreignness or nationality.[69]

As a term, integration indicates available narratives about belonging in Italy. Yet importantly, integration is also something on which migrants themselves insist. Migrants I spoke with also understood integration as a right and as a process that should connect them with each other and with local communities. Rather than a passive process, it's one that migrants were ready to help define.[70] It's also an undertaking some choose to take into their own hands. Given the extreme uncertainties of limbo, the paradoxical expectations of integration, and in some cases given the despicable conditions of reception centers, it is no surprise that some migrants exit the formal system.

## CONCLUSION: ACCOGLIENZA AND ABANDONMENT

Although conceived as a system for managing migrants and migration "emergencies," accoglienza often perpetuates limbo and extreme uncertainty: people seeking better lives in Europe have ended up in holding patterns in its southernmost spaces. Asylum seekers depend on local and state authorities for their very survival. Yet so often these are spaces of abandonment—places where Europe's racialized others are left to wait—to waste—and sites overdetermined by people's deportability, that is, sites where someone is always potentially deported and where many are refused legal recognition.

My conversation with Bakary and Sulayman in the city center was prompted by an asylum rejection. Bakary had received a negativo (formally, a *diniego*) at his commission hearing. Although he was still awaiting the official results of his appeal, he had already gotten word of the decision: on the morning of our interview, when he went to the roster where CAS residents sign in each day, next to his name someone had written the word *dimesso*: dismissed. For Bakary, the message was clear: his appeal had been denied and he was to leave the CAS. No formal deportation, no transfer to another center or escort to the border. When you receive the negativo, they said, you have to leave the camp. Bakary said he was devastated and frightened. He said that he could not return to his home country; he wanted to stay in Italy. But now he found himself undocumented and on his own. We discussed how these rejections affect migrant precarity. Without papers, he had few options for securing housing, aid, or work.

As long as Italy's asylum system remains overwhelmed, insufficiently funded, and regularly revamped, migrants will experience the waiting period as one of extreme uncertainty in which they struggle to understand their place within the system and have limited say in how their cases are heard. This is especially complicated at the appeal stage. One point of confusion for Bakary was that he had been in Italy long enough that the relevant laws had changed. When he first arrived, multiple appeals were possible, and migrants attended their appeals. In 2017, the Minniti-Orlando Law restricted the number of possible appeals to one and allowed officials to judge an appeal based on a video recording of the original interview—no new testimony required. To Bakary, it seemed absurd that his chances for asylum might change so radically while he awaited a decision. He understood the appeal as, essentially, a second opinion on his original case. Despite all efforts and intentions, how did he ever stand a chance?

Bakary's situation was typical of the migrants I spoke with who feared the new stage of precarity that a denial would usher in. They understood the dimesso as an order to disappear into the growing networks of undocumented, unaccounted-for migrants making their way in Italian cities or across the border into France. Bakary's experience speaks to how the treatment of migration as an emergency produces a growing population of undocumented migrants. Asylum courts in Italy have managed increases in migrant arrivals by alternately stalling or accelerating the review of asylum claims. The CAS cannot legally house migrants whose claims have been rejected, but the government does not arrange detention or deportation for everyone in that category, thus expanding a population of illegalized, deportable subjects. Here, as with reception, counts are likely incomplete, but to offer a sense: In 2017, Italian authorities deported 6,514 migrants; an additional 11,805 were issued "leave" papers and told to exit the country.[71] In 2022, authorities ordered 28,185 people to leave the country but only deported 2,790 people.[72] Given slow processing and low deportation rates, the number of people living without papers continues to grow.

For Bakary and Sulayman, the state's production of deportable subjects ruptured their sense of rights and deservingness. When they first described learning about Bakary's rejected appeal, they did not use the word *dimesso*; perhaps they could not remember it exactly. Instead, they said *abbandonato*: abandoned. This was the word Bakary initially recalled having seen written by his name. He understood both that he had to abandon the CAS and that Italy had, through this rejection, abandoned him. *Abbandono* is also the term the Interior Ministry uses to describe when migrants leave a reception structure before completing their formal period of accoglienza. Abandonment, and the "ban" to which it refers, might recall Agamben's notion of the sovereign ban and how it positions refugees outside the body politic—yet this "abandonment" explicitly rejects even the idea of refugeeness, instead pushing the migrant into unnamed, unrecognized status, where they may well remain within national borders. Recalling Fanon on colonizers' rejection of the self-determination of the colonized, this is exclusion through invisibilization—a way of rejecting newcomers' self-determination.[73]

The rejection of an asylum claim without the possibility of recourse is a legal witnessing limit that enacts necropolitical border regimes through abandonment: a ban on further testimony, and banishment to illegalized status. Rather than exclude migrants from the life of the nation, these processes of abandonment produce an invisibilized labor force critical to Italy's economy. Accoglienza and abbandono are two sides of the same coin.

Shocked and disheartened, Bakary said he knew no one else in Italy and did not know where to go. Left with no real options, he talked about heading north as his only choice. Without papers and without savings or regular income, he hoped to find work that would pay enough for him to maintain himself and, gradually, to build a life in which he could live safely. The day after our interview, he left the CAS.

3

———

# Emergent Practices of Hospitality
# in the Camp

Walking through Rome, it can feel like water is everywhere. It flows from centuries-old fountains and from *fontanelle*, street corner spouts where people fill bottles and, on hot days, stop to rinse their faces. But at Piazzale Maslax, an unofficial migrant camp near the city's Tiburtina train station, water wasn't so accessible; it had to be brought in so that camp residents living in tents on the occupied asphalt lot could drink, wash, and cook. Still, in the camp's first months, that wasn't so hard. While visiting in the summer of 2017, I helped residents and volunteers with activist collective Baobab Experience, which operated the camp, ferry large coolers in a grocery cart to a loose hose at the edge of the station. The coolers were cumbersome, but the source was within walking distance. By 2018, the hose had been blocked, and residents depended on volunteers who could drive to collect water at a more distant fountain.[1] The decision by municipal officials to shut off the water source was strategic: it made people's stay on the isolated lot all the more challenging, while temporarily allowing the encampment itself to stay put. Since the city refused to open additional accommodations for its growing population of migrants in transit to or through Rome, Baobab Experience's operations were simultaneously essential and, for officials, uncondonable.

Improvised encampments expanded in both size and number across Europe in the mid-2010s, from "The Jungle" in Calais, France, where people waited for a chance to cross the Channel to England; to camps along the Bosnian border, where crossing meant entry into the EU; to the settlements on Greek islands that grew around overcrowded official camps. In Italy, informal (unofficial) encampments were not new. The camp is a familiar site, associated with farmworkers from Eastern Europe, Africa, and South Asia who have built or been housed in camps

84

during seasonal labor since the 1980s. Worker camps and dormitories have a longer domestic history, for instance with the *mondine*, Italian women who moved seasonally to work in the rice fields. In addition, Romani and Sinti communities have long lived in settlements throughout the country, either by choice or when local regulations enforce settlement living.[2] For decades these camps have featured in debates about statelessness, mobility, and the use of space, with their residents subject to discrimination, surveillance, and eviction, or what I recognize in this chapter as *intentional unsettling*. Nonetheless, the expansion of camps as a consequence of emergency responses to Mediterranean migration in the 2010s brought renewed visibility to their existence—and to the precarious legal, social, and working conditions of their residents.[3]

In Italy's capital, the intersection of local and national politics shone a spotlight on migrant homelessness. In the 2010s, amid widespread acknowledgement of a "refugee crisis" in Europe, Rome remained the only European capital lacking an official plan for accoglienza, or migrant reception.[4] As migrants continued to arrive, the municipal government refused to open additional centers or formally recognize groups providing assistance on a volunteer basis. The NGO Baobab Experience is one such group, a collective born in response to the lack of formal aid available for migrants in transit. The accoglienza Baobab offers is unofficial, administered without government funding or support. This term has multiple meanings: as I discuss in the previous chapter, *accoglienza* names official systems and structures of reception; it also refers to practices of welcoming, care, and in this case, solidarity. The support Baobab offers substitutes what migrants would have received at official centers, had there been space for them. For instance, the group coordinates meals, language lessons, and legal and medical services. Other forms of accoglienza, like musical and circus events they have organized, represent practices of welcoming that treat migrants not as strangers but as coinhabitants of the city or as friends. Baobab welcomed people who arrived on their own or were evicted from other sites, first at its center in the San Lorenzo neighborhood, then at a series of improvised encampments near the Tiburtina station, including at the lot they named Piazzale Maslax, where they operated an informal settlement from May 2017 to November 2018 (map 3). A core volunteer, herself originally from France, was nearly always at the camp when I visited, serving as a key point of contact. With some regularity, volunteers led small groups to a museum or historical site, and, almost daily, to the *questura* for appointments with immigration officials.

Surrounded by trees, two dilapidated buildings, and a low grassy hill, Piazzale Maslax was largely invisible to the outside, but local, national, and international news of the site and the collective supporting those who lived there brought attention to it. The resulting tensions of visibility and invisibility shaped the life of the camp, which people without access to the formal reception system made their home for anywhere from several days to several months. Baobab volunteers—a

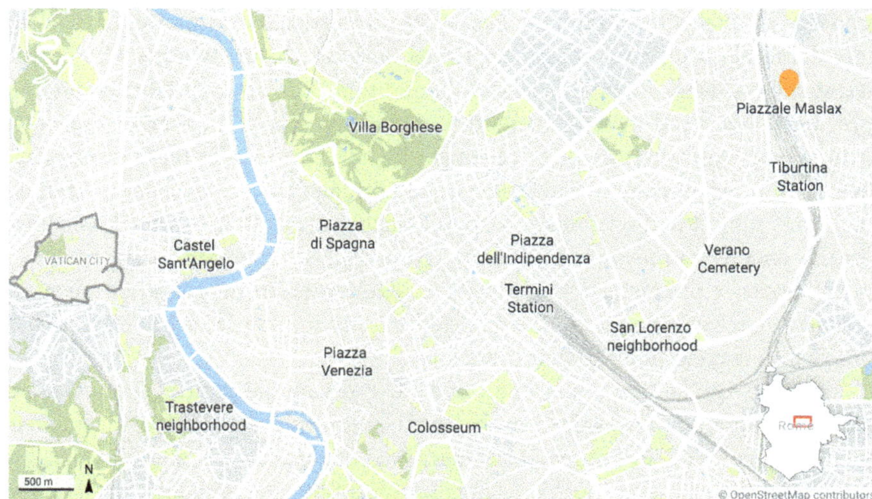



MAP 3. Piazzale Maslax in relation to Rome's Centro Storico. Made by the author with Datawrapper.

transnational group that included local Italians and migrants—referred to camp residents outside of legal status terms as *transitanti*: people in transit. Whether they stayed days or months, everyone was en route to somewhere else or to something more permanent. (I think of Palestinian poet Yousif M. Qasmiyeh's words: "In the camp we arrive not, nor do we remain.")[5] The transitanti at Baobab and camps throughout Europe challenge common conceptualizations of transit migration developed by the International Organization for Migration (IOM), that frame transit in terms of the countries people traverse *en route* to the EU. With Baobab, it's clear that Europe *itself* is a site of transit.[6] They included people in situations like that of Bakary, whose newly undocumented status I discuss in chapter 2; "dublinati" who, thanks to the EU's Dublin Regulation (table 2, appendix), were sent back to Italy from another European country for asylum processing; asylum seekers and refugees who could not find steady work or afford housing; and people who had left formal reception because conditions were intolerable.

Camp residents and volunteers employ a "politics of survival," enacting individual and collective efforts as part of what Abby Wheatley describes as "the process of surviving, subverting, struggling with, and sometimes overcoming the border."[7] Here I extend this idea to describe the processes at play in people's navigation of the borderzones within a country. Camps like Piazzale Maslax reveal the politics of survival to be often also a politics of (in)visibility. Baobab volunteers and residents—meaning people residing in the camp—navigated the necessity to be seen and heard as they appealed for rights, and, simultaneously, the need to remain out of sight from authorities and locals who viewed their presence as a problem. In the process, Piazzale Maslax became an icon for migrant rights movements and a target for right-wing politicians.

FIGURE 10. Piazzale Maslax entrance after authorities added barricades, 2017. Photo by the author.

Through these frictions, informal settlements like this one are sites where the emergency apparatus takes shape in relation to the limits of witnessing.[8] They are places where multiple gazes operate with especially high stakes, from the state that watches and regulates the camp; to camp residents themselves, who choose to bear witness (or remain silent) to their experiences of precarity; to volunteers who speak on behalf of the camp before wider publics. In this chapter, reflecting on the camp as a key site of witnessing, and drawing on oral and written testimony, I discuss *emergent* forms of accoglienza that residents and volunteers at Piazzale Maslax practiced as they fought against the constant threat of erasure (figure 10). The experiences, negotiations, desires, concerns, tensions, acts of violence, and forms of solidarity that shaped the camp on a daily basis are not only reflected in testimonies *about* it. Witnessing practices themselves shaped the camp, as I illustrate here through a discussion of multiple witnessing acts and testimonials, including voyeuristic gazes that further marginalized residents, oral history interviews I conducted with residents, residents' own testimonial writing, and public testimonials used by organizers in a plea to save the camp from destruction.

Piazzale Maslax continually morphed, depending on who was passing through the city, how recently police had evicted camp residents, and what provisions volunteers were able to offer. When it took shape in spring 2017, the lot housed around seventy migrants of varied legal status in shared tents—mostly single men,

FIGURE 11. Piazzale Maslax, 2018. Photo by the author.

reflecting migration trends and because the group worked to secure spaces for women in local shelters or centers, where there might be one or two beds, but never enough to take in everyone. There was no running water, no chemical toilet, no real protection from rain, heat, or cold. In summer, in the heat of the day, people napped or went to the station or city center. Those staying longer than a few days took language classes or looked for work. For however long they stayed, they also made the camp their home: sharing stories, hosting performances, pulling pranks, cooking over makeshift stoves, laughing at YouTube videos, arguing, and helping each other navigate obstacles (figure 11).

My discussion of this camp through multiple testimonies and witnessing acts contributes to recognition of camps beyond their common framing, via Agamben, as spaces of exception. While camps are, indeed, spaces shaped by bio- (or necro) political violence, the idea of bare life so central in Agamben's theorization of the camp does not fully capture a place like Piazzale Maslax, where people come and go who inhabit a range of legal positions, and whose collective construction of the camp troubles simple or fixed notions of sovereignty. Recognizing the camp as a site of emergent forms of accoglienza, this chapter understands these improvised sites as neither defined by bare life nor existing in opposition to the official reception system. Rather, informal camps are fundamental to that official system. An informal settlement like Piazzale Maslax emerges in response to exclusion. But it survives—so long as it can—driven by an abolitionist politics that is in many ways counter to the migration governance strategies represented in formal accoglienza, and emergent practices of accoglienza may shape forms of "abolitionist sanctuary."[9] Yet, as people who have lived across these centers and camps know well, they exist in relation to one another and to necropolitical governance and its central impulse to abandon—or, as Bakary put it, make people "abbandonati" (abandoned). That is, Italy's emergency management of migration produces the need for these camps by creating the legal uncertainties and delays, homelessness, and inefficient systems that leave migrants few options other than occupying abandoned sites. In turn, local and national authorities depend on the camps as part of the broader management of recently arrived migrants, both in controlling their movements and in getting them necessary aid.

While daily life differs significantly between unofficial camps like Piazzale Maslax and official, government-funded reception centers (centri di accoglienza) like the CAS I discuss in chapter 2, both kinds of sites comprise the emergency apparatus that shapes and reflects discursive and material understandings of Mediterranean migration to Europe via Italy. CAS residents who referred to the reception center as the *campo* (camp) drew out these connections explicitly. In this blurred role, informal camps are shaped by the frictions of visibility and invisibility, as residents navigate the need for recognition and the risks that come with being seen. They are thus important sites for tracing the relationship between emergency logics, accoglienza, and witnessing possibilities.

## VOYEURISM AND THE COLONIAL GAZE

The encampments Baobab operates are the collective's own emergency response strategy. Piazzale Maslax, to date still the group's most established camp, stood near Rome's Tiburtina train station between May 2017 and November 2018.[10] During multiple visits throughout this period, I spoke with volunteers and camp residents; helped serve meals prepared and delivered by other volunteers; attended assemblies where residents and volunteers discussed the asylum system, the city's plans for the camp, or camp dynamics; and participated in several actions and events the collective organized. In June 2017, many residents had escaped civil conflict in the former Italian colonies of Eritrea and Somalia, or in North or South Sudan. In 2018, the group included more West Africans and a growing Maghrebi community, and some had already been in Italy for several years. Consistently, most residents arrived via the Mediterranean after a journey of a few months or longer, and most hoped not to stay in Italy. The camp offered a modicum of stability during their limbo, though its set-up was precarious and its longevity constantly threatened by local authorities.

As a witness myself to life in the camp during periods of organizing and collective activity as well as downtime, I observed how the Baobab community responded to people's immediate material needs and also created forums for larger conversations about accoglienza and rights. This activism took multiple forms, from coordinating legal and medical services and cultural programming, to hosting an annual conference, to leading demonstrations, and this was strategic in at least two ways. First, the group garnered broad international support for the plight of unhoused migrants in Rome. Second, being vocal about the struggles of both migrants and the collective as a whole was a way of preventing their erasure: broader awareness of their existence made it harder to ignore the dire circumstances that so many migrants confronted and the lack of response on the part of city government. Invisibility in diaspora can function, as Carter notes, as "a corrosive social erasure."[11] Processes that invisibilize migrants function within the emergency apparatus, enabling a disregard for migrants' well-being, and even their presence. But visibility also poses risks. Politicians campaigning on anti-immigrant platforms also kept Baobab's efforts on their radar, making the camp's visibility both urgent and politically charged.

Informal settlements that garner media attention have a fraught relationship with testimony: acts of witnessing can serve advocacy or enact a kind of voyeurism. Early on, when people were still able to enter the camp by car, many residents told me they felt like zoo animals when journalists or locals stopped by for a quick story or out of sheer curiosity. A couple of times, before the city barricaded the camp's perimeter, I myself saw cars drive in, slowly circle in front of the tents, and leave again. Already a space of extreme precarity and anxiety, the camp in this sense was also an object of public suspicion and political animosity, and space of crisis voyeurism.

What were people coming to see? In part, I imagine, their curiosity was piqued following news coverage of Baobab's efforts. The anticipation of a spectacle of suffering holds a fetishizing appeal, especially in the case of Black suffering in spaces defined as white. This can be the case whether coming to gawk or to quickly drop off donated goods—and researchers can be just as complicit. The issue, as residents described it, arose when people passed through to catch a glimpse, without engaging in the actual life of the camp. Like in human rights media that attempt to spread awareness, images of suffering may position viewers as voyeurs rather than people poised to take action.[12]

As several residents pointed out to me, the "zoo" visitors—especially those who came and went midday without interacting with residents—were conspicuously absent during the camp's calmest moments or didn't stay long enough to recognize the camp as a site of everyday life. One evening I sat with a few residents, watching a game of football unfold across the asphalt. An Italian dad had brought a couple kids along, and they kicked the ball back and forth with residents. A few migrants stood in line to visit doctors on call with MEDU (*Medici per i Diritti Umani*, Doctors for Human Rights), there with their mobile clinic. A man from Nigeria talked with me about how people came to take pictures, to see "how it is," and then quickly leave again. How they came looking for evidence of misery. But much of the time, the camp was calm and quiet, with some people napping, some playing games or cutting hair, some at appointments in the city, others accessing aid there on the asphalt lot, a few Italian volunteers around and others on their way to set up the next meal.

The voyeur's gaze is a colonial gaze, one that sees suffering through processes of "thingification" and erasure (recalling Césaire). The voyeur's observation of otherness reifies difference, producing the camp as a site of strange encounters in which the migrant is "already recognized" as an unknowable or undesirable other.[13] As George Yancy defines it in the context of historical colonialism, "the white colonial gaze . . . constructs the Black body into its own colonial imaginary."[14] Media coverage risks reproducing this gaze, depicting migrants through an "'alien' world . . . filtered in" through photographs described as representing crisis.[15] Saidiya Hartman calls out this challenge directly. In *Scenes of Subjection*, examining representations of experienced, observed, or imagined violence against enslaved people in the United States, she asks: "Are we witnesses who confirm the truth of what happened in the face of the world-destroying capacities of pain, the distortions of torture, the sheer unrepresentability of terror, and the repression of the dominant accounts? Or are we voyeurs fascinated with and repelled by exhibitions of terror and sufferance?"[16] In other words, the voyeur is a witness capable of reproducing only problematic narratives that sensationalize suffering and reify difference. Voyeurism marks the failures of empathy to lead to real change.[17]

Integral to emergency imaginaries, the colonial gaze disregards the past and perceives the (formerly) colonized as objects out of context, out of history.[18] The colonial imaginary that shaped ideas of foreignness in Europe continues to shape the present, in racialized notions of belonging and in the simultaneously widespread refusal, in dominant discourses, to recognize race and racism as persistent issues.[19] It's a gaze legitimized in a city like Rome through imperial formations such as colonial-era monuments and streets named after colonized territories, as well as in the fleeting encounter of the car passing through the camp.[20] The mix of curiosity and suspicion, violence and solidarity that shaped the relationship between the Piazzale Maslax camp and the surrounding city reflects the colonial gaze and its production of Europe's so-called refugee crisis as a spectacle where Black lives are rendered disposable not in secret but in everyday media coverage, in national and international policies, and in public discourse. Despite that residents were free to come and go, Piazzale Maslax and the migrants who stayed there remained under the eye of the state, and so even the autonomously run camp was a space of limited freedom of movement.

What does it take to upend abandonment or dismantle the zoo? In Brand's contemplation of grammar in *The Blue Clerk*, the author-narrator talks about being trapped inside a zoo in which she must always perform and is always dissected by the gaze of others. "The vocabulary of what is called resistance," writes Brand, "you will notice later only reinforces the zoo."[21] Disrupting the colonial gaze requires not simply recognition but the creation of new means of bearing witness to one's presence and experience. In relation to Brand's search for a new grammar, uses of witnessing in the camp that trouble voyeurism, abandonment, and the violence of unsettling can be understood as attempts to articulate a new language—of belonging, of solidarity, of the right to be present.

Baobab Experience and Piazzale Maslax residents regularly challenged their enforced precarity, including in the protest with which I open this book, when migrants stood on the steps of the Campidoglio holding a banner that read, "We are not dangerous, we are in danger." Their public testimony illustrates their sense of shared belonging, a kind of "campzenship," a concept Nando Sigona develops in the context of Italy's Romani encampments to describe "the specific and situated form of membership produced in and by the camp."[22] Campzenship and the forms of political solidarity that the collective employs themselves rely on testimony and witnessing—that is, on bearing witness and bringing visibility to migrants' plight. As such, they foster a politics of survival that speaks back to the coloniality of the camp and of residents' marginalization.

Given the pervasive treatment of migrants as emergency figures, the camp may appear to be a contemporary "contact zone," a space of encounter between "disparate cultures."[23] Yet for the objects of the colonial gaze, shared histories and the entanglements of camp and colony stand in plain view. For camp residents, and for many African migrants and Italians of African descent, Italy palpably represents the colonial present. This was clear in my conversations with a group of Eritreans at Piazzale Maslax. Several of these men, when they introduced themselves to me, also immediately invoked Eritrea's colonial ties to Italy. Two men cited the specific years of colonial rule: "We're from Eritrea. You know Eritrea, it was an Italian colony from 1890 to 1941." Another man opened his palms, touching the pinky side of his hands together and saying, "Italy and Eritrea are like this": Italy and Eritrea are connected. One Sunday, I accompanied the group to a nearby boxing gym where owners opened their doors so migrants could shower. Walking there through the station and the San Lorenzo neighborhood, we continued to talk about these connections, including words that bear the mark of Italian rule. Eritreans often count with *uno due tre*, they told me, and the Tigrigna words for some household objects come directly from Italian.

The men's familiarity with Italy and the Italian language was unlikely to lend favor to their cases for asylum.[24] By emphasizing these connections, they did not underscore the immediate reasons they had fled Eritrea. Instead, they marked their position within Italian spaces through historical ties that link them to Italy, but that also recall Italy's racial logics and violent conquest of the Horn of Africa. Marked as unrecognizable "strangers" by emergency discourses and their colonial gaze, and living in extreme legal, physical, and social precarity, they claimed *a right to be present* in Italy, inscribing their presence through colonial relations.

Their appeal to history defines their mobility beyond the immediate emergency terms of Italy's migration management and inscribes the camp as a site of colonial memory. Their positioning also speaks to how improvised settlements coalesce around claims about the right to stay, including the right to occupy particular spaces and not be continually displaced. While not every camp resident claimed ties to Italy as directly as these Eritreans, there was a collective sense there that people's right to have rights, and their right to be present, were under constant threat of erasure: Italian authorities failed to respond to their need for aid and protection, and police repeatedly cleared the camp. In addition, locals complained about their presence, projecting stereotypes of criminality and chaos onto this group whose occupation of an asphalt lot was a consequence of emergency responses to migration, not a cause of *emergenza*. Activists and residents at Piazzale Maslax created space to recognize those histories and combat how their erasure has enabled racialized, ahistorical discourses about identity and foreignness that do not account for Italy's own colonial campaigns in Libya and the Horn of Africa, or Europe's colonial presence across the countries from which many migrants today have fled. Testimony by camp residents responds to the need to counter imminent and ongoing erasure with acts of imagining otherwise, making the camp a space for understanding border crossing outside dominant emergency discourses.

## CHOOSING THE CAMP

The Piazzale Maslax camp grew through word of mouth. While it existed because of the insufficiencies of the Italian system, it was also a place migrants actively chose over official centers, either because they were in transit to other European countries or because conditions in the CAS were unacceptable, as people repeatedly told me. In interviews, the way that camp residents positioned themselves in relation to sites and practices of reception underscores the informal settlement as a key site within the emergency apparatus and also a space where alternative possibilities emerge. Emmanuel (pseudonym), a man in his mid-twenties from Côte d'Ivoire, had come through a reception center in rural Sicily, where he found conditions to be so poor that he opted to live on the streets:

> *Emmanuel:* I was in Italy [in] January. And I live in [a center in Sicily] one month. . . . But it was a prison. Because we cannot go outside, we cannot see nothing, and we are sleeping there and they give you some cigarettes to get money.[25] If you smoke or you don't smoke, they give you the cigarettes to sell to get money.
>
> After one month they threw me outside, to live in Italy. I don't have anywhere to go. I was asking them, do you save me? You know I don't have anybody else. . . . They was asking me, inside/outside, what do you think? I say, okay, no problem, I prefer to stay outside because it's my god who helped me to come here, and if God said I'm going to sleep in the streets forever, I will stay there, but if God said I'm not supposed to sleep in the streets, but I'm going to move, I move.[26]

Emmanuel, whose story I return to later in this chapter, struggled for weeks to file an asylum claim in Rome. While he framed his arrival in Rome as a kind of destiny ordered by God, his position at the camp was anything but passive. He was outspoken about his own needs and his anger about repeated police raids at the camp. He argued with volunteers and also celebrated with them, and he became a vocal spokesperson, taking the megaphone at demonstrations and leading a petition effort to request that the mayor grant Baobab Experience a building. One week he joined a group of US volunteers who visited the camp to offer Bible study; he also regularly interpreted for other French speakers at camp assemblies. While not everyone assumed such an active role in camp activities, Emmanuel's account of his arrival to Baobab and his participation there exemplify how rights claims were tied to ongoing practices of hospitality that included both official aid and legal procedures, as well as collective efforts to create the forms of hospitality missing from formal and public reception of migrants—that is, accoglienza as a set of practices of survival and care.

Emmanuel's account also illustrates camps and official centers as together comprising a complex network of reception sites—and more broadly, as fundamental sites within the emergency apparatus that shapes the legal and social realities of precarious migration in Italy. Because informal settlements take shape without explicit government consent, they are often discussed by authorities and publics alike as existing outside the official system, and therefore as abusive or criminal. Scholarship on informal settlements has challenged their framing as sites of exception, recognizing that they emerge as a consequence of state neglect but are also sites of collective action and agency.[27] Yet this work still tends to treat unofficial (unsanctioned) camps as wholly distinct from formal structures.

Instead, in our conversations, residents described Piazzale Maslax as one camp among several where they had spent time, including formal accoglienza structures like the CAS and SPRAR I describe in chapter 2. Some of the people I met at Piazzale Maslax in fact resided in centers but came to Baobab regularly for solidarity and to socialize. While informal camps are defined by their residents' strategic decision-making, they are also rendered necessary and shaped by local- and state-led migration governance that sorts migrants into hierarchies of deservingness and polices their mobility long after they have crossed a national border.[28] At the same time, these sites are spaces of possibility: people's futures depend on what happens during accoglienza. I highlight connections between formal centers and informal settlements to underscore that migrants advocating for the right to keep their tents in Piazzale Maslax were not simply claiming the right to live in the margins; they were claiming a place within formal systems of recognition, just as they inscribed the camp with broader, more heterogeneous understandings of mobility and collective belonging.

At Piazzale Maslax, migrants lived within a major neighborhood of a European capital yet legally and socially just outside Italy, just outside Europe, in *proximal distance* from local communities, like with the CAS. Baobab's location meant that migrants passed through Tiburtina Station regularly. They took advantage of its cooler public spaces in the summer (or winter heating) and its Wi-Fi connection. While the camp was a site of solidarity, life there wasn't easy; people were struggling to survive. Many had suffered severe trauma and loss. It didn't help that locals complained, projecting neighborhood issues onto the camp and its residents. Such complaints are easy to circulate within a broader context that sees migration as a problem or threat. After a knifing incident involving two Italians near Tiburtina Station, for example, media covered locals' concerns for the area's degeneration. One piece quotes a representative of the Comitato Cittadini Stazione Tiburtina (Citizens' Commission of Tiburtina Station) who complained about a lack of security and blamed groups like Baobab for "the illegal administration of food and drink to stragglers," claiming

> most of the participants at these gatherings are *clandestini*, drunks, illegal squatters, Roma, and every other type of problematic person. We have asked again and again to the authorities, including the Prefecture, the questura [police headquarters], and city government to prohibit the passing out of meals and drinks on the street by these little unofficial groups.[29]

Here migrants are termed only "clandestini," slang for illegal or undocumented immigrants, used here as if synonymous with drunkards. The list implicitly distinguishes upright citizens from "every other type of problematic person," associating behavior with legal status. The representative cites illegality as a character trait to be condemned rather than a condition produced by the policing of mobility and borders. Associations of legal status with moral character position locals and migrants in a never-ending strange encounter in which the migrant "other" is always already unknowable and undesirable in the community.[30] Regular police raids and the city's refusal to provide adequate accommodations only fed these associations.

Meanwhile, the asphalt lot baked or flooded. Days there were often monotonous, and despite regular opportunities for classes, training, and cultural activities, the wait was long and heavy. Collective living required collective rulemaking. There were moments of shared celebration, from breaking fast at dusk during Ramadan, to artist performances, but fights also sometimes broke out, for instance when people cut in line for meals or attempted to take extra items from a clothing donation bin. Baobab paid a few migrants for extra help with meals or maintaining order in the camp, but volunteers struggled with how to respond, for example, when those residents showed up late for a shift. As word got out about Piazzale Maslax, organized groups of volunteers came to serve lunch for a week, for example, or to lead an activity with residents. I met groups of US college students and a French volunteer organization, each there to help for a few days. The volunteers were appreciated, but with such variability in the amount and nature of help they'd have on any given day, it was also challenging to maintain consistency.

At the same time, as an autonomously run site, the camp was a space of community and exchange, shaped also for instance by humor. In the tense summer of 2018, following the rise of La Lega party in national elections, there was a contrast in energy between the CAS and the camp. The camp felt like a space where humor was more possible; this was also, perhaps, a survival tactic. As national elections neared, people ridiculed politicians, especially populist leaders Matteo Salvini and Luigi Di Maio. They'd knock on someone's tent: "Excuse me! Can you give me asylum?" "Get out, get out!" the tent resident would shout. "Get out" as in, get away from my tent, and also, get out of Italy. They poked fun by calling one another Salvini or Di Maio. Joking, teasing, and being teased were part of my own interactions with residents, as we sat in the shade or shared food, and they were tactics people adopted to create camaraderie—and to be themselves—in this space where survival depended on the will of the community.[31] Still, the anxieties and frustrations of waiting lingered between tents, between meals, into the morning.

Piazzale Maslax was both a refuge and a site of friction, and I don't mean to romanticize the camp or the efforts of volunteers. As a grassroots movement, Baobab Experience is also comprised of myriad challenges, tensions, and losses. As the camp grew, volunteers and residents disagreed on how to negotiate with authorities, how to support families with young children, how to carry out the constant battle for donations, and whether to remain open to truly anyone who needed a place to sleep. They debated how to deal with violence in the camp, where, on principle, they ID'd no one. The group's own expansion and their increased public visibility also brought questions of reach, and not everyone stayed with the group. In 2020 and 2021, when they operated near the Verano cemetery, the COVID-19 pandemic challenged their efforts, as they sought to uphold safety protocols, support unhoused migrants without ready access to care, and continue this work during Italy's severe lockdown restrictions. In this period, some organizers kept working with migrants in Rome through Baobab or other organizations; others instead traveled, taking Baobab Experience to Bosnia and other EU borderzones to document pushbacks and assist people on the move. In early 2022, they went to Moldova to help people fleeing Ukraine. They continued offering meals to transit migrants in Rome. These multiple efforts reflect the complexity of the work of accoglienza outside formal systems—unfolding in opposition to state violence, but not reducible to a simple binary.

Here the overlapping meanings of *accoglienza*, from reception structures to practices of welcoming, are significant. As Ida Danewid points out in a foundational essay on the Black Mediterranean, "hospitality" can uphold a citizen/noncitizen binary and the nation-state as the dominant frame for understanding identity. That is, attention to racial politics and the colonial present point us away from practices that welcome "the other" in ways that reify difference. With this in mind, Danewid calls for "abolition, not hospitality."[32] Drawing on lessons from Piazzale Maslax, I want to suggest that such a politics does not require the eradication of

FIGURE 12. Tea at Piazzale Maslax, 2018. Photo by the author.

hospitality, but its reconceptualization. The informal camp teaches us that abolition and hospitality are not strictly oppositional, and that alternative practices of hospitality that do not align with official modes can upend borders and create spaces of sanctuary. Forms of witnessing are especially significant within the camp, from facilitating individual testimony to enabling wider recognition of the obstacles people in transit face, especially in a site often framed in dominant narratives as a singularly abject and anonymous experience. I see these practices as pointing us toward what Danewid describes as "a transfigurative and abolitionist politics that rearticulates the struggle for migrant justice as a struggle against racial capitalism and state violence."[33]

Beyond official and volunteer-driven forms of aid and assistance, multiple conceptualizations of hospitality circulated in the camp, including practices people brought from their home countries and communities, such as the Senegalese notion of *teraanga*. Loosely translated as generous hospitality, teraanga is widely understood as a way of life, a practice of solidarity and respect.[34] Unlike the CAS, the camp was a space migrants themselves built and managed, and with a culture of "hosting"—tea brewed over a makeshift coal stove, rice and chicken cooked on a small fire, and invitations to escape the heat under someone's tarp (figure 12). These seemingly small gestures are significant; they shape daily life and relations within a space that residents are aware could be cleared at any moment.

They nurture possibilities for what A. Naomi Paik calls an "abolitionist sanctuary" that works in solidarity with migrants "with the deep envisioning and building of a new society where we . . . not only fight systemic oppression but also advance shared liberation."[35]

## FROM CULTURAL CENTER TO IMPROVISED CAMP

How Baobab Experience ended up operating the Piazzale Maslax camp is, in part, a story about housing and mobility issues that affect poor and marginalized communities throughout Italy, and, in part, a story about how corruption and exploitation drive the emergency apparatus of migration. Baobab Experience formed in 2015 while operating an unofficial reception center in a former glass workshop in the San Lorenzo neighborhood where Rome's original Baobab center served in particular African communities since the early 2000s. As a cultural center and, in the 2010s, as a reception center, Baobab hosted translation services, musical events, a restaurant that served *"cucina africana"* (African cuisine), and a dormitory. The center was closed at a crucial moment in its operations, however, as part of Mafia Capitale investigations that uncovered how an organized crime syndicate enlisted politicians to profit from contracts in migrant reception and waste management in Rome and elsewhere. It came to light that the owner of the cooperative overseeing the cultural center—not directly running it—was Salvatore Buzzi, a key figure in Mafia Capitale who was famously recorded telling an associate, "Do you have any idea how much we make from immigrants? Drugs bring in less."[36] When investigators determined that Buzzi was using his cooperative to take advantage of migration funds, they closed the Baobab reception center.[37]

Following its closure as an official center, volunteers—including Italians and migrants—transformed the center into an autonomously run space, without state funding. They expanded the dormitory and coordinated legal and medical aid for the transitanti who stopped by for meals or stayed a few days before continuing their journeys north. Volunteers' efforts were tolerated by authorities; at the time, given concerns about Italy's capacity for hosting increasing numbers of asylum seekers, migrants were sometimes encouraged to move on without registering in Italy.[38] But as the center accommodated more people, its relationship with the municipal government grew tenuous. In fact, Baobab expanded in part because of the city's ongoing *sgomberi*, or evictions, elsewhere.[39] The last straw for authorities came after Baobab welcomed migrants whom police had evicted from a camp in the Ponte Mammolo neighborhood, nearly doubling the center's nightly capacity of 150–200.[40] In December 2015, citing overcrowding and complaints from the neighbors, the city closed the center, promising that an official aid structure would shortly be opened. It never was.

In the meantime, with the timeline for the promised center unclear, volunteers erected a camp in the street outside, which has the ironic name of Via Cupa, or "gloomy street." For the next nine months, a group of approximately forty regular volunteers arranged tents, mattresses, and seven chemical toilets.[41] They continued to provide meals and coordinate medical and legal counseling, and to lobby for government aid. Despite not having a permanent physical space, they organized football tournaments, concerts, and tours of ancient Roman sites, activities that brought migrants and locals together.

Informal settlements are sites of "violent inaction" by authorities and regular *unsettling*, via evictions, and while Baobab vied for an official center, police cleared the Via Cupa camp three times, blocking the street and removing the tents, mattresses, and other items. Meanwhile, as volunteer Francesca Del Giudice explained to me, Baobab volunteers sent proposals to city government officials and issued press releases updating the public on the lack of adequate response.[42] In these communications, the group highlighted the distinction between *accoglienza* and *assistenza* (assistance/aid) and their commitment to offering both hospitality and specific forms of assistance, for instance in this April 2016 blog post (originally in Italian) laying out their vision:

> Our project does not offer simple assistance, but a complete reception that involves the necessary professional figures necessary in the medical, psychological and legal fields, and that has among its objectives the spread of a cooperative, community-based culture, through the creation of a museum of migration and the involvement of schools in educational activities.[43]

While the collective continued to offer hospitality and build community among transitanti and locals, a mix of active unsettlement and violent inaction on the part of municipal and national governments kept the group moving. In the two years following Via Cupa, Baobab residents were evicted from encampments more than twenty times. Police conducted additional raids and document inspections as well, including during the occupation of Piazzale Maslax.

## PIAZZALE MASLAX AND *ACCOGLIENZA* AGAINST ERASURE

The collective named the asphalt lot they occupied near Tiburtina Station beginning in May 2017 after Maslax, a young Somali who stayed with Baobab in Via Cupa. He then made his way to Belgium, where he was caught and sent back as a "dublinato," having first entered the EU via Italy and registered with authorities there. Maslax died by suicide near Rome in 2017 around the time Baobab occupied the lot.[44] I didn't meet him, but his loss, and the risk of repeated loss, was present in the camp in those first months. Far from the strange grief of state memorials and tokenizing references to migrant deaths, Piazzale Maslax gave a name to the haunting that shaped the solidarity work and struggles unfolding there. On Google Maps, "Piazzale Maslax" still directs users to wherever the collective is operating, a trace of the encampment and a symbol of its transformation of local spaces, despite that authorities cleared the camp multiple times and permanently closed it in November 2018.

Before that November, local authorities tolerated the settlement but didn't allow it to develop any semblance of permanence, for instance by limiting access to water. The camp was, after all, handling problems the city refused to address. Yet the threat of erasure was constant, and tensions between the camp and officials remained high. In 2018, tightened national borders within Europe meant that migrants who would have preferred to move on to another country instead stayed longer in Italy, and with Baobab. Municipal officials and police used evictions and document inspections as tools to manage camp residents. During evictions, police rounded up residents, seizing their belongings (regardless of their legal status), and taking some residents to the questura, the local police headquarters that handles initial asylum claims. Evictions were especially unsettling for asylum seekers awaiting word on their status while processing traumatic experiences from their journeys or their home countries. And to unsettle is, of course, the point. The camp, like the colony, "is marked by unsettledness, and forced migration."[45] Official and unofficial migrant camps populate an "imperial network" that includes multiple forms of detention, and even an improvised camp reflects colonial dynamics of control.[46]

These realities underscore camps like this one as "more-than-camps," connected to other spaces and times.[47] Like the emergency frame itself, this period of Mediterranean migration was not the first time Italian authorities resorted to sgomberi to police people's mobility and hold their rights hostage. In recent memory, the Berlusconi administration declared an *emergenza nomadi* or "nomad emergency" in 2008 to close multiple Romani and Sinti settlements in several Italian regions. As Hom reminds us, these evictions, too, recall colonial-era displacement practices.[48] Hom links the "emergenza nomadi" to the uprooting by Italian forces of nomadic communities in Libya in the 1930s. In this way, emergency logics link people with distinct histories—in these examples, Bedouins in North Africa, Romani and Sinti in Italy, and today's African immigrants—via narratives that posit these groups as criminal and threatening, and their mobility and use of space as part of the problem. Containing and controlling their movements through sgomberi is justified as a solution. In the "emergenza nomadi," the uprooting and destruction of Romani and Sinti settlements included census, increased surveillance, some camp closures, and some deportations. Until it was declared unconstitutional by Italian courts in 2011, this decree displaced and unhoused thousands of people and exacerbated tensions between local Italian and Romani communities.[49] A common political tactic, sgomberi maintain appearances of order and control while keeping people already living at "Italy's margins" in precarious positions.[50]

These evictions are often spectacular in nature, a display of control of "unwanted others." Like other instances of border spectacle, they attract media attention but are fundamentally acts of erasure. Evictions are orchestrated events that attempt to create public witnesses who will see the state as taking action against a "migrant problem," and by criminalizing the evicted, seizing their belongings, and withholding resources, they also restrict the possibilities for those affected to bear witness to their circumstances. The violence of evictions thus shows how the limits of witnessing are entangled in broader understandings of the limits of the human—that is, of whose lives count.[51]

In interviews, camp residents' oral testimonies underscored the contradictions of these practices. As Emmanuel, the man who had left an official center in Sicily, explained, the sgomberi functioned to create insecurity and uncertainty. They made clear to migrants that their movements remained under the control of authorities who were also actively working to keep Africans out of Italy. When Emmanuel and I spoke, the group was, it turned out, between evictions. Through Baobab, Emmanuel had been able to meet with lawyers and apply for asylum, a process that repeatedly brought him to the questura. Yet it was also police who raided the camp and, more than once, took his paperwork.

> *Emmanuel:* When I was sleeping in the street, every time when the police was coming, or we go to them, every time—I was in the questura seven times—and they never give me nothing, no place to stay. They leave you in the streets.
>
> *Eleanor:* Had you applied for asylum yet?
>
> *Emmanuel:* Yes, and I applied to stay here [in Italy] because I don't have anywhere to go. They're supposed to take my fingerprints but they never ask and they give you some appointment, for next month, this month, the twentieth.
>
> After that, I was sleeping here [at Piazzale Maslax] when they come last week. And everything we get to go to questura, like appointment [documents], they took everything. They give you some contact [information], to talk to see their lawyer. And when I was meeting them they say they cannot do nothing. I say, Why? Even in my country when you lose some documents you're supposed to go to the police station. After that you go to see God, because it's him who will make you have your documents.
>
> *Eleanor:* So your documents were in the tent.
>
> *Emmanuel:* Yeah, and they took the tent. And they threw everything. On Tuesday.
>
> *Eleanor:* And what did you have in there?
>
> *Emmanuel:* I have my money. . . . And my shoes and my clothes, everything important for me . . . yeah, everything, they throw it. Now they say they cannot do nothing. [I'm] supposed to start again to get another appointment. And I ask them, how am I supposed to start again? See my condition, I am living here three months. Do you want me to stay here maybe seven months?

FIGURE 13. Signs at Piazzale Maslax about the regular camp assembly, 2018. Photo by the author.

Emmanuel calls attention to the temporal, spatial, and legal precarity he has experienced since arriving in Italy, a limbo he recounts as a form of abandonment. His experience of formal accoglienza was procedural and disruptive, hindering his potential integration. He describes his transition out of prima accoglienza as being "thrown outside . . . to live in Italy." He came to seek protection in Italy and yet was abandoned to it, in it, by it. In Rome, his life in Baobab's informal settlement was the result of being "left in the streets." He was thrown out, and his belongings, too, were thrown out. For authorities, Emmanuel's presence at the camp is a symptom of the emergency overwhelming the country, and therefore a problem to be dealt with by removal, or at least by repeated disruption. For Emmanuel, instead, these interventions render his personal situation an emergency and exacerbate his already precarious situation.

The hospitality Emmanuel found and participated in with Baobab was made necessary by gaps in the official system, and also exceeded what official accoglienza offered. An emergent set of collective practices of care anchored people like Emmanuel to this transient site. One such example was the regular camp-wide assemblies that Baobab coordinators held to convey important information to residents and facilitate collective decision-making (figure 13). Founding member Andrea Costa would call everyone together, saying, "We have some things to tell you, and then we want to hear from you—you tell us what you think." He called out information in English, turning every few sentences to translate into Italian to an Eritrean resident, who called out the information in Tigrigna. Emmanuel and another volunteer translated from English into French, and other volunteers interpreted for Arabic speakers.

At one such meeting, Italian volunteers shared their concerns about a statement made by Mayor Raggi that the city would be closed to new arrivals. In addition, since police had raided the camp less than a week before and seized the tents, they had to be careful. That said, there were new donated tents. They were large and would make the camp more visible, which meant risking additional disruption. Did residents want the tents? Yes, they quickly decided; it was worth the risk.

Here accoglienza involves emergency response, meeting people's immediate and urgent needs, but it does so through collective action and adaptation. Hospitality practices at Piazzale Maslax encompassed challenging the group's repeated displacements and working to make the camp not a site of abandonment but an active community space and a node in a larger network. To this point, as the camp gained international recognition, politicians and activists including former Greek economic minister Yanis Varoufakis and French-Beninese writer and pan-Africanist activist Kémi Séba visited, meeting with camp residents and, with them, hosting conversations about freedom of movement that were open to the public. This is accoglienza as radical hospitality, to invoke Paik—accoglienza that both provides aid and works to eradicate borders. Like in other makeshift camps and collectives that provide this kind of hospitality, such practices can "enable residents . . . to escape the camp's limiting and dehumanizing conditions."[52] These practices of accoglienza are emergent, taking shape within an evolving vision of solidarity that produces the camp as a space where claims to history, to presence, to work, and to autonomy of movement might be heard.

## COLLECTIVE TESTIMONY AS HOSPITALITY

The camp swelled and shrank: in winter, fewer people cross the sea; in spring, arrivals increase. When I met Emmanuel, Baobab was home to approximately 150 migrants, most of them single young men. Because of the constant threat of eviction, there were few tents up; residents slept in the open, on mattresses or blankets. By the summer of 2018, the camp had doubled in size, becoming home to three hundred people, including several families with women and young children and a couple of Italians. Many residents no longer lived in simple donated tents but had built more elaborate structures with the intention of staying longer. Fethi, for instance (pseudonym), a Tunisian I met that June, had set up an old TV on a plastic crate.

Through Fethi I encountered yet another form of emergent hospitality. When I explained my project, he brought me to his tent to share the book he kept, a kind of collective diary by camp residents and volunteers. He had titled it *La vie des immigration* (*Immigration Life* or *The Life of Immigration*). At the top of each page, he had saved space for a note by writing the name of a country. By some countries, he had listed the names of other Baobab residents. By others, residents and volunteers had themselves written a note about their journey or their experience at the camp, in their own language. There were pages for Afghanistan, Germany, Italy, Côte d'Ivoire, Palestine, Senegal, and many others, with notes in nearly that many languages. Some countries were repeated; some pages remained to be filled (figure 14a).

The notebook is simultaneously a documentation of struggle and a celebration, and in this way, it exemplifies the forms of accoglienza that emerged within the camp to create space within "crisis" for claiming rights and belonging. Turning the pages, Fethi proudly noted the number of places and languages it represented. A man from Bangladesh wrote in Italian:

> I've been here almost a week. I live with friends from Pakistan, Bangladesh, Morocco, Senegal, etc. Here I've found a different world. I have really kind friends and there are more than 400 people here. Like a real family. Here no one asks you for money. Here they ask you only for kindness. Thanks my friend [Fethi].

While a shared notebook could be circulated in reception centers, too, this set of testimonies reflected the ethos of self-built community and freedom of movement so fundamental to the approaches to accoglienza at Piazzale Maslax. As this author's entry illustrates, the notebook's collective testimony reflected the camp as a transnational community in ways that countered depictions of such sites as homogeneous spaces of exception or as reproducing an us/them binary. As such, the notebook, while not a work of literature in the traditional sense, intervenes in dominant discourse in ways aligned with the "creative critique" of autobiographical literary and filmic works produced and circulated for broad audiences, speaking back to monolithic crisis narratives.[53]

Still, the book also includes passages that recall the bare life so often ascribed to camps. An Italian volunteer wrote:

> Baobab is a piece of asphalt that holds the world. Here I've seen incredible smiles despite suffering. Here, more than any other time or place, I've understood what freedom means and what people are capable of doing to obtain it. Here I've learned what a person becomes when they no longer have anything to lose. Here I've seen people punch each other and then shortly after help each other out.
>
> Here I've cried, gotten angry, gotten upset, I've laughed, I've done my part to fight because I don't want world peace, which is utopia, but I want Baobab to exist here and elsewhere.

Here the camp is a space where people have reached absolute loss, yet it is not defined by that loss but by the paradoxes and tensions enacted through and around it.

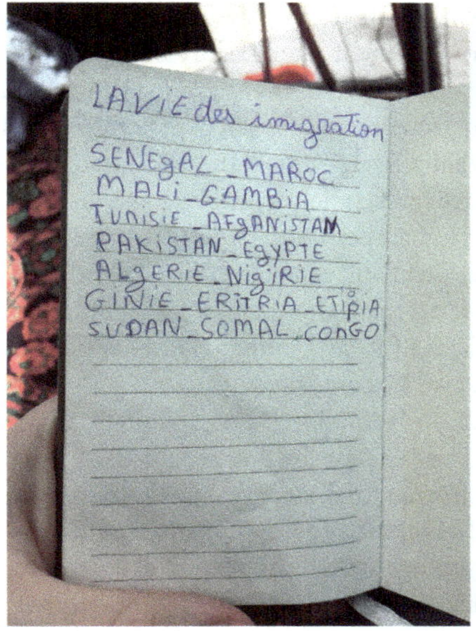
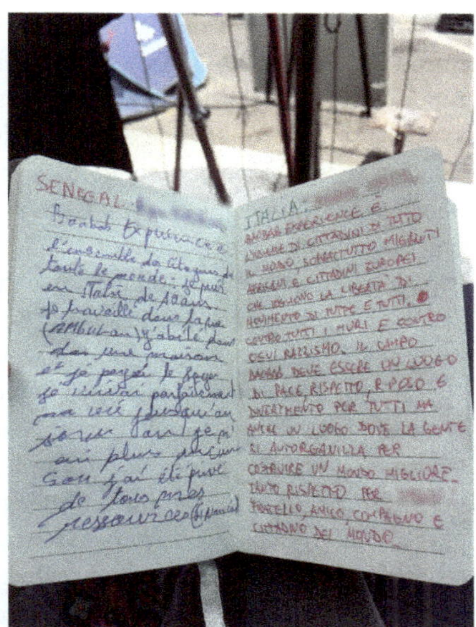

FIGURES 14a and 14b. *La vie des immigration*. Photo by the author, with permission.

The notebook also documents how the camp expanded beyond its original transit population or changed what *transitante* indicated. By mid-2018, many residents were still navigating initial asylum procedures or hoping to head north, but multiple residents had arrived several years before. Fethi himself had reached Italy seven years earlier. This was a sign of the city's larger housing insecurity issue, which affects migrants and citizens alike, and which emergency-response approaches to migration exacerbated. When the city stopped offering beds to newcomers, they abandoned a growing number of people to the streets.

The notebook also speaks to Baobab as a community people chose (figure 14b). As a Senegalese resident noted in Fethi's book (translated from French):

> Baobab Experience is all the cities of the world. I've been in Italy for ten years, working as an ambulant vendor. I lived in a house and I paid my rent. I lived my life perfectly. But over the years I was deprived of all my resources.

Describing Baobab as "all the cities of the world" seems to gesture both to global community and to the problems of big cities. Page after page, writers define this space and community for Fethi and for each other. The witnessing relations here are primarily internal: residents and volunteers share mutual appreciation and mark this community as it existed, knowing it was fleeting. As a collective record of the camp, the notebook also illustrates the importance of testimony as a form for enacting community.

What is the life of such a book, and what do its testimonies enact? It was produced for Fethi, who had the impulse to document the diversity of experiences represented in Piazzale Maslax, and also for everyone at the camp who turned the pages of the book while deciding what to write in it themselves. Perhaps most striking about *La vie des immigration* is that it bears witness to the camp on residents' own terms—not in response to police raids, not for crowds at a public demonstration, but for one another. While many authors addressed Fethi directly in their entries, they wrote in languages that Fethi and other authors (me included) might or might not read. And so they wrote especially for themselves, signing their presence in ink, not knowing who would read it, and perhaps never seeing the completed version—if such a book could ever be completed.

The "analog" notebook, as opposed to something people might access through their cell phones, for example, is a perhaps fleeting record that people held in their hands within the limbo of the camp. In this sense, I posit, the passing of the book from person to person is itself a practice of reception, or accoglienza— a practice of hospitality created within settings where people had lost access to official reception spaces and a transnational practice that contrasts explicitly with more widely circulating narratives and images produced in global media. The practice of writing itself and of sharing the book was a way of facilitating solidarity and care with those present and those who had passed through and would still arrive.

As individual testimonies literally bound together, Fethi's notebook offers reader-witnesses a sense of the heterogeneous and collective experiences of the camp. It also illustrates how, in contexts of precarious migration, testimony itself transits: changing form and finding new audiences, differing in this case from the testimony residents were required to give about their past and present circumstances repeatedly to police. With the camp and its residents constantly under threat, the notebook can be read as an act of resistance, an attempt to inscribe these experiences in a way that might outlive the camp itself. As Whitlock observes, asylum seeker testimony that emerges from situations of extreme hardship may "impa[ct] thinking about citizenship, obligation, and responsibility in the community of the nation."[54] As the notebook illustrates, the politics of survival in the camp were a constant exercise in articulating the right to be present and the "right to have rights."[55]

As an Italian member of the collective wrote in Fethi's notebook (figure 14b),

> Baobab Experience is a community of citizens from all over the world, above all African migrants and European citizens who want freedom of movement for all. Against all walls and against all racism. The Baobab camp should be a place of peace, respect, rest, and enjoyment for all, but also a place where people self-organize to build a better world. Much respect for [Fethi]: brother, friend, comrade and citizen of the world.

The first line echoes the Senegalese street vendor's entry cited above, describing Baobab as "all the cities of the world." The call to self-organization signals the ethos of hospitality that distinguishes this camp from official centers, despite their entanglements within Italy's migration governance regime.

The accoglienza produced through the notebook concerns the intimate attention of testimonial exchange. In this way, it contrasts with the high-stakes testimonial transactions of the asylum court, or even with the public-facing testimonies given by Baobab residents and volunteers before the press or at demonstrations. The book and these practices constitute a form of accoglienza that enables a form of ethical communication, which, thinking with Ahmed, concerns "holding proximity and distance together. . . . It is through getting closer, rather than remaining at a distance, that the impossibility of pure proximity can be put to work, or made to work."[56] That is, it is not through stasis but through movement, and movement together, or toward one another, that a more ethical communication becomes possible.[57] The notebook is a reminder that cultivating these practices within the camp is as important as facilitating ethical communication between camp residents and outsiders.

If the accoglienza administered in official centers like the CAS is, essentially, an exercise in reproducing national sovereignty, this notebook represents forms of accoglienza that cultivate the kinds of individual and collective sovereignty that abolitionist sanctuary works to realize. The informal settlement is, in this way, both an object of necropolitical violence and a site where hospitality and resistance might be reimagined and practiced together.

## TESTIMONIAL ETHICS AS ACCOGLIENZA

Baobab has turned to witnessing practices not only to document the lived realities of the camp but also as a strategy to counter the increasing criminalization of migration. This trend became especially marked in Italy with the retreat of Italian and EU-sponsored rescue missions at sea following the end of Mare Nostrum. It includes, for example, security decrees that threaten the viability of independent rescue operations, Italy's deals with Libya and Tunisia to prevent migrants from attempting to cross the sea, and documented pushbacks across the Mediterranean. Baobab Experience has been a kind of public testing ground for these efforts through regular threats to shut down the group's operations and even criminal charges brought against core organizers.[58]

The group's survival depends in part on people seeing and recognizing it on its own terms, without projecting other notions of migration or deservingness onto it. In this vein, the group's activism necessarily involves the search for "an adequate witness," or one who, in Leigh Gilmore's words, "receives testimony without deforming it by doubt, or substituting different terms of value than the ones offered by the witness themselves."[59] For questions of group survival, the adequate witness is often a public witness—not a public that exerts a colonial gaze on the camp but one that recognizes and might even be moved to speak for the rights of camp residents and, by extension, of migrants everywhere—that is, witnessing not for empathy that condemns suffering yet reifies difference but as a call for structural change. Through social media—including regular posts and stories on Twitter/X, Instagram, and Facebook—and demonstrations in the city center, the group's strategic uses of testimony attempt to create "social connections to the public sphere," influencing debates about migrant rights and housing rights. These testimonial transactions allow the camp to "emerge as a 'house of witness,'" rather than a space defined by abandonment.[60]

Another genre the group regularly employs is the press conference, utilizing this form in a testimonial way to bear witness to their own experiences of transit and accoglienza as ways of challenging the criminalization of migration. One such example dates to the early days of Salvini's #PortiChiusi (Closed Ports) campaign, in which the newly appointed interior minister repeatedly blocked rescue ships from docking and disembarking at Italian ports—a practice that continued after his tenure and that has reinforced an anti-immigrant agenda.[61] In late August 2018, the *Diciotti*, an Italian Coast Guard ship, remained docked in Catania with 157 rescued migrants on board. Despite that most of the migrants were Eritrean and were therefore likely to be granted asylum, they were not allowed to disembark or file asylum claims but were kept on the ship for ten days, in view of Italy but not allowed to set foot there, their appeals for help treated instead as threats.[62]

Salvini was later charged with kidnapping for this incident. At the time, however, there was little recourse. Once the migrants finally disembarked, they were sent to a CAS south of Rome. Unsurprisingly, some opted to stay clear of official Italian structures and made their way to Piazzale Maslax instead. Rumors and debates circulated about Baobab's role in providing shelter for them. On September 7, police arrived in riot gear at Piazzale Maslax with "4 armored vehicles, a bus, and 7 DIGOS [special operations] military cars."[63] At the time, a number of people were waiting for appointments with Doctors Without Borders at the organization's mobile clinic. Pulling people out of line, agents took sixteen people presumed but not confirmed to have been on the *Diciotti* to the questura. The militarized border operated in the heart of the capital city.

Baobab organizers turned to testimony as a way to take control of the *Diciotti* narrative.[64] In a press conference (held in Italian) a few days after the incident with police, representatives from medical NGO MEDU read testimonial accounts of several Eritrean men who had been aboard the *Diciotti*. Before they took the floor, Andrea Costa addressed the need for Baobab to share its testimony, "to tell our own version."[65] He justified the group's choice to drive migrants to Ventimiglia, a site known as a transit point for people heading to France but still within national borders.[66] And he framed the press conference as an act of counter-witnessing:

We decided to convene this press conference to say our part, to tell our version, compared to what we read in too many newspapers, heard across too many media, about the fact that there was allegedly a brilliant police operation that intercepted a bus full of migrants headed to France with Baobab Experience, which was thus complicit in an illegal act. None of this; we are unfortunately forced to take credit instead for a very simple gesture, that is to say, to have rented a bus to bring forty-eight migrants . . . to accompany them as was their wish, to the Red Cross camp in Ventimiglia, a camp managed by the operators of the Red Cross, a camp considered official [governmental], with law enforcement at the entrance . . .

  Why did we do it? We did it for a number of reasons. First, for the protection of these people . . . especially those of the *Diciotti* . . . they were in a truly difficult situation, they were still tired from the long journey from the Horn of Africa to here, from the sequester/detention they had to suffer on board the *Diciotti* ship in the port of Catania. . . . We also wanted to protect them from the media [reporters] that had begun to appear with increasing frequency at the camp, stopping anyone who looks like they might be from the Horn of Africa, asking where are you from, how did you get here, why did you escape.

Costa's words verge on the confessional, though he underscores that the group committed no crime. I cite him at length because of how he uses the press conference to articulate migrant rights and Baobab's work: he explains that movement within Italy is within the rights of asylum seekers and that the collective violated no laws by renting a bus, and he describes migrants as moving in a state of fugitivity, a constant escape. He also highlights how multiple gazes converge on the camp—of the state, journalists, migrants, and activists.

Costa uses the phrase "a very simple gesture" to summarize the group's approach to accoglienza: working to meet people's basic needs by listening to them. I want to suggest, in the simple gesture, a resonance with the "small and stubborn possibility" that Baldwin posits as the possibility for a different future, and of witnessing as a practice of desire for that future: "I wish to be a witness to this small and stubborn possibility."[67] In Costa's immediate framing, the small and simple gesture is a defense. Might it also signal possibility, an opening?

Of course, the gesture Costa calls simple is also symbolic, as the group models forms of accoglienza outside state-sanctioned protocols. The drive to Ventimiglia served immediate needs and made a point about freedom of movement, countering the idea that migrants should be detained or confined in centers.[68] This is accoglienza geared toward abolitionist sanctuary, practices of hospitality that disrupt state-sanctioned violence and enact alternative visions of mobility—in this case, refuting the idea that a person held captive by the state must continue to seek the state's permission to move.

Testimony is not inherently good; it can appeal to anti-immigrant stances, just as it can reify notions of migrant vulnerability or innocence.[69] But acts of witnessing can also be an important tool for the radical work necessary to create spaces of sanctuary through the work of "tearing down structures of oppression and creating a just, equitable society."[70] Baobab organizers position their testimonial acts as part and parcel of the group's accoglienza practices: as articulated in Fethi's notebook, to create a space of self-organization that works toward realizing freedom of movement. Because testimony also depends on reaching an audience "who will register and witness its truth,"[71] addressing multiple publics is also part of this work. The drive to the border demonstrates hospitality as an enactment of rights.

## CONCLUSION: ENCLOSURES

This case is also a reminder of the ways that freedom of movement is regulated, surveilled, and controlled across many stages of a migration journey, especially for those seen as undesirable outsiders. While press conferences and demonstrations established Baobab's perspective on events, they did not protect the camp from political scrutiny. In November 2018, police raided the camp one final time, pushing everyone out and destroying what was left in Piazzale Maslax. They erected a high steel and concrete barricade, outlining the space where the camp had been (figure 15). The group relocated multiple times and at the time of writing now serves meals near the Verano Cemetery but does not operate a camp there.

When I returned in the summer of 2019, several months after the barricade went up, I arranged to meet Yousef, a former Piazzale Maslax resident from the Gambia, at the station. He was living outside the city by then but stayed in touch with Baobab and returned fairly regularly to hang out and help. We walked together between benches where people tried to sleep through the afternoon heat, winding our way down the road to the former encampment. The enclosure loomed before us, marking Piazzale Maslax for passersby with striking visibility, both for the concrete barriers and metal fence, and for the banners that, now seven months after the eviction, still hung from what is effectively a border wall. One read "FREEDOM" and another "MIGRATION IS NOT." It should have read, "MIGRATION IS NOT A CRIME," but the last two words had fallen off in the intervening months, and the wall now attested to blocked border crossing.[72] The fence made the former camp even more visible than when it was in operation, materializing legality/illegality via "the tactile border."[73] Ironically, the barricade had placed migrants on the same side as locals. As I write this, it still stands, though the banners have disappeared.

In its more than eighteen months, the Piazzale Maslax camp was home to tens of thousands of transitanti. If the final closure of the camp is an emboldened attempt at erasure, these signs are a reminder that experiences of transit, recognition of the rights of transitanti, and representation of these issues are not a foregone conclusion, but one constantly negotiated through a range of witnessing acts. The traces of the camp that lingered in signs and fragments are reminders that the forms of hospitality that shaped this space emerged in response to the constraints placed on witnessing—the limits of (self-)representation in such precarity. They illustrate once again how emergency responses to migration operate through the

FIGURE 15. Piazzale Maslax entrance after its final closure, 2019. Photo by the author.

control of people's movements and of witnessing possibilities. At the same time, those very controls prompt testimonial practices that speak back to this violence and offer alternative forms of hospitality—however temporary, fraught, or precarious they may be.

In the following chapters, I consider how emergency imaginaries of foreignness and emergency responses to migration affect migrants outside the parameters of arrival to Italy, in their daily routines and relationships to labor and to urban space whether they have arrived two months ago, or twenty years.

# PART II

# The Right To Remain

*We . . . are greatly indebted to the "sans-papiers" who, refusing the "clandestineness" ascribed to them, have forcefully posed the question of the right to stay. . . . We owe them . . . for having recreated citizenship among us.*
—ÉTIENNE BALIBAR, "WHAT WE OWE THE SANS-PAPIERS"

4

———

# Street Vendor as Witness

In 2018, the national campaign *Operazione Spiagge Sicure* (Operation Safe Beaches) directed €2.4 million to support seaside communities in policing the beaches during the summer tourism season, clearing out any unauthorized commercial activities. In practice, that meant fining, arresting, or seizing the goods of the immigrant vendors who pace the beaches selling sunglasses, books, jewelry, and toys to locals and vacationers enjoying the seaside.

While Operation Safe Beaches emphasized unauthorized commerce, it was part of a set of anti-immigrant policies rolled out that year by recently appointed Interior Minister Matteo Salvini. Salvini, of the right-wing Lega party, had won support on promises to close Italian ports to rescued migrants and criminalize rescue itself. Now he made clear in rallies that this policy would guarantee beachgoers "molti meno vu cumprà a rompere le palle"—using offensive slang associated with African migrants to proclaim that there would be "a lot fewer immigrant street vendors bothering you" during the summer holidays.[1] Celebrating the operation's success at a press conference that September, Infrastructure Minister Danilo Toninelli commented, "In two months approximately 620,000 square meters of beach were liberated and returned to citizens, the equivalent of more than 100 football fields."[2] The idea that Operation Safe Beaches consisted in "liberating" land from migrant vendors and returning it to Italians feeds pervasive associations of migrants with invasion, illegality, uncleanliness, and the sense that *these* foreigners have no right to move within Italian spaces.

The migrant vendor remains a figure onto which notions of unknowability, risk, and danger are projected—key affective dimensions of the emergency apparatus. Operation Safe Beaches is just one example of how the figure of the street vendor

115

returns again and again in popular and political discourse as an object of blame used to catalyze the criminalization and racialization of migration. In Italy, political uses of the migrant vendor to forward narratives of "emergenza immigrazione" legitimize crisis racism, or the idea that some foreigners are the bearers of crisis and don't deserve to live in Italy, let alone receive legal protection. Migrant vendors are an easy mark onto which notions of undeservingness can be projected, especially because their labor necessitates their visibility and mobility in public spaces. In 2018, shifting public focus from national borders to cities and vacation spots was strategic. Arrivals had in fact decreased significantly from the high numbers of 2015 and 2016. Focusing on street vendors reassured publics that the emergenza immigrazione was still a problem being managed.

Border and migration "crises" bring questions of foreignness into sharp relief: Whose bodies, movements, and voices are cast as embodying dominant notions of belonging and nonbelonging? These are of course never new issues; they are constitutive of national identity and the images and narratives that uphold it. But the heightened sense of urgency that accompanies crisis discourses moves people to make bold and extreme claims about borders, rights, and identity. In this sense, emergency *appears* as a sudden rupture of normative ways of life and a threat to the nation-state; like crisis, it marks out new time.[3] It is, however, better understood as an apparatus whose various discursive, political, and material components continually participate in the production of national belonging by honing emergency imaginaries that "recognize" foreignness in particular settings or encounters.[4] Part 1 of this book examines circumstances immediately tied to arrivals by sea and the asylum and reception processes that hold the recently arrived in limbo. In Part 2, I consider witnessing practices that challenge the sense of an interminable present that emergency and crisis framings impose by in fact masking continuities, obscuring the longer entangled histories that link Africans and Europeans and shape transit routes today. As Balibar demonstrates in his work on the *sans-papiers* in France, people without citizenship status or other legal recognition "recreat[e] citizenship among us," having long demonstrated through resistance and solidarity movements, as well as the actions of everyday life, that *belonging* concerns, first and foremost, collective practice and a shared recognition of the right to remain.[5]

In this chapter I take up the figure of the *venditore ambulante*, or street vendor, which illustrates how this masking functions and speaks to how racializing assemblages have produced citizens and others in Italy over time. The vendor holds a major place in Italian imaginaries of foreignness as a cultural icon that has long been the object of racist and gendered stereotypes. While plenty of Italians sell goods in this way, the migrant venditore—often a man—is its own archetype, a figure simultaneously visible and invisibilized in everyday and touristic spaces. But vendors are not simply archetypal, imagined others; their labor materially shapes Italian spaces, just as Italian spaces and communities shape their lives. Vendors include newcomers, but many have lived in Italy for years, even decades, obtained legal residency, and mastered a knowledge of Italian spaces and cultural practices.

The migrant street vendor is also a global figure, representing rural to urban mobilities within countries, international migration the world over, and the trade of goods ranging from art to falafel to designer bags. Migrant vendors' work combines entrepreneurship and cultural exchange, as labor migration scholars have established, and is often a form of precarious labor.[6] Here I recognize ambulant vendors' labor within a contemporary capitalist context, via Kathleen Millar's framing of precarity as "both the tenuous conditions of neoliberal labor as well as states of anxiety, desperation, unbelonging, and risk experienced by temporary and irregularly employed workers."[7] Within these constraints, workers also exercise agency and, as I discuss here, strategize about the nature, possibilities, and limits of their labor. While the vendor's reality—and precarity—is shaped by local circumstances, vendors who inhabit the intersections of precarious migration and precarious labor share the experience of having to navigate the risks of working in public spaces, especially if they don't have a vending permit or a visa. Rocío Rosales's observations about the strategies adopted by Mexican *fruteros*, or fruit vendors, in Los Angeles applies to West African and South Asian vendors in Italy: the risks they confront "are met with distinct survival strategies developed by *fruteros* both to minimize risk and to maximize profit. On their street corners, *fruteros* must forge alliances, engender sympathy or solidarity, and establish and maintain trust with their customer base."[8] Together, these dynamics position the vendor as a witness to the daily life of a city, and as someone whose livelihood depends on the transactions—financial, conversational, testimonial—they carry out with customers.

This chapter recognizes the ambulant vendor as an observer of Italian life and a producer of memories, via souvenirs, conversations, sales, and other interactions in Italy's city centers and tourist destinations. An "emergency" figure that is simultaneously a figure of everyday life, the venditore ambulante is also a worker whose livelihood depends on testimonial transactions, as vendors market goods by bearing witness to their own identities, especially when their wares include autobiographical narratives, as I discuss here. The migrant vendor is also a figure of transit: while previous chapters address transit in terms of transnational border crossing and the limbo of reception, here we see emergency in transit in the local, everyday movements of the venditore ambulante. Having relocated from another country, and moving continually for work, the vendor's labor is intimately tied to specific geographies. This transit is transnational and translocal, connecting Italian spaces with those where vendors may have learned their trade—many Senegalese migrants worked as or grew up around ambulant vendors in their hometowns, for instance.

Here, I consider the figure of the migrant street vendor as cultural icon and as a heterogeneous group of workers whose precarious labor positions them to be

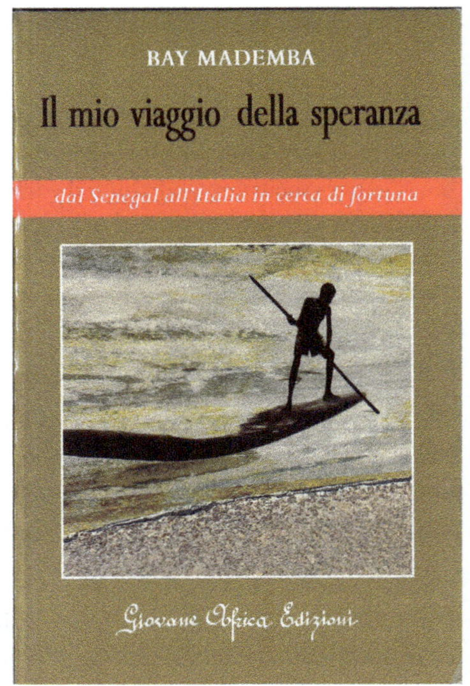


FIGURE 16. Cover of *Il mio viaggio della speranza*, by Bay Mademba. Photo by the author.

critical witnesses of and participants in everyday Italian life, within and outside of crisis framings. I focus on the work and witnessing of Senegalese vendors in the Tuscany region who sell books, including the 2011 memoir *Il mio viaggio della speranza: dal Senegal all'Italia in cerca di fortuna* (*My Voyage of Hope: From Senegal to Italy in Search of Fortune*), written in Italian by a Senegalese immigrant known as Bay Mademba, in collaboration with an Italian editor (figure 16). Directed at Italian speakers, the testimony presented in *Il mio viaggio* exists in relation to the witnessing exchanges initiated by vendors who hawk the book to potential customers. How does testimony operate in the context of this small-scale circulation? How does it engage with or reject notions of "migration crises"? What visions of Italy and of migration emerge through the nested testimonies of vendors who spend their workdays observing, engaging, and bearing witness within key spaces of Italian cultural heritage?

Unlike more widely celebrated literature about migrants in Italy, such as work by Pap Khouma (addressed later in this chapter), Mademba's memoir circulates locally, through vendors who often market the book by identifying with its narrative. Thus, while *Il mio viaggio* is an example of Italian literature of migration and can be read within that growing body of work, it remains outside mainstream circuits of consumption and critique. This small-scale movement and the transactions that enable it—testimonial transactions within the narrative and forms of witnessing that vendors use to sell the book—are the focus of this chapter. Giovane Africa Edizioni, the small Tuscan press that published *Il mio viaggio*, produces writing by Senegalese migrants and provides them with work. Between 2017 and 2019, I visited Florence and the nearby town of Pontedera several times, interviewing press editors and book vendors.

Analyzing Mademba's memoir as a work of migration literature that moves outside standard literary circuits, and drawing on interviews with vendors and editors, this chapter employs testimony as method to trace the racialization of migration and anti-Black sentiment as they manifest in relation to vendors' paradoxical (in)visibility. As I elaborate in the following sections, Mademba presents a narrative that in part aligns with neoliberal, multicultural notions of deserving migrants, and in part subverts those ideas. In what follows, I first present the book and the work of the press. Then I alternate between the two spheres of witnessing that overlap in this case: within the book, and between vendors and potential customers. I close by reflecting on how a focus on the street vendor also illustrates how immigration policies alternately criminalize and legalize African migrants, and how restrictive policies have rendered precarious journeys essentially the only viable means for entering Europe. Recognizing the street vendor as a critical witness of Italian life and the place of the foreigner within it offers a window into understanding mobility outside the strict terms that emergency framings impose.

SITUATING *IL MIO VIAGGIO DELLA SPERANZA*
AND THE SCALE OF THE SMALL PRESS

Because ambulant vendors often occupy precarious legal, social, and financial positions, they navigate multiple dimensions of (in)visibility, including the need to be visible (for work) yet remain out of sight of authorities, as well as their erasure within discourses of Italian identity and belonging. Vendors without a permit for setting up their wares have to stay on guard not only for potential customers, but for police who might chase them off, seize their goods, or arrest them. "Selling only brought me fear and anguish because I had to run away from the police an infinite number of times," Khouma writes in his 1990 autobiographical novel *Io, venditore di elefanti: Una vita per forza fra Dakar, Parigi e Milano* (*I Was an Elephant Salesman: Adventures between Dakar, Paris, and Milan*), "because they confiscated my merchandise, because I ended up in jail, because people looked at me assuming the worst—that is, when they weren't cursing me for setting up my elephants and necklaces in front of their store."[9] At the other extreme, Italians and tourists often treat vendors as part of the urban landscape, as if the vendor were functionally invisible to them or to avoid any interaction. For decades now, travel guidebooks and forums have offered tourists techniques for avoiding vendors, bringing them up strictly as a nuisance: likely criminals and people to be avoided. Armed with this knowledge in my own first visits to Italy in the early 2000s, I assumed I was a potential victim. "Be rude and adamant," the guidebooks say. "Hold up your hand and walk away." It's no surprise that vendors have to be insistent to make a sale.

These entrepreneurs and their suppliers depend on local circulation and individual exchange.[10] This is certainly the case for booksellers who rely on small presses for their stock, and who then market the books by connecting with potential customers about their contents. It is through this local circulation that I first encountered *Il mio viaggio*: I acquired the book and got to know the press by meeting a vendor in 2017 in Florence, where I was attending a seminar. The vendor, originally from Senegal, had arranged a dozen books on a sheet on a sidewalk. When I asked whether he was selling any autobiographies, he showed me *Il mio viaggio* and suggested that if I wanted to know more, I might reach out to the press editors, who were local. I interviewed cofounders Giuseppe Cecconi and Fatou N'Diaye that summer and again in 2019, and I spoke with vendors in Florence during those same visits.

Giovane Africa Edizioni (Young Africa Editions) is a small, independent press that Cecconi and N'Diaye, who are married, run out of their home. On this very small scale, Giovane Africa Edizioni proposes literature for social change, selling books through which press editors aim to stem discrimination and spread awareness of the cultural backgrounds and humanity of Italy's African residents. Cecconi and N'Diaye have each authored some of the books they produce, and while they don't focus exclusively on memoirs, their catalog includes several, such as N'Diaye's *Il cielo sopra Ibrahima: come gli immigrati giudicano gli italiani* (*The Sky Over Ibrahima: How Immigrants Judge Italians*, written under the pseudonym Penda Thiam), and *Il mio viaggio della speranza*. Their children's books include an illustrated story of Aeneas as a refugee and a collection of African fables; novels include translations of celebrated Senegalese author Mariama Bâ; and they offer several Senegalese cookbooks. Cecconi, a white Italian man and Tuscan native, and N'Diaye, a Senegalese woman who ran a restaurant near Florence before joining forces with Cecconi, have long collaborated with the local Senegalese community. Via the press, they supply the books to Senegalese newcomers, mostly men from their late teens through their thirties, who can then sell them for the cover price (€6–8) or whatever they agree upon with customers. Giovane Africa Edizioni is by no means the only such press in Italy, but they are exemplary of this model of local circulation that supports migrant employment.

*Il mio viaggio della speranza* participates in this mission as Bay Mademba's 2011 account of his struggles to reach Italy and his strategies for responding to the anti-Black, anti-immigrant discrimination he faces as he settles in Tuscany. Mademba recounts his own precarious journey, his work as a book vendor for the small press that then published his memoir, and his interactions with white Italians who alternately reject or appreciate his presence in Tuscany. Mademba's approach is in part didactic, modeling anti-racist behavior for readers. Narrator-Mademba also recognizes his position as a Black African in Italy as necessarily shaped by colonialism, a message reinforced in the book's second, epilogue-like chapter added by Cecconi (though not marked as such). Where the main chapter recounts Mademba's journey to Europe and his encounters as a bookseller, these final pages situate his experiences within Senegalese migration to Europe more generally, including by observing that travel by boat from Senegal to the Canary Islands is a more typical route and one that has repeatedly proven fatal.

Mademba's memoir is not the first such narrative. Some readers may recall earlier works such as Khouma's *Io, venditore di elefanti*. Indeed, Senegalese-Italian cultural production has made an important mark on Italian literary and cultural studies, from work explicitly about precarious migration and labor, to work on identity and belonging, such as short stories by Aminata Aidara, novels by Cheikh Tidiane Gaye, or more recent essays by Khouma.[11] Autobiographical and fictional texts have expanded the counter-archive of works that bear witness to experiences of mobility and belonging from the perspective of those on the move. *Io, venditore di elefanti* is widely recognized as one of the first works of Afro-Italian literature. Like Mademba's *Il mio viaggio*, Khouma authored *Io, venditore di elefanti* "a quattro mani" (with four hands) in collaboration with journalist Oreste Pivetta. The book was published by the major press Garzanti and subsequently translated into English,[12] and it marks witnessing as a key aspect of the vendor's life and a key literary mode for Italian narratives of migration and belonging. "I was a good seller," Khouma writes, "because I was a good observer."[13]

The two texts have had very different reception, especially given their different modes of circulation. Khouma's book, available in English, is taught in North America and was recently featured in an issue of the journal *Transitions* focused on the Black Mediterranean. Mademba's book is available only in its original Italian form and almost exclusively via in-person exchange with a vendor in Italy. Taken together, they nonetheless highlight the ongoing significance of particular themes across more than two decades and, moreover, the choice some migrants make to challenge their marginalization by bearing witness to it through writing, situating their experience in a broader cultural moment. Both authors describe using their personal background to market the "Africanness" of their wares to Italian and foreign customers alike. And both underscore how a vendor's movements expose the vulnerabilities and invisibilities that so many migrants experience when their livelihood depends on the outcomes of overtly precarious legal and social situations.[14]

It's important to hold in mind that Mademba's memoir was written not for publication by a major press but in order to be sold by vendors whose stories it represents. This necessarily shapes how narrator-Mademba addresses readers, who are implicitly also customers purchasing books from vendors. It is with a range of reader-customers in mind that Mademba employs multiple strategies for describing and celebrating his work. Most overtly, the novella-length memoir broaches neoliberal ideals of multiculturalism—his wares as objects of cultural exchange that might promote cross-cultural understanding—and of the productive citizen. Yet just as readily, the narrative subverts those tropes by focusing on Mademba's strategic uses of his own foreignness to make a sale. Given how narrative and material transactions converge in the book, readers who purchase *Il mio viaggio* from a vendor who identifies with the narrative may find it resonates in unexpected ways.

## WITNESSING THROUGH THE (POTENTIAL) SALE

As witnesses, vendors use testimony in ways that illustrate its transactional nature: they are, fundamentally, hoping to make a sale. Yet, as transnational and transcultural texts, these testimonies also "mobilize" cultural encounters and postcolonial perspectives, to borrow from Whitlock, in contexts otherwise shaped by emergency imaginaries.[15] As *Il mio viaggio* illustrates, vendors create witnessing platforms where none were available, (re)claiming space and authority as people not simply projected onto but using labor to transform social relations.

Aware that their witnessing authority affirms the product's authenticity, Senegalese book vendors in Florence often foreground their own foreignness to market their wares, even as their own legal and social precarity imbues those transactions with risk. Transactions are frequently both commercial and conversational; the vendor suggests books the consumer might enjoy and may share parts of his own story. Viewed in terms of the pressures to assimilate, this insistence on one's own heritage and nationality could be understood as a form of resistance to narratives that position foreignness as the problem. In *Il mio viaggio*, narrator-Mademba describes himself as proudly Senegalese. He makes no claims to being or becoming Italian but understands Italian culture and can relate to Italians and, it follows, should be able to live a happy, successful life in Italy.

Within the book, like in his work, Mademba centers the individual encounter. "Before selling a book I ask: 'Who are you?'" he writes. He credits his initial success at bookselling to his "excellent idea" to call his customers "fratelli" (brothers). "Thanks to the idea to engage everyone like a brother, I was immediately successful and managed to really invest in my work." He acknowledges this gesture as a Senegalese tradition not necessarily common in Italy, and he describes using his Senegalese background to engage potential customers through familiar salutations that, he recognizes, cross national boundaries: "So I use my culture, my ethics, my spontaneity in dealings with clients."[16] Here the narrator posits his foreignness as a point of connection with Italians, especially given his own capacity for intercultural understanding. He's proud of the relationships he's built with shop owners and locals he meets regularly at a café:

> Along the street where I sell books, there are lots of people who love me. Sometimes shopkeepers come to me to change money . . . often they confide their troubles to me; they tell me they were misled by something or that they are unhappy because of this or that. I give them advice and I sense that they trust me.[17]

In showcasing his bookselling as (multi)cultural labor, Mademba describes how he began selling books to earn money for himself and to send funds home to his mother and says he was attracted to the work because through these books, he would "help people with a product that is culturally enriching for its customers."[18]

Yet this early account of trust serves primarily to foreground the problem of being treated as a stranger. The mission to "overcome distrust" seems to motivate the telling of his story. "All these acquaintances are often useful for overcoming the distrust of those who don't know me."[19] Throughout the main chapter, Mademba reminds readers how dedicated he is to his work, presenting himself as stand-up and trustworthy. In this sense, as a testimonial work of life writing, *Il mio viaggio* reflects how Mademba positions his narrated self to be perceived by white Italian readers. The narrative that emerges envisions a multicultural Italy where foreignness is welcomed and respected, rather than treated as suspect.

For the street vendor, narrative and material possibilities converge in an act of interruption. On the one hand, the interruption is a critical sales move, with a vendor approaching a potential customer, calling out to passersby from wherever they've set up their wares, or approaching with a stack of books, asking, "Where are you from?" "Would you like to look at a book about Africa?" On the other hand, vendors are often seen as interrupting space: occupying the corner of a central square or passing through where they are unwanted. These interruptions are necessary aspects of the work. They are also a gesture of potential: an exchange of words, of cultures, a possible sale. The vendor's interruption insists on a "small and stubborn possibility" for change.[20]

Texts such as *Il mio viaggio* potentially expand testimonial networks that document migrant experiences. Yet to find "adequate witnesses"—that is, to have even the possibility of meaningful impact—these narratives must themselves transit between readers, across regions, and within different social contexts.[21] Here transit depends on the street vendor as witness, both within and outside the memoir. In facilitating this transit, the interruption bears not only potential but also risk. It announces foreignness. Like the "transruptions" that Bernor Hesse describes in his critique of postcolonial multiculturalism, the interruption "unsettle[s] social norms and threaten[s] to dismantle hegemonic concepts and practices." In the convergence of narrative and material transactions, the memoir is "transruptive," participating in "the recurrent exposure of discrepancies in the post-colonial settlement."[22] The vendor, who depends economically on book sales, also depends socially on the contents of the narrative to shift perceptions of himself from stranger to neighbor as it transits "in search of witnessing publics." Vendors rely on the power of testimony to move, in Whitlock's words, "as a social and political force in the public sphere that commands recognition and ethical response from both institutions and individuals."[23]

Migrant vendors who assume this task also face its sometimes violent consequences. This came up in my 2019 interview with Lamine (pseudonym), a Senegalese vendor who had arrived eight months earlier and was selling Giovane Africa Edizioni books in Florence.[24] We recorded an interview in Italian while Lamine was on a break in Piazza della Repubblica. As he put it, "When Italians don't buy these books, we can't survive in Italy, without working. But this ambulant work is too difficult. You have to learn the language, stop people, chat with them." A vendor may spend the morning near Florence's Duomo without a sale; other days he might sell three or four books, bringing in perhaps €20. Nearly every sale depends on the vendor initiating conversation with a potential customer, and therefore making himself especially visible before strangers and as a foreigner. In a political climate increasingly hostile to migrants, those exchanges feel especially risky. Lamine was struggling to make ends meet. "You try to sell," he told me, "but often it's not so easy. So many people say terrible things to you."

## VENDORS IN TRANSIT, HISTORICALLY AND CULTURALLY

The ambulant vendor is a transhistorical figure, appearing in Renaissance accounts as peddlers whose mobility was critical to their trade—including the selling of print materials—and who were often foreign.[25] The vendor's prominence in contemporary imaginaries of foreignness dates to Italy's new status as a primarily destination country beginning in the 1970s. As more people arrived from North and West Africa, street selling was (and is) a common trade, including men and women selling art, handmade objects, fabric, and other items. Ambulant trading includes vendors from a diverse set of countries and reflects changing immigration trends. For instance, Moroccan migrants dominated this line of work in the 1980s and 1990s; it's now also a relatively common sector for people from Bangladesh.[26] While undocumented labor, like undocumented migration, is difficult to quantify, economists estimate that informal markets make up at least 14 percent of Italy's economic output.[27] Ambulant trading likely comprises a very small part of that percentage but is viewed as pervasive in part because it is so visible.

Senegal–Italy migration is one of the oldest continuous trends in contemporary Italy, and many traders bring their experience throughout West Africa into Italian spaces. As Carter documents in his study of Senegalese immigrants in Italy in the late 1980s and early 1990s, these newcomers represent diverse backgrounds, with some coming from rural Senegalese communities that were, already thirty years ago, dealing with the consequences of drought and various pressures to relocate to growing cities. Today, some have reached Europe as they realize they cannot survive as traders in Senegal. This was pointedly clear following 2007 demonstrations by vendors in Dakar. As one protestor told reporters, "We are tired. Today, I cannot eat because I haven't sold anything. . . . That's why everyone wants to go to Europe."[28]

Many are followers of the Mourid Brotherhood, a Sufi order that views travel as part of its adherents' calling.[29] Their skills and experience in a range of trades often go unrecognized by potential Italian employers, which, coupled with the complications of work and residency visas, can lead migrants into precarious and exploitative labor. In the case of the Senegalese, many vendors "define themselves as commerçant and . . . enter this occupation as their line of work on all official documents."[30] At the same time, ambulant work is also a job migrants can readily pick up and abandon if they find something more stable or better paying.

Multiple kinds of transit are at play here, from international border crossing, to travel between towns, to the daily movements along train lines and streets that inscribe a city with meaning.[31] These movements remind us that precarious migration involves a constant act of translation—between languages, spaces, futures, between the seen and unseen, between those who speak and those who are spoken to. Migrant vendors are simultaneously hypervisible and also made anonymous, their presence generalized as illegal economic migration that threatens Italian institutions and publics. In Carter's words, it is when people are "designated 'superfluous,' imponderable as a human presence, that they become invisible."[32]

In my conversations with Senegalese vendors in Florence, they described how crucial their visibility was to making a sale—hence their set-up near the Duomo or at major pedestrian intersections. Yet this is a superficial visibility, one that gets construed in public discourse in ways that erase individual identity and uphold a racial order[33] through stereotypes that depict all immigrant vendors as a homogeneous group of undesirable others and use the ambulant vendor as a proxy for all migrants, as the fervor for "cleaning" and "liberating" Italian beaches also demonstrates. In Florence, vendors told me that even as they approached potential customers, they braced themselves for the racist comments they often received in response. Bay Mademba describes his commute from a small town near Florence into the city center as a regular site of racist encounters. As Rosales and others note for migrant vendors more broadly, this (in)visibility is a common issue.[34] The Italian case illustrates the extent to which emergency imaginaries of foreignness exploit that (in)visibility, projecting notions of illegality, criminality, and unbelonging onto people whose work is in fact of very little consequence for most Italians.

Like the asylum seekers I discuss in chapter 2 who appear out of place when they leave the reception center and visit the heart of the city, vendors' movements are treated with a mix of suspicion and the invisibilizing gaze of intentional disregard. These workers can rarely afford to live in the areas where they labor. Khouma speaks at length about sharing crowded apartments with a constantly changing set of tenants in the late 1980s and early 1990s. In his study of the same period, Carter describes a house in which 120 Senegalese immigrants live in close quarters in Barriera di Milano, an immigrant neighborhood in Torino long neglected by city officials.[35] This segregation means that as residents, migrants' lives are fairly invisible to broader, white, middle- and upper-class publics, but as workers, their labor in touristic urban centers and other vacation destinations is instead hypervisible.

From the 1980s on, this work made some migrants especially visible as foreigners in a moment marked by immigration from outside Europe, and with it, issues related to the language and notions of foreignness. In particular, Moroccan and Senegalese vendors' visible presence positioned these foreigners as *the* foreigners in the Italian imaginary, as illustrated by the confused and problematic colloquialisms for foreignness, including *marocchino*, Moroccan, to mean "African foreigner," or words such as *vu cumprà*, slang for street vendor, to indicate "immigrant." Their visibility made them a familiar figure in everyday Italian life and thus a key icon in Italian imaginaries of foreignness, coming to represent the fears and concerns of Italians as the country grappled with its changing demographics and its role as an immigrant destination. In recent and seemingly readily forgotten memory, Italians emigrated to France and Germany for work and were themselves the marginalized migrant other.[36] In today's dominant cultural narratives, the migrant vendor has become synonymous with "illegal migration" and with migrants of color, evident in the very language used to describe foreigners. In reference to Operation Safe Beaches, Salvini's use of *vu cumprà* holds power before his audience because it refers to the conflated figures of "illegal" and "black" in the public consciousness.

The offensive term contains traces of Italy's particular racial history. *Vu cumprà* represents a version of southern dialects for "vuoi comprare?" *Do you want to buy?* The peddling of goods itself becomes a name.[37] It also reflects two racist associations: the more overt idea that migrants do not speak "proper" Italian, and the more implicit link between today's African migrants and the Southern Italian migrants of previous decades, who were themselves racialized as other and treated as uneducated, disorderly, and fit only for manual labor. The racialization and stigmatization of the street vendor serves as an important reminder that "current dynamics of anti-Black racism have been developing since the mid-nineteenth century in conjunction with Italians' fragile and liminal racial status."[38] Questions of African otherness did not arise with today's sea crossings but have been enfolded into debates about Italian identity and belonging since Unification and colonialism. Negotiating its position in Europe's South, the newly unified Italy relied on Africa to distinguish itself as European.[39] From the late-nineteenth-century post-Unification period into the twentieth century, Southern Italians were referred to as "Africans" by Northern leaders and prominent scholars such as criminologist Cesare Lombroso as a way of distinguishing them from the "white" citizens of Northern Italy.[40]

While multidirectional mobilities have always shaped Italian society, today's emergency imaginaries of foreignness reflect the intersections of migration and racial thinking over time. As Italy transitioned from a country defined largely by internal south-north movement and by departures to a destination country, newcomers from Africa, the Middle East, and Asia occupied the place of the undesirable, threatening "other" in dominant imaginaries. The declarations of emergency that Italian leaders made to control Southern and colonial populations are echoed in emergency discourses that have described contemporary migration from the 1990s through the present, defining foreigners from the global south as embodying crisis and emergenza.

Senegalese migrations to Italy are importantly related to colonial-era West Africa–Europe mobilities. The French recruited colonial subjects, including Senegalese men, for their infantry in World War II and, beginning in the 1950s, for their expanding labor force. This recruitment established a migratory route, and numbers increased over time, including through family reunification. As France began to limit these movements, especially via labor immigration restrictions in the 1980s, Italy became a destination.[41] The racialization of certain forms of labor in Italy aligned with the creation of what Nik Theodore terms the "regime of precarious employment" in post-Fordist economies.[42] In this environment, norms and stereotypes associate particular sectors with specific ethnic groups or with migrants in general.[43] Informal economies are multifaceted, and migrants working in the agricultural or domestic labor sectors certainly outnumber ambulant vendors. Yet street vendors' visibility makes this role a popular icon. As Russell King observed through survey data in the early 1990s, "the predominant picture of immigration . . . is the one represented by the African street vendor, a finding which confirms that the collective imagination is focussed mainly on the more visible side of immigration which is easier to stereotype."[44]

Italy's informal economy is robust, for example compared to France,[45] and for many migrants these jobs remain their only options for earning money. The ensuing racialization of specific lines of work such as ambulant vending also reifies stereotypes about those who "look like" they would work in such jobs.[46] On the one hand, migrant labor "reshap[es] . . . the metropolitan economy and the development of social struggles."[47] On the other hand, the racialization and stigmatization of street vendors extends to encompass anyone who looks like a vendor, reiterating associations of nonwhiteness with undesirable foreignness.

In popular culture, vendors remain "one of the most despised social categories of immigrants,"[48] and caricatures of migrants use the image of the vendor in ways that recall colonial iconography, representing blackness as buffoonery. A common image of African vendors involves their escape from police; having spread their wares on sheets in city squares or along sidewalks, they can grab everything quickly and run if police approach. This image of pursuit has become a comical trope that reifies racialized and gendered stereotypes through caricatures of Black African men. These stereotypes are compounded by assumptions of illegality; presumed to be in Italy illegally, street vendors take the blame for criminality, even as they supply Italians with beach wares, earrings and sunglasses, and books. But the need to pick up and run is very real: as a vendor, you don't want to be ticketed for selling without a permit, and you probably also don't want to be questioned about your papers.

Like Khouma writing twenty years earlier, the work of Mademba illustrates that the precarity migrants experience en route does not end with the crossing of an EU border, where "European apartheid" holds some migrants in the margins.[49] This came up in my interview with Lamine, who mentioned his frustration at stereotypes he hears about African migrants, including that they are drug dealers. He talked about the insults he hears on a daily basis, and how he chooses not to respond. "It's about dignity," he said. "There are people, the people who do this work [selling books], who don't have anything, but they carry their dignity inside them, and they do this work [as opposed to selling drugs or robbing] because it's cultural work." This cultural work remains a form of precarious labor, even as it positions ambulant vendors as key witnesses of Italian everyday life and shifting politics. Witnessing can place a burden on those narrating their own experiences of trauma and marginalization. As we know from studies of the diaries and other testimonies by formerly enslaved people, and from refugee testimony, witnessing is potentially retraumatizing. As I emphasize in part 1 of this book, witnessing prompts a reckoning between what Hartman describes as "the precariousness of empathy and the uncertain line between witness and spectator." At the same time, those who do opt to bear witness can use their narrative power strategically and position readers not as voyeurs but as witnesses who might be moved to "confirm the truth" of past and present.[50]

## WITNESSING AS COUNTERNARRATIVE ACT

For these reasons, it's significant that Mademba's memoir resists the temptation to portray a simplified view of "the good migrant" or "deserving refugee."[51] This prevalent trope is regularly invoked by well-intentioned journalists, humanitarian workers, and sometimes politicians who challenge the erasure or negative portrayals of migrants by suggesting they are good, productive citizens. In doing so, however, they implicitly invoke what Didier Fassin terms "humanitarian reason" and its "moral sentiment," suggesting a hierarchy in which "good" refugees stand out but are still beneath the citizens able to recognize and cultivate their goodness.[52] Literature, film, and media can uphold or subvert these hierarchies in their engagement of cultural memory and understandings of belonging and mobility.[53]

*Il mio viaggio* may not be the antidote to the problem of erasure, but it illustrates cultural work enacted through the production and circulation of testimonies that go against the grain, on whatever scale those transits and transactions occur. With this in mind, I don't claim to measure the transformative potential of a single text or sale, but to underscore the testimonial ethics at play here: how vendors and narrators position tellers, sellers, and consumers informs the "conditions of possibilities of hearing" that render these testimonies possible, or that delimit their circulation.[54] Throughout the book, the narrator tries several approaches, some focused on entrepreneurial success, others foregrounding the journey, and others oriented around confronting discrimination. None of these approaches is framed to cultivate pity or compassion for the narrator.

To be clear, the memoir is not entirely subversive; narrator-Mademba directly posits a vision of an Italy in which people with different backgrounds live alongside one another in harmony. He sees his purpose as at least in part didactic, challenging the notion that, as a migrant, he is necessarily an alien other. "I don't sell books just to make a little profit," the narrator says, "but I sell them to get to know people, to teach them what I know, to share what I have in my soul."[55] The idea of the book sale as a cultural exchange contrasts importantly with Khouma's descriptions of selling in *Io, venditore di elefanti*. Khouma's narrator is a proud vendor, but he is frustrated at having to sell to Italians who exoticize him. Selling "African statues" and jewelry, he laments that "my Africa is for sale." Instead, Mademba's narrator foregrounds the sale of goods as potentially transformative—and again, he's writing this for readers who will have likely acquired the book through just such an exchange and so might see themselves in these transactions.

Still, it's striking that in presenting this vision, the book doesn't hinge on a "good refugee" narrative. The story conforms neither to emergency framings nor to deservingness tropes. In that sense, it avoids reinforcing a kind of neoliberal multiculturalism in which *some* foreigners are desirable because of their potential to integrate or to benefit society through entrepreneurship or other economic contributions, on the one hand, or because their vulnerability is seen to represent a kind of innocence that "promises a space of purity," on the other.[56] Per his own telling, Mademba did not arrive as a vulnerable refugee. Rather than seek empathy for past suffering, the narrator matter-of-factly recounts details including that along his journey he lied to border authorities and falsified documents.

In this spirit, one way Mademba subverts deservingness tropes is by positing his story not in terms of strict migration categories but as aligned with multiple mobilities. He is inspired to reach Italy by a brother who has lived there for some time, and his own story certainly fits within the longer history of Senegal–Italy migrations. The memoir's second chapter refers to the number of people who crossed from Senegal to the Canary Islands in the mid-2000s—increasing from fifty-four hundred to twenty-seven thousand between 2005 and 2006—and how many have died trying, estimated between five hundred and three thousand in 2006.[57] As Carter writes of Senegal–Italy migration in the 1980s, these mobilities "must be seen in the context of African internal and international migration of the past and, in that, of a crisis of West African agriculture, prolonged drought, urbanization, and the fluctuation of international market outlets."[58] These patterns of routes and labor were established before Italy implemented formal immigration legislation. Indeed, Mademba's and Khouma's memoirs bookend a more than twenty-year period of Senegalese migration to Italy and speak to how that border crossing changed in response to increasingly restrictive EU and Italian border policies. While Khouma reached Europe by plane, overstayed a visa, and finally received residency through the 1986 amnesty that regularized so many Senegalese migrants, two decades later, Mademba instead had no safe option.

In fact, this precarious journey links Mademba's experience not only with other Senegalese migrations but with the journeys of so many migrants who cross the sea today. Like them, he was unable to secure an EU visa and understood reaching Türkiye and then traveling by boat to be the only feasible way to arrive. Rather than conform to a ready-made narrative of either vulnerability or criminality, the narrator crosses borders to survive, adapts his story as he moves, and aligns his movements with multiple contemporary and historical mobilities, from his invocation of colonialism to his account of crossing from Greece to Italy, which he describes in terms of passengers' diversity. When the motor dies, he says, they "bowed in prayer, each to his own god. Some asked help of Serigne Touba, some of Allah, some of Jesus, some of Buddha."[59] Descriptions like this portray migration as a global phenomenon, rather than in terms of linear movements between fixed points. He describes his own navigation of borders as a matter of strategy, not merit. In Greece, he allows a friend to speak for him, claiming that they have fled violence in Côte d'Ivoire; they are then granted political asylum. In Italy, he and a friend use fake identity documents and pretend to be French tourists looking for work.

Far from a straightforward deservingness story, the account that Mademba and the press choose to circulate confounds easy categorization, aligning his narrated self with refugees, via his precarious travel by sea; with so-called economic migrants, as he describes his decision to move largely in terms of a need for employment; and with so-called irregular migrants, having crossed multiple national borders without documents or with false documents. In this way, *Il mio viaggio* frustrates the refugee / economic migrant binary—a dichotomy at least as old as the 1951 Refugee Convention that established grounds for determining refugee status and one that operates with particular force in contexts deemed crisis, circulating in public and political discourse with a moral valence.[60] This dichotomy is part of popular and political discourse; Salvini, for instance, campaigned on promises to expel "economic migrants."[61] As Bohmer and Shuman elaborate in their discussion of the suspicion imposed on asylum seekers, migrants regularly incorporate falsehoods or exaggerations into their asylum narratives to persuade officials of their need for protection.[62] As awareness of this potential deception has seeped out of the courts and into mainstream discourse, it feeds notions of deservingness among publics generally unaware of refugee realities or asylum processes. By sharing—not confessing or justifying, but simply stating—how he arrived, Mademba's narrator opts out of the deserving/undeserving binary. He regularly refers to his pride at being Senegalese and his expertise at selling: *these* are the reasons he deserves recognition.

That is, in Mademba's view, the point is not whether he has suffered enough to merit residency or financial stability but that he has reached Italy and can now share his story. The memoir's lessons concern racism within Italy, not migration routes or visas. The narrator describes a series of encounters that illustrate how he and other Black migrants are not a threat to Italians but are instead regularly wronged by them. A (presumably white) Italian teenager approaches him for drugs, assuming that because he's Black, he deals. A (white) Italian couple verbally attacks him as they pass on the street, telling him to "go back to your country."[63] In both instances, Mademba is calm and patient. Rather than dismissing the teen, he talks with him and convinces him to stop using (another example of the book's didacticism); later the young man returns and buys several books out of gratitude. When the couple yells at him, he does not respond in anger but reflects to himself (and to readers) on xenophobia.

In an especially striking scene at a bar in the Tuscan seaside town of Follonica, where Mademba has gone to sell books, he is verbally attacked by an Albanian man. "He looks at me and says: 'Another black man!'"[64] Mademba looks to the Italian barista, who calls out, "Ora basta!" (Now that's enough!). It's not clear whether she is defending him or simply quieting the exchange. Of particular interest here is the representation of anti-Black racism by another (white) migrant. The episode illustrates the prevalence of anti-Black racism in Italy. At the same time, it can also be understood to reflect changing understandings of otherness in contemporary Italy. Albanians were the subjects of emergency discourses in the 1990s, when they crossed the Aegean to the Puglia region following the fall of communism. Italian stereotypes of these migrants racialized Albanians as amoral, lazy, and deceitful.[65] In this account, two decades after those arrivals, the Albanian seems to align himself with whiteness—a reminder of the power of whiteness and that Italy's "racializing assemblages" are not monolithic.[66]

*Il mio viaggio* also responds to discrimination by situating the vendor's work within the colonial present. This is a Black Mediterranean memoir: Mademba describes racialized encounters in Italy within the duress of colonialism, or, via Stoler, the tangible and intangible ways that the colonial past continues to shape lives, spaces, and temporalities in the present.[67] As a Senegalese migrant to Italy, colonialism marks his movements in historically and linguistically different terms than it might in France, and his experiences could represent what Teresa Fiore has described as "indirect postcolonialism."[68] Yet Mademba does not make the claim expressed by some Senegalese migrants, including Khouma, that moving to Italy was an explicit choice *not* to live in the land of the former colonizers. Instead, the longue durée of colonialism readily informs the narrator's understanding of his position in Italy and his encounters with Italians.

Near the end of the main chapter, Mademba recalls the words of a white Italian he met on a train, who spoke up on his behalf when another passenger made racist comments. The man begins to discuss historical Italian emigration and the need to recognize climate refugees today. "The whole time they were talking," Mademba says, "I didn't speak. I listened and thought. I was thinking about Gorée, the island of slaves, from where ships loaded with Africans were taken to labor camps in America."[69] He recalls his own visit to Gorée, historically a major point of departure for transatlantic slave ships, and how struck he was by the traces of Europe still present in the architecture there. The short epilogue-like chapter expands this discussion, aligning Mademba's journey narrative with broader Senegalese migration trends, including that Gorée is now a point of departure for hundreds of Europe-bound migrants at a time. Through these references and his account of his movements to and within Italy, Mademba's narrative links the colonial present with European racial politics.

Vendors who market this book are offering readers the lessons of the seller-as-change-agent.[70] Narrator-Mademba addresses Italian publics with the knowledge and authority he's gained through his travels and work, and speaks to reader-consumers as "implicated subjects" who "occupy positions aligned with privilege and power without being themselves direct agents of harm" and who might therefore be moved to reconsider their positions.[71] In other words, this is not the narrative of how Mademba learned about Italian culture or developed his multicultural outlook but of how his awareness of these issues has empowered him in the role he has assumed of cultural ambassador. While readers may respond to this didactic approach with enthusiasm or skepticism, on a fundamental level, *Il mio viaggio* validates the presence of the people marketing it on Tuscan streets, creating a narrative that explains their movements and that they can also associate themselves with directly.

## TESTIMONIAL TRANSACTIONS AND COLLABORATION

The book and its circulation represent multiple interconnected testimonial transactions, from Mademba's initial oral account given to Cecconi, to the transactions that vendors set in motion as they sell the book to passersby. Production "a quattro mani" has a relatively long tradition in Italy. Khouma's collaboration with journalist Oreste Pivetta, for instance, involved recording oral accounts that they shaped into the written *Io, venditore di elefanti*, which was published in 1990 and translated into English in 2010, reaching wider readership. These practices often facilitate the print publication of personal narratives before the author has mastery of the Italian language and may enable the entry of migrant-authored texts into Italian literary canons.[72]

Collaborative processes also raise important questions about whose story is in fact exchanged through the vendor's labor—that is, to what extent the narrator/ protagonist represented in the text corresponds to the migrant narrator's experiences or the Italian editor's views. Unlike other books published by Giovane Africa Edizioni, *Il mio viaggio* does not include any acknowledgment of collaboration, but the process is evident in the sharp shift of tone, focus, and narratorial voice between the book's two chapters, from the personal account of Mademba's journey and interactions, to the broader social and historical context of Senegalese migration to Europe. In our interviews, Cecconi confirmed that he added the brief second chapter to contextualize Mademba's story and also to fill out the requisite number of pages per signature for printing purposes. In focusing on *Il mio viaggio* as part of a web of testimonial transactions that vendors use in their work across Italian urban spaces and tourist destinations, I'm interested in the person the book presents to readers, and I don't presume that the Mademba represented within the book corresponds to a single author named Bay Mademba. On the contrary, the book is itself part of multiple collaborative acts of witnessing and necessarily reflects the aims of the press. Identifying the narrator/editor balance is challenging, if not impossible. For the vendors I spoke with, it's also beside the point.

To vendors, the book is available as both narrative and product, offering an account they use in positioning themselves before potential customers. Cecconi told me that "everyone who sells Bay Mademba's book says, 'I am Bay Mademba. It's my story.'" If they don't assume Mademba's name, they might claim to be the author's cousin or brother. The matter of ownership here exceeds editor-author collaboration. These booksellers know the power of testimony, Cecconi said, and associate their presence as migrant vendors with the narrative recounted in the memoir. In addition, the figure of Mademba as author and narrator reflects shared ownership. Bay Mademba is, in fact, the original author's brother. According to Cecconi, the original author honored his brother and effectively dedicated the book to him via named authorship, in a sense gifting narrative ownership.[73] "Mademba" thus refers to at least two subjects, as well as others who claim ownership of the narrative. As a sales technique, claiming ownership through authorship or connections to the author positions the vendor as the one offering testimony. This sense of shared ownership, Cecconi explained, "aligns completely. [The vendors] know what they went through. . . . What they read, they relive, recounted by each other. It's not a problem." These vendors understand that narratives such as Mademba's are tellable because they are not simply individual but speak to shared experiences,[74] and they know that testimony can be a powerful means of interpersonal connection.

The memoir's collective ownership forms a critical part of the in-person transactions that facilitate the book's circulation as both product and narrative. In Florence, as in other cities, street trading is a forum in which multiple mobilities converge, as immigration, internal migration, tourism, and everyday movements meet on the streets of historic city centers. With a population of less than four hundred thousand, Florence is a relatively small city but a major tourist destination with more than twelve million visitors per year, the home of an important university, and a key site for national corporations and organizations. It also has a high cost of living, and many migrants live on the outskirts or in nearby towns, reachable via regional trains. Pontedera, where Giovane Africa Edizioni is located, is one such town.

The circulation of *Il mio viaggio*, while in one sense quite limited, is importantly marked by the convergence of the memoir's narrative and material transactions.[75] In this narrative *of* transit, about Mademba's journey from Senegal to Italy, Mademba's narrator positions interlocutors within the text and the book's readers as witnesses to the experiences he recounts. The memoir is also a compelling example of a narrative *in* transit, via local circulation that depends on an in-person exchange of conversation, product, and cash, between a migrant vendor and a (usually Italian) passerby.

## PRECARITY OUTSIDE THE BOOK

As Italy continues to manage Mediterranean arrivals as an "emergenza," it makes sense that *Il mio viaggio* has continued to be the press's best-selling book: reader-consumers seeking narratives that help them understand migrant experiences find this story through vendors who themselves made such journeys. Lamine told me that it is popular among migrants, as well, who read it while learning Italian and can recognize their own experiences in its various episodes. Texts like this one expand testimonial networks that document migrant experiences and shape public witnesses.

Yet this is a complicated witnessing role, especially if the ideal customer is someone potentially transformed by Mademba's story—that is, someone in need of persuasion. As anti-immigrant sentiment grew throughout the 2010s, the work of the press and of its vendors became more challenging. When I interviewed press editors in 2017, they were looking for new projects and excited at the prospect of more autobiographical work. By May of 2019, they had temporarily stopped publishing new books. The months between our visits had seen the rise to power of a right-wing, anti-immigrant government and accompanying shifts in public discourse. Cecconi noted that in more than two decades of living in Italy, N'Diaye "always noted this racism, but everyone [Italians/whites] kept it in." N'Diaye agreed: "They kept it frozen," she said. But things had changed. "Now . . . it's an everyday dish. . . . Before no one had the courage to say, 'I'm racist.' Today, instead, they do, there are people who say, 'I'm racist.'" The editors were concerned about Salvini's security decree, which would criminalize rescue at sea.[76] When we spoke, the decree was in its proposal stage; they worried that this criminalization would eventually affect work like theirs, preventing them from helping recently arrived migrants with legal status or employment. Acts of witnessing seemed ever more important and ever riskier.

This climate and a lack of new publications added pressure to vendors' work. The vendors I spoke with said the main challenge was that their customer base does not grow or change very quickly. They market to Italians, and once someone

FIGURE 17. "Uno a caso" ("One at random"), by Mauro Biani (www.mauro biani.it). Reproduced with the artist's permission.

has bought a book, they are unlikely to acquire a second or third copy. The men sometimes supplemented their offerings with texts from other small presses that print African-authored stories, but it remained hard to pay the bills with book sales. Some days it seemed that despite the crowds, there was no one to approach.

For the venditore ambulante, precarity in labor is also precarity of the body.[77] On March 5, 2018, the day after national elections that would put Salvini and his La Lega party in power, fifty-four-year-old Senegalese immigrant Idy Diene was shot to death on the Ponte Vespucci, the bridge in Florence where he was setting up his wares for sale—in his case, objects sold as "African souvenirs." Diene had lived in Italy since 2001. He was murdered by a white Italian who claimed to have left his house with suicidal plans, only to fire instead "randomly" at Diene (the murderer was later sentenced to thirty years in prison). Political cartoonist Mauro Biani published a panel on March 6 in the nationally circulated newspaper *Il Manifesto* that underscores the impossibility of this claim (figure 17). Depicting a small crowd of people, six white and one black and wearing a cap, words above the figures read "uno a caso" ("one at random"). The incident seems even less random when one

FIGURE 18. Memorial display for Idy Diene on the Ponte Vespucci, July 2018 (four months after his murder). Photo by the author.

considers Diene's immediate family. For Diene's widow, Rokhaya Mbengue, this was a second marriage. Her first husband, Samb Modou, was shot in Florence on December 13, 2011, by activists from the neofascist organization CasaPound.[78] This is not a bizarre coincidence. The men's visibility as street vendors did not guarantee safety or security.

Given the longer history of Senegal—Italy migration, Diene and Mbengue are not unique in having lived in Italy for nearly two decades. Diene's death made headlines in the context of the heightened anti-immigrant discourses circulating during Italian elections—and in general within "crisis" debates. Diene, though, was in a relatively stable position. He had his papers in order; his wife had recently become an Italian citizen. Florence's large Senegalese community, which has grown since the 1990s, rallied after the murder, holding public events and marches to commemorate Diene and also to speak out against racism (figure 18). One demonstrator blamed recent political rhetoric, saying, "Salvini has sold his hate throughout the country, and this is the result." Diene's nephew, a high school student in Italy, invoked colonialism in his comments to journalists about racism: "Europeans still treat us like slaves, as they did our ancestors. They consider us inferior when we come to Europe to work. They hate us because we want to live as they do."[79] These statements and demonstrations refuse empathy for Diene or his family as a finite answer and recognize Diene's murder within broader systemic violence.

Vendors' labor exemplifies the paradoxes of proximity that describe their positions in relation to Italian institutions and communities: like reception center residents held in legal limbo yet expected to "integrate," vendors who may have arrived years before move within the same spaces as Italian citizens, yet their presence is often defined by otherness. Diene's murder underscores the extent to which emergency responses to migration erase longer histories of mobility and established diasporic communities, as well as the violence to which vendors are exposed. And while the killer said he shot "someone at random," it's no coincidence that the other person on the bridge that morning was a Senegalese man setting up his wares. As an icon of undesirable foreignness in Italy, the migrant vendor also exemplifies politicized notions of deservingness that posit certain lives as outside normative society, or normative discourses, and therefore expendable. This is a manifestation of the same expendability enacted in borderzones where governments knowingly allow migrants to die in the desert or at sea or neglect them in camps.

## CONCLUSION: VENDORS AMID EMERGENCY

While this chapter has focused primarily on Senegalese ambulant vendors in Tuscany, the venditore ambulante is a common job for border crossers of many backgrounds and a widely racialized icon of foreignness throughout Italy. Amid ongoing emergenze, this work and the forms of fugitive witnessing it involves are a survival strategy for many migrants, and as Operation Safe Beaches showed, it remains a case through which migrants are criminalized.

Vendors might also attend pro-migrant demonstrations to sell their wares to sympathetic crowds. I acquired additional books at such events in Rome until I learned that police were targeting vendors among the crowds of pro-migrant marchers. One especially hot summer afternoon in 2018, after a demonstration in the city center, I made my way back to Tiburtina station and the Piazzale Maslax camp I discuss in chapter 3. The demonstration followed the murder of Malian farmworker and labor union organizer Soumaila Sacko. The crowd was substantial; L'Unione Sindacale di Base, a national union, had brought demonstrators in busses from several other regions (figure 19). We walked from Piazza della Repubblica to Piazza San Giovanni—not an especially long walk but one that, with thousands of marchers stopping to chant and listen to speeches, can take a couple of hours.

Back at Piazzale Maslax, I sat with a few residents near the camp entrance. After a while, three men from Bangladesh showed up and approached us. One of them held out a piece of paper. He didn't live at the camp; the other two had suggested that this might be a place where he could seek help. They asked in English for help reading an Italian document.

FIGURE 19. Demonstration in Rome following the murder of Soumaila Sacko, 2018. Photo by the author.

It turned out that during the demonstration, this man had carted water through the crowd, selling cold bottles for €1—a common-enough sight. He was stopped by police, who asked to see his papers. From what I could make out from our exchange—a kind of telephone chain of interpretation between Bengali, Italian, and English, with some commentary in French from others sitting nearby—the man's initial asylum claim had already been rejected. He hadn't known what to do and didn't have his documents with him at the demonstration—not that they would have made a difference. At the station, they issued him a two-sided document. What does it say? He wanted to know. He was almost hopeful, as they hadn't arrested him. Did the paper have another court date? A new possibility?

Yousef, seated near me, glanced over the paper but struggled to make sense of it. I took a look and saw that each Italian paragraph was in fact translated into English directly beneath. Still, the Italian and English versions both read like a foreign language—a succession of "whereas" clauses, incredibly difficult to follow. It was the second page, I realized, that mattered: there, at the end of the document, was the order to leave.

I had not held a *foglio di via*, "leave papers," before then. It seemed such a cruel act: issuing papers demanding that a person vacate a country without bothering to tell him what the papers said. The withholding of language illustrates how emergency responses to migration impose severe limits on witnessing, in this case by masking the very meaning of the document itself. And yet the document still seemed so long, nearly two pages, and was handed without explanation to a person for whom the return home appeared unfathomable. A person who, minutes before, had been selling water on the street in order to afford a meal. We put the man in touch with lawyers who volunteer with Baobab and who would try to push back against the order.

The street vendor as a racialized symbol of undesirable foreignness has persisted over periods of massive change in immigration policy and bordering practices. The once circular migrations with which migrants came to Italy for seasonal labor, then returned home, are now only possible for European Union residents. Periodic regularization of migrants throughout more than three decades of emergency-response legislation should evince the constructed nature of legal categories, especially given Italy's clear dependence on migrant labor,[80] but the emphasis on "crisis" as the fault of "economic migrants" prevails. Through witnessing, the vendor participates in reimagining mobility and belonging beyond these binaries, as Mademba's memoir illustrates. Yet the work of reframing and shifting narratives remains challenging.

The Italian context aligns with wider shifts throughout the global north. Tightened borders and criminalizing rhetorics have gradually "fragmented" the figure of the refugee,[81] supplanted by the securitization of borders and the illegalization of migration. The vendor exemplifies how these shifts affect people's everyday movements, regardless of their legal status. In the next chapter, I consider uses of witnessing that center mobility to instead reimagine our relationship to urban spaces.

# 5

# Seen and Unseen in the City

Precarious migration in Italy is often treated as a crisis of space. Mainstream news pushes invasion narratives, making it seem as if boats are arriving on all sides of the peninsula, delivering crowds who overwhelm the country. Rome's Mayor Virginia Raggi repeatedly claimed Rome could not tolerate the "continual flow of foreign citizens."[1] In mid-2017, Raggi imposed a moratorium on migrant arrivals to the city and, soon after, approved the eviction of eight hundred to one thousand residents of a building they were occupying near the central area of Piazza dell'Indipendenza (see map 3).[2] Most of the residents were refugees and asylum seekers from Eritrea and Ethiopia. On August 17, forced to abandon the building but not given alternative accommodations, they occupied the piazza. On August 19, police dressed in riot gear and armed with hoses dispersed the crowd. Photos of this incident are still used today in articles about Rome's *emergenza abitativa*, or "housing crisis"—a reminder that the emergency apparatus of migration does not operate in isolation. Following the police intervention, authorities offered shelter to only 80 of the building's former residents. At least thirteen migrants required medical treatment for injuries. Unhoused, many made their way to improvised settlements, including Piazzale Maslax.[3]

The building's residents included survivors of the October 3, 2013, wreck that in many ways initiated Europe's recent "migration crisis" period.[4] Following that wreck, which I discuss in chapter 1, global sympathy poured out for Mediterranean migrants, and Italy announced the Mare Nostrum military-humanitarian operation for surveillance and rescue at sea. For survivors, arrival in Italy was the opposite of clandestine: they were contacted by news crews and politicians, and the wreck seemed to mark a turning point in policy and public sentiment.

Still, they had ended up in the occupied building and now, four years later, they were again displaced, treated without concern for their rights, needs, or histories.

Despite that access to housing is crucial for newcomers to develop stability, secure work, and care for loved ones, emergency responses to migration have folded migrant housing into Italy's larger emergenza abitativa.[5] The denial of accommodations is perplexing in a country with a famously low birthrate and significant emigration. Recent years have seen, simultaneously, ports closed to migrants from the global south and real estate campaigns hawking €1 homes in small towns to Western tourists. Some cities have promoted a culture of welcoming—Palermo is a good example—but in the capital, the refusal to accommodate more migrants was matched by the simultaneous policing of occupied spaces, as I elaborate in chapter 3 in the case of Baobab Experience. These practices align notions of spatial crisis with discourses of security and cleanliness, suggesting that housing migrants disrupts public decorum.

These violent evictions are framed as crisis solutions but in fact perpetuate conditions of extreme precarity, underscoring how the emergency apparatus leaves migrants in transit, without a stable footing, even years after they have disembarked on European shores. In addition, the Piazza dell'Indipendenza sgombero (eviction), like the many sgomberi that clear unofficial camps, produced a spectacle that portrays migrants as "illegal" and literally out of place. In other words, the emergency apparatus draws a thick border around the nation and national identity, excluding migrants from former colonies from its "social and symbolic boundaries."[6] The refusal to accommodate asylum seekers is directly linked to the refusal to consider the stranger as a potential citizen. Upholding the idea that culture and identity are fixed, rather than in flux, these emergency imaginaries also presuppose that non-Christian migrants and nonwhite Italians do not or cannot possess full cultural fluency. That is, their knowledge of Italian spaces is not recognized as having currency, let alone authority.

Yet precarity is also a site of activism. As Maribel Casas-Cortés has discussed in the context of social movements throughout Southern Europe, people operating within precarity are also actively theorizing their circumstances and efforts and challenging dominant discourses that marginalize their experiences.[7] In line with this understanding, this chapter shows how the movements of migrants and G2 Italians (seconde generazioni, or second generations), disrupt whitewashed, heteronormative notions of identity and citizenship.[8] As they intersect with the movements of citizens and tourists and draw attention to the longer histories of mobility inscribed into monuments, street names, businesses, and the people who frequent them, they make transnational Italy newly visible. By claiming a right to the city, and the right to remain, they also redefine citizenship outside the strict, exclusionary bounds of the national frame.

Citizenship has a fraught place in narratives of precarious migration, as a legal status that reifies the nation whose border governance renders some journeys especially precarious. In Italy, citizenship remains a matter of ongoing political debate and a site where racial politics play out on a national stage.[9] Italy's *jus sanguinis*, or bloodline, stipulation famously allows the grandchildren of Italian emigrants abroad to claim Italian citizenship but makes naturalization for more recent immigrants and their Italian-born children incredibly difficult and sometimes impossible.[10] Meanwhile, emergency responses to migration treat migrants and their children as here temporarily. Despite their supposed focus on "integration," Italian and EU-level policies offer little in the way of imagining or enabling a long-term future for the country, or for the EU, that genuinely includes those born elsewhere and their Italian-born children and grandchildren.

Yet, as migration and border studies scholars have long noted, citizenship is not an exclusively legal phenomenon but also a collective practice.[11] Engin Isin and Greg Neilsen call this "substantive," as opposed to legal, citizenship, articulated not through a singular person or static identity, but through "acts of citizenship," or "collective or individual deeds that rupture social-historical patterns."[12] This chapter focuses on acts of citizenship that describe belonging in relation to specific urban geographies. I take up witnessing texts and practices through which people marginalized as migrant others or marked as noncitizens claim a right to the city, not only through their presence in it but by establishing forms of authority on its cultural practices and histories. I discuss three cases based in Rome in which migrants and Italians of African descent who are treated as "foreigners in their own country"[13] use forms of witnessing to establish their authority on its spaces, and therefore their right to move within them. The *Guide Invisibili*, or Invisible Guides, is a soundwalk initiative in which migrant narrators lead participants through central neighborhoods, retelling Roman history through their own experiences in the city and in their home countries. I then turn to the work of Somali-Italian author Igiaba Scego, which returns colonial memory to a broad Italian, and increasingly global, readership. And in the city periphery, at the occupied site of Metropoliz, residents claim the right to the city via a politics of survival that includes their transformation of an abandoned space into a museum.

These cases move us between multiple spaces—public, monumental, occupied—and enact belonging in the city through what Michel de Certeau describes as "spatial practices."[14] My engagement of urban sites builds on de Certeau's understanding of the city as constructed through movement, and of places as comprised of "fragmentary and inward-turning histories" and "accumulated times that can be unfolded but like stories held in reserve."[15] Acts of citizenship reenvision the city through narrative and embodied experiences that lift these multiple story fragments and temporalities to the surface.

As with the vendors I discuss in chapter 4, these witnesses are not peripheral figures simply working for their own survival. They are key witnesses of contemporary Italian life whose spatial practices make apparent the construction of society around (in)visible geographical, legal, cultural, and historical borders. But their translocal, transhistorical narratives and practices also call those same national frames into question. Their testimonies, produced for a range of audiences, exemplify what Isin and Neilsen describe as the normative ruptures that acts of citizenship make possible.

By bearing witness to their experiences in Rome, these guides, narrators, and curators enact substantive citizenship and position audiences to witness the city in ways that disrupt emergency imaginaries of foreignness. In the process, they redefine who curates, who visits, and who possesses the capacity to create cultural sites in a city both celebrated for its art and architecture and constantly battling the so-called crises of housing and migration. They also disrupt the expectation that embracing the right to the city means assimilating into normative life.[16] Aligned with the understanding that identity is "perpetually under construction,"[17] these projects refute the presumption that migrants and outsiders should aspire to assimilate; instead, they suggest that genuine recognition of the right to remain, and freedom of movement within urban space, requires that all residents and visitors reconsider their relationship to its geographies, histories, and ongoing construction. The following examples function on a relatively small scale, and I am interested in the intimacy of these gestures. They are nevertheless critical illustrations of how acts of citizenship invoke a person's belonging by demonstrating their fluency in a space, including practices by migrants who "actively create a new situation, a new social reality."[18]

## LISTENING TO THE CITY

In the soundwalk project Guide Invisibili (Invisible Guides), migrants exercise the right to the city by narrating soundwalks through central neighborhoods, flipping the script on assumptions about who can be a tour guide and who possesses cultural fluency in an ancient city like Rome. This grassroots initiative was founded by Italian Marco Stefanelli, himself a transplant to Rome from the Calabria region, along with collaborators at Laboratorio 53, housed in the *centro sociale* (autonomous community center) Città dell'Utopia. The multivocal soundwalks feature guides self-described as "new citizens." Participants listen to the prerecorded hour-long tours via the intimacy of headphones while moving through the winding cobblestone streets of Trastevere or past vendors near Termini station. Migrant author-narrator-guides direct listeners from place to place, mixing their own stories and memories with historical information about the areas through which the tour passes.

The Invisible Guides soundwalks are acts of citizenship that emerge through acts of witnessing. That is, centering the often-marginalized voices and experiences of migrants, and structuring the recorded narrative around the physical space through which participants move, these soundwalks bear witness to multiple experiences of belonging and moving in the city, with testimony emerging through the transactions of narrator and listener-participant.[19] This is not simply a case of migrant narrators sharing perspectives on Rome that participants might find interesting; in these soundwalks, narrators position participants to reenvision the city and participants' own places within it. Here sound and movement join in a spatial practice that constructs the city and gives it meaning as participants transit its streets.[20] This is especially significant because, as Black studies scholars have argued, projects that attempt to challenge marginalization by appealing for recognition within given frameworks or grammars—of freedom, or of the nation-state—can reify oppression. Hartman states this directly in a conversation with Frank Wilderson about blackness, subjectivity, and racialized positionality: "So much of our political vocabulary/imaginary/desires have been implicitly integrationist even when we imagine our claims are more radical." What Hartman elaborates in the US context resonates in the context of Africa-Europe migration: "Ultimately the metanarrative thrust is always towards an integration into the national project, and particularly when that project is in crisis, black people are called upon to affirm it."[21] To imagine belonging outside emergency imaginaries of foreignness is to disrupt the push for assimilation into the heteronormative nation and the linear, whitewashed narratives of its own development. What other ways of knowing and moving in the city shape its communities and spaces?

Near the beginning of the Monti neighborhood tour, a narrator named Amadou Doumbia from Côte d'Ivoire directs listeners' attention to a door in Via delle Sette Sale. "That's the entrance for the *mensa*," a cafeteria run by the Caritas charity. He describes how glad he was to learn about this soup kitchen in the city center; otherwise he would have had to stay close to the reception center where he lived, which is ten kilometers away. Tourists—Italian and foreign alike—who may have meandered the streets of Monti to shop the boutiques or in search of a traditional trattoria are unlikely to have realized the significance of this address for Rome's poor and migrant residents. Like other migrant-led tour initiatives across Europe—for instance, Berlin's Refugee Voices walking tours, or Amsterdam's Lampedusa Cruises, canal tours on recovered migrant vessels—the Invisible Guides offer an alternative to the standard city tour, distinguishing themselves for their use of personal testimony and their centering of mobility to make racial and class disparities visible elements of these landscapes.[22] Unlike both standard tours and other migrant-led walks, the Invisible Guides soundwalks play overtly with elements of (in)visibility; via headsets, narrators like Doumbia offer listener-participants an intimate experience in which they are closely guided and in a sense on their own to take in the city—and their place in it—through new perspectives.

Rome thrives on both domestic and international tourism, with more than nine million international visitors per year (pre–COVID-19). The capital city is a key site in "Destination Italy" and the romanticized version of Italian history and culture it embraces.[23] As participants witness the city through migrants' words, the tour sets in motion a series of testimonial transactions that challenge pervasive racism and xenophobia. They do so by positioning authors not simply as present but as guides in spaces associated with the idealized Italy of *La Dolce Vita* (e.g., the Trevi Fountain) or "authentic" Italian neighborhoods (as in the area of Trastevere)—spaces in which refugees are generally seen as out of place. Although the Guide Invisibili initiative operates at a relatively small scale, it hosted more than two thousand participants in its first two years and continues to reach audiences through six Italian- and English-language tours. Participants include everyone from locals to people visiting Italy for the first time; Italian and foreign school and university groups; even, at least once, a group of police officers.[24]

Many of the invisible guides themselves arrived by sea after 2014, in the years of Europe's recent "migration crisis." Their own journeys inform the soundwalks, but these accounts avoid linear narratives. Instead, they weave memories from childhood, the journey, and life in Italy into the city tour, suggesting resonances across specific places and moments. By engaging space transnationally and translocally, the soundwalks subvert the ways in which, as McKittrick has argued, "the placement of subaltern bodies deceptively hardens spatial binaries, in turn suggesting that some bodies belong, some bodies do not belong, and some bodies are out of place."[25] The experiences of tour authors, many of whom are awaiting a decision on their asylum claim when they record, are not generally recognized as part of the social fabric in the historic, central areas where they offer tours. Yet in these tours, they are not only present in the city, they are guides, directing participants through historic spaces. In this way, the Invisible Guides also exemplify one answer to the critical question Vang raises for critical refugee studies scholars: "How can we map refugee presence without relying on the very humanitarian data that present them as objects of rescue?"[26] In the case of these narrators, autobiographical and collectively produced narratives refute migrant categorization and reenvision the city itself.

In some soundwalks, narrators present their familiarity with a particular neighborhood, as in the Monti tour, which begins with several migrant narrators who describe meeting other migrants at the Colle Oppio park by the Colosseum, or sometimes sleeping there. Other tours highlight the division of Rome's public and touristic spaces between locals, tourists, and migrants. In welcoming listener-participants to the Spanish Steps tour, Ghanaian guide Abdul asks participants to notice that the area is filled with "foreigners," but hardly any "migrants like me": "Look around again. Do you see African faces? Do you see any migrants like me? Here the foreigners are tourists: Germans, Americans, Chinese."[27] His comment reflects pervasive perceptions of Black subjects as outsiders in Italian spaces, in ways accentuated by class difference.

At the same time, he also stakes claims on Italian belonging: "How do I know there are rich people here? Because they can leave their countries and come here to Italy on holidays and go back home. I can't go back. That's why I am Italian by now." Like other narrators, Abdul emphasizes how his position differs from those of tourists and expats. Later in the tour, another narrator, Ali, explains, "But in Europe it is different. Here we often feel rejected for our skin, for our color. Many of us want to become Italian. We want to perceive ourself as Italian. In the reception center, when someone wins his documents, he says he has become Italian." These claims to Italianness concern the nature of the narrators' mobility, their legal status, and a sense of identity linking them to the physical spaces of the nation. In addition to these direct claims to belonging, narrators' navigation of the city as guides marks their fluency in Italian spaces via their own curiosities and memories. Their authority is a form of substantive citizenship. It is, crucially, also never simply about the singular nation or its borders but about transnational movement and transhistorical memory.

These narratives are always negotiations, as narrators determine what to tell and how to tell it in line with what their potential audiences may find persuasive.[28] In general, migrants' marginal status is reinforced by their association with nonmonumental, nontouristic spaces, including reception centers, tent cities, and occupied buildings in more peripheral locations, or the rural camps where they live while working the harvest.[29] As I discuss in the previous chapter, the popular imagination often recognizes migrants within city centers and touristic spaces only through the figure of the ambulant vendor. The racialization of this figure in the Italian imaginary relegates Black African and South Asian migrants in particular to either unseen or hypervisible status, their presence largely ignored or treated as a nuisance in the dominant cultural landscape. The Invisible Guides project subverts these tropes by centering the very invisibility of "new citizens." Present during the tours primarily through the audio recording rather than physically, the guides call attention to how Italian legal and social systems "overdetermine" their otherness and effectively invisibilize them from mainstream society and from dominant ideas about who belongs in the places through which the tour passes.[30]

Participants join a tour by registering in advance and learning when and where to meet up with the guides (figure 20). I myself first heard about the tours from a Roman friend and learned more at the centro sociale Città dell'Utopia, where the tours are produced. For the Spanish Steps soundwalk, two guides met our set of about twelve participants by the Barcaccia fountain, introduced themselves, handed each of us an iPod, divided us into three smaller groups—I assume for less conspicuous wandering—and then disappeared. I followed the soundwalk with two other women—one Italian, one Argentinian—and as a group, we donned headphones and coordinated hitting the "play" button to begin. We moved slowly through the neighborhood, following the audio directions about where to look, when to stop, what sounds to pay attention to. As we wandered from Piazza di Spagna to just past the Trevi Fountain, we encountered the guides only a few

FIGURE 20. Flyer for the Invisible Guides soundwalks. Photo by Ginevra Sammartino for Guide Invisibili. Reproduced with permission.

times: at the beginning; at the end, to collect the iPods and tips and facilitate a brief reflection session; and once in the middle, when my trio got a bit turned around.

Yet multiple guides shaped our walk. As tours proceed, when one narrator finishes their story, they instruct participants where to walk next, and another narrator carries on the tour. Over the course of an hour-long soundwalk, participants hear from six or seven narrators from multiple countries; most are African men, from West Africa in particular, but the soundwalks also include women's voices and narrators from the Middle East. On the Monti tour, for example, two Syrian-Palestinian sisters describe how their experience fleeing the war in Syria made them closer, and how they navigate being young Muslim women in Italy, where many people treat the hijab with suspicion. On all soundwalks, narrators link the spatial and the personal, using neighborhood sites as a cue to present an aspect of their own story, for instance letting participants know why migrants frequent a particular address, or how the detail of a façade reminds them of a structure in the town where they grew up. There is no single formula for these recordings, which narrators produce together with Italian facilitators through a series of oral history, writing, and sound editing workshops.[31] In the Monti soundwalk, narrators focus primarily on details from the history of their home country, recalled as they move down Rome's Via dei Serpenti. The Spanish Steps tour instead includes a significant amount of Roman history.

The tour's enactment via the transaction of recorded tour and individual listener both documents narrators' experiences and perspectives *and* positions listener-participants to reconfigure their own relationship with urban space. It is an act of co-constructing the city, in line with Doreen Massey's notion of place as "woven together out of ongoing stories, as a moment within power-geometries, as a particular constellation within wider topographies of space, and as in process, as unfinished business."[32] In this way, the soundwalks illustrate understandings of testimony as an intersubjective form that differs for each participant, including that it emerges in relation to the contingency of ambient sounds, the presence of other people, the movement of traffic, despite moving along the "same" route.[33]

Two aspects make this especially salient. First, the soundwalk narrative unfolds via headphones in what Peter Salvatore Petralia terms "headspace,"[34] which blurs the boundaries between participants' thoughts and senses and the space through which they move. Listener-participants simultaneously inhabit the space they see and the space evoked by narrators' words and memories. Second, narrators are not the primary object of attention; rather, via headspace, they help listener-participants see the city. This avoids what could otherwise be a kind of fetishizing exercise, were guides the (visible) focus of the tours.[35] The soundwalks are not an exercise in producing compassion for the (objectified) tour guide, but in repositioning the self through the experience of witnessing the city through multiple voices and memories, constantly aware, too, of one's own position in space. In this way, walkers might engage Rome as a space in flux rather than as the site of fixed narratives and identities. This matters in creating the conditions of possibility for reconfiguring understandings of belonging and the entanglements of past and present.

In reenvisioning the city, narrators carve out space for themselves as "address-able and response-able" citizen-subjects, and they center belonging as co-constructed and relational, and rights as, in part, participatory processes of social transformation. This makes it important to read the project not in terms of the cultivation of empathy across difference but as an exercise of citizenship and the right to the city. In other words, the guides' subjectivity and belonging do not come into being because tourists or white Italians "recognize" them. To invoke bell hooks, "We are not looking to that Other for recognition. We are recognizing ourselves and willingly making contact with all who would engage us in a constructive manner."[36] As I learned from a conversation with a guide named Efe, the collaborative process of producing the tours is as important to many guides as the "live" tours themselves.

The resulting recordings narrate Rome through personal and collective histories that inscribe Europe's colonial past within Roman spaces, for instance when one narrator notes that when Rome's Galleria Sciarra was constructed, "in those same years, France was occupying my country." The soundwalks employ oral testimony and aural and visual witnessing to write invisibilized stories into lived, popular, touristic spaces, becoming visible in ways that potentially transform listeners' engagement with the city, its famous and familiar sites, and its residents. These listening practices recognize migrants' personal histories, including the journeys that brought them to Italy, without utilizing emergency and crisis frames. For instance, narrators in both the Colle Oppio and Piazza di Spagna tours make multiple references to sea crossing and to traumatic experiences that prompted their initial departure, or that they survived while traveling—but the soundwalks' focus on Roman neighborhood landmarks refuses to define narrators' presence in Italy through the experience of arrival. Instead, these testimonies acknowledge that experience but focus on moving through the city itself, as a shared space with multiple overlapping histories.

As asylum seekers, narrators also present an unexpected portrait of refugeeness: not outsiderness or exception, and not assimilation, but authority, knowledge, and curation that do not simply recount familiar history but retell and reshape those histories. The cultural authority that migrants perform through their narrations is a form of fluency, both in the sense of expertise and also of fluidity and flow, as the soundwalk produces testimonial transactions.[37] The acts of witnessing that unfold across headphones and physical space construct the city by "enunciating" it[38] through narrators' and participants' "chorus" of movement, in de Certeau's terms.[39] The soundwalks also illustrate invisibility as both a problem and a strategy, as narrators use their imposed invisibility to challenge "conventional boundaries such as citizenship, sovereignty, colonialism, modernity, representational regimes, identity, and language."[40] Moreover, the soundwalks illustrate our relationship with space as constructed through movement and memory, implicitly challenging the notions of cultural and historical fixity that can enable racist, dehistoricized, exclusionary practices. Soundwalks as lived experience make the ubiquity of borderzones visible and audible.[41] They also reveal these borderzones to be both transnational and translocal, enabling "ways of understanding the overlapping place-time(s) in migrants' everyday lives" as well as a kind of "'groundedness' during movement."[42]

In material terms, the soundwalks offer an alternative way of (re)encountering Rome and questioning what belonging there might look—or sound—like. Sometimes this is done by highlighting particular frictions in the urbanscape. The Spanish Steps tour ends, for instance, by moving participants from the Trevi Fountain to wrap up outside the nearby questura office—police headquarters where immigrants register, in an office that tourists might not even notice but that, in practical terms, everyone knows must exist. As Baldwin says of the artist as witness, "You're bearing witness helplessly to something which everybody knows and nobody wants to face."[43] These stories are not secrets, but unheard and often unasked for. (Re)centering them is the risk and the point.

## MAPPING THE CITY

The work of Somali-Italian writer Igiaba Scego offers another example of testimony that braids histories together to prompt audiences to reenvision their own positions in the city. A "second generation," or G2, writer born in Rome whose parents fled Somalia in the 1970s, Scego works to combat racism and pushes for changes to Italy's citizenship laws.[44] Across her oeuvre, encounters with specific monuments and neighborhoods remind readers that G2 and migrant issues are linked and illustrate the set of social and historical entanglements that Camilla Hawthorne describes as "Black Mediterranean diasporic politics."[45]

Scego focuses on Italian identity itself as heterogeneous, and collective memory is the subject of much of her work, in particular the widespread silence among Italian publics and institutions regarding the country's colonial past and its influence on the present. While France and Germany have conducted some form of reckoning with the past, however limited, in Italy "instead silence reigned, accompanied by a solid dose of delusion."[46] This topic is central in *La mia casa è dove sono* (*My Home is Where I Am*, the 2010 memoir that I cite in chapter 1 in the context of a funeral scene). There, she writes,

> In many [other countries] after World War Two there was discussion, squabbling, the views exchanged were bitter and impetuous; societies interrogated themselves about imperialism and its crimes; studies were published; the debate influenced literary production, research, film, music. In Italy, instead, silence. As if nothing had happened.[47]

This silence feeds emergency imaginaries, which position the subjects of former colonies as unrecognizable foreigners—strangers whose arrival to Italian coasts is framed in dominant narratives as a question of African vulnerability, African crisis, or African threats. Migrants and Italians of African descent are presumed to have no connection to Europe or Italy, and no relation to national publics, presumed to be a (white) homogeneous collective with a linear history.

At the same time, Scego draws critical connections across these borders, not limiting her appeal in ways that reify nationalisms. Writing for weekly news magazine *Internazionale* during the uprisings of 2020, following the murder of George Floyd in Minneapolis, Scego charged Italian readers to pay attention to the toppling of confederate monuments in the United States: "Fighting for the bodily safety of people of African descent has always been intimately linked to care for the body of the city, and therefore of a country. . . . Urban space is not neutral."[48]

Today's arrivals could well prompt a reckoning among Italian publics with the country's colonial history, but emergency imaginaries mask this past. This colonial aphasia positions publics to view those from former colonies now arriving to Italian shores as if out of nowhere, possessing what El-Tayeb has described as

> a flat, one-dimensional existence in which she or he always has just arrived, thus existing only in the present, but like a time traveler simultaneously hailing from a culture that is centuries (or in the case of Africa, millennia) behind, thus making him or her the representative of a past without connection to or influence on the host society's history.[49]

In *European Others*, El-Tayeb explains the "alternative community building" that emerges from these erasures and exclusions as "queering ethnicity," and writers like Scego certainly participate in these processes.[50] Scego's writing reckons with historical erasures and becomes a site "from which to transmit traumatic memory, forge cultural identity, and re-narrate national history."[51] In both her 2010 memoir *La mia casa è dove sono* and the 2014 collaborative book *Roma negata*, Scego portrays Rome's historic center as a postcolonial space, moving readers through the city and prompting readers to question their own relationship to particular sites, and their understanding of Italian history. Like the Guide Invisibili, Scego's narrators invite audiences to become witnesses to their place in these histories through a reencounter with urban space. As works of "literary witnessing,"[52] *La mia casa* and *Roma negata* use the possibilities of autobiographical writing to enact the transactions of testimony between narrator, reader, and additional witnesses.

*La mia casa* unfolds as a map; each chapter is built around a key site in Rome that anchors a discussion of entangled history and Scego's own understanding of self and home.[53] Scego's life in the Italian capital is shaped by her experiences growing up in its neighborhoods and schools—a reminder that G2 youth are themselves reshaping Italian spaces and notions of belonging, their presence marked in quotidian routines like the route to school, as well as through activist practice. Scego's life in Rome is also shaped by her family's relationship with Somalia, by

Italy's colonial relationship with Somalia, and by racism in Italy, which she experiences through encounters in which she is marked as other in the country of her birth. We learn early on that, following Siad Barre's rise to power and his attacks on dissidents in 1969, Scego's parents fled the country in political exile, reaching Rome. Broadly, the book moves from Igiaba's birth in Rome in the mid-1970s to Somalia's civil war in the 1990s (I use "Igiaba" to refer to the narrated persona and "Scego" to the author). Yet the book's memory work is primarily spatial, not chronological: the narrative is organized most overtly around specific sites, moving between Rome and Somalia (primarily Mogadishu) and finds form through their resonances in multiple historical moments. For Igiaba, Rome's colonial and imperial monuments speak loudly, rendering the city a living map of the long histories joining Europe and Africa—an archive of imperial formations that are both physical and psychological, "slash[ing] a scar across a social fabric that differentially affects us all."[54] She writes from within this context of duress that affects all who live there, shaping how white Italians see Scego and how she sees herself.

The memoir is, in one sense, a series of acts of excavation: Scego's narrator moves between physical sites to access her own memories of specific incidents and the intergenerational memory that informs her understanding of the present. As she narrates her long walks through the city, Igiaba essentially educates readers about Italy's presence in Somalia, from colonial rule in the late nineteenth century, to Italy's post–World War II protectorate role leading up to 1960 independence.[55] In addition, she forwards a critical discussion of Italian identity as multivalenced and shifting. Throughout *La mia casa*, Scego utilizes the autobiographical form to "expand the limits of what it means to acknowledge and grieve the losses of history."[56] In testifying to her own experiences as a Black Italian woman, she reveals how the country's lack of reckoning with colonial history and its related emergency imaginaries construe people in positions like hers as foreign in the city of their birth.

Scego's work exemplifies a key cultural turn in twenty-first-century Italy, where writers and artists of African descent have worked to highlight how urban space already contains the histories often displaced from collective historical consciousness. Since the early 2000s, Scego's novels, short stories, essays, and autobiographical writing have illustrated how multiple mobilities and temporalities intersect to construct Italy in transnational terms. In an environment in which work by Italian writers of African descent is forever categorized as "migrant literature," national and international recognition of Scego's work matters. Nominated in 2023 for the prestigious national literary prize Premio Strega for her autobiographical novel *Cassandra a Mogadiscio* (*Casssandra in Mogadishu*), Scego has, together with writers like Ubah Cristina Ali Farah and Gabriella Ghermandi, carved out a place for Italian writers of African descent within mainstream literary circuits both within Italy and abroad.[57] Scego's writing has been translated into at least nine languages. The circulation and reception of her work is understandably different than that of

Bay Mademba, whose small press memoir I discuss in the previous chapter as a testimony shared on a small scale as a physical product supporting the livelihoods of migrant vendors. Of course, Scego's narratives also differ because she writes from her position in the G2 movement; Mademba, instead, emphasizes his foreign birth and upbringing. Where Mademba draws connections across Senegalese and Italian spaces to underscore the coloniality of racial politics, Scego is interested in making readers see Italy itself as a postcolonial space.

*Roma negata* (2014), for which Scego collaborated with photographer Rino Bianchi, is in many ways a visual companion to the memoir, extended to other migrant and G2 subjects. Text by Scego appears alongside Bianchi's portraits of immigrant and G2 Italians with heritage in the Horn of Africa standing before different spaces in Rome, including some of the same sites so critical to *La mia casa*. Scego has described *Roma negata* as creating new living monuments, as it were—posing people in front of these colonial monuments and traces. In the portraits, Italian-Ethiopian model and actor Tezeta Abraham gazes up at the top of the fence that surrounds the Palazzo della Civiltà Italiana, a building that serves as a monument to "Italian civilization," erected under Mussolini and inaugurated in 1940. Director Amin Nour stands on a small block of concrete as if a statue on a plinth outside Termini station, in Piazza dei Cinquecento, an area often misremembered and miscited by Italians who assume it is Piazza *del* Cinquecento, or Renaissance Square, rather than the square of the five hundred, named for the Italian victims in the Battle of Dogali. Filmmaker Dagmawi Yimer stands outside the building of the former Ministry of the Colonies. In the accompanying text, Scego narrates these sites through their often untold histories, including that immigration between the Horn of Africa and Italy has been continuous since the 1970s, as today's migrants include large numbers of Somalis and Eritreans.

The now infamous wreck of October 3, 2013, becomes a critical example of how colonial aphasia shapes public responses to migrants' presence in Italy, and to deaths in crossing:

> On 3 October 2013, the Mediterranean Sea swallowed 369 Eritreans, women, children, young men. All the dreams of those people shipwrecked in that cold and inhospitable sea. But no major newspaper wrote, "Those boys, those girls, those children are ours." The historical link between Italy and Eritrea wasn't felt or recognized. Faced with this terrible tragedy, Italy never declared its historic responsibility towards Eritrea. Everything has been silenced, forgotten, erased. And if the asylum seekers of Somalia and Eritrea know about this connection, Italy does not want to know anything about it. . . . In fact, the device of colonial racism in Italy has never been dismantled.[58]

Here the links between history and the present, colonial violence and contemporary border deaths and anti-immigrant racism, could not be clearer. Racism is a colonial device, a technology employed in the present as migrant deaths are ignored and migrants continue to be excluded from the Italian national body.

In her elaboration of the wake, Sharpe describes this violence as "dehuman-ing": not *dehumanizing,* as if an attribute that could be assigned or removed, but *dehumaning,* as in the removal of the human from a body, a space, a history.[59] With this in mind, we might understand a project like *Roma negata* as *re*-humaning—returning real bodies and lived experiences to accounts of history and to the present. This is what I mean when I refer to Scego's life writing as an act of citizenship: to underscore the extent to which it disrupts normative notions of belonging.[60]

Embodied in the portraits and spelled out in the text, this retracing of colo-niality within present-day spaces, like in *La mia casa,* charges Italian readers to reconsider their own positions in these spaces and in relation to those they pre-sume to be outsiders. Those who, like me, read these works as foreigners with passports that let us come and go with ease are also invited into these processes, to see Rome not only through the romanticized lenses of Destination Italy. While colonial violence may have unfolded largely outside of today's Italian national bor-ders, the records of those campaigns and their inscription into dominant narra-tives of identity and race have literally shaped Italian cities. Monuments, street names, and buildings stand as present-day imperial formations. Streets like Viale Libia, Rome's Quartiere Africano (African neighborhood), monuments to Italians killed in the Battle of Dogali against Ethiopian forces, and language of empire that appears in business names and popular songs all present opportunities to remem-ber the disregarded colonial past and to recognize its continued influence on the present. Yet, as Scego writes in *Roma negata,* "The city's colonial sites are left in the void (Axum), uncared for (Dogali), misunderstood (African Neighborhood). What's too uncomfortable is erased. It's uncomfortable for Italy to admit to having been racist. It's uncomfortable to admit that today's racism has strong roots in the racism of the past."[61]

Here the city of Rome appears as a colonial archive in which people's daily movements are shaped by encounters with such monuments—and by the modi-fication and erasure of their significance. This is a kind of spatial practice that transfers from the page to lived geographies. Urban space itself is a reminder that multiple Africa-Europe mobilities have shaped Italy as a nation—and that Italy is a transnational space in flux, a site of diaspora, linked to diasporic spaces across borders. Monuments like the Dogali statue have inscribed urban space itself with narratives of "italiani brava gente," writing colonialism into collective memory as a time of Italian generosity toward those it colonized. Such sites, Scego argues, should not be celebrated but are instead tangible reminders that "Africa has been important not only historically, but in Italian daily life."[62] In line with this claim, a clear aim of the work is to establish witnessing relations that prompt read-ers' reengagement with familiar spaces and a reconsideration of their relationship with or within diasporic communities in Italy, and perhaps their role as "impli-cated subjects" who, by virtue of various forms of social privilege, "help propagate the legacies of historical violence and prop up the structures of inequality that mar the present."[63]

Like other wake work that makes the Black Mediterranean present for multiple publics, this memory work is nonlinear and layered. One clear example involves Piazza di Porta Capena, which features in both *La mia casa* and *Roma negata*. This piazza near Rome's Circus Maximus is a (post)colonial site that links Italy and the Horn of Africa. The Stele of Axum, an obelisk originally from Axum, in modern-day Ethiopia, stood there from 1937 to 2005. It's one of several monuments that anchor Scego's portrayal of blackness and African heritage within italianità, and of diaspora as reflecting complex histories and multiple emergent identities.[64] The monument was seized by Mussolini's troops in 1937 and brought to Rome, then returned to Ethiopia nearly seven decades later.

Recounting these movements in *La mia casa*, Scego illustrates a web of relations between Fascist-era colonialism, Rome's geographies, and her own position as a Black Italian woman. When Italian authorities finally removed the obelisk and returned it to Ethiopia in the early 2000s, following years of negotiations, the empty plinth came to evoke a kind of haunting for the narrator, who both celebrates and mourns its removal and return. The stele belongs in Ethiopia, but its unmarked absence in Rome triggers memories of other absences, namely those of her grandfather and of an uncle who was assassinated in Somalia: "Every time I pass through Piazza di Porta Capena I fear the oblivion."[65]

Through the stele's transit across time and space, she also grapples with the legacy of her family's own relationship to colonial violence, which she poses as a potential complicity that other Italian readers might also confront. Scego's narrator reflects on her Somali grandfather's employment as the interpreter for Italian General Rodolfo Graziani. As she explains for readers unaware of this history, Graziani is the same general who in 1937 used poison gas on Ethiopians under direct order by Mussolini.[66] Before leading troops in Ethiopia, he had overseen the construction of concentration camps in Libya. While Grandfather Scego's employment with Italian forces ties the family still further to Italy, his role in giving voice to the orders of such a notorious, violent figure raises troubling questions: "So was my grandfather a fascist, then? Or better yet, was he a collaborator? Was he guilty of the crimes he had to translate?"[67]

These questions speak to how a culture of colonial aphasia impacts these very personal reckonings. In this case, Igiaba's grappling with personal and collective histories is itself a layered process affected by a lack of language or discourse that adequately captures the complexities of history. This is another iteration of aphasia, which Stoler observes is marked by "the *irretrievability* of a vocabulary, a limited access to it, a simultaneous presence of a thing and its absence, a presence and a misrecognition of it."[68] For Scego the problem of irretrievability—troubled or blocked access to history or language—manifests in the stele and appears as a problem of inheritance across generations: With what words or framings can she make sense of her own positionality, given her grandfather's work? To what extent must she also own the words he voiced as Graziani's interpreter? What does she inherit from her grandfather's body as the "almost white" body that channeled Graziani's orders?[69] Here, imperial formations take hold not only through national institutions and physical structures, but through language and its transmission via the body. Scego's work, too, involves the work of translation—translation as part of the "Second Generation condition."[70] These questions, which Scego says she has "posed [her]self many times," model the kinds of questions that readers who undertake their own mappings might pursue: What is their relationship to the colonial past? How does it shape their perception of themselves and others?

In *Roma negata*, Scego arrives at the Stele of Axum instead through a more recent event: the 2009 dedication of a monument for September 11 across from the grassy area where the stele stood for more than sixty-five years. This newer monument, comprised of two small columns, commemorates

> the victims of the attack of New York and Washington on
>     September 11, 2001
> the city of Rome for peace against every form of terrorism.

The presence of a September 11 memorial in Rome is, at first glance, unexpected, even bizarre. The new monument reminds us that the space has always been marked by empire and nation: overlooking the Circus Maximus, the columns themselves are ancient; recovered in the Renaissance, they flanked the fountain on the exterior of the pontifical court, which became home to the Italian Parliament. Brought to Porta Capena to represent the fallen Twin Towers, the columns are a palimpsest heralding the post-9/11 world in imperial terms. Nearby, the site of the missing Stele of Axum marks the ruins of colonialism. The columns speak to the 9/11 attacks in global terms but effect additional erasures. Ironically, engraved above the main plaque is George Santayana's line, "Those who cannot remember the past are doomed to repeat it." As the narrator explains in *Roma negata*, in her view the monument adds insult to injury as yet another symbol of Italy's insistence on ignoring colonial history, with a memorial to distant events at a site that long held a colonial monument and where the victims of colonialism have yet to be commemorated.[71]

Who is mourned and who is remembered are questions intimately related to the (in)visibility of those living in Italy's social and legal margins. They are also key challenges for writers, scholars, and artists. As Espiritu posits, reflecting on the charge of critical refugee studies: amid fragmentary and "imperfect" memories, "how do we write about absences? How do we compel others to look for the things that are seemingly not there? How do we imagine beyond the limits of what is already stated to be understandable?" Espiritu invokes Toni Morrison's call to "be mindful that 'invisible things are not necessarily not-there.'"[72] In recovering fragments, partial testimonies, and displaced memories, work like Scego's rewrites notions of identity and belonging in ways that disrupt the accepted borders of citizenship.

## TO THE MOON AND BACK

The final example in this chapter takes us from Rome's historic center out to its eastern periphery, and from monumental space to abandoned and occupied space. On March 27, 2009, an unexpected collective occupied a former sausage factory in the Tor Sapienza neighborhood, claiming it as their residency: immigrants and refugees from South America and Africa, along with several Italians, joined a few months later by a group of Roma. United largely through their institutional exclusion from public housing and their social exclusion as members of marginalized, racialized groups, some two hundred people founded the collectively run community now known as Metropoliz.

Amid the industrial ruins at Via Prenestina 913, residents have found shelter and safety in numbers but live with the constant threat of eviction by city authorities. And so, the story goes, in 2011, recognizing that they were unwanted in Italy and on planet Earth, they decided to go to the moon. The moon, they knew, did not discriminate; the moon accepted all arrivals. They studied, built a telescope, and mounted it atop the factory building. Eventually, they constructed a rocket.

Life on the moon was just as they hoped, a kind of utopia. And yet, after some time, looking back at Earth, they realized that they could perhaps make a difference here: change how people think about belonging, model a kind of living to which others might aspire. And so, though moon life was hard to leave, they returned to Earth, and to Metropoliz.

This is the story I learned while on a tour of Metropoliz and the museum that the collective operates there, in collaboration with curators from Rome's MACRO museum organization. MAAM, the Museum of the Other and Elsewhere (Museo dell'Altro e dell'Altrove), is generally open to the public once a week. When I visited on a Saturday morning in the summer of 2019, I joined a couple dozen visitors, including Romans from different neighborhoods and a small group of US students and their instructor. Gianluca Fiorentini, the Italian guide, recounted the collective's history, including the moon expedition, tracing this chronology through a mural painted on the outside the main building (figure 21). He pointed up to the roof, where the telescope still stands. Later, in line for lunch in the resident-run cafeteria, I found myself before a wall decorated in photographs documenting the voyage—residents testing the rocket, donning spacesuits—then bought an abundant plate of rice and vegetables from the residents running the kitchen that day.[73] It felt like wandering through a Calvino story come to life. But I was constantly aware, too, of the dilapidated state of the space in which they had built this world.

The collective curation of the museum is an act of citizenship that claims space and challenges emergency responses to precarious migration. Europe's racialized

FIGURE 21. Rocket on the mural outside of MAAM, which tells the story of the group's moon landing. Photo by the author, 2019.

others are written out of dominant narratives, yet they are not "a people without history." Rather, they exemplify how, as El-Tayeb argues, "the creation of narratives of identity, both for communities and individuals, is not a linear, affirmative process of authentication, but rather rhizomatic and preliminary instead."[74] Yet claiming the right to the city often relies on people's ability to document a history. At MAAM, this history is a co-authored work of speculative fiction, or an aspirational narrative created for engaging with visitors.

This history also materially shapes residents' routines. Between hearing about the telescope and sharing lunch, I took in a fraction of the more than five hundred artworks that adorn the concrete and brick walls and steel beams of the former sausage factory. Installations weave art throughout the site and are curated for visitors, but galleries and the communal cafeteria are also used as meeting and event spaces for Metropoliz residents (figure 22). As he walked us through, Fiorentini pointed out highlights of the collection, which includes multiple large installations, many directly related to questions of otherness and borders. Some are dramatic and difficult; not all are signed, though Fiorentini seemed to hold the full catalogue in his head. When I first visited, the most recent addition was an

FIGURE 22. *Rane infinite* ("infinite frogs"). MAAM spaces double as meeting rooms and learning space for young residents. Photo by the author, 2023.

installation (this one signed) by Vittorio Sordi, produced through a performance piece in which participants had donned the shoes of Syrian migrants, stepped in paint, and walked across long scrolls, which now hung next to a crate holding the shoes themselves. Other works are whimsical, such as the alien face painted on an upstairs window that invites visitors to gaze out at the city through alien eyes.

Some works are integrated into the structure. A flight of stairs leading between the main floor and a couple of large upper rooms is stenciled with "MIGRANT 4 LIFE / LIFE 4 MIGRANT." Along the tracks that once ferried hanging swine carcasses for processing, someone has painted a series of bleeding pigs, titled "Cappella porcina: E-MAAMcipazione," or "Porcine Chapel: E-MAAM-cipation." Fiorentini pointed to murals by well-known street artists like Alice Pasquini and talked about how museum collaborators and residents determined where to place works. I was especially struck by several boats within MAAM, including a wall of painted wood scraps taken from the remains of migrant vessels that reached Lampedusa; a small boat installed by Sara Bernabucci and "repaired" with drums, or transformed into an instrument via drums inserted into its hull (figure 23); and a small rubber dinghy set up on the floor of a smaller room such that visitors have to navigate around it to cross. On one side of the dinghy sits a cloth mannequin, posed as if a silhouette or a ghost.

FIGURE 23. Inside MAAM, artworks including the boat by Sara Bernabucci. Photo by the author, 2023.

As a third example of acts of citizenship that challenge the coloniality of border regimes, these works index government practices of exclusion and the displacement and unsettling of non-Italians in a space curated by those excluded subjects. This collective exemplifies precarity as a site of action that "flip[s] vulnerability upside down in such a way that experiences of insecurity and dispossession lead to initiatives of collective agency and organized resistance."[75] One of the attributes uniting Metropoliz residents is their exclusion from formal modes of belonging in Italy, both spatial and legal: the collective includes members of marginalized and racialized groups who lack access to housing and, in many cases, lack full citizenship rights. They also represent communities whose struggles for rights recognition often unfold separately, in particular in the case of immigrants and Roma, with Romani communities more often living in separate camps of their own making or designated by local authorities (case in point: the Roma first reached Metropoliz after being evicted from their nearby camp). In the former factory, they share a common cause, establishing their right to the city and fighting for housing rights while repurposing the abandoned site as their home. In the public interface they maintain, they play with the idea of the alien gaze in their role as curators, turning the question of outsiderness on its head, as migrants and Roma are not unknowable strangers but hosts and curators inviting Italian and other visitors into their space.

In the 1980s, when the Fiorucci sausage company ceased operations in via Prenestina, it was easier for the owners to desert their factory than sell it, and so they abandoned the building, taking their production elsewhere. Fiorucci finally sold the premises to a developer in the early 2000s, but the buildings remained untouched. Since Metropoliz took up residence in 2009, its longevity has been uncertain. In 2018, the same security decree that criminalized independent rescue ships at sea also increased penalties for the "illegal occupation" of sites and enabled swifter eviction procedures. Eviction was legitimized as a security measure. Metropoliz was determined by a judge to have been occupied illegally but, as of this writing, has avoided being cleared. Campaigns to protect Metropoliz from eviction have featured resident children with lines like, "I live in a museum. Protect my hybrid/mestiza city."[76]

The collective movement is a fiction, an aspiration, but also a material transformation of space. Still, the structure remains incredibly run down. When I returned with a friend in December 2023, I was struck by how little it had changed, and also by how uncomfortable the winter must be for residents living in apartments configured within the factory's walls. As is true in other informal settlements, some residents are long term; others come and go. At Metropoliz, not everyone shares the same ideology or participates in the public-facing aspect of this cause with the same enthusiasm. Metropoliz is not a paradise but a site of active struggle that refutes romanticized ideas of migrant realities.

The reality of Metropoliz is also one of friction with the city.[77] Located in Rome's outskirts, Metropoliz may seem far from political debates and news cycles about border issues and Mediterranean crossings. Yet the exclusion of these residents is intimately tied to the emergency imaginary that fails to envision arriving migrants as future citizens. Those arriving by sea are commonly portrayed in dominant media and political discourses as illegal, defined by clandestine movements.[78] Residents of Metropoliz, the self-dubbed *città meticcia*, or hybrid or mestiza city, confront the same "racializing juridical assemblages"[79] and are held outside of formal and normative recognition within Italy's capital. "Meticcia" evokes notions of hybridity and constant, ongoing processes of identity formation elaborated by Gloria Anzaldúa and others, and in this spirit, the narratives Metropoliz puts forward are the flip side of those that center national identity as the primary form of collective belonging. The città meticcia rejects the colonial gaze and its designation of hierarchies of belonging, or its division of those allowed to move freely through urban spaces, from those seen as mistakenly or criminally present and without a right to the city and its spaces and histories. Residents of the mestiza city offer a version of fugitivity through which they, to borrow from Vang, "imagine ways of being in but not of the nation-state and its 'official' history."[80]

While the collective navigates its own internal frictions and multiple agendas, as might be expected given the pressures of precarious living, they use the former factory as a space for creating and enacting forms of belonging that give them some security and also model alternative conceptions of belonging. The collective presents itself to visitors in ways that subvert strange encounters, with Italy's racialized and marginalized others as hosts and curators. This is akin to what El-Tayeb terms the "queering" of ethnicity in that it exemplifies a survival strategy that is "largely invisible in dominant discourses" and should be understood as a form of resistance that functions in part by "a creative (mis)use [of categories], rearranging a variety of concepts and their interrelations, among them time, space, memory, as well as race, class, nation, gender, and sexuality."[81] The collective's journey narrative, their repurposing of the former factory, and their insistence on engaging the world outside the factory as a transnational, multigenerational group exemplify this resistance; their curation of the space as a home and museum are forms of cultural production through which they enact their claim to the right to the city. As they described themselves in a 2016 statement (issued in Italian),

> We come from Africa, Eastern Europe, Latin America, Italy. Many of us are refugees whom the corrupt accoglienza system didn't know how to help, or people made homeless when we could no longer pay exorbitantly high rents, or Roma who rebelled against the ghettoization of camps. A complex living reality that is enriched by the presence of MAAM (Museo dell'Altro e dell'Altrove di Metropoliz città meticcia), an experience that has consumed residents and the neighborhood, creating another layer of defense for this courageous endeavor.[82]

Their recognition of solidarity across struggles that transgress the categories imposed by legal regimes and hegemonic narratives highlights the conditions in which they fight and speaks to the need for further recognition of the links between refugee and second-generation rights movements.

Looking into the site after my 2019 visit, I learned that the moon expedition and museum were realized in collaboration with Italian artist, anthropologist, and filmmaker Giorgio de Finis, who in 2018 was tapped to run Rome's MACRO museum organization. That kind of endorsement involves a version of what some have critiqued as the "artification" of Rome's working-class neighborhoods.[83] But while the reframing of peripheral areas into a kind of off-the-beaten-path tourist destination is certainly relevant for this museum housed in an occupied factory in the eastern part of the city, the transformation of Metropoliz is not simply an example of creating alternative tourism schemes. Crucial to the longevity of Metropoliz is residents' curation of the museum, with the support of people like de Finis, both as an interface with non-Metropoliz residents and as a strategy to protect their own occupation of the space. According to de Finis and collaborators who continue to work with MAAM, transforming the squat into a museum was a strategy to combat harassment and eviction from police. In an interview with English-language online magazine *Romeing*, collaborator Carlo Gori explained:

> Do you know what the police do when they want to kick you out of squatting? The first thing they do is to destroy the walls in order to make the place uninhabitable. So we had to find a way to protect the walls. This is how the museum was born. . . . There are more than 500 artworks between these walls. Some of these walls are worth more than 150.000€. If they destroy them, they become the bad guys.[84]

Metropoliz is "a social experiment that serves as a powerful example of how to remould an industrial wreck into a place of living and a powerful 'super-object and a subject of collective art.'"[85] Art curation is, in this case, a strategy of survival that transforms urban space and positions publics—museum visitors—to witness that transformation and the way of life it represents. Resident "outsiders" invite nonresident "outsiders" to contribute art and to view their space—an invitation to intimacy, if curated intimacy—and visitors validate the site by donating an entry fee and joining a tour. This does involve a version of artification processes, with Metropoliz residents transforming the occupied factory into a site of cultural heritage, and using the processes and mechanisms of tourism to protect and enable their own citizenship practices. The witnessing transactions that unfold here between residents, visitors, institutions, and municipal authorities disrupt the dominant gazes of the citizen and the tourist alike and establish ethical relations that have, at their core, the possibility of recognition for Metropoliz as a legitimate community and site. In other words, these transactions establish a set of conditions of possibility for recognition of residents' right to the city. That recognition, however, remains precarious; residents and organizers continue to protest their potential eviction.

I first visited Metropoliz as emergency politics effectively closed Italian borders, stoked racist sentiment, and rendered legal citizenship more difficult to obtain, and the museum appeared to me to illustrate belonging as one of the paradoxes that the emergency apparatus sets in motion: presence as a contested right, community building as a fraught process, and citizenship as a legal and social act always potentially threatened by policies that treat mobility as a problem rather than a way of being. La città meticcia enacts citizenship from within the extreme precarity of its position as a city within the city.

## CONCLUSION: ON CITIZENSHIP

The various claims to ownership of and authority within the city that I have discussed in this chapter emerge via testimonial transactions: migrant narrators position soundwalk listeners as ambulant witnesses to their testimonies; Scego's life writing bears witness to individual and collective pasts for readers; and Metropoliz residents welcome visitors who will perceive their ongoing struggles through artworks that celebrate migration and challenge abuses of power, and, through their visit, participate in transforming the site itself into a cultural space that resists closure. As acts of citizenship that emerge through acts of witnessing, these texts and practices make space for narratives of belonging that defy emergency framings of migration and foreignness. That is, they disrupt or expand the "available narratives" of foreignness and precarious migration in Italy or, to invoke Shuman, they participate in processes of negotiation concerning "what gets told and what doesn't" and what stories "become tellable" about belonging in Rome, Italy, or

Europe.[86] With emergency and crisis discourses as the primary modes for representing people on the move, and given the obscuring of the historical movements and ties to Italian and European cultures and communities, there are no readily available narratives for migrant belonging in the everyday life of the city, or through the monuments that celebrate national history or sites of cultural production and exchange. Yet through testimonial transactions and spatial practices, these guides, curators, and citizens create the potential for forms and practices of mutual recognition to emerge that exceed those dictated by state-sanctioned labels or that dominate public discourse.[87]

These are examples of witnessing that begin from Italy's margins, whether literally, in the case of Metropoliz, or in social terms, as is the case for the soundwalk narrators who speak from places of legal and social precarity. Scego's work, too, despite international recognition and her Italian citizenship, is often assigned the default label of "migrant literature," suggesting it does not fit within national or European literary canons. Such narratives are especially important in illustrating the limits of traditional citizenship, which may appear to offer the stability that "emergency" precludes. Appeals for more inclusive national narratives often do important work to promote equal rights. As Balibar has observed, it is thanks to the bold resistance of the marginalized and excluded that citizens might grasp the significance of debates around legal and social belonging and the right to remain.[88]

But if the nation is already a problematic frame through which to understand belonging, these appeals face potentially harsh limits. The possibilities that citizenship seems to offer narrow drastically as nationalism and racial politics intersect. As Hawthorne observes in her study of citizenship and race, "in the context of an ethnonationalist resurgence in Italy . . . Black activists are increasingly confronting the limitations of citizenship as a strategy for combatting institutionalized, state racism in Italy."[89] Citizenship, as a project developed through Enlightenment notions of self and nation, legitimizes a disregard for the gaps of history, a lack of reckoning with duress. If the Italian nation has been shaped in part through colonialism and colonial aphasia, then notions of national identity are imperial formations. Including some as citizens always necessarily excludes others: an expanded national citizenship serves the immediate goal of extending rights to those previously excluded, yet it also risks reaffirming normative citizenship and the privileges it bestows.[90] Another model of citizenship might refuse to identify with the national form of the former colonizing power and instead gesture to the postnational or the translocal. As postcolonial and border studies scholars have discussed, these forms could at a minimum acknowledge that national culture emerges through movement rather than fixity or, as Bhabha argues, through liminality and within borderzones rather than from homogeneous centers.[91] Given colonial history, in other words, is it possible for Italian identity to be truly transnational or translocal? Can a national imaginary possibly invite in the subjects and imaginings of the undercommons, the people who necessarily resist normative borders for their own survival?[92] Does the geographically and socially peripheral space of the città meticcia offer another model of belonging?

Let me turn the question: What happens to the limit case of the refugee when we consider it from the cafeteria at MAAM? What form does the state of exception take within a map that ruptures dominant historical narratives? Within the intimacy of headspace? In *The Universal Machine*, Moten argues that notions of the state of exception developed by Agamben and others (e.g., Santner) potentially reify sovereign power. That is, Agamben's framing presumes an "originary sovereign," but as those always excluded from the sovereign body know well, the foundations of such sovereignty are "originarily disturbed": "To say that the suspension of law in the name of the law's preservation *is* the regular situation is to erect a rickety bridge between forms of life whose historical nonconvergence defies the commerce between them." Put another way, the insider/outsider binary that a state of exception invokes does not encompass the fundamental exclusion of Black subjects. Therefore, Moten refutes the idea that a subject comes into being through recognition by the sovereign power.[93] It is instead in spaces outside the bounds of the nation and the social borders denoted by national identity and citizenship—in "a common underground"—that resistance and imagination can take shape. And it's at the boundary between these spaces—at the literal edge of the city, or at the borders of visibility and invisibility, or where history and the present converge in physical space—that this work becomes possible.

The interventions I have discussed in this chapter reveal the limits of emergency frames, offering alternative ways of recognizing and appreciating how mobility shapes lives. The transactions through which their testimonies emerge function at the intimate scale of the individual encounter, through a set of headphones, engagement with the printed page, or a small group visit to the periphery of Rome. These small-scale exchanges and seemingly small gestures offer their own "stubborn possibilities" as practices that write the future outside the bounds of crisis. By modeling the kinds of work necessary to create new conditions for hearing, these transactions enable what Ahmed discusses as "ethical encounters," or encounters that resist simplistic labels of otherness or strangeness.[94]

As ethical encounters, the testimonial transactions I have discussed here rely on memory and proximity. The racializing assemblages that keep migrants and their children outside of national and European recognition are key to the very notion of nation. Reconfiguring space through narrative, movement, and encounter—to know space as relational—is one way of challenging those borders.[95] As these guides, narrators, and curators demonstrate, witnessing acts can utilize the intimacy of testimony to expand the archive of such stories and, in doing so, to reconfigure our relationships with the city and its inhabitants, recognizing mobility as central to the making of space and community, and reimagining belonging through interrogations of memory and of space. These movements are also tied to questions of labor, and in the next chapter I turn to the labor precarity migrants confront as they seek to establish more permanent lives in Italy.

6

———

# Oranges and Riot Gear

Ousmane Sangare held up a small pair of clippers in one hand, an orange in the other. "This is how you cut them," he said, snipping the stem to leave a few centimeters attached to the fruit. "If you cut them wrong, they don't count, and you don't get paid."

He addressed the crowd of thirty or so people gathered around long tables at Rome's collective space la Città dell'Utopia. We were there to learn about the labor and exploitation of the *bracciante*, the farmworker. The *braccianti*—a word that refers to the "braccia," or arms, for manual labor—are seasonal workers. Historically a category for internal migrants, Italians who moved within or between regions to harvest for day wages, braccianti today are a diverse group increasingly made up of foreigners of many legal status designations. With this shift, in the twenty-first century the category of bracciante has become strongly associated with precarious migration and illegalized border crossing, and with African and South Asian border crossers who arrive by sea.

I first met Sangare, a twenty-nine-year-old from Mali, at Piazzale Maslax, the improvised camp run by Rome-based activist collective Baobab Experience that I discuss in chapter 3. In late spring 2018, he visited a camp assembly to share from his own experience of finding employment. He had spent several months working the harvest in Rosarno, in the southern region of Calabria, and vowed not to return. Back in Rome, he had recently landed a paid internship at IKEA. Now, having achieved some stability, he hoped to help others avoid the trap of labor exploitation.

The oranges were a small prop but a significant symbol of Italy's dependence on migrant labor and, within the country's large agricultural sector, of the *caporalato* network of "gangmaster" middlemen who coordinate day labor for organized criminal syndicates and mafia-like organizations. These working conditions have been described as a form of enslavement.[1] Sangare described the physical toil, low and sometimes absent pay, and despicable conditions of improvised settlements where workers eat and sleep. He testified to his own experiences of exploitative harvest labor, he said, because he could finally speak out and wanted to mobilize others to stand up against these practices.

Migrant farmworkers are transit laborers, moving to follow growth and harvest cycles. Farmworker transit, in turn, enables the transit of goods over international borders that workers themselves would have trouble crossing. In addition, their labor is largely invisibilized: braccianti harvest the fruits and vegetables that appear on dinner tables throughout Italy and around the globe, yet workers remain largely out of public view. During the COVID-19 pandemic, farmworkers briefly shared the spotlight with other "essential workers," but in general, their labor does not often take center stage. People across this especially diverse workforce, which includes Eastern Europeans, South Asians, and Africans, regularly face discrimination. Multiple violent deaths of braccianti in recent years, including a number of Black African men, underscore anti-blackness and racism in general as not only pervasive in this sector but structural to it, holding workers in precarious working and living conditions, and making some workers especially vulnerable to attacks.[2]

While orange groves and tomato fields may appear distant from the spectacle of arrivals by boat or the fraught limbo of reception centers, the emergency apparatus enables and relies on the exploitation of the labor that sustains these spaces. That is, emergency discourses, policies, and related practices together maintain a deportable, exploitable, and largely invisibilized workforce. One way they do so is through the "refugeeization" of labor. As Nick Dines and Enrica Rigo explain in their elaboration of this term, "The failure of the quota system [of work visas] to meet the agricultural demand has been offset by the growing number of asylum seekers making the decision to cross the Mediterranean Sea."[3] As the emergency management of migration has led to increasingly restrictive policies and the closure of safe, established modes of entry, precarious migration means people reach Italy as both asylum seekers and as part of a continuous supply of workers. As is the case across sectors, migrants' legal precarity puts them in readily exploitable positions. In maintaining these vulnerabilities, the emergency apparatus thus also upholds systems like the caporalato. In a context in which Black suffering and death are central to dominant narratives about who deserves to reach Europe and to survive there, the intertwined refugeeization and racialization of labor constitute a crucial lens for understanding how this exploitation operates, and for combatting it.

This chapter situates the plight of migrant braccianti within the emergency apparatus of migration through the words of farmworkers themselves in testimony shared in interviews, film, and social justice campaigns. For farmworkers, advocating for better working conditions means putting their livelihood—and sometimes their lives—on the line. Yet many have spoken out about their experiences, including in interviews and by bearing witness to their experiences through a range of performative testimony. Through testimony as method, after offering context on migrant farmworkers and exploitation within the caporalato system, I elaborate the struggles of the braccianti through a Black Mediterranean lens in two ways. First, I discuss how the emergency apparatus facilitates the refugeeization of labor through testimony shared by a camp resident in Rome about his experience working the harvest in Southern Italy.

Second, I argue that the struggles of migrant braccianti represent a kind of limit case in terms of witnessing. That is, forms of witnessing used to combat this suffering also articulate the limits of (self-)representation in such circumstances.[4] The heightened extremes of visibility and invisibility that "emergency" sets in motion render it especially difficult for migrants to challenge their exploitation. Moreover, given the long history of the caporalato, along with news coverage and films that feature farmworker exploitation and public acknowledgement of migrant deaths during the harvest, invisibility in this case is not a problem of broader awareness but of an obscuring from view. This is a case of experiences "*relegated* to invisibility," as Carter puts it.[5] The challenge in disrupting this invisibility, then, is not to educate the public as if from scratch but to reshape how publics already understand these issues, and to challenge the structures, systems, and willful ignorance that facilitate and normalize that invisibility. To elaborate this limit case, I examine how (in)visibility informs uses of testimony for broader publics through a discussion of Jonas Carpignano's 2015 film *Mediterranea*, set in Rosarno, and make reference to several social justice campaigns.

Across these different testimonial modes, I address how migrant farmworkers position themselves individually and collectively in relation to Italian and global publics and to issues of violence and exploitation. The witnessing relations these narrators invoke don't simply call attention to their invisibility as workers; by illuminating how (in)visibility and deservingness operate in their lives, they point to how racial capitalism powers the emergency apparatus of migration.

## HARVEST LABOR AND THE CAPORALATO

Farmwork is but one example of the kinds of precarious labor to which migrants turn, but it is a significant one.[6] While harvest work has long involved seasonal and day labor, the neoliberalization of food economies and agribusiness models in recent decades has solidified the agricultural industry's dependence on short-term, low-wage workers. This favors the underpaid and often undocumented labor taken up by migrants who, in turn, play a critical role in the global food economy but benefit little from their efforts.[7] Migrant labor in Italy fits within a wider reliance on "permanent temporary" workforces to support agricultural industries in high- and low-income countries in and beyond the Mediterranean region.[8] These workers represent a mix of people with and without visas. Spain regularly recruits Moroccan women to harvest strawberries on temporary work visas, for instance. In the United States, H-2A visas support temporary seasonal harvest work. Undocumented workers also have a strong presence in these workforces, and exploitation affects workers across the legal spectrum.

Italy remains in the top three countries in the EU for agricultural production and for number of workers in the sector,[9] employing more than 1.1 million people in cultivation and harvest work. Nationwide, at least 37 percent of agricultural workers are foreign. Official counts, however, are notably incomplete, given the prevalence of uncontracted work; in some areas, migrants outnumber Italians.[10] Since Eastern European nations joined the EU, their citizens, who have long been among Italy's primary foreign farmworkers, can travel freely across national borders as Schengen citizens, coming for seasonal work without the residency or legal status issues that many Africans face.[11] As of 2018, at least 59 percent of foreign farmworkers are African.

The sector relies heavily on irregular labor, with more than a third of farmwork uncontracted, and more than 40 percent in the South (sometimes much more).[12] In my conversations with migrants who had worked the harvest in Calabria or Puglia, *caporalato* and *caporali* were familiar terms. This is the system that has long taken advantage of poor workers, including Italians who moved locally or between regions to work and, increasing, migrants who arrive from abroad.[13] Individual caporali are the middlemen on the ground, the ones who check that oranges have been properly cut. They recruit and transport day laborers to work sites with piecemeal pay, enforcing strict hours and low wages. In some cases caporali—some of whom are migrants themselves—retain workers' documents for the season, essentially holding them captive.[14] At upper levels, the agricultural sector has strong ties with *agromafie* and other organized criminal syndicates who control (depending on the area) ports, equipment contracts, and transportation and waste systems, and who enforce oppressive labor conditions to keep prices low.[15] Links between some reception centers and organized crime funnel migrants into this work. Despite a 2016 law criminalizing the caporalato, it remains pervasive, now controlling approximately one fourth of Italy's agricultural workforce.[16] A system that has long profited from Italy's poorer classes now also exploits postcolonial migrations, joining in the conscription of migrants to benefit global north economies.[17]

As the caporalato's exploitation of multiple marginalized groups shows, these practices are infused with class issues and are also racialized, exemplifying Ruth Wilson Gilmore's definition of racism as "the state-sanctioned and/or extralegal production and exploitation of group-differentiated vulnerability to premature death."[18] In fact, these conditions have been widely recognized as a form of enslavement and denounced by politicians, activists, and international bodies including the UN.[19] Low-to-no-wage pay and abusive living and working conditions reflect Mbembe's definition of "slave" as a person "whose body can be degraded, whose life can be mutilated, and whose work and resources can be squandered—with impunity."[20] Exploitation and violence in the agricultural sector today carry on the extractive processes through which European colonial powers first established a hold over African subjects and territories. As these processes are reproduced in contexts of precarious migration and organized crime in Italy, they illustrate how individual migrants can so readily become casualties of the systems linking global capitalism, national sovereignty, and the regulation of bodies.[21] Local and regional structures, including the caporalato, "mediate the relationship between global capital and local labor," maintaining a precarious workforce of racialized laborers by exploiting people who are already legally and socially marginalized.[22]

This is an instance of what Mezzadra and Neilson term the "multiplication of labor," which manifests in part as an *intensification* of labor and of exploitation. As they contend, ongoing shifts in the composition of workforces and the multiple borders that differentiate people in turn shape labor and living conditions through the colonization of time and the manipulation of space.[23] Through this lens, we can understand the exploitation of African migrant workers in Calabrian orange groves as occurring within the very specific context of caporalato exploitation and as entangled in broader global shifts. This underscores the idea that the emergency apparatus does not simply concern arrivals at Italian borders but fits within a broader web of interconnected racial capitalist processes and practices.

Precarious work keeps people mobile across regional borders they might not otherwise cross so frequently. For instance, migrants who live in Calabrian reception centers while awaiting word on their asylum applications often imagine leaving the region, joining friends and family in larger cities or in northern European countries. Yet outside of accoglienza, the region is a destination, at least seasonally. Calabria employs the second highest number of agricultural workers (following Sicily) and relies heavily on migrant labor.[24] For those without permanent European residency, seasonal work is often their only option for obtaining the necessary funds to support themselves and, perhaps, as several people explained to me in interviews, to pay the debts they owe to those who funded their journeys.

Irregular labor does not necessarily mean irregular status; working local harvests, mostly without work contracts, are refugees, asylum seekers, immigrants with shorter-term humanitarian visas, and undocumented migrants. In major agricultural areas such as the Piana di Gioia Tauro, near Rosarno, migrants are generally unable to secure or afford housing and squat in makeshift camps outside of city centers, sometimes in the countryside, which local authorities generally tolerate and periodically evict. These camps may be entirely improvised, built by migrants as a set of lean-tos with salvaged metal and wood, housing hundreds of people at a time. Anticipating the arrival of seasonal workers, NGOs and local governments sometimes construct temporary encampments that offer slightly more humane conditions (e.g., sturdy tents, running water, electricity access) but do not forestall exploitation and never suffice for all workers. Working alongside one another, migrant laborers with protected status and those without papers bear the risks of exhaustion and injury that accompany physical labor. Unions exist and support multiple movements, demonstrations, and legal reforms but lack the power to usher in sweeping changes.

Bearing public witness to reprehensible working conditions in this context necessarily means speaking out against systemic violence and corruption—which is especially challenging from precarious positions. While Italian publics are generally well aware of this system and the realities it encompasses, farmworkers and their labor are still readily invisibilized. For migrants, the invisibilization of labor is facilitated through the manipulation of categorical binaries such as "refugee" versus "economic migrant"—that is, through a focus on migrants' individual deservingness as the fundamental issue shaping the so-called crisis. Within such logics, it's easy to conflate workers' invisibility with what is presumed to be their *clandestinità* or clandestine status. The very word *clandestino*, a common derogatory term for *migrante*, or "migrant," suggests a kind of secretive or sneaky illegality. While invisibility can also be a right, invisibilization as a process of obscuring and erasure can enable violence to continue.

Migrant farmworker struggles remain invisibilized from mainstream concerns given how the refugeeization of labor is tied to the legal and political production of the Afro-European borderzone as one in which Black death is common, subject to either spectacle or disregard. As Carter explains, invisibility "often operates in plain view." The invisibilization of undesirables helps normalize *emergency* because it is "orchestrated in such a way that it becomes part of a naturalized set of practices, supported by an economy of indifference."[25] The association of migrants with both the security threat of "emergenza" and undesirable work reinforces public support for exclusionary policies that treat migrants as a problem, while ensuring they continue to arrive.

Farmworker invisibility became globally salient in 2020, during the COVID-19 pandemic. As many scholars, journalists, and activists remarked, farmworkers were "'essential' yet expendable,"[26] their perceived deservingness of legal residency bound up in their status as workers who provide fundamental goods and services. In Italy, early pandemic lockdown prompted a labor shortage; migrants were both unable to move and concerned about the risks of relocating for work at that time. In May 2020, lawmakers passed a bill intended to temporarily regulate up to six hundred thousand migrant workers if they could demonstrate an employment contract.[27] Yet implementation failed, and abuse increased during this time. Of the only two hundred thousand applications filed, 85 percent were for domestic workers. One key problem was the necessity of the advance contract, which caporali offered in exchange for a hefty fee.[28] A failed amnesty amid the high stakes of converging public health and migration "crises" illustrates a kind of systemic captivity that holds migrants within an exploitative and racialized system of labor—a "precarity trap" in which they move from one exploitative situation to another and which reinforces their invisibility.[29]

## THE REFUGEEIZATION OF LABOR

The week Sangare spoke about the orange harvest, his words felt especially urgent. Just a few days before, Soumaila Sacko, also from Mali and active in a labor union supporting migrant seasonal workers, was shot to death near Rosarno while collecting materials to use to build a shelter. The white Italian man eventually convicted of killing him and injuring two others claimed to have been defending his property, the grounds of a factory closed several years earlier for toxic waste pollution. Sacko's June 2 death did not lead to extensive statements by the newly instated Conte administration, which included Salvini as interior minister. Nor did it prompt state memorials—a marked absence even of strange grief. It did, however, prompt demonstrations where people marched for migrant worker rights, as I mention in chapter 3. It was also what led people to gather at the Città dell'Utopia to hear directly from braccianti about their experiences working the harvest and from humanitarian groups operating in the area. Struggles for migrant rights, worker rights, and racial justice intersect in these responses and campaigns.

Several people I met through Baobab Experience had worked the Rosarno orange harvest. Their experiences of hardship and exploitation illustrate how the refugeeization of labor positions them for precarious work. Yousef, whom I mention in earlier chapters, is among a significant number of African harvest workers who do have papers. A legal resident of Italy originally from the Gambia and in his late twenties, Yousef had spent several seasons doing this kind of work while awaiting his protection documents, and later while awaiting renewal. When we met in 2018, he was living in a tent at Piazzale Maslax while waiting for a document renewal appointment. He talked about how the costly, lengthy process of waiting for documents made precarious labor necessary. We recorded an interview upon his return from a short visit to Milan to meet with fellow organizers supporting migrant rights.

Yousef came to Rome after two years of harvest work. He needed to renew his passport at the consulate there in order to proceed with extending his humanitarian documents. Unable to afford a hostel or rent, he had come to live at Baobab while waiting for his questura appointment. One of the challenges he articulated about living there was the absence of work options:

> So that's the way I came to Roma. Before I will see [the consular officer] it takes me almost one week. So the money I came with, it's finished. I can't get money to go back to Foggia [Puglia region] again. . . . [The consular officer] also told me that I need to pay money there also. That was forty euro. Plus the passport photos, that is almost forty-five euro. So at that moment I [didn't] have money, I came to Baobab and I

asked help, for them to help me. So they give me that money, I went to take pictures, and I pay [the consular officer] also to get this paper, to the *questura*. So from there it's a problem . . . since then I cannot leave. I am here for almost ten months.[30]

Here Yousef describes his position as an uncontracted manual laborer and when we spoke, as the occupant of a tent in Rome, as inextricably linked with the lengthy, costly asylum process. His words highlight waiting as an active process, but one in which his sense of his own agency fluctuates.[31] His situation is almost paradoxical: he came through the Italian reception system to become a legal resident of Italy, only to live in occupied spaces, performing uncontracted work.

When I asked him to talk about his experiences in the Calabrian orange groves, he spoke through a collective "we," bearing witness to his own struggles by framing his personal history as part of shared experience:

> We are moving season to season because when the season is finished, we have to find farming assistance [elsewhere]. Because in Rosarno they work for oranges. . . . When the orange season is finished, maybe in Rosarno in a few months you have . . . asparagus. So there we work for *asparagi*, but that work is very painful and the money they pay people also is [much less].

Following the logic of emergency response, a migrant exiting Italy's formal accoglienza system no longer resides within emergency purview: their case has been adjudicated and a status assigned or denied, and while they may count within the total number of arrivals, they no longer result as part of a population in need of immediate aid. For migrants, authorities' decision on their asylum claims often instead marks a transition or the beginning of new uncertainty.

Legal recognition matters: it opens up a number of doors for foreigners, including access to healthcare and other forms of aid, to contracted work, to fair housing. Those granted refugee status in Italy can move freely among Schengen countries. At the same time, however, as Yousef's case illustrates, obtaining papers does not guarantee stability. While reception processes enable people like Yousef to obtain protection, the pressure to resolve the "crisis" of thousands of annual migrant arrivals by processing asylum claims more swiftly and denying at high rates has also bolstered the production of a precarious workforce. In Italy, the high number of people who exit accoglienza without papers—in recent years, 50–80 percent of first-instance asylum cases were rejected annually—lose access to aid and benefits and cannot obtain legal work contracts.[32] Undocumented status severely limits the options available for finding housing and work, and for crossing borders.

At the same time, as Yousef attested, in the caporalato system, refugee or humanitarian visa status does not protect a worker from exploitation. When Yousef was injured on the job, for instance, he received no compensation. To obtain work in the first place, he had to forego any official contract. Now he had to find ways to continue working in order to survive:

A machine's supposed to do that work . . . not human beings, you know? But we force ourselves because we don't have money to eat, we don't have nothing to help ourselves [for] our health. . . . And we are in the document process also . . . you need to pay the lawyer also to take out the documents [for] you. All those things. You have to go to the field and you work [for low wages] and you give it to the lawyers. So you pay the lawyers and those lawyers also still they don't do nothing for your document process, with all the sufferings that you have [gone through]—so it's very stressful.

So this is the problem, you know, when I was there—so I decided that I cannot do this *campagna* [rural] work and so I created a business also. . . . I'd go to the supermarket, I'd buy things and sell them. Maybe I get a two cent profit or three cent profit. . . . It's not much, but I cannot do that power work [in the fields], it cannot go for my health, but I need to help myself . . . maybe not to go steal, not to go and tell lies to people, you know, to get money from them. But if I can solve my problems, it is better than being in another situation. This is why I'm involved in a business.

While moving for seasonal work, Yousef continuously looked for alternative opportunities. He also opted to work as an ambulant vendor but found it not very fruitful. He was navigating these obstacles on his own but aware that his participation in informal economies was a common one among newcomers. Like many people seeking asylum and humanitarian protection, he hadn't arrived with a work permit. Moreover, people applying for asylum and protection have limited work options while their case is in process. They can only begin working two months after filing their claims, and given the uncertainties of that wait, potential employers understand asylum seekers to be temporary workers. In these circumstances, many opt, like Yousef, for uncontracted positions and day labor.

What's more, it would have been difficult for Yousef to arrive with a work permit, even if he hadn't had to flee his home country. In Italy, seasonal work visas fall under a country-based quota system. However, the annual limits placed on these visas since 2002 have not matched the constant need for workers, especially in agriculture. While the 1998 Turco-Napolitano law established visas for entering Italy to obtain work, the 2002 Bossi-Fini law tied many immigrant visas to work contracts; that is, one has to secure employment before reaching Italy (table 2, appendix). Bossi-Fini, implemented with the aim of eliminating "irregular migration," is instead credited by migration scholars as part of a web of policies and practices that led to growth in precarious migration. Since its implementation, visa quotas have been consistently lowered. By way of example: in 2007, Italy offered 170,000 visas for non-EU foreign workers. A decade later, the *decreto flussi* (official quota decree) offered 30,850 visas, not all of which were finalized within the year.[33] Not only are visas fewer in number; the contracts on which they depend are difficult to come by. These factors have accelerated the refugeeization of workforces: with fewer visa options and fluctuating annual quotas, the agricultural industry increasingly relies on people with precarious or uncertain legal status, and more people have resorted to reaching Italy by sea and applying for asylum.

This work, in turn, keeps migrants in transit between Italian regions, which holds them in further precarity. Even though the government's "distribution" of asylum seekers to reception centers throughout the country's twenty regions has expanded the foreign population in rural areas, and while those in small villages may not have to travel far to find cash-paying harvest work—because the work is seasonal—many braccianti do travel.[34] Yousef described moving between Calabria and Puglia, living in encampments that were at constant risk of sgombero, or eviction. In Foggia (Puglia), Yousef described how "police brutality also came there and they destroyed [the migrant encampment]." He was referring to the so-called Gran Ghetto in Rignano Garganico, near Foggia, where up to three thousand migrants lived until it was razed by Italian authorities in 2017, in the act he describes as police brutality. Other camps have since been built and occupied.[35]

With a term like "police brutality" (which does not have a direct Italian corollary), Yousef analyzes what happened at the Gran Ghetto through the language of anti-racist, abolitionist movements across the English-speaking world. In this way, he links his experience as a Black migrant navigating Italian spaces with experiences across the African diaspora, perhaps most overtly in police brutality against Black communities in the United States. In situating experiences like his in the broader context of struggles against anti-blackness and state violence, testimonies like Yousef's illustrate lived experiences of the refugeeization of labor and speak to how, as white supremacy crosses borders, anti-racist struggles link across geographies.

The refugeeization of labor transpires amid multiple economic shifts that are themselves related to mobility. Calabria is one of the country's poorest regions and continues to see significant out-migration of locals to northern regions and to other European countries. While the caporalato operates throughout the country, Southern Italian regions have higher rates of uncontracted agricultural labor and higher unemployment rates in general.[36] Hiring and leasing without contracts, however problematic, are relatively common practices: landlords avoid paying taxes on unregistered rents and can maintain lower prices for tenants. But to maintain their visas, migrants need official residence contracts. In interviews, women and men I spoke with in Calabria described how hard it was to obtain a housing contract that would have allowed them to live near a better job. Redeem, from Nigeria, lamented having to close the business she had opened because once she exited official accoglienza and lost access to state support, she would not be able to afford to live in the town where her shop was, and she was struggling to find anyone who would rent an apartment to her. Studies spanning the 1990s through the present have established that immigrants often face higher rental costs and a narrower set of possibilities, as rental ads may say outright "*no extracomunitari*" (no non-EU foreigners).[37] Black migrants report this housing precarity as a particular hardship.[38]

In 2018, medical NGO MEDU observed that more than 90 percent of migrants who visited its Rosarno-area clinics were in Italy legally, with most migrants possessing protected status or awaiting a decision on an asylum application. Despite their ability to work legally, fewer than 30 percent of migrants that MEDU met with had obtained a contract for their work. The grave conditions in which migrants live and work "has a serious impact on seasonal workers' physical and mental health," including respiratory and digestive conditions and, often, psychological issues from their experiences in Libya.[39] In the informal settlements where most workers live, the cold, rainy fall weather and lack of running water or heat exacerbate their symptoms.

These conditions are grave enough that deaths are a regular part of the story of migrant harvest labor. To name but a few from recent years: In 2018 alone, the year I recorded the interview with Yousef, Italian news media repeatedly covered camps in the Rosarno area following the separate deaths of three residents there. Soumaila Sacko was killed on June 2. Two other people died in fires: Becky Moses, a Nigerian woman of twenty-six, died on January 27 in a fire in the camp she had made home after her asylum application was rejected; and Suruwa Jaithe, an eighteen-year-old from the Gambia, burned to death on December 2 in another such camp. These fires were likely started by other residents seeking to stay warm; in the makeshift settlements, they quickly spread.[40] In August that year, workers went on strike following the death of sixteen braccianti in two separate incidents involving overcrowded vans transporting migrant workers. In addition, precarious conditions include working in increasingly extreme temperatures with little reprieve. In the summer of 2023, at least two farmworkers died while laboring in record-breaking heat: Nasser Al Masoudi from Tunisia, who died in Lazio, and Famakan Dembele from Mali, who died in Puglia.[41] In 2024, when Satnam Singh, from India, lost his arm in a machinery accident in Lazio, his employer left him to die outside. A number of additional deaths on the job, including suicide, should be added to this list.[42]

These deaths are consequences of the emergency apparatus that has long operated not only in the Mediterranean Sea but within Italian orchards and fields. In fact, today's braccianti deaths should be understood as occurring in the wake of the 1989 murder of Jerry Essan Masslo, the South African refugee I mention in chapter 1 who was living in a camp for tomato harvesters when he was shot to death. Like these more recent deaths by attack, neglect, and fire, Masslo's murder signaled more than thirty-five years ago how racism and exploitative labor practices are linked in the disposability and ungrievability of migrant lives and bodies.

Popular media representations of migrant precarity often focus on incidents of violence or degrading circumstances that reiterate negative stereotypes without addressing the systemic issues that produce these circumstances. In fact, while common knowledge, farmworker precarity still often only becomes more widely visible in the immediate aftermath of violence, as they did in news coverage of Sacko's murder, or of the 2010 demonstrations in Rosarno that turned violent, which I address in the next section as a touchstone for the interconnected issues of labor exploitation and racism. These acts of violence reflect the interconnected-ness of precarious mobility with global agribusiness, local economic strife, racism and anti-immigrant discrimination, and organized crime.

## TESTIMONY AND (RE)INSCRIBING PUBLIC MEMORY

Amid the failures of empathy and this ongoing violence, how do those who bear witness about their circumstances choose to tell their stories? How are the limits of witnessing related to the politics of deservingness? Witnessing can bring visibility to a situation—from revealing unknown aspects of a situation, to telling another side of a story. This is one reason so many advocacy campaigns employ testimony.[43] Migrant farmworkers represent a kind of limit case: the stakes of their witnessing necessarily reflect the politics of (in)visibility. Moreover, while exploitation in this sector is common, not exceptional, migrants' differential treatment shows that it is racialized. Given that the living and working conditions of braccianti often only make the news in connection with acts of violence, *how* such incidents are written into public memory is critical. Media coverage of these issues often sensationalizes violence or further criminalizes migrants, and news and political debate rarely center migrant perspectives beyond quick clips.

One set of events that remain present in public memory is the migrant-led dem-onstrations in Rosarno in January 2010. Here I focus on this episode as one that suggests how testimony can (re)engage publics in recent history and related social issues. These incidents remain a common reference point in the Italian national imaginary for debates about racialized violence, but they are often remembered through one-sided tellings as migrant riots. Initially, migrants protested after a drive-by shooting by local Italians of two Africans living in Rosarno, like many, as farmworkers. The protest quickly became violent, with incidents carried over three days, including locals hurling rocks, wielding metal rods, and physically attack-ing the protesting migrants, and migrants smashing shop windows, beating in car frames, and also fleeing the city. At least fifty migrants, several locals, and several police officers were wounded. Authorities arrested and prosecuted ten migrants in what an article in the *Guardian* referred to as a "bloody ethnic cleansing."[44] News coverage of the incidents included multiple images of Black migrants marching and visibly angry, with captions describing the violence and damage to the town. Even stories addressing attacks against migrants still focused on the violence and disorder of those days. While these stories document actual events, they also offer a narrow representation of the broader issues behind the demonstrations and risked affirming racist associations of Black migrants with violence.

In following, a counter-archive of testimonials and more in-depth coverage has documented the events of January 2010, and the broader circumstances in which they unfolded, through the perspectives of migrant workers.[45] The 2010 docu-mentary film *Il sangue verde* (*Green Blood*) directed by Andrea Segre incorporates interviews in which migrant harvest workers describe their legal and social precarity, and their relationship to the spaces of the orchard and the camp, in connection with the demonstrations. We hear migrants testify to what happened in 2010, and their narration of the memories of those days offers a fuller, more complex picture of worker exploitation in Rosarno. The film also situates these narrations historically, including through footage of Fascist-era braccianti labor performed by Italian locals, emphasizing how despicable working conditions have affected citizens and foreigners for generations. Historicizing labor within Italy offers viewers a way of understanding migrants' struggles outside standard representations that figure migrants as outsiders detached from Italian history. That is, the film expands the tellable narratives about migration.

But changing tellable narratives is not simply about a need for more context. The forms testimony takes can shape the ways that alternative or more complete representations engage audiences. In what additional ways might documentary forms expand or transform tellability, especially considering the problem of migrant (in)visibility and the challenges it poses for witnessing? Here I turn to the 2015 docudrama *Mediterranea*, which reenacts the 2010 events through the eyes of migrants. The film uses layered forms of witnessing in ways that reject dichotomies of deservingness and highlight invisibility as both condition and political strategy. The film is based on the experiences of migrants who live in the area, several of whom act in the film and have worked as citrus harvesters. Directed by Italian-American filmmaker Jonas Carpignano, *Mediterranea* follows the journey of Ayiva, played by Koudous Seihon performing a version of his own story, and Abas, played by Alassane Sy. Given the use of nonprofessional actors, Carpignano's work has been described as a kind of new neorealism; that actors draw on lived experience is certainly crucial to their performances.[46] Through this layered witnessing, the film illustrates two approaches to repositioning publics and rewriting public memory: first, it offers testimony through reenactment and through the use of actors who perform versions of their own experiences. Second, through these doubled acts of witnessing, its retelling of the 2010 demonstrations counter dominant narratives that portray precarious migration as an "invasion" of "fakers" and challenge associations of Black migrants with violence and degradation.

Ayiva and Abas are two friends who travel from Burkina Faso to Italy. They cross the desert, and then Ayiva steers the crowded dinghy on which they cross the sea. In Rosarno, they live in an informal settlement with other migrants, and they struggle to find steady work and to earn enough to afford better housing. The men's new acquaintances reflect the diversity of Rosarno's migrant community: men from several West African countries, the Maghreb, and Eastern Europe, and a group of women from Nigeria. The film's languages alone reflect the heterogeneity of experience and background, as characters move between English, Italian, Arabic, French, and Bissa. Ayiva befriends a kid-hustler from the local Romani community who helps him navigate the Rosarno scene, where it is not clear who

FIGURE 24. Abas harvesting oranges. Still from *Mediterranea*, by Jonas Carpignano. Used with permission from Stayblack Productions.

is safe to approach for help. He looks after his boss's child, who is the only Italian character who expresses curiosity about Ayiva's home country or family; for others, Ayiva is simply Black, a worker, or a "clandestino." The child also reminds him of his own daughter in Burkina Faso, with whom he chats periodically via Skype. We see the men harvesting oranges and their mistreatment by the caporali who monitor their work (figure 24).

One especially remarkable aspect of the plot is that, apart from a brief scene alluding to a conversation with legal advisors, the narrative does not coalesce around questions of legal residency, asylum, or other visas. As the film resists criminalizing migrants, it also resists victimizing them, instead foregrounding their agency within legal and labor precarity and their physical exclusion from local communities. Part of a trilogy in which Carpignano recounts the complex racial and class politics in the area of the Piana di Gioia Tauro, *Mediterranea*'s central story concerns the racial tensions amplified through the intersections of labor precarity, poverty, organized crime, discrimination, and migration to and within Southern Italy—tensions that erupted in the violent clashes between migrants and locals.[47] In the film's climax, Ayiva and Abas march with other migrants in the January 2010 demonstrations. In this telling, multiple testimonial acts shape viewers as witnesses who "see" these circumstances through the eyes of migrants, and of Ayiva in particular.

*Mediterranea* performs a specific kind of memory work that, I'd argue, differs from that of other films that nevertheless embrace related ethics of representation. Matteo Garrone's 2023 Oscar-nominated *Io Capitano* (*Me Captain*), for instance, also tells the story of two friends (cousins) who traverse the Sahara to Libya and then cross the Mediterranean. Like *Mediterranea*, it employs the layered witnessing of amateur actors. Seydou Sarr and Moustapha Fall, who play characters Seydou and Moussa, have spoken in interviews about having themselves reached Italy through lengthy, precarious journeys, experiences surely recalled in different ways in their performance of the journey from Senegal. While both films recount these journeys in compelling ways, *Mediterranea* differs as a docudrama reenacting specific historical events. In this way, its narrative works not only to shift broader narratives of migration—challenging stereotypes about West African men reaching Italy, for instance—but to rewrite Italian collective memory of the events of January 2010. The film builds its account of those events both by recreating actual scenes and by drawing on the power of fictionalization to represent unknown or otherwise untold aspects of the story, raising provocative questions about the borders of testimony.

Given its 2015 release at what many recognized as the height of Europe's "refugee crisis," *Mediterranea* offers contemporary viewers an opportunity to look to the not-so-distant past for perspectives on the social and historical entanglements that perpetuate this violence. By aligning viewers with the film's migrant protagonist—we see through Ayiva's eyes, and we follow his story—the film functions in ways similar to the docudramas that film scholar Leshu Torchin has described as having "a witnessing function, producing eyewitness testimony, a narrative of suffering, trauma, and injustice in encounters designed to summon politically, morally, and socially engaged publics."[48] The story emerged through Seihon's oral testimony to Carpignano, and so the final production is, in one sense, Carpignano's own act of witnessing, based on these testimonies. Yet it also offers the embodied testimony of several actors who perform versions of themselves to reenact historical events at which they were present.[49] These layered testimonies emerge through relations of witnessing partly enabled by the film's publicity, which featured Carpignano's collaborations with survivors in press releases and festival interviews. Carpignano's work has been supported by the Sundance Festival and director Martin Scorsese, and while the film was not as widely celebrated as other migration cinema—for instance, Gianfranco Rosi's *Fire at Sea*, which came out around the same time—*Mediterranea* still represents Hollywood funds and interests and is now available to stream on Amazon. To that end, the film bears witness to the January 2010 events for an Italian and global audience simultaneously—rewriting history for some, and for others, telling it for the first time.

By (re)inscribing January 2010 events, and migrant exploitation more broadly, into public awareness in a moment when global attention was newly (and has repeatedly) focused on precarious Mediterranean mobilities, the film potentially prompts viewers to recognize how ongoing sea crossings are linked to other precarities within Italy, including in labor. The audience's awareness of migrant farmworkers' lived realities, and in particular Seihon's reenactment of his past—for instance, his own role steering the boat across the sea, or his work harvesting oranges—enables viewers to recognize the film "as an extension of [survivors'] testimony."[50] There is a sense of intimacy here that can alter viewers' memories of the events depicted, reconfiguring their representation—especially since for most viewers the January 2010 events were not experienced directly but were always a matter of representation. These new, revised, or expanded memories "have the capacity to transform one's subjectivity, politics, and ethical engagements."[51] The resonance of the film's reenactments with viewers—that is, its potential to produce new or revised memories—is one way of understanding how "extensions of testimony" function in the world. This is witnessing not to evoke sympathy or pity for "the other," but to reconfigure and expand memory.[52] The layered witnessing of the docudrama frustrates the tendency of the white colonial gaze to abstract or objectify, to render a subject either one among *any*, or to treat the subject as thing.[53] By making the matter of invisibility part of the production itself, *Mediterranea* resists this urge.

Even if viewers aren't aware of the film's layered acts of witnessing, *Mediterranea*'s mise-en-scène establishes its witnessing authority. Shots in which Ayiva and Abas appear with a group of other border crossers reenact Seihon's personal experiences and, at the same time, echo images familiar to viewers from media coverage of migration between Africa and Southern Europe. Upon nearly reaching the Italian coast, the migrants jump from their small boat and cling to a tuna net, a scene which recreates a 2007 photograph that captured global attention. This image, published in news outlets including the *Guardian*, the *BBC*, and *La Repubblica*, and featured in *The Independent* with the headline "Europe's Shame," accompanies the story of twenty-seven migrants rescued after having hung onto the steel rails of a tuna net for three days.[54] In the photograph, taken from an Italian navy helicopter, migrants visibly cling to the net, but all detail is lost to distance. In the film, instead, viewers first glimpse the net from below, as people swim from their sinking raft to the rails. Near the close of this sequence, a wide shot recalls the newspaper photograph, as the camera cuts to a view of the whole structure, with migrants holding the rails; it then cuts back underwater, where two bodies float. Italian audiences' conscious or unconscious recognition of the famous scene is reimagined through this more intimate view, through the characters of

Ayiva and Abas, and through this haunting acknowledgement of death. In these examples of "media witnessing," the medium itself essentially assumes the position of interlocutor, "aid[ing] in the transmission of the experience to an audience" and enabling viewers to sense an intimacy with these current events, in their portrayal through individual characters.[55] These recognizable shots depict crucial details in the protagonists' lives. They also simultaneously recall and question media coverage of precarious migration, reinterpreting those visual and narrative memories.

As a docudrama, *Mediterranea* is concerned with representing history, but its main project involves "performing a memory of the past," making history "accessible not so much as static 'fact' as [via] a process of remembering."[56] *Mediterranea's* portrayal of the demonstrations recognizes them as a moment of violence and, critically, as a moment of anti-racist action, a portrayal that contrasts with the emphasis in much media coverage of the riots on the physical violence of the demonstrations and the damage inflicted on private property. Such coverage often elides or obscures the crucial role that migrants' individual and collective agency plays within the constraints imposed by these circumstances, and the extent to which such incidents indicate entangled systems of exploitation and discrimination.

In Carpignano's retelling, and in Seihon's portrayal of Ayiva, the demonstrations mark a turning point for the protagonist. By this point in the film, viewers know why the migrants are upset, having seen their exploitation by local employers, the abuses hurled at them by locals, and the gunshots aimed at their friends as they walked to their camp. Still, Ayiva resists marching; he tries to convince the others not to protest. Yet he follows them, and viewers see, from his perspective behind the group, the migrants gathering and walking into town. Their chant, in English, of "Stop shooting Blacks!" carries across the scene before any shot portrays the signs or the migrants' faces. As viewers, we walk with the migrants, looking up with them at the balconies from which a few locals throw rocks. Ayiva watches, in silence, as rocks hit two of the women with their group. The camera follows his gaze from friend to friend, as migrants help their wounded comrades away from the scene. When Ayiva grabs a metal rod and smashes car windows, this action does not come as a surprise, though its decisiveness is notable.

Here again the film recreates images that circulated globally, repositioning them as moments within the story of Ayiva and Abas. A photograph by Franco Cufari shows migrants marching with street signs, dark smoke rising behind them. Although taken from some distance, their angry expressions are still visible (figure 25). At the time, the image was reprinted in Italian, US, and UK papers. In the years since, it has also been miscited, for instance appearing in memes that circulated in Australia suggesting that the photo represented Black protesters in Melbourne ("where the locals live in fear," one meme reads). When *Mediterranea* presents a version of this recognizable shot, we as viewers are brought physically closer to protesters, and we have already been marching with them for several

FIGURE 25. This photograph of the January 2010 riots by Franco Cufari circulated widely. Reproduced with permission.

FIGURE 26. Recognizable scenes were recreated with a different perspective in *Mediterranea*, by Jonas Carpignano. Used with permission from Stayblack Productions.

minutes and witnessing their exploitation throughout the film (figure 26). It's not about excusing violence but about seeing the violence alongside them, with fury at the conditions we know they confront.

This work challenges invisibility not simply by making visible, but by "locating" the specific modes and harms of that invisibility, in the sense Moten invokes of locating as a kind of seeing that responds to "crisis." Defining crisis as "deprivation on a global scale" that is shaped by policing, Moten argues for *seeing* as a form of criticism that recognizes both the crisis and its production within a specific set of dynamics.[57] Applied to this episode, the generative possibilities of criticism-as-seeing (as locating) can create modes for viewers to *see*—to witness—just how these events and the dynamics that shape them unfold in relation to individual lives, collective experiences, and histories. Testimonial documentary work could also reify crisis—could orient debate around the question of representation. Seeing *beyond* crisis, or understanding migration beyond emergency framings, is not simply about "the constant disruption of the normal." Rather, it is about creating new ways of seeing, finding new grammars, resisting the need to counter "crisis" on its own terms.

Such acts of witnessing are a reminder that, as Hall writes, "rioting and civil disorder are only the outward, if dramatic, symptoms of this inner unravelling of our social, political and community life."[58] To respond to migration as emergency is to pretend that border crossing is an isolated act of individual choice rather than part of a web of relationships, histories, and structures, including these systems of exploitation. As Alessandra Corrado argues in her discussion of the post-Fordist politics of Rosarno and the agricultural industry, "The Africans of Rosarno, by claiming their dignity and rebelling against this complex local racist system . . . have revealed the contradictions and limits of national and European immigration policies."[59] In doing so, they also speak to the "contradictions and limits" of their imposed invisibility—one that aligns migrant farmworkers with precarious laborers more generally, while also taking shape through racialized forms of exploitation. *Mediterranea* articulates this invisibility as a potential platform—as migrants join forces to challenge their invisibilization—but also as a condition that limits the actions they can take, as we see in both the narrative the film recounts and in the layered witnessing it adopts to tell this story.

## THE POLITICS OF (IN)VISIBILITY AND THE LIMITS OF WITNESSING IN THE BLACK MEDITERRANEAN

Bearing witness to how anti-Black, anti-immigrant racism upholds labor exploitation and frustrates the efforts of individual workers to assert their rights, individual testimonies like Yousef's interview and more widely circulated cultural texts like *Mediterranea* make clear that this violence doesn't transpire in a vacuum. Nor are the January 2010 protests or the deaths of Sacko, Moses, Jaithe, Keita, Al Masoudi, Dembele, Singh, and others exclusive to the agricultural sector. Rather, attacks on agricultural workers in Italy, and the lack of structural changes in response, are part of the continuum of racialized suffering and death shaping the borders of Europe and reifying the otherness against which Europe defines itself. The perceived expendability of Black subjects in particular is directly related to the deportability of the asylum seeker or undocumented migrant *and* to what P. Khalil Saucier discusses as *carne nera*, or black flesh:

> Black flesh is not simply and only the point of departure, but the vortex of struggle. . . . Europe needs the Black but is allergic to its existence. . . . Thus when only one or more than a thousand move across the aquatic threshold of the Mediterranean, we are witnessing the drift of boundaries between the human and non-human.[60]

Saucier calls us to recognize that the stakes of these precarious crossings are not only a matter of individual lives and deaths but also encompass the very definition of the human. These boundaries "drift" and articulate not only at sea but throughout Italy, throughout Europe. In this vein, the stakes of (in)visibility are not confined to a single worker or moment. To *witness* farmworker exploitation— to attend to these testimonies—is to be asked to account for the construction of the human, or the reassurance of one's own humanity, through the suffering and "dehumaning"[61] of Black migrant workers. And to tell one's story from a position of border crossing or enslavement is to make this "drift of boundaries" visible.

Unfolding within the racial capitalist mechanisms of contemporary border regimes, these experiences of exploitation are directly related to the violence of sea crossings. Seen through Sharpe's framing of the wake, these harvest testimonies are "accounts of the hold in the contemporary"[62] that show the farmworkers' camp to be an iteration of the hold of the slave ship where "the logics and the calculus of dehumaning" repeat and augment over time, with repeated deaths "fill[ing] the archives of a past that is not yet past. The holds multiply." Yet, Sharpe underscores, "so does resistance to them, the survivance of them."[63]

A Black Mediterranean perspective makes explicit that the solution to the problem of worker exploitation is not simply to regularize workers, as Italy has done periodically since the late 1980s. Maintaining an industry through the intermittent legalization of workers does nothing to move us beyond the violent idea of migration as an ongoing emergency, and migrants as sortable into categories of deservingness. Instead, responding to the refugeeization of labor requires a shift in perspective, following Saucier, to recognize "carne nera" as the site where "the continuum of violence and theft of the body locate ground zero for the conceptualization of the human."[64] Migrant farmworker-led movements that challenge their invisibilization reveal Italian spaces to be one site of this ground zero. We see that in their representation in *Mediterranea*, and in continued work on the ground.

For example, just a year after the Rosarno protests, a month-long strike involving hundreds of farmworkers in Nardò, Puglia, prompted a number of local farmers to issue work contracts and was part of efforts that led to the national anti-caporalato law, ratified in 2016 (Law 199/2016). Arguably one of the most successful farmworker-led campaigns, workers protested not only in city centers but in spaces where their presence disrupted the movement of goods—for instance, blocking key roads used for transport. This kind of embodied witnessing shifted where and how workers appear in the public's line of sight and drew attention to the system's dependence on migrants' actual presence, so that their demands for an end to corruption and slavery-like working conditions would find an audience of "adequate witnesses." The 2016 law has not ended corruption but does give authorities and activists a means for denouncing abuses. Yvan Sagnet, originally from Cameroon and a key organizer in this movement, was inspired to take action when he worked the harvest while in Italy earning a university degree. He also founded NoCap, an organization that certifies goods sold in supermarkets that are produced under fair labor conditions.[65] NoCap media campaigns position viewer-consumers as witnesses to the need for such a network, and Sagnet continues to draw on his own experience as a bracciante in meetings with activists, politicians, consumers, and university students who plan to work in agriculture in some capacity.[66]

Yet as a set of ethical relations, witnessing is tenuous, volatile, especially in a context where national (white) publics are accustomed to the comfort of disregard, or of suspicion. This has played out in the case of Aboubakar Soumahoro, who, like Sagnet, has used his own narrative as a former farmworker-turned-activist to work for migrant rights and to build a movement that embraced invisibility itself as a political platform. Soumahoro, born in Côte d'Ivoire, became a recognized voice following the murder of Soumaila Sacko, when Soumahoro began speaking more regularly at anti-racist and migrant rights demonstrations. He has a strong social media presence, has collaborated with reporter and television host Diego Bianchi, and published a memoir (*Umanità in rivolta*, or *Humanity in Revolt*, Feltrinelli 2019). The movement he helped build, "Gli Invisibili," or The Invisibles, gained international recognition during the pandemic when organizers brought protective equipment to migrant farmworkers, among other critical and much-needed work—and as media beyond Italy covered a short documentary about the movement (I heard about the documentary on NPR).[67] In 2021, Soumahoro formalized the movement by founding the Lega Braccianti (the Farmworkers' League), a platform for advocacy and fundraising to support the rights of the Invisibles. He was elected to Parliament through the Green and Left Alliance party in 2022.

A widely circulated photograph of Soumahoro's arrival in Parliament shows him standing outside Montecitorio wearing a suit and muddied work boots, his fist held high. It's an image that communicates both his literal embodiment of this cause, as well as his entry into at least the lower rungs of the political establishment. This victorious, defiant rhetoric made it even more devasting to his supporters—me included—when, shortly after his appointment, his wife and mother-in-law were investigated for embezzlement and corruption in their oversight of migrant reception centers. They have since been indicted. Soumahoro denied knowledge of these deeds, but the case cast suspicion over the new MP, one of the few Black parliamentarians to serve in Italy. It also threatened the causes he was seen to represent, through suspicion and by removing the spotlight from those causes.

As the voice and face of a movement he then shepherded into his Parliamentary work, Soumahoro embodied the movement's successes but also established the conditions for its failure. As journalist Annalisa Camilli astutely pointed out at the time, part of the problem for Soumahoro was that he came to embody Gli Invisibili in a moment when he was also widely seen to embody oppositional, moralistic politics—"campaigning on values, rather than policies."[68] The Soumahoro fiasco did not suddenly reveal problems with the MP; rumors had circulated earlier about his own lack of transparency in union leadership and fundraising, for instance. Instead, this case points to systemic issues, including how racism pervades political party structures and discourse—as Soumahoro's race made it that much easier for people to discount him and the work he represents. As Camilli argues, Parliament had all but dropped the focus on criminality in the accoglienza system, until those problems could be pinned on an MP of African descent. Moreover, discourse surrounding this case has failed to address broader structural issues within accoglienza, including the gradual reduction in funding since 2018.

I raise the Soumahoro example because it illustrates another kind of limit case, as political heroics may utilize witnessing to gain visibility but are still subject to the operations of systemic racism. They can also distract from ongoing movement work and from "the collective visibility of invisibility."[69] The image of Soumahoro in his work boots may be about representation and the promise of visibility, yet it does not wholly counter the complex problem of invisibilization—a set of processes that have only continued to obscure the issues facing farmworkers and people living in reception centers. (We might think, too, of how an emphasis on persona-based visibility contrasts with other movements built around invisibility, such as the Zapatistas' decision to wear masks *in order to be seen*, obscuring their own faces to move collectively and "undermine hierarchy.")[70] Instead, by channeling the movement through his persona—a tactic not uncommon in politics—Soumahoro essentially made the issues he stood for contingent on his own story, in a moment of widespread suspicion against African migrants.

The further suspicion cast on farmworker movements and precarious migration also distracts publics from recognizing what is in fact longstanding collective work. And this work continues. A number of translocal, transnational efforts are organizing for change in ways very rooted to place and community. Actions include a range of locally based collaborations in which migrants produce and obtain social and legal support. In Campobasso, several Italian employees of a local CAS started a small farm where they work alongside newcomers. This small-scale farming operates in a system almost wholly separate from the national and global markets that large-scale agriculture supplies. It doesn't compete with agribusiness, but it does create alternative forms of agricultural employment for those involved. In Palermo, the NGO Porco Rosso and the restaurant and workspace Molti Volti ("many faces") are hubs for migrants and Italians to build solidarity and support one another in work and through community, and through food produced in just, sustainable ways. One answer these groups offer to the problem of (in)visibility is orienting their efforts toward recognition, at least in part, on a local scale. Through a focus on the (trans)local and on intersections across multiple issues, these efforts challenge social erasure and the withholding of rights.[71]

## CONCLUSION: WITNESSING BEYOND VISIBILITY

Transnational migrant and racial justice movements are bringing renewed global attention to the exploitation of migrant workers in agribusiness and other sectors. These activists' efforts exemplify the possibilities for migrants to exercise agency despite the limits placed on their autonomy by the severe social borders that divide, for example, the realities of global agribusiness managers from those of the laborers harvesting their products. These borders highlight "a fracture at the very heart of the concept of citizenship"[72] that is further enunciated by the mobility of Mediterranean migrants, by the policing and exploitation of their movements, and by the solidarity, activism, and cultural production that emerge in these same spaces.

These are ongoing struggles that manifest not only in demonstrations and media campaigns but in everyday labor and the routines that accompany it. As Carter points out in a discussion of African diaspora and (in)visibility,

> working against invisibility and insisting on one's social presence is what people do all the time—Senegalese migrants create an African market on the streets in an Italian shopping district, where police detain them and sequester their wares, colonial soldiers insist on their right to equal pay, and others everyday refuse to succumb to the indignities of social exclusion, immigration restrictions, discrimination, and neglect.[73]

Again, witnessing is not simply about making visible, just as the stakes of witnessing in contexts of precarious migration do not come down to empathy. The conditions in which migrant farmworkers live and labor index the failures of empathy to sustain material change. If change depended on empathy, then the fall of Soumahoro would devastate farmworker rights movements. They will struggle, but they will also persist.

Crucially, the case of braccianti also reveals how embedded the emergency apparatus is beyond immediate sites of migration. The so-called emergency of Mediterranean migration is neither a sudden, unprecedented rupture, nor an isolated set of issues. Rather, it involves a multiscalar set of interlocking systems of exploitation and exclusion that function in part through a reliance on the invisible farmworker, and that connect death at sea to the single orange clipping and to the more than 1.7 million metric tons of oranges harvested in Italy each year.[74] The emergency apparatus serves globalized Western economies by maintaining a labor force about whom publics not only don't have to care but, crisis framings suggest, should be wary. Emergency imaginaries ignore and exacerbate the structural and systemic issues that hold *some* lives in precarious conditions—tightening borders for people while facilitating the movement of goods, capital, and services.[75] Put another way, the racialization of those presumed to a source of "crisis" for Europe allows European and Italian publics to ignore their perpetual dehumaning, for the traveler who drowns and for the migrant filling crates.

Europe's reliance on deportable workers shows the colonial present to be an age of emergency—or put another way, shows how integral "emergency" is to maintaining the colonial logics and structures that define the present. Working for stability from Italy's margins, the people whose experiences I have discussed here challenge the boundaries imposed on them by the asylum regime, by racist structures and practices, and by Italy's emergency politics. Their testimonies present the right to remain in Italy as the right also to have one's presence and work recognized through contracts and fair wages. Just as these testimonies show the urgency of the issues that intersect in the orange groves, they also show the need to find ways not simply to address repeated "crises." Framing their stories and experiences not through categories of "legal" or "illegal" migration, but in ways that expose the structures linking precarious crossing and migrant worker exploitation, they illustrate how exercising these rights in the colonial present requires a shift from emergency to emancipatory politics.

# Epilogue

*Mobility in an Age of Emergency,
or, A Small and Stubborn Possibility*

In recent years, the area of jungle between Colombia and Panama known as the Darién Gap has regularly made international news as a treacherous passage for people making their way north to Mexico and the United States. This site of transit is also a site of border externalization and control, via surveillance, detention, and collaboration between US, Panamanian, and Colombian governments to prevent people from moving any further north.

Attesting to how such dangers resonate across contexts, in the last decade, scholars, journalists, and activists have increasingly referred to the Darién Gap as "the new Mediterranean."[1] *Mediterranean* as global metonym for deadly crossing, for policed borders, for journeys of extreme risk.

To invoke one "crisis" to explain another: at the surface, this rhetorical move contains no future but simply trades in labels that convey migration as a rupture, a threat, an emergency. It also reflects a trade in kind. In the 1990s, the Mediterranean was called "Europe's Rio Grande," a label used in part to make a point about divisions, that is, about the border—the sea, the river—as separating regions entirely distinct.[2]

What if we instead understood the analogy not as concerning division or the disruption of norms, but as pointing to the porosity of borders and to ongoing entanglements across geographies? After all, crisis and emergency discourses orient European and North American attention to southern borderzones not only figuratively but because these crossings are among the very few options available to tens of thousands of people on the move each year. The Darién Gap is "the new Mediterranean" not simply because it is a dangerous borderzone, but as a now frequent transit corridor for Africans who opt to fly to Brazil, Ecuador, or

Colombia and make their way north via the Americas rather than via the Mediterranean Sea.[3]

As this book has shown in the case of Italy, how a so-called *emergenza immigrazione* or border or refugee crisis takes shape is not simply a matter of how people cross borders but is the product of a complex and shifting apparatus of policies, discourses, and practices that obscure some voices and experiences while making others hypervisible, and that operate together to perpetuate circumstances of risk and precarity. In other words, crisis begets crisis. Asylum itself is increasingly under threat. In Italy and throughout Europe, the criminalization not only of migration but of rescue and aid transforms practices of care from ethical obligations and community practices to exercises in risk. Emergency and crisis rhetorics shape the experiences of migrants and local communities; they also limit broader understandings of mobility by positing migration as the cause of dire circumstances and by construing rights as negotiable or not always applicable.

In this age of emergency—of climate change, pandemics, wars, race- and gender-based violence, economic disparity—migration articulates the intersections of multiple overlapping issues and how they impact individuals and communities. Matters of real, material urgency—genocide, wildfires, a lethal virus—become recognized "crises" as they are managed, mediated, and manipulated over space and time. This is not to say that they don't require radical, immediate intervention, but that the constant treatment of these issues within emergency frameworks defines them through emergency imaginaries, operating as a "counterrevolutionary force" that holds the future hostage, making it difficult to recognize how contemporary issues are interwoven with longer histories and linked injustices, or to envision possibilities for care and community that do not rely on the logics and temporalities of emergency.[4] It's hard not to perceive emergency as a way of being and its accompanying structures, risks, and acts of violence as the terms to which we are collectively bound.

As emergency transits through regions, languages, and lives, how to see outside the grammars and logics it imposes? How to know the world beyond the constraints of crisis—or to create such a future?

Moving from the understanding that "emergency" is both experienced materially and produced through our collective imaginaries, this book has investigated the workings of the emergency apparatus through testimony as method. The makers and narrators whose testimonies I document, analyze, respond to, and in some cases coproduce, make evident some of the violence of emergency migration governance and also signal alternative ways of understanding mobility and its intersections with history, belonging, identity, and rights. These testimonies shift our understanding of the Mediterranean from a sea of "crisis" to a critical site of production of race, where notions of rights and refugeeness are being tested. In Italy, where precarious migration has long been framed in emergency terms, refuting the notion that migrants are the bearers of crisis requires seeing beyond the interminable present of *emergenza*. As I have shown through oral, written, and filmic testimonies, and examples that illustrate migration realities via material space, this work of witnessing is already in play, actively reinscribing interactions, discourses, spaces, and memory with displaced histories and transforming what narratives of migration are available to broader publics.

. . .

One of the most widely circulated images of Europe's "migration crisis" is an aerial photograph of a migrant boat in the Central Mediterranean. It's a photograph you have most likely seen; it continues to be reproduced under headlines around the globe. As viewers looking down from above, we see the faces of dozens, perhaps even hundreds of migrants packed in together, gazing up at the camera from the boat. It's a colorful image, with people in bright clothes. Viewed on a laptop or cell phone, it seems to capture a crowd, but zooming in, individual faces become visible. Some grin at the camera. Some hold infants in their arms. Some raise their hands as if surrendering, or make the peace sign with their fingers. It's an image that invites us to ask, Who is witnessing whom? That is, what relations of witnessing does the photograph capture or invoke? To what ends does such witnessing aim?

This image was circulated by newspapers and activists as a call to action to resolve the "humanitarian crisis" of contemporary Mediterranean migration. Taken in 2014 by Italian photographer Massimo Sestini, its caption in *Time Magazine* read, "Italian navy rescues asylum seekers traveling by boat off the coast of Africa on the Mediterranean, June 7, 2014." It was recognized with a World Press Photo award that year and seemed to cultivate compassion; an effort followed to identify the people in the photograph.

Some six years later, the same image appeared in a campaign ad for Silvia Piani, running for office with Salvini's Lega Party in the Lombardia region. Calling up pandemic-era politics, the ad reads: "When you forget your mask: €1,000 fine. Arrive in a *barcone* [migrant boat]: room, board, and phone plan."[5] The photograph is flipped, so that the boat is moving in the other direction. Banking on viewers' perhaps subconscious memory of the original image, Piani's ad turns the boat around, as she would, sending it back to Africa.

Proof that, as Sontag argued, photographing atrocities does not guarantee their singular reception, this image and its subsequent manipulation remind us to understand witnessing not as a straightforward exchange of objective evidence but as a transaction always contingent on the people involved and the circumstances of their seeing (or hearing, or reading, etc.).[6] The crucial question is not what the photograph means but how it circulates, who owns it, whether those photographed are aware their faces have traveled the world. Simply seeing the image, while it may sometimes enable compassion or empathy, will not resolve border violence or racial injustice. Witnessing is not always transformative. As I have emphasized throughout this book, the violence of emergency is itself evidence of the failures of empathy. The point is not to redeem empathy, but to rethink the work of witnessing itself.

. . .

Emergency is everywhere, experienced differentially and also circulated through a range of media. Yet as much as it stuns, emergency shouldn't surprise us. For Benjamin, recognizing our present as an age of emergency means refuting the temptation to see today's circumstances as unexpected. "The current amazement that the things we are experiencing are 'still' possible in the twentieth century is *not* philosophical," he wrote shortly before fleeing Vichy France. "This amazement is not the beginning of knowledge—unless it is the knowledge that the view of history which gives rise to it is untenable."[7] Likewise, we should recognize the ongoing dehumaning and deadly violence that today's emergency-response border regimes impose not as ruptures but as emerging from longer histories and efforts that created no space for what Ahmed terms "the conditions of possibility of hearing" that testimonial ethics can open.[8]

Where do the failures of empathy leave us?

They leave us in a police car in North Macedonia with Abu Bakar, the husband of Fatmata, a woman from Sierra Leone shot to death by a border guard as she tried to cross from Greece with a small group of people. They leave us with the death of Soumaila Sacko in Calabria, trying to gather building materials to build a shelter to sleep in after harvesting tomatoes. They leave us with blocked ports and abandoned boats, with barbed wire buoys in the Rio Grande and US governors campaigning for reelection by bussing asylum seekers to distant cities, with asylum seekers imprisoned on a barge in the English Channel, with live-streamed genocide as Palestinians document their own violent erasure. The failures of empathy leave us with the strange grief of states and authorities who pretend empathy while depoliticizing violence. They leave us with a perplexing sense that "crisis" is both inevitable and unpredictable, that national borders trump individual rights.

At the same time, this age of emergency is also a time of transnational movements and reconfigured practices of care. I'm thinking of how I learned of Fatmata's death, from comrades at Greece-based NGO Second Tree, which mobilized to support Abu Bakar, sending staff to be with him those first weeks and to ensure Fatmata's body was returned to her family for burial. Or of the organizations by and for migrant women, like the Donne di Benin City in Palermo, which helps people exit trafficking networks. Our age of emergency is also a period of protest and organizing, of solidarity encampments, of migrant-centered art, of expanding dialogues on race, borders, and decoloniality. It is a time of accountability, with activist collective Alarm Phone running a hotline for sea crossers and inspiring related efforts in the Sahara. And it is a time of storytelling—of reclaiming narrative through a range of media—from Kurdish-Iranian journalist Behrouz Boochani's memoir *No Friend but the Mountains*, written via WhatsApp from the

Australian detention center on Manus, to documentaries made by border crossers on cell phones, to graffiti inscribed onto prison walls and culverts en route.

Witnessing is not only about testifying to or documenting the past; it's also about seeing the potential for change. Writing in response to the US war in Vietnam, Baldwin argued that "when the black populations of the world have a future, so will the Western nations have a future—and not till then." He was protesting the US conscription of Black Americans into an imperial war, sent to defend a nation that holds them in harm. Until such a reckoning occurs, he wrote, "Western populations . . . will precipitate a chaos throughout the world which, if it does not bring life on this planet to an end, will bring about a racial war such as the world has never seen." This warning, a recognition of the racial violence that structures the colonial present, echoes in today's intersecting "crises." It's also his point of departure for that slimmest line of hope: "I think that mankind can do better than that, and I wish to be a witness to this small and stubborn possibility."[9]

A small and stubborn possibility: amid widespread violence and uncertainty, this is the scale on which a different future might be set in motion. I don't mean this as a metaphor for resilience. Rather, I mean to take Baldwin at his word, to invoke a small and stubborn possibility as what might emerge through the kinds of witnessing I have discussed throughout this book. Witnessing is about making visible, about seeing differently, but it is equally about imagining otherwise. To imagine—to create—a world that no longer perceives migration as an inherent threat requires reckoning not only with the individual law or shipwreck or discriminatory act (though all of these merit direct response), but also with how these acts fit within a broader apparatus that posits them as solutions to the sudden, unprecedented "problem" of migration, and that renders such acts always possible and increasingly likely. It is to center mobility as a way of being, to mourn and care in ways that defy strange grief, to practice radical hospitality, to challenge systems that build borders as violent, racialized spaces of hypervisibility and erasure, of extreme risk, of nationalisms. This is what we might think of as witnessing for abolition: engaging the world in ways that practice emancipatory rather than emergency politics, that participate in imagining a future not structured by crisis logics.

. . .

Amadou Diallo led me on a walk through Palermo, his adopted city. We meandered past the Quattro Canti; stopped into Ciwara, an African café in the famous *Vucciria* market; walked past a couple of African-owned stores as we made our way to the waterfront. There, I accompanied him to a meeting of local organizations connecting around creating an anti-racist network. Diallo was there representing Stra Vox, the NGO he cofounded on June 6, 2020, amid the initial massive uncertainties of the pandemic, in response to the murder of George Floyd.

For Diallo, this work is about migrant rights and anti-racism, but it's also about Italy and Europe, now his home. It's about Italian youth who are leaving because

FIGURES 27a and 27b Across the street from each other are this mural of George Floyd and the entrance to BarConi (2022). Photos by the author.

they don't see a future here, while Africans arrive by boat to build a better life. He sees these movements as connected—not analogous, but linked, yet another reason to think expansively about what belonging looks like in the world these movements are both responding to and building.

In the Ballarò neighborhood, Diallo introduced me to the staff of a new gelateria run by newcomers from the Gambia and Nigeria, with the support of restaurant and community center Molti Volti. They named the spot BarConi, a pun that recalls the boats on which they crossed the sea to reach safety—*barconi*—and that alludes to the ice cream *coni* they fill for happy customers (figure 27b). They see the name, they said, as signaling a shift "dalla disperazione alla speranza"— away from the despair of the boat and toward hope for the future.

That gaze toward a different future is akin to what I imagine Baldwin had in mind in hoping to be a witness to a "small and stubborn possibility" for change, for "doing better than that." His is a statement about surviving, and also about imagination.

The reorienting gaze of wordplay—a pun that contains lives and livelihoods— offers a small and stubborn possibility for yet another reason. When BarConi employees look out the front of their shop, they see a mural of Floyd, by local artist Cristian Picciotto, the words "no racism" emerging from Floyd's mouth (figure 27a). This positioning—Floyd's face before a migrant-owned gelateria named after precarious vessels that move in the wake of colonial violence— recognizes the structural violence linking Mediterranean crossings and anti-Black racism across regions. It's a juxtaposition that makes present the entanglements of today's precarious crossings, global anti-blackness, the Movement for Black Lives, evolving debates about who belongs in Italy, and the ways that Africans in Europe are creating solutions and services and imagining other ways of being together, via transnational networks and local actions. It's a perhaps small, perhaps stubborn act of reframing that asks passersby to reflect on the relation between the boats, the city, the presence of migrants, and questions of rights and justice, and to orient themselves—ourselves—in relation to these struggles and possibilities.

# Appendix

In a book that addresses the multiple temporalities of migration and the problematics of anonymization and erasure, it feels both crude and important to include maps, lists, and numbers. Migration and refugee "crises" and border "emergencies" are often invoked through counts, but these numbers are themselves fluctuating approximations that tell an incomplete story. Death tallies are an important part of humanitarian appeals for revised laws and the decriminalization of rescue and migration. Arrival counts are regularly cited in fearmongering discourses of invasion. In the United Kingdom, movements to block small boat crossings of the English Channel have relied on these discourses; the Texas governor used precisely such language to justify defying a Supreme Court order in early 2024, blocking the border with Mexico and preventing the US Border Patrol from processing asylum seekers; Italian Prime Minister Giorgia Meloni has worried aloud about a migrant "invasion" in Italy should Tunisia not stop departures from its ports; and Tunisian Prime Minister Kais Saied has condemned the "hordes" of Black migrants reaching Tunisia. In other words, like any data point, a count is readily politicized.

On their own, counts are abstractions, turning people into ciphers, anonymous groups, percentages, trends. Timelines suggest a straightforward chronology, when instead people experience passing months and years with different rhythms, different (re)encounters with the past, and changing ideas about the future. Migration maps often rely on arrows that replicate notions of invasion or that oversimplify what are in fact lengthy, complex journeys that people experience both individually and collectively. Tables, timelines, and maps need context, and—I will say it emphatically—border crossing counts should be understood as guesses under constant revision that, depending on several factors, may serve the causes forwarded by authorities, humanitarian agencies, or people on the move.

How data are collected and shared reflects operations of power. In research for this book, I was repeatedly frustrated by the lack of ready availability of certain kinds of information. For instance: How many people have died crossing the Sahara in recent years? How reliable are data on interceptions at sea along the different Mediterranean routes? How many interceptions go unrecorded? What about pushbacks? Given Italy's nationwide reception system, why is it so difficult to know with any regularity how many people are housed in which kinds of centers, for how long? What opportunities and programs have different centers offered to asylum seekers? How should we understand counts of Italy's foreign population, and references to those counts, given that the children of immigrants who feel and identify as Italian may not have Italian passports? Likewise, I was perplexed by what I worry is the ease with which certain counts and data points get cited without question—information about a particular wreck reported in one newspaper article, for instance, gets recycled in other news and academic publications, without a return to original sources—though source counts and other data cannot always be taken for granted as final facts.

I am constantly struck by the fact that the International Organization for Migration refers to their map of the dead as the documentation of "missing migrants." It's a phrase, common enough in these arenas, that gestures to the inherent incompleteness of the project—to unrecovered bodies, and to the fact that we cannot always know for certain how many people were crossing or how many people drowned—but it also suggests that they might somehow be found again.

We can't understand border violence through death tallies alone and their dehumaning appeal. At the same time, obscured information—nonknowledge—and the lack of ready access to more complete information powers the emergency apparatus and makes counts and linear narratives both suspect and necessary.[1] In the following tables, in an attempt to offer a more comprehensive—if always incomplete—picture, I have assembled information that is often shared only selectively: a chronology of policies that show, when seen together, how the Italian government has relied on emergency framings of and responses to migration for decades; estimates of arrivals and deaths across the Mediterranean; and some of the structures in which people live while waiting to hear what fate authorities will assign to them. To understand how the information in these tables manifests in lived life, we need the stories that have preceded them in this book, and others.

TABLE 1. Precarious Mediterranean migration to Europe: Arrivals and deaths, 2013–2023

| Year | Western routes to Spain* | | | Central routes to Italy and Malta | | | Eastern routes to Greece | | |
|---|---|---|---|---|---|---|---|---|---|
| | Sea arrivals | Land arrivals | Dead & missing | Sea arrivals | Land arrivals† | Dead & missing | Sea arrivals | Land arrivals | Dead & missing |
| 2013 | 3,237^ | 4,235 | — | 42,925 | — | 636 | 11,447 | 1,122 | — |
| 2014 | 3,264 | 964^ | 59 | 170,100 | — | 3,126 | 41,038 | 2,280 | 405 |
| 2015 | 5,312 | 11,624 | 67 | 153,946 | — | 2,913 | 856,723 | 4,907 | 799 |
| 2016 | 8,162 | 6,443 | 102 | 181,461 | — | 4,578 | 173,450 | 3,784 | 441 |
| 2017 | 22,103 | 6,246 | 209 | 119,392 | — | 2,873 | 29,718 | 6,592 | 56 |
| 2018 | 58,569 | 6,814 | 811 | 24,815 | — | 1,311 | 32,494 | 18,014 | 187 |
| 2019 | 26,168 | 6,345 | 685 | 14,877 | — | 754 | 59,726 | 14,887 | 71 |
| 2020 | 40,326 | 1,535 | 821 | 36,435 | 4,100 | 955 | 9,714 | 5,982 | 105 |
| 2021 | 41,979 | 1,218 | 1571 | 68,309 | 9,400 | 1,545 | 4,331 | 4,826 | 115 |
| 2022 | 29,895 | 1,868 | 1221 | 105,575 | 198,000‡ | 1,453 | 12,758 | 6,022 | 343 |
| 2023 | 57,071 | 467 | 1,148 | 157,545 | 11,000 | 1,897 | 41,561 | 7,160 | 710 |
| TOTALS | 292,849 | 42,560 | 6694 | 1,075,380 | 222,500 | 21,405 | 1,261,513 | 74,454 | 3,232 |

SOURCES: UNHCR 2024 and UNHCR annual country fact sheets; International Organization for Migration, Missing Migrants 2024.

NOTE: The above estimates are for people making precarious journeys to the EU via the Mediterranean and Southern Europe. They represent people with a range of legal status, including refugees and people seeking asylum and humanitarian protection. In the Central Mediterranean, most arrivals are in Italy; annual arrivals in Malta range from 23 (2017) to 3,406 (2019). Land arrivals in Italy largely represent people who traveled the Balkan route, then crossed into Italy from Slovenia. "—" indicates unavailable data. Not included here are data on interceptions at sea. In the Central Mediterranean, interceptions by the Libyan and Tunisian coast guards have totaled more than 50,000 per year since 2021. Note that death counts are underestimates.

* Sea arrivals include the Canary Islands; land arrivals are via Ceuta and Melilla

^ Frontex estimates

† Arrivals in the Central Mediterranean are almost entirely by sea; UNHCR data on land arrivals are included where available

‡ Includes 173,638 Ukrainians fleeing Russian invasion, many reaching Italy via Slovenia, granted temporary protection status by the EU

TABLE 2. Emergency measures: Major asylum, immigration, and rescue policies affecting migrants in Italy, 1986–2024 (selection; EU policies in italics)

| Year | Policy | Focus |
| --- | --- | --- |
| 1986 | Foschi Law (946/1986) | Addresses migrant worker rights; establishes study and family reunification visas; includes amnesty to regularize undocumented migrants |
| 1990 | Italy signs Schengen Agreement | Freedom of movement between EU Schengen countries (established 1985) |
|  | Martelli Law (39/1990) | Expands geographic bounds of asylum; regularization amnesty |
|  | *Dublin Convention* | *Regulates asylum procedures across the EU* |
| 1991 | Ordinance, 26 June (2144/FPC) | Initiates "urgent measures" to "confront the emergency" of Albanian arrivals |
| 1992 | State of Emergency (19 May) | Addresses migration from Bosnia-Herzegovina that "threatens to spill over into Italian lands"; additional decrees follow |
| 1994 | Decree (n. 318, 27 May) | "Urgent provisions" for continued humanitarian support for displacement from former Yugoslavia; becomes law 174/1994 |
| 1995 | Puglia Law (563/1995) | Authorizes the deployment of military forces for border control along the coast of the Puglia region |
|  | Dini Decree (n. 489, 18 Nov.) | "Urgent measures" to confront ongoing arrivals; never converted into law but issues amnesty and establishes detention precedent |
| 1997 | State of emergency (19 Mar.) | Issued following *Katër i Radës* wreck and "fear of mass arrivals from Albania"; law 128/1997 solidifies aid measures from this declaration |
| 1998 | Turco-Napolitano Law (40/1998) | Establishes deportation centers, job seeker visas, family reunification for refugees; includes amnesty rule |
| 2002 | Bossi Fini Law (189/2002) | Criminalizes "illegal" immigration; requires employment contracts for visas; establishes country-based quotas, SPRAR system; issued under state of emergency |
| 2003 | *Dublin Regulation (Revised)* | *Stipulates that cases must be decided within two months* |
| 2004 | *Frontex* | *Establishes the European Border and Coast Guard Agency* |
| 2005 | Civil Protection Ordinance (n. 3476, 2 Dec.) | Implements "urgent measures" to handle "clandestine" migrant arrivals |
|  | *Prüm Convention* | *Multiple EU countries agree to share identification and DNA information to protect against "terrorism, cross-border crime and illegal migration"* |
| 2008 | Italy-Libya Friendship Treaty | Italy pledges €5 billion to Libya to combat terrorism, organized crime, drug trafficking, and "illegal" immigration; signed by Berlusconi and Qaddafi |
|  | Security Package (21 May) | Set of policies that establish harsher penalties for "illegal" immigration; requires DNA samples for family reunification; subscribes Italy to Prüm Convention |

TABLE 2. *(Continued)*

| Year | Policy | Focus |
|---|---|---|
| 2009 | Anti-crisis Law (102/2009) | Post-financial crisis measures include amnesty for immigrants in domestic labor and home healthcare |
| 2011 | Emergenza Nord Africa (12 Feb.) | State of emergency concerning North African migration following Arab Spring uprisings; used to open large reception centers; ended 28 Feb. 2013 |
| 2013 | *Dublin III, Revised Dublin Regulation* | *Stipulates that an asylum seeker may apply for asylum in only one EU member state* |
| | *EU Directive on reception (2013/33, 26 June)* | *Establishes EU-wide standards for the reception of applicants for international protection* |
| | Operation Mare Nostrum | Military and humanitarian patrol and rescue mission; Oct. 2013–Oct. 2014 |
| 2014 | Memorandum of Understanding between national, regional, local authorities (10 Jul.) | Issued in response to "extraordinary flow of non-EU citizens" into Italy; basis for Extraordinary Reception Centers (CAS) |
| | *Operation Triton* | *Frontex surveillance mission; replaces Mare Nostrum; Nov. 2014–Feb. 2018* |
| 2015 | *Emergency Trust Fund for Africa established* | *Reserves €5 billion for efforts addressing "root causes of irregular migration and displaced persons"* |
| | *Emergency Relocation Schemes (EU Council Decision 2015/1523)* | *Establishes plan to relocate 160,000 migrants from Greece and Italy to other EU member-states (largely unrealized)* |
| | *EUNAVFOR MED / Operation Sophia* | *Military mission in Southern Mediterranean targeting smugglers for arrest; Jun. 2015–Mar. 2020* |
| 2016 | *EU-Turkey Statement* | *EU pledges €3–6 billion to Türkiye for deterrence; stipulates that for every Syrian deported to Türkiye, another can enter EU* |
| 2017 | Italy-Libya Memorandum of Understanding | Funds and supplies Libyan border control |
| | Code of Conduct for NGO maritime rescue | Regulates rescue and rights on board rescue ships |
| | Minniti-Orlando Law (46/2017) | Increases expulsion centers from 4 to 20; limits asylum appeals to 1 |
| 2018 | Security Decree (n. 113, 4 Oct.) | Abolishes humanitarian protection status; extends possible time in detention; limits SPRAR access; adds Italian language requirement for naturalization; excludes asylum seekers from Italian residency |
| 2019 | Security Decree "Bis" (n. 53, 14 June) | Criminalizes rescue at sea; establishes grounds for denying entry to rescue ships; establishes harsher penalties for disruption of public order during demonstrations |
| 2020 | Rilancio (relaunch) Decree (n. 34, 19 May) | Pandemic-related emergency measures include amnesty rule for domestic workers and farmworkers in response to worker shortage |

*(Continued)*

TABLE 2. (Continued)

| Year | Policy | Focus |
| --- | --- | --- |
|  | *EU Pact on Migration and Asylum* | *Incentivizes distribution of asylum claims among member states; aims to streamline asylum processes across EU* |
| 2022 | Emergenza ucraina | Beginning in March, multiple policies regulating the state of emergency for Ukrainian arrivals, including temporary protection, and COVID-related protocols; extended in 2024 |
|  | *Temporary Protection Directive* | *Grants temporary protection status and related aid to people fleeing Ukraine* |
| 2023 | Code of Conduct for NGOs Decree (no. 1, 2 Jan.) | Limits rescue; restricts how NGO-operated ships request safe port of entry; becomes law 15/2023 |
|  | State of emergency (11 April) | Declared for arrivals by sea |
|  | Cutro Decree (Law 50/2023) | Under emergency measures, limits protection forms; increases penalties for "aiding illegal immigration"; establishes separate procedures for asylum seekers from "safe countries," including €4,938 fee to accelerate process |
|  | *Revised EU Pact on Migration and Asylum* | Streamlines asylum procedures across EU; member-states can accept distribution of migrants or pay hosting countries; implementation under discussion in 2024 |
|  | *EU-Tunisia Memorandum of Understanding* | Funds and supplies Tunisian border control; EU admits "highly-skilled" Tunisians and promises economic support; Tunisia readmits deported Tunisians |
| 2024 | Italy-Albania Memorandum of Understanding | Agreement whereby Italy manages asylum processing centers in Albania for people rescued in Italian waters |

TABLE 3. Main reception categories and center types

| Accoglienza Category | Center Type[*] | Abbreviation | Years Active |
|---|---|---|---|
| *Prima Assistenza /* First Aid | *Centro di Primo Soccorso e Accoglienza /* Center for Emergency Response and Reception | CPSA | 2006– |
| | Hotspot | | 2015– |
| *Prima Accoglienza /* Primary Reception | *Centro di Accoglienza /* Reception Center | CDA | 1995– |
| | *Centro di Accoglienza per Richiedenti Asilo /* Reception Center for Asylum Seekers | CARA | 2008– |
| | *Centro Emergenza Nord Africa /* Center for the North African Emergency | Centro ENA | 2011–2013 |
| | *Centro di Accoglienza Straordinaria /* Center for Extraordinary Reception | CAS | 2014– |
| *Seconda Accoglienza /* Secondary Reception | *Sistema di Protezione per Rifugiati e Richiedenti Asilo /* System of Protection for Refugees and Asylum Seekers | SPRAR | 2002–2018 |
| | *Sistema di Protezione per Titolari di Protezione Internazionale e per Minori Stranieri Non Accompagnati /* System of Protection for Holders of International Protection and Unaccompanied Foreign Minors | SIPROIMI | 2018–2020 |
| | *Sistema di accoglienza e integrazione /* System of Reception and Integration | SAI | 2020– |
| *Detenzione e Rimpatri /* Detention and Expulsion | *Centro di Permanenza Temporanea e Assistenza /* Center for Temporary Permanence and Aid | CPTA | 1998–2008 |
| | *Centro di identificazione ed espulsione /* Center for Identification and Expulsion | CIE | 2008–2017 |
| | *Centro di Permanenza per i Rimpatri /* Detention Center for Deportation | CPR | 2017– |

[*] This list is not comprehensive but offers a sense of the multiple structure types implemented within Italy's accoglienza system. See also Open Polis (2021) and European Council on Refugees and Exiles (2023)

# NOTES

## INTRODUCTION: EMERGENCY IMAGINARIES

1. de Haas 2021.

2. Colucci described emergency in this way at a roundtable on Annalisa Camilli's book *La legge del mare* (*The Law of the Sea*) at Nuovo Cinema Palazzo in Rome on June 5, 2019.

3. Albahari 2015.

4. Gregory 2004, xv.

5. Roitman 2013, 70.

6. Leogrande 2019, 25.

7. Via Mezzadra and Neilson's "border as method," as I elaborate later in this chapter.

8. While I am critical of dominant media narratives, I am also indebted to the careful work of journalists who operate with an ethics aligned with critical refugee studies approaches.

9. Proglio et al. 2021; Smythe 2018; Sharpe 2016, 58–59; Di Maio 2012.

10. Walia 2021, 122.

11. Benjamin 2019 [1940].

12. Agamben's *Homo Sacer* (1998) remains an important and common reference for the state of exception, though as scholars have noted, colonialism, global inequalities, and "capitalist developments" are relatively absent from Agamben's discussion of refugees and the exception (Mezzadra and Neilson 2013, 148). Recentering these matters underscores the fundamental coloniality of the camp and related spaces and processes of containment and control (cf. Anam 2020; Davies and Isakjee 2019).

13. Nyers 2013, 1.

14. Espiritu 2014, 12.

15. Espiritu, 11.

16. Hodžić 2017, 158.

17. Calhoun 2010, 22.

18. See, e.g., Squire 2020; D. S. Massey 2020; Crawley and Skleparis 2018; Campesi 2018; Pallister-Wilkins 2016; Mountz and Hiemstra 2014.

19. Mountz 2020; Nyabola 2019; Rutinwa 2010.

20. Fanon 2004 [1961], 38.

21. Again, "emergency" marks continuity: these dynamics unfolded in the wake of other recent shifts—namely, the 2011–2013 *Emergenza Nord Africa* (North African Emergency) addressed migration prompted by the Arab Spring uprisings (di Costantini 2014). This program concluded just as the EU's revised Dublin Regulation went into effect, stipulating that asylum seekers file their claims in the country in which they enter the EU. In 2015, Germany suspended the Dublin regulation to accommodate Syrians, but in general, the policy has placed significant responsibility on Italy, Greece, and other border nations. See Table 2.

22. *European Commission* 2019.

23. FitzGerald 2019, 2–5.

24. "Missing Migrants" 2024.

25. Sontag 2003; see also Slovic et al. 2017 on the fleetingness of empathic responses to incidents like Alan Kurdi's death.

26. Levi 2017 [1986], 63–64

27. Following the 2011 Arab Spring and the US-led, NATO-supported unseating of Qaddafi, multiple militias have vied for control of Libya, and Africans who once saw Libya as a destination for work struggle to survive there. Nevertheless, EU migration governance enlists the Libyan Coast Guard in policing maritime borders and detaining migrants, with severe consequences. For instance, as arrivals to Italy decreased in 2019, the number of people detained in Libya swelled to more than seven hundred thousand at a time (IOM 2019). For more on political change in Libya, see Lacher 2020.

28. Mezzadra and Neilson 2013, 6–18.

29. Mezzadra 2006.

30. Butler 2006, 25; see also Ettlinger 2007, 320.

31. Brand 2018, 208.

32. Moten 2018a.

33. Baldwin 1985, xi–xiii, reflecting on his experience covering the murders of Black children in Atlanta.

34. Rothberg 2019, 3.

35. Throughout this book, I capitalize "Black" in line with parameters discussed by scholars including Camilla Hawthorne, who recognizes "Black" as indicating "shared histories of subjugation and struggle" that lead to contextually specific forms of "political collectivity and subjectivity" (2021, 172).

36. Gregory 2004, xv.

37. Gregory, 16.

38. On racial borders in the global north, see Achiume 2022.

39. Fanon 1986, 116.

40. On multidirectional movements as a crucial point of reference for transnational Italian studies, see Fiore 2020.

41. On constructions of race in twentieth- and twenty-first century Italy, see Merrill 2018, 56–62; Welch 2016, 29; Carter 2010, 244–50. More broadly, this narrative problem

aligns with the shaping of modern liberalism across Europe and North America through processes of colonization, racialization, assimilation, and forgetting (Lowe 2015, 6–7).

42. Also during this period, as Suzanne Stewart-Steinberg observes, forms of internal colonization significantly shaped the Fascist project, including through land reclamation and (re)settling (2016).

43. Until Italy's economy grew in the mid-1970s and early 1980s, Italians were among the large labor force moving to Northern Europe (Caponio 2008). As immigrants in the Americas, Italians were racialized as other and negotiated their whiteness over time (Guglielmo 2012). On decolonization, see Ballinger 2020.

44. With "coloniality" I intend, following Ahmed, processes of extraction, exploitation, and dehumanization that reflect the "relationship between histories of colonialism and contemporary modes of encounter" (2000, 14; see also Gregory 2004).

45. For a more extensive overview of this framework, see Proglio et al. 2021 and other work by members of the Black Mediterranean Collective and by Alessandra Di Maio.

46. Pratt 2008, 7–8.

47. See, e.g., Fogu 2020; elhariry and Talbayev 2018; Chambers 2008, citing Fernand Braudel.

48. Historical debates on "the Mediterranean race" took up the place of Africanness within Italianness (Cerro 2022).

49. Italy exerted colonial control (in various configurations) in what are today Somalia, Eritrea, Ethiopia, Libya, the Dodecanese Islands, and concession territory Tianjin, China. For more on this chronology, see Ben-Ghiat and Fuller 2005, 2.

50. See Del Boca 1986. The Italian case illustrates how emergency responses to migration today recall the historical development and application of emergency laws and codes by European colonizing forces in the colonies (Shenhav 2012).

51. Forgacs 2014, 185; Carter 1997, 205–9; Pinkus 1995.

52. Italy has of course long policed mobility, via documents and checks. For example, an 1869 ruling required people to obtain a passport to leave Italy; in 1931, Royal Decree 773 required foreigners to register with police and carry identification papers.

53. On Schengen and the securitization of borders, see Bigo 2002; Walters 2010.

54. Servizio Studi del Senato 2015; see also Angel-Ajani 2000; Meloni 2014.

55. These images have also been miscited as representing migration today (Capron 2015).

56. Mezzadra and Neilson 2013, 179.

57. This period is marked by the 1994 election of Silvio Berlusconi and the partisan and legislative shifts of the "Second Republic" (Paynter 2024).

58. UNHCR 2024.

59. Heather Merrill discusses how this imagery normalizes death and suffering (2018, 64–66).

60. Stoler 2016. Colonial memory is also a critical site of "Italy's divided memory" (Foot 2019). On the temporality of emergency in humanitarian contexts and how it limits acknowledgment of historical connections and future possibilities, see Ticktin 2016.

61. Unlike France and Britain, Italy saw rebellions but not anticolonial wars (Ben-Ghiat and Fuller 2005, 2–3).

62. Larebo 2005; Lombardi-Diop 2021, 3.

63. Weheliye 2014.

64. Hall 2021a, 375.

65. Baldwin 1985, xiv.

66. According to IOM data, men typically comprise 60–70 percent of those crossing, and youth 15–30 percent. On migrant deservingness, see, e.g., Abdelaaty and Hamlin 2022; Zetter 2007.

67. Carter 1997, 187; Cariello 2021, 167.

68. Anderson 1983. On emergency imaginaries, see also Craig Calhoun's elaboration of this term (Calhoun 2010). Whereas he discusses the emergency imaginary that defines the humanitarian sphere, here I recognize emergency imaginaries as constructing notions of foreignness much more broadly, though humanitarian responses are certainly a part of it.

69. As Bonnie Honig observes, "emergency" also prevents us from embracing "the afterlife of survival" because it is ahistorical and forecloses futures (2009, 10).

70. Foucault 1980, 194.

71. "Emergencies" 2023.

72. Mountz 2020. On the Australian case, see the work of Behrouz Boochani—e.g., his 2019 memoir *No Friend but the Mountains*.

73. As Joe Masco contends in the context of multiple "crises" in the United States, "crisis talk" saturates publics with images of disaster such that our relationship with the collective future is defined first and foremost by fear (2017, 66).

74. Agamben 2009, 3. As Timothy C. Campbell and Adam Sitze note, many of the "crises" that define our contemporary era center biopolitical questions—that is, "the encounter between the concepts of 'life' and 'politics'" (Campbell and Sitze 2013, 2). Here, in borrowing the concept of "apparatus" in broad terms to describe the operations of emergency, I acknowledge the rich debates that interpret and interrogate the implications of Foucault's *dispositif* for a range of philosophical and political questions. For more on these debates, see Campbell's reading of *dispositif* across the work of Agamben, Esposito, and Deleuze, which underscores its significance for processes of (de-)subjectification. Campbell's reading also confronts the risk that biopolitics leads inevitably to thanatopolitics, with a focus on death supplanting that of care, prompting "a truly staggering extension of death through the production of docile bodies" (Campbell 2011, 60).

75. As Franck Düvell observes, transit migration has been defined in multiple ways and in the European context is often conflated with migration to Europe via EU-adjacent countries. In this sense, it gets cited as an issue in policies that externalize EU borders in attempts to stem "irregular" migration (2012). However, Italy itself is effectively a transit country for many; see, e.g., Belloni 2019, on Eritreans who continue their journeys to Northern Europe.

76. On Dublin, see Fullerton 2016. The EU pact adopted in April 2024 aims to address "burden-sharing" and streamline asylum procedures across member-states but does not prioritize migrant rights and will likely increase detention rates in border countries (Crisp 2024).

77. Byrd 2011, xvi–xvii.

78. Moten 2018a, 35.

79. Moten 2018b, 39. Resonances between "fugitivity" and "refugeeness" include the idea of mobility as "a way of knowing attached to fugitivity" (Vang 2021, 8); fugitivity as a state of being essential to Black life (Moten); and metaphorical connections between the Underground Railroad, freedom seeking, and today's migrations. On this last point I am grateful for conversations with Gerard Aching.

80. Squire 2020, 37.

81. Lynes, Morgenstern, and Paul 2020.

82. *Ministero Dell'Interno* 2022.

83. Besteman 2020, 74. See also Bigo 2009; del Grande 2006; Balibar 2004.

84. Carney 2021; Cusumano and Villa 2021; Mainwaring and Debono 2021.

85. These perspectives inform scholarship across disciplines from geography and political science (e.g., Davies, Isakjee, and Dhesi 2017; Tazzioli and Garelli 2018) to literary and cultural studies (e.g., González Ortega and Martínez García 2022; Sellman 2022). On the fraught relationship between migration research and policy, see Stierl 2020.

86. See, e.g., Hawthorne 2022; Declich and Pitzalis 2021; Campesi 2019; Hom 2019; Merrill 2018; Fiore 2017; Lombardi-Diop and Romeo 2012.

87. Walia 2013.

88. Vang 2021.

89. Gandhi 2022, 3.

90. Agier 2011, 149.

91. Calhoun 2010, 30.

92. Hall et al. 1978, 217.

93. Renga and Cooper 2013.

94. Past 2013.

95. Alexander 2019.

96. Bassi 2018.

97. On the problematics of these labels, see Hamlin 2021.

98. Mezzadra and Neilson 2013, viii.

99. Krämer and Weigel 2017.

100. Bohmer and Shuman 2008, 6.

101. Fanon 1986, 116.

102. Roitman 2013, 41.

103. Shuman 2005.

104. Malkki 1996, 389–90; Powell 2015, 102.

105. On available narratives, see Shuman 2006.

106. Levi 2017, 63.

107. Johanna Sellman observes that Arab literatures of migration use "creative defamiliarisation, new forms of testimonial narratives, and ventures into speculative genres" (2022, 28). On adequate witnesses, see L. Gilmore (2017, 5).

108. Shoshana Felman, quoted in Caruth 2014, 322.

109. Brodzki 2001, 870, emphasis mine.

110. Bhabha 1986.

111. Lester 1984.

112. Baldwin 2010b, 202.

113. Powell et al. 2016, 78.

114. Smith and Watson 2012, 592.

115. Beverley 2008, 572.

116. Shuman 2005, 145.

117. Baldwin 2012 [1955].

118. El-Tayeb 2011, xxxviii.

119. Sellman 2022, 50.

120. L. Gilmore 2017.

121. Whitlock 2015, 169, citing Shoshana Felman.

122. Portelli 2003.

123. M. M. Clark 2014, 7, English version shared with me, in translation from the Italian.

124. Morrison 1993, 6.

125. Oral history interview, Rome, June 2018, English.

126. Mezzadra and Neilson 2013, 3.

127. Balibar 2010, 316.

## 1. STRANGE GRIEF AND ELEGIAC POSSIBILITIES IN THE BLACK MEDITERRANEAN

1. Smythe 2018, 5.

2. De Genova 2011, 1181.

3. Hartman 2019, xiii.

4. Chambers 2017, 110.

5. My conceptualization of "strange grief" is indebted to Sara Ahmed's discussion of "strangerness" and the idea that "through strange encounters, the figure of the 'stranger' is produced, not as that which we fail to recognise, but as that which we have already recognised as 'a stranger'" (S. Ahmed 2000, 3).

6. Squire et al. 2021.

7. See also Giulia Bertoluzzi's documentation of these practices in the 2018 film *Strange Fish* and Amade M'charek's work on this subject.

8. For instance, fishermen from Mazara del Vallo were held captive in 2020; see Puglia 2020.

9. Forensic Architecture 2012.

10. Andersson 2014, 78.

11. See Robinson 2000, 11–16. The Black Mediterranean framework is often traced to Robinson and the Black radical tradition, and to Alessandra Di Maio's 2012 discussion of its relevance for contemporary migration to Italy.

12. Mbembe 2003.

13. J. Butler 2009, 38.

14. Given ongoing political turmoil between militias in Libya, many journalists and activists refer to this entity as "the so-called Libyan coast guard."

15. R. Jones 2016. See also Soto 2022; Squire et al. 2021; FitzGerald 2019.

16. This is by no means the first such threat, but it's notably tied to these contemporary externalization policies.

17. Christedes et al. 2016.

18. Williams 2015, 13.

19. Mengiste 2016. Note that I use "victims" to refer to those who died in transit but do so within the autonomy of migration approach, which understands border crossing as a social and political act. I also recognize, in line with Mezzadra and with Black Mediterranean frameworks, that these dynamics should be understood within the operations of capitalism, as Europe relies on the precarious labor force that arrives via sea crossings, no matter the rate of death. See Mezzadra and Neilson 2013; Mezzadra 2011; Proglio et al. 2021.

20. These narrative negotiations are tied to what John Foot recognizes as "Italy's divided memory," as disputes about the past and its significance have long shaped public perceptions and collective memory (Foot 2009, 3).

21. Mattone 2003. This case also underscores emergency as a structural facet of the present via performances of strange grief that span the political spectrum, from center-left politician Veltroni to right-wing leaders.

22. Lombardi-Diop 2012, 182–83.

23. Ahmed 2000.

24. In the second wreck, which occurred near Malta just eight days later, thirty-four people died.

25. On the visual politics of Mare Nostrum, see Musarò 2017. On how this shift blurred the line between policing and humanitarianism, see Cuttitta 2015.

26. Pop 2013. See also Francesca Soliman's discussion of Lampedusa and the friction between initial public responses to this wreck that condemned EU culpability, and the government's insistence on bringing criminal charges against individual migrants it accused of trafficking, including for having "captained" the boat (Soliman 2024). On both tensions and "solidarity work" in Lampedusa, see also the work of Megan A. Carney (2021).

27. Responses were also contentious within Eritrea: "The Eritrean government has already stated it will pay for all costs needed to bring them [the deceased] home. The biggest obstacle to this seems to be the 'Eritrean opposition' groups who want to drag on this tragedy to capitalize on the grieving state of Eritreans for political consumption" (*Tesfa News* 2013b; see also *Tesfa News* 2013a).

28. Espiritu 2014, 86.

29. Angel-Ajani 2000; Colucci 2018.

30. Pompei n.d.

31. Baldwin 2010d, 5.

32. Lester 1984.

33. Scego 2010, 42.

34. Powell 2015, 15.

35. Romeo 2012, 223.

36. Smith and Watson 2012, 21–30.

37. Ali Farah 2011, 13, trans. Giovanna Bellesia-Contuzzi.

38. Ali Farah, 14–15.

39. Ali Farah, 16.

40. Ali Farah, 14.

41. Portelli 2008, as translated by and quoted in Triulzi 2012.

42. Riccò 2020.

43. *Redattore Sociale* 2003.

44. *The Straits Times* 2013.

45. Ticktin 2016, 263.

46. There are colonial echoes here, too. Ali Abdullatif Ahmida writes that Italian colonial forces did not record the names of the Libyans they killed in concentration camps (2021, 88).

47. Cubilié and Good 2003, 9.

48. Hartman 1997, 74.

49. Torchin 2012.

50. Ponzanesi 2017, 125, quoting from the Archivio Memorie Migranti.

51. Sharpe 2016, 13–14.

52. Sharpe, 19–20.

53. Brand 2018, 59, citing Deleuze on elegy.

54. Smythe 2018, 8.

55. Hall 1993, 225.

56. Mazzara 2016, 5.

57. Torchin 2012, 3, 218.

58. For more on the "afterlives" of the October 3 wreck in art and humanitarian practice, see Horsti 2023.

59. Stierl 2016. One controversial example is the June 2015 funeral coordinated by Berlin-based collective Center for Political Beauty (Zentrum für Politische Schönheit; ZPS). ZPS worked with authorities for a stunt they called The Dead Are Coming (Die Toten Kommen), in which they had the body of a migrant woman exhumed in Sicily and brought to Germany, where her relatives waited, and where ZPS had arranged to hold a proper Muslim ceremony (Itagaki and Gully 2017, 281).

60. Jackson 2002, 91.

61. On racial justice organizing and the Movement for Black Lives across contexts, see Beaman 2021; Shahin, Nakahara, and Sánchez 2021. On the invocation of names, see Lebron 2023, xii.

62. Hartman 2019, xiv.

63. I have in mind SA Smythe's discussion of the Black Mediterranean as "offer[ing] a political paradigm shift that is radical, anarchic, collective, Black and queer," and as a site of "emancipatory citizenship" that counters the centrality of the nation-state (Smythe 2018, 8–9).

64. Ponzanesi 2017, 125.

65. Oral history interview, Calabria, 2018, English.

66. Glissant 1990, 6.

67. Sharpe 2016, 59. Sharpe's expansive understanding of the ship extends beyond the physical boat. Explaining that "the hold" also manifests in the transit camp in Calais and on the streets of Berlin, Sharpe emphasizes that transit *within* Europe also occurs in the wake (2016, 71).

68. Gladstone 2016.

69. García Peña 2022, 230.

70. Brand 2018, 82.

71. Yimer 2015.

72. Hartman 2006, 6.

73. McKittrick 2006, 59; see also Gilroy 1993, 17.

74. Carter 2010, 60, citing Fanon.

75. Foucault 1984.

76. Gandhi 2022, 7–8.

77. Andersson 2014, 79.

78. Sharpe, 90.

79. Fofana 2020.

80. See Ismail 2017. It is worth noting that the English translation I quote, by Charis Bredin, differs from the original Arabic version, for example with several passages appearing in a different order. I thank Johanna Sellman for conversations about its original edition.

81. Khaal 2014, 60–61.

82. Khaal, 121.

83. Ali Farah 2011, 35.

84. Calabrò 2015.

85. Scego 2015, 30. This last phrase could also be translated as "remember that I'm not dead."

86. Gregson 2008, 269–70.

87. Delgado 2012.

88. M. Ahmed 2007, 3.

89. "U.S. Administration Proposes Legislation," 2006.

90. As many pointed out at the time, that same week a boat carrying at least seven hundred people wrecked near Greece, but the vessel and its victims were left where they sank (Sharp 2023). This recalls Fogu's discussion of the Mediterranean as *mare aliourum* (sea of others) (2020, 241).

91. For a longer discussion of these points, see Paynter and Miller 2019.

92. Walcott 2021, 71.

93. Migrant boats and life jackets have periodically been recovered and displayed around Europe. Artist Arabella Dorman hung a rubber dinghy in a church in London; Ai Weiwei wrapped Berlin's Konzerthaus in life jackets; Sara Bernabucci "repaired" a wooden boat with drums in a display I saw in Rome (see chapter 5). Still, the boat as a more permanent memorial object is less common.

94. Salerno 2016, 136.

95. Leogrande 2011, 210–11.

96. Walcott 2021, 71–72.

## 2. HOSPITALITY AS EMERGENCY RESPONSE

1. The CAS, established in 2014, are part of a shift to using larger reception centers, dating to the 2011 *Emergenza Nord Africa*, a response to migrations following the Arab Spring uprisings (Colucci 2023).

2. CAS housed approximately 50 percent of the 154,000 migrants who arrived in 2015 and 86 percent of the more than 76,000 who arrived in 2018 (see Villa, Corradi, and Villafranca 2018; Doctors Without Borders 2016, 3).

3. Derrida's notion of (un)conditional hospitality helps elaborate this paradox: *un*conditional hospitality would mean dissolving distinctions between guests and hosts. But guests must remain guests; otherwise, they threaten the host's sovereignty. Derrida explains this argument through the etymology of *host*, which in Latin (*hostis*) refers to both guest and enemy, and the entangled notions of hospitality and hostility (Derrida and Douformantelle 2000).

4. S. Ahmed 2000, 3.

5. See also Declich and Pitzalis 2021.

6. Stephanie Malia Hom has discussed the related paradoxical notion of "temporary permanence," the name assigned to earlier accoglienza structures (2016).

7. Abrams 2010, 7.

8. Giuseppe Campesi describes this system as "humanitarian confinement," as it integrates humanitarian practices with state security and border governance (2015).

9. Religious organizations also run reception centers, and some operate donation-funded centers outside the official accoglienza system, which enables them to support migrants during transitional periods after they obtain documents. I thank the Agenzia Scalabriniana per la Cooperazione allo Sviluppo in Rome for introducing me to these realities.

10. Oral history interview, Acquaformosa, 2018, Italian.

11. Khosravi 2020a, 203.

12. Beni 2017, 34.

13. "Pocket money" (the term used in Italian) has been a source of criticism and confusion from the public, who sometimes see it as an undeserved handout. Center residents use pocket money to pay for goods and services including clothes, bus tickets, snacks, debts owed for their voyage, and remittances for relatives.

14. Emergency funds are released with little oversight. At some centers, staff did as much as they could for migrants; others tried to profit. When Salvini's 2018 Security Decree decreased daily funding from €35 to €21–26 per resident, centers with more robust cultural programming had to radically tighten or cut services. For an account of daily operations with one cooperative in Prato, see Trentanove et al. 2019.

15. Oral history interview, Campobasso, 2017, Italian.

16. S. Ahmed 2000, 88, emphasis mine.

17. *The Dick Cavett Show* 1969.

18. Baldwin 2012 [1955]. He also notes how processes of projection are revealing: "It's one of the ironies of black-white relations that, by means of what the white man imagines the black man to be, the black man is enabled to know who the white man is."

19. For more on cultures of suspicion concerning asylum seekers, see Bohmer and Shuman 2018.

20. According to ISTAT, as of 2023, 17.5 percent of families in the region live in poverty, compared to 11.8 percent nationally (Redazione ANSA 2023).

21. Decisions to keep migrant arrivals out of sight reflects broader techniques of incarceration, including, as Hana Maruyama pointed out to me, the World War II-era use of trains traveling in off-hours to transport Japanese Americans to the camps where they were incarcerated.

22. S. Ahmed 2000, 37.

23. Khosravi 2021, 14.

24. Merrill 2018, 64.

25. Derrida and Douformantelle 2000, 53.

26. Rigo 2019.

27. Women comprise a minority of people crossing the Central Mediterranean (10–20 percent), but sheer numbers show that while overall asylum requests doubled between 2014 and 2017, the number of women requesting asylum quadrupled. In addition, gendered representations of migration obscure the longer history of women migrating to Italy. Women shaped the country's 1980s transition to a migrant destination, including domestic workers

(*badanti*, or nannies and caregivers) from Eastern Europe and West Africa. They often arrived with visas, something restrictive quotas have inhibited. On gendered migration to Italy, see Olivito 2017, 45; Paynter 2023.

28. Oral history interview, Campobasso, 2018, English. These examples of discrimination mark shifting racial politics in Italy, where discrimination against Southerners historically invoked Africa as a proxy for undesirable otherness. Today, Southern Italians are "in a position of greater privilege as citizen insiders vis à vis 'blacks' ('*Neri*' and '*Marrochino*')" (Merrill 2011, 1543).

29. Carter 2010, 5.

30. Krause 2022, 143.

31. Jacobsen and Karlsen 2021, 13.

32. See the discussion of waiting in Shahram Khosravi 2020b, 303. This paradox also illustrates the complexity of experiences within what Ticktin describes in the humanitarian context as the temporality of emergency (2016, 9).

33. Mbembe 2001, 15–16.

34. Khosravi and Yimer 2020.

35. As Espiritu notes, the focus in scholarship on suffering or listlessness in camps can contribute to crisis discourse. Centering migrant perspectives and a heterogeneity of experiences offers a critical counterpoint (2014, 190).

36. Smith and Watson 2010, 90.

37. Waiting is an active state in multiple senses, including "being in a state of consciousness" (Khosravi 2020a, 205).

38. Oral history interview, Campobasso, 2017, English.

39. Viviano and Ziniti 2018; Urbina 2021.

40. Shuman 2005, 5.

41. Bohmer and Shuman 2008, 16–18, 27–28.

42. This violence is neither new nor newly documented. For example, Yimer's 2008 documentary *Come un uomo sulla terra* (*Like a Man on Earth*, dir. with Andrea Segre) features the testimonies of people who experienced such violence in the mid-2000s.

43. CAS staff includes psychologists, but it is difficult to ascertain what uses migrants make of their services. For some, these services are significant, but for others, the forms of therapy or consultation offered in an Italian context do not represent familiar values and practices, or migrants may suspect staff of serving the interests of authorities. See Giordano 2014.

44. Vang 2021, 14, citing Stefano Harney and Fred Moten on fugitivity.

45. Quoted with the author's permission.

46. Initially shared with me by the teacher; quoted with the author's permission.

47. Oral history interview, Campobasso, 2018, Italian.

48. On deservingness and Europe's "refugee crisis," see Holmes and Castañeda 2016.

49. This may be because of competing views; it can also simply be a problem of linguistic translation (Jacquemet 2019).

50. See also Paynter 2022b, where I discuss language learning and the CAS environment in terms of deservingness and crisis racism.

51. In fact, the system sometimes allows for one's adjustment to "count." As Isabella, with the SPRAR in Acquaformosa, explained, if someone's appeal is rejected but the applicant has made measurable progress with integration, then they could submit a "*reiterata*," or

"reiterated application," essentially a chance to start the process over from the beginning. In the CAS system, however, I never heard it cited; since the 2017 passage of the Minniti legislation, the sense was, one appeal only.

52. Reuters 2018.

53. *La Repubblica* 2019.

54. *Fortune Magazine* 2016. I witnessed similar efforts in the nearby town of Camini.

55. Giuffrida 2018.

56. Derrida and Douformantelle 2000, 77.

57. Ciullo 2017. Such corruption persists, with cases continuing to come to light, as I also discuss in chapter 6.

58. Bassi 2018.

59. Goldberg discusses dehumanization as racialization (2001, 87, citing Fanon).

60. Balibar 1991; see also Paynter 2022b.

61. Shuman 2006.

62. Hom 2016, 92.

63. Albahari 2015, 12, 50–51.

64. This idea also recalls guest worker programs implemented in northern European nations to attract laborers, including Italians, following World War II (cf. Castles 2006, 742).

65. Hom 2016, 92.

66. Between 1929 and 1934, Italian colonial forces carried out genocide in Libya, including in concentration camps in which they imprisoned Bedouins whose nomadism they saw as a threat to their imperial aims (Hom 2019, 65, 85).

67. "Integration" is used in multiple countries, e.g., the Netherlands, Germany, and Sweden, as part of citizenship processes, including exams that test linguistic capacity and rely on specific kinds of cultural knowledge. Salvini's 2018 Security Decree instituted an Italian language requirement for those obtaining citizenship.

68. Paik 2020, 28–30; Marinari 2020.

69. El-Tayeb 2011, xxxi; Balibar 1991; M'charek, Schramm, and Skinner 2014; Goldberg 2006.

70. NGOs across Europe have launched projects with municipalities to do just this; I encountered such initiatives through the Greece-based organization Second Tree.

71. "Nel 2017 6.500 Migranti Rimpatriati" 2018.

72. Blasco et al. 2023.

73. See Gordon, Sharpley-Whiting, and White 1996.


### 3. EMERGENT PRACTICES OF HOSPITALITY IN THE CAMP

1. In 2018, members of transnational collective No Name Kitchen operated a van there for this purpose.

2. Forgacs 2014, 272–73; Hom 2019; Sigona 2015.

3. Doctors Without Borders 2016.

4. E. Camilli 2017a.

5. Qasmiyeh 2021, from "Function of Inhabiting."

6. As Franck Düvell observes, official EU and IOM reports conflate transit migration with illegality and insist that people "transit" through countries bordering the EU (2012).

The experiences of migrants suggest otherwise. On transit in France, see Luca Queirolo Palmas 2017.

7. Wheatley 2021, 256. This notion of a politics of survival is intimately related to the Italian idea of "politica solidale," or solidarity politics. On emergent solidarity practices in contexts of transit, see, e.g., Giliberti and Queirolo Palmas 2020.

8. With "friction," I refer to Anna Tsing's discussion of multiscalar (inter)connections, sometimes in tension, sometimes in generative mode (2005).

9. Paik 2020, 113.

10. My discussion of Piazzale Maslax is informed by my visits to other camps and services that Baobab supported before and after.

11. Carter 2010, 5.

12. Hesford 2011, 56.

13. S. Ahmed 2000, 22–24.

14. Yancy 2008, 6.

15. Carter 2010, 108.

16. Hartman 1997, 3.

17. Hartman 1997, 22; Shuman 2005, 5.

18. Gregory 2004, 9–11; Kelley 2000, 9.

19. M'charek, Schramm, and Skinner 2014.

20. Stoler 2016, 77–78.

21. Brand 2018, 83.

22. Sigona 2015, 1.

23. Pratt 2008, 7.

24. At the time, Italian asylum officials readily recognized Eritreans' flight from political unrest and forced military conscription as meriting political asylum. It is even more striking, then, that the men insisted on voicing their rights via linguistic and other cultural ties.

25. In some notorious centers, operators profited off government funds, for instance by giving residents cigarettes and keeping their pocket money.

26. Oral history interview, Rome, June 2017, English.

27. Katz, Martin, and Minca 2018, 2. See also Kandylis 2019; Davies, Isakjee, and Dhesi 2017; Belloni 2016.

28. Davies and Isakjee 2019.

29. Coletti 2018.

30. S. Ahmed 2000.

31. Wheatley 2021, 257.

32. Danewid 2021, 158.

33. Danewid, 161.

34. Thanks to Rachel Beatty Riedl and Aliou Gambrel for conversations about this concept.

35. Paik 2020, 113.

36. Pasciuti 2014.

37. Mayor Virginia Raggi would later refer to Buzzi when explaining why Rome continued to fail to provide additional accommodations for transit migrants, saying, "It will take longer. Buzzi's not around anymore" (*Redattore Sociale* 2016).

38. The center appears on regional lists from 2014 to 2015 as a site providing migrant aid with the support of local authorities, even receiving some funds to provide meals (Ufficio immigrazione 2014; see also Bock 2018, 162).

39. The history of occupied spaces in contemporary Italy is connected to movements across the political spectrum. It is also a history of crackdowns; authorities regularly threaten eviction and clear these structures, especially in recent years. Cf. Herzfeld 2009.

40. Baobab Experience 2017.

41. Frequent coverage by Italian media brought Baobab into public view. *Vanity Fair Italia* covered the center closing; news media highlighted the Mafia Capitale scandal and the city's unrealized promises for more accommodations. National weekly *Internazionale* regularly covered Baobab as a window onto changing migration dynamics.

42. Skype interview, January 2017, Italian. On "violent inaction," see Davies, Isakjee, and Dhesi 2017.

43. Baobab Experience 2016.

44. A. Camilli 2017.

45. Stoler 2016, 117.

46. Stoler 2016, 77–78; see also Hom 2019.

47. Fiddian-Qasmiyeh 2020, 289.

48. Hom 2019, 3.

49. For more on the nomad emergency, see Hom 2019, 124–27.

50. Forgacs 2014.

51. Whitlock 2014, 82.

52. Gueguen-Teil and Katz 2018, 94. This radical hospitality stands in contrast to what Miriam Ticktin critiques as humanitarian regimes of care that, while intended to help people on the move, nevertheless rely on hierarchies of deservingness and innocence (Ticktin 2016).

53. Fiore 2018, 525.

54. Whitlock 2014, 94.

55. Arendt 1953.

56. S. Ahmed 2000, 157.

57. On listening, see also Powell 2015, 116–17.

58. In 2022, Andrea Costa and two volunteers face charges of facilitating illegal migration for having purchased bus tickets for migrants to travel from Rome to Genova in 2016. Charges were eventually dismissed.

59. L. Gilmore 2017, 5.

60. Whitlock and Kennedy 2020, 484–85, citing John Durham Peters and writing about migrants' uses of social media while detained in Australia's island centers.

61. Salvini claimed this move would force the EU to distribute migrants more equitably between member states rather than requiring countries of first arrival like Italy to accommodate all asylum seekers who disembark on their shores.

62. Rannard 2018.

63. Baobab Experience 2018.

64. For more on witnessing and narrative control, see Powell 2014.

65. Baobab Experience 2018.

66. Giliberti and Queirolo Palmas 2020.

67. Baldwin 2010b, 202.

68. In fact, Baobab would again transport migrants, including when, in 2022, they drove Ukrainians fleeing war across Europe to Italy.

69. Whitlock 2015, 9.

70. Paik 2020, 132.

71. Whitlock 2015, 82.

72. For more on these "traces of displacement," see Paynter and Powell 2023.

73. Hamilakis 2016, 9.

## 4. STREET VENDOR AS WITNESS

1. Vista Agenzia Televisiva Nazionale 2019.

2. *La Repubblica* 2018.

3. Roitman 2013, 18–19.

4. S. Ahmed 2000.

5. Balibar 1997.

6. L'Hote and Gasta 2007; Gasparetti 2012.

7. Millar 2014, 34.

8. Rosales 2020, 18.

9. Khouma 2010, 5.

10. The question of supply is also a source of rumor in popular Italian narratives that question the legality of this trade, including how and where vendors obtain their goods—amplifying the "culture of suspicion" surrounding migration more broadly (Bohmer and Shuman 2018).

11. See, for instance, his 2020 book *Noi italiani neri: Storia di ordinario razzismo* (*We Black Italians: An Account of Everyday Racism*).

12. Parati 2010. In addition, this and other works often also exist in French translation or even French-Italian bilingual editions, making them available to more Senegalese across the diaspora.

13. Khouma 2010, 2

14. For more on the writing and selling of these works in the 1990s, in Italy's early days as a net destination country, see Lombardi-Diop 2005.

15. Whitlock 2015, 1.

16. Mademba 2011, 29.

17. Mademba, 30.

18. Mademba, 28.

19. Mademba, 30.

20. Baldwin 2010b, 202.

21. L. Gilmore 2017, 5; see also Whitlock and Kennedy 2020.

22. Hesse 2000, 17.

23. Whitlock 2015, 169.

24. Oral history interview, Florence, 2019, Italian.

25. Salzberg 2011, 738, 752.

26. Nicholas Harney discusses this in the context of Naples (2004).

27. *The Economist* 2020.

28. Khadyi Tall, quoted in Thomson and Tattersall 2007.

29. Carter 1997, 45–47.

30. Carter, 50.

31. de Certeau 1984, 93–95.

32. Carter 2010, 23.

33. Carter, 24

34. See, e.g., Rosales 2020; N. Harney 2004.

35. Carter 1997, 90.

36. Daly and Barot 2020, 36.

37. On this etymology, see also Carter 1997; Khouma 2010; Ponzanesi 2004, 130; Parati 1999, 40.

38. Pesarini 2021, 51.

39. Carter 1997, 209–12; Ballinger 2020, 28–29.

40. Pesarini 2021, 37–38; Hawthorne 2022, 98.

41. Baizán and González-Ferrer 2016, 343. This period also coincided with major political shifts in Senegal, influenced by leaders' "thick connections" to France (Riedl 2014, 74–75).

42. Theodore 2003; see also Carter 2010, 267.

43. Mosoetsa, Stillerman, and Tilly 2016, 13.

44. King 1993, 290.

45. Baizán and González-Ferrer 2016, 348.

46. Gasparetti 2012, 263.

47. Mezzadra and Neilson 2013, 2.

48. Carter 1997, 83.

49. Balibar 2010, 319.

50. Hartman 1997, 3–4.

51. Fassin 2011; on "ideal refugees," see also Fiddian-Qasmiyeh 2010.

52. Ticktin 2017, 578. As Yến Lê Espiritu argues in the context of the US invasion of Vietnam, a media emphasis on the United States and on white US soldiers as "innocent" and "benevolent" has made heroes out of this conflict while erasing numerous atrocities from US collective memory and obscuring the significant and heterogeneous experiences of refugees who fled that violence (2014, 91).

53. Aronsson 2022, 61, citing Bhabha.

54. S. Ahmed 2000, 157.

55. S. Ahmed, 157.

56. Ticktin 2017, 578

57. Mademba 2011, 54.

58. Carter 1997, 5.

59. Mademba 2011, 17.

60. Paynter 2022b.

61. *Stranieri in Italia* 2018.

62. Bohmer and Shuman 2018, 25–26.

63. Mademba 2011, 35.

64. Mademba, 51.

65. Albahari 2015, 42; King and Mai 2009.

66. Weheliye 2014.

67. Stoler 2016, 7.

68. Fiore 2017, 17.

69. Mademba 2011, 49.

70. These examples also speak to testimonial life narrative as a genre that can be used to "demand recognition, advocacy, responsibility, and accountability" (Whitlock 2015, 203).

71. Rothberg 2019, 1.

72. Parati 2010; Romeo 2015.

73. I did not contact the original author for reasons including his desire for privacy.

74. Shuman 2005, 5–8.

75. Copies are also available online on used book sites, though Cecconi suggested to me that these are likely pirated copies or resales. The press does not have an online presence.

76. Salvini's 2018 and 2019 security decrees were especially harsh and accompanied by overtly racist discourses. They should also be recognized within a broader emergency apparatus and the longer trend of tightening Italian borders and enlisting Libya's collaboration under governments on both the left and right of the political spectrum.

77. This was palpably true during the COVID-19 pandemic, when face-to-face exchanges brought serious health risks, and then curfews and public distancing regulations effectively closed many public spaces. Vendors lost access to their income, and because they were largely operating in informal economies, they had no recourse for the supplementary aid the state offered to furloughed employees during that period. To address these problems, Senegalese communities in Italy rallied for support and to stay informed (Di Rienzo and Angeloni 2021).

78. A. Camilli 2018.

79. A. Camilli 2018.

80. Pradella and Cillo 2021.

81. Mezzadra and Neilson 2013, 144; see also Fassin 2011.


## 5. SEEN AND UNSEEN IN THE CITY

1. See *Il Messaggero* 2017.

2. Occupying buildings and abandoned sites has a significant social and political history in Italy, especially since the occupations of the 1960s and 1970s (Grazioli 2021). It's a practice that groups across the political spectrum have long used to combat the lack of official support for their causes and to operate outside the purview of systems that refute them. For more on migrant occupations and the emergenza abitativa, see Belloni, Fravega, and Giudici 2020.

3. Ficocelli 2017.

4. E. Camilli 2017b.

5. Underscoring how pervasive these "emergencies" are, a number of municipalities have webpages dedicated to assisting locals in confronting the *emergenza abitativa*.

6. Beaman 2017, 11.

7. Casas-Cortés 2021.

8. I use "seconde generazioni" or G2 in reference to the names of formal and informal networks of people working for citizenship rights and invoking this term (e.g., Rete G2). While "G2" is one way those in the movement for citizenship rights refer to themselves, I don't mean to adopt it as an all-encompassing term. In that sense, the plural "generations" is important, as strict generational definitions here would be too limiting.

9. On racial politics and the history of Italy's *jus sanguinis* framework, see Hawthorne 2022, 32–37.

10. Italy is not unique in its *jus sanguinis* framework; other EU countries also pass on citizenship through parentage and do not automatically assign citizenship to those born within their territory. Still, Italy's paths to citizenship for those with foreign parents are especially strict. In France, the children of migrants can obtain citizenship upon turning eighteen if they have lived continuously in France for five years. Germany requires eight years. In Italy, when the children of migrants turn eighteen, they have one year to claim citizenship and must prove continued residency in Italy for the prior eighteen years. Meeting these criteria can be especially difficult for immigrant families. As *jus soli* advocates have pointed out, "it is remarkable that several common documents certified by state administrations, such as degrees, cannot be considered sufficient evidence to allow a person's continued presence on Italian soil" (Ceravolo and Molina 2013).

11. I use the term "citizenship" to underscore the significance of multiple, heterogeneous modes of belonging beyond strictly legal, nation-bounded status. Related work has also discussed belonging in terms of "denizenship" (cf. Mezzadra 2006).

12. Isin and Nielsen 2008, 2. In a related discussion, Mezzadra and Neilson discuss "practices of citizenship" and underscore how race and sexuality, along with border politics, shape understandings of the citizen (2013, 257–58). See also Balibar 2004; Brandzel 2016; Belloni, Fravega, and Giudici 2020.

13. El-Tayeb 2011, citing Italian rapper Amir Issaa; see also Scego 2010, 46.

14. de Certeau 1984.

15. de Certeau, 108.

16. Focusing on acts of citizenship is also a way of recognizing migration as a social and political act and, as autonomy of migration scholars observe, "a force that is capable of social and political transformations" (Nyers 2015, 27; see also Walters 2008, 189).

17. Carter 2010, 265.

18. Nyers 2015, 27.

19. Cf. Felman and Laub 1991, 76.

20. Cf. de Certeau 1984.

21. Hartman and Wilderson 2003, 185.

22. For more on oral history and walking tours, see, e.g., High 2013.

23. Hom 2015, 5–6.

24. Zoom interview with Marco Stefanelli, May 21, 2020, Italian.

25. McKittrick 2006, xv.

26. Vang 2021, 180.

27. I quote from English versions of these tours.

28. Hartman describes how Harriet Jacobs "brackets" her status as a slave in order to narrate in ways that are "meaningful in a white dominant frame" (Hartman and Wilderson 2003, 187).

29. Doctors Without Borders 2016; Mazzara 2019, 29–30.

30. Fanon 1986, 116.

31. For more on the Invisible Guides' soundwalk production processes, see Paynter 2022a.

32. D. Massey 2005.

33.  Brodzki 2001, 871; on contingency, see also DiPiero 2022, 7–8.

34.  Petralia 2010, 97.

35.  Of course, aural encounters could reproduce strangerness, but the tour orients participants not to imagine the lives of individual narrators, but instead to experience Rome through their words.

36.  hooks 2014, 50; also cited in Oliver 2001.

37.  See also Tom Western's discussion of the sounds of migration and sonic citizenship practices, including uses of sound to evoke belonging (2020).

38.  de Certeau 1984, 98; Paquette and Mccartney 2012, 138.

39.  de Certeau 1984, 99.

40.  Carter 2010, 23–24.

41.  Mezzadra and Neilson 2013, 5–10.

42.  Brickell and Datta 2011, 4.

43.  Baldwin 2010a, 43.

44.  In interviews, Scego has repeatedly refuted the activist label, emphasizing instead her role as a writer.

45.  Hawthorne 2022, 161.

46.  Bianchi and Scego 2014, 107–8.

47.  Scego 2010, 9.

48.  Scego 2020.

49.  El-Tayeb 2011, 4.

50.  El-Tayeb, xxx.

51.  Espiritu 2014, 125.

52.  L. Gilmore 2011, 79.

53.  See also Paynter 2017b.

54.  Stoler 2016, 8.

55.  Ben-Ghiat and Fuller 2005, xv–xviii.

56.  L. Gilmore 2001, 154.

57.  This literature also explicitly connects experiences across the African diaspora and across histories. For instance, Scego's 2020 novel *La linea del colore* (*The Color Line*) brings Indigenous North American history, African American history, Italian unification, Italian colonialism, and contemporary precarious migration into dialogue. With broader diasporic connections in mind, Christopher Hogarth refers to Scego as an *Afropean* writer (Hogarth 2022).

58.  Bianchi and Scego 2014, 21–22.

59.  Sharpe 2016, 74.

60.  In other work that ruptures these norms, Scego also addresses sexuality.

61.  Bianchi and Scego 2014, 107.

62.  Bianchi and Scego, 69.

63.  Rothberg 2019, 1.

64.  Brah 1996, 193.

65.  Scego 2010, 40.

66.  Sbacchi 2005, 50; Labanca 2005.

67.  Scego 2010, 36.

68.  Stoler 2016, 157.

69. Scego 2010, 36.

70. See Lorgia García Peña's discussion of translation across histories, borders, and cultures as a definitive aspect of second-generation lives and one that can serve or challenge "the project of the nation-state" (2022, 218–219).

71. Bianchi and Scego 2014, 16–18.

72. Espiritu 2014, 19–20, quoting from Morrison's 1989 essay "Unspeakable Things Unspoken."

73. Following our tour, Fiorentini encouraged us to stay and spend time in the museum, then gather for a meal in the cafeteria. This is one of the ways visitors both interact with residents and financially support the collective.

74. El-Tayeb 2011, xxx.

75. Casas-Cortés 2021, 511–12.

76. Sina 2020.

77. Gabriele Salvatori's thesis on Metropoliz carefully documents the complex and conflictual relations of residents (Salvatori 2021; see also Grazioli 2021). These are crucial aspects of life within the occupied site; here, however, I focus on the ways Metropoliz appears to outsiders and on that particular witnessing work.

78. Cusumano and Villa 2021; Atoui 2020; Paul 2020; Heller and Pezzani 2020.

79. Weheliye 2014, 79.

80. Vang 2021, 6.

81. El-Tayeb 2011, xxxvi.

82. "Dalla parte di Metropoliz Città Meticcia!" 2016.

83. Baudry 2017, 134–35.

84. Palermo 2021.

85. Grazioli 2017, 399.

86. Shuman 2006.

87. Cf. Powell 2015, 121.

88. Balibar 1997.

89. Hawthorne 2022, 159. On the French context, see Beaman 2017, 201. The regulation of migration and citizenship is, as Nandita Sharma argues, part of the construction of the nation itself and the "Postcolonial New World Order" (2020, 3–6).

90. On gender, asylum, and (non)normative citizenship, see Brandzel 2016, 3–4.

91. Bhabha 1990, 299.

92. Harney and Moten 2013.

93. Moten 2018b, 50.

94. S. Ahmed 2000, 158.

95. D. Massey 2005, 130.

## 6. ORANGES AND RIOT GEAR

1. Cf. Jones and Awokoya 2019.

2. Colucci 2022.

3. Dines and Rigo 2015, 165.

4. Leigh Gilmore uses the notion of "limit case" to describe trauma-informed autobiography and the related constraints of self-representation (2001). In applying this term to the

context of migrant labor, I mean to suggest the (limited) range of self-representation that people in precarious legal or social positions may find possible.

5. Carter 2010, 15.

6. Other examples of precarious labor include construction, sex work, and domestic labor. These sectors can provide a contract, decent pay, and some stability, but they are also rife with exploitation, and recently arrived migrants are prime targets for this work, as they seek income to establish themselves in Italy or, as many told me in interviews, to pay off debts incurred in transit.

7. Corrado, de Castro, and Perrotta 2017, 5.

8. Venkatesh et al. 2023.

9. "The Economic Performance of Agriculture in Italy" 2017.

10. Avallone 2017, 219.

11. Leogrande 2016, 67–69.

12. Gaudio et al. 2020, 39–44. In a 2011 article, Alessandra Corrado cites an INPS figure stating that more than 90 percent of worked hours in the South are from irregular labor (195).

13. Monti 1998.

14. Palmisano and Sagnet 2015, 29–30.

15. Corrado 2011; Nagle 2020; Leogrande 2016.

16. Testore 2019.

17. With "conscription," I have in mind Christopher Ian Foster's framing: "Imperialism set the global conditions that dictate how and where one moves, while neoliberal capital continues to destabilize the Global South for the direct benefit of the North. This directs, shapes, and interdicts movement" (2019).

18. R. W. Gilmore 2007, 247; see also Raeymaekers 2021, 121.

19. Bhoola 2018; see also Jones and Awokoya 2019. In 2023, the Global Slavery Index estimated that at least 197,000 workers in Italy were enslaved (in and beyond agriculture), up from 145,000 in 2018, when that number included at least 50,000 agricultural laborers. Conditions in Italy (pop. 60 million) reflect specific social and geographical contexts while also marking a global issue. To compare to nearby countries, the GSI estimates that 135,000 people live in conditions of enslavement in France (pop. 65 million); 66,000 in Greece (pop. 10 million); 108,000 in Spain (pop. 47 million); and 1,320,000 in Türkiye (pop. 84 million).

20. Mbembe 2001, 235; see also Pradella and Cillo 2021.

21. Corrado, de Castro, and Perrotta 2017, 4.

22. Kelly 2001, 2; see also Walia 2021, 7–8.

23. Mezzadra and Neilson 2013, 21–23, 92.

24. Gaudio et al. 2020, 44.

25. Carter 2010, 32, 28.

26. Cf. Handal et al. 2020.

27. Morlotti 2020; Roberts 2020.

28. Human Rights Watch 2020.

29. Lewis and Waite 2015; see also Samaddar 2020, 68.

30. Oral history interview, Rome, June 2018, English.

31. Khosravi 2021, 17.

32. Blasco et al. 2023.

33. Annual *decreto flussi* are available via the Ministry of the Interior. On how these counts changed in the 2000s–2010s, see Dammacco 2018.

34. This was even more the case following the closure of a number of urban reception centers beginning in 2018. These closures, ordered under Interior Minister Salvini's leadership, served political optics: fewer centers in cities made it look like the "problem" of migration was being handled.

35. For more on the Gran Ghetto, see the work of Timothy Raeymaekers, e.g., in Proglio et al. 2021.

36. For instance, in 2017 Southern Italy had an unemployment rate of more than 20 percent, triple that of the North and double that of Central regions, and including a 24.6 percent unemployment rate for women ("Economie regionali: L'economia di Calabria" 2018; *Gazzetta del Sud* 2019).

37. Marra 2012, 62.

38. Dotsey and Chiodelli 2021.

39. Locatelli et al. 2018, 6–7.

40. Morosi 2019.

41. These deaths are also linked to the deaths of exploited farmworkers globally—for example, to the heat-induced death of Efraín López García in Florida in 2023.

42. Mira 2020.

43. Advocacy witnessing may aim to increase awareness of suffering but inevitably confronts the limits of trauma testimony (Schultheis Moore 2014).

44. Hooper 2010; see also Donadio 2010.

45. One more recent example comes from the weekly television program *Propaganda Live*, where reportage has included collaborations between host Diego Bianchi and local migrant activists and unions to document ongoing worker exploitation in the Piana di Gioia Tauro.

46. On the recent use of nonprofessional actors in Italian cinema and its role in films' global reception, see O'Rawe 2020.

47. The other two films are *A Ciambra* (2017), about the Romani community, and *A Chiara* (2022), about organized crime. *A Ciambra* was considered for an Oscar nomination.

48. Torchin 2012, 3.

49. I discuss these layered testimonial aspects of the film at more length in Paynter 2017a.

50. Torchin 2012, 7–8.

51. Landsberg 2009, 222.

52. Baldwin 2010c, 189–90.

53. Césaire 1972 [1950].

54. See, e.g., Hooper 2007.

55. Torchin 2012, 7.

56. Lipkin 2011, 13.

57. In *Stolen Life*, Moten defines criticism as "the capacity to see things in their branching and unfolding and generative differentiation," as opposed to forms of critique that instead foreclose possibilities and regulate behaviors and ideas. "Seeing things doesn't hide the crisis that critique discloses; rather, it locates it more precisely, within a general tendency for upheaval that it constitutes" (2018a, 183–84).

58. Hall 2021b [1981], 77. Building on Hall, Moten defines "crisis" as having "a policing function" (2018a, 184).

59. Corrado 2011, 200.

60. Saucier 2021, 112.

61. Sharpe 2016.

62. Sharpe, 71.

63. Sharpe, 73.

64. Saucier 2021, 111.

65. "Yvan Sagnet | No cap" 2023.

66. Liguori 2018.

67. Poggioli 2020.

68. A. Camilli 2022.

69. Thanks to Amrita Wassan for this phrase, which came up in a conversation that clarified this point for me.

70. Olguin 2002.

71. Raeymaekers 2021, 140.

72. Mezzadra and Neilson 2013, 153, 151.

73. Carter 2010, 22–23.

74. "Larger European Orange Crop Expected" 2021.

75. Bigo 2009, 580.

## EPILOGUE: MOBILITY IN AN AGE OF EMERGENCY, OR, A SMALL AND STUBBORN POSSIBILITY

1. Lowal 2019.

2. Montanari and Cortese 1993; King 1996.

3. The risks of this crossing are so well known that some people now opt to fly instead to Nicaragua, to avoid that step in the journey.

4. Masco 2017, 67.

5. *La Repubblica* 2020.

6. Sontag 2003.

7. Benjamin 2019 [1940].

8. Ahmed 2000, 157.

9. Baldwin 2010b.

## APPENDIX

1. Krause 2022.

# BIBLIOGRAPHY

Abdelaaty, Lamis, and Rebecca Hamlin. 2022. "Introduction: The Politics of the Migrant/Refugee Binary." *Journal of Immigrant and Refugee Studies* 20 (2): 233–39.

Abrams, Lynn. 2010. *Oral History Theory*. New York: Routledge.

Achiume, E. Tendayi. 2022. "Racial Borders." *Georgetown Law Journal* 110 (3): 445–508.

Agamben, Giorgio. 1998. *Homo Sacer: Sovereign Power and Bare Life*. Redwood City, CA: Stanford University Press.

———. 2009. *"What Is an Apparatus?" And Other Essays*. Translated by Stefan Pedatella and David Kishik. Redwood City, CA: Stanford University Press.

Agier, Michel. 2011. *Managing the Undesirables: Refugee Camps and Humanitarian Government*. London: Polity Press.

Ahmed, Masqood. 2007. "Satellite-Aided Search and Rescue (SAR) System." *IEEE Aerospace and Electronic Systems Magazine* 22 (8): 3–8.

Ahmed, Sara. 2000. *Strange Encounters: Embodied Others in Post-Coloniality*. London: Routledge.

Ahmida, Ali Abdullatif. 2021. *Genocide in Libya: Shar, a Hidden Colonial History*. London: Routledge.

Albahari, Maurizio. 2015. *Crimes of Peace: Mediterranean Migrations at the World's Deadliest Border*. Philadelphia: University of Pennsylvania Press.

Alexander, David E. 2019. "L'Aquila, Central Italy, and the 'Disaster Cycle,' 2009–2017." *Disaster Prevention and Management* 28 (2): 272–85.

Ali Farah, Cristina (Ubah). 2011. *Little Mother*. Bloomington: University of Indiana Press.

Ali, Zakaria Mohamed, dir. 2012. *A chiunque possa interessare*. Italy, Archivio Memorie Migranti.

Anam, Nasia. 2020. "Encampment as Colonization: Theorizing the Representation of Refugee Spaces." *Journal of Narrative Theory* 50 (3): 405–36.

Anderson, Benedict. 1983. *Imagined Communities*. London: Verso.

Andersson, Ruben. 2014. *Illegality, Inc.: Clandestine Migration and the Business of Bordering*. Oakland: University of California Press.

Angel-Ajani, Asale. 2000. "Italy's Racial Cauldron: Immigration, Criminalization and the Cultural Politics of Race." *Cultural Dynamics* 12 (3): 331–52.

Arendt, Hannah. 1953. *The Origins of Totalitarianism*. Cleveland: Meridian Books.

Aronsson, Mattias. 2022. ""Migrant Literature Migrating: The Case of Fatou Diome's *Le Ventre de l'Atlantique* and Its Reception in Sweden." In *Representing 21st-Century Migration in Europe: Performing Borders, Identities and Texts*, edited by Nelson González Ortega and Ana Belén Martínez Garcia, 102–34. London: Berghahn Books.

Atoui, Farah. 2020. "The Calais Crisis: Real Refugees Welcome, Migrants 'Do Not Come.'" In *Moving Images: Mediating Migration as Crisis*, 211–28. Bliefeld: transcript Verlag.

Avallone, Gennaro. 2017. "The Land of Informal Intermediation." In *Migration and Agriculture: Mobility and Change in the Mediterranean Area*, edited by Alessandra Corrado, Carlos de Castro, and Domenico Perrotta, 217–30. New York: Routledge.

Baizán, Pau, and Amparo González-Ferrer. 2016. "What Drives Senegalese Migration to Europe? The Role of Economic Restructuring, Labor Demand, and the Multiplier Effect of Networks." *Demographic Research* 35 (1): 339–80.

Baldwin, James. 1985. *The Evidence of Things Not Seen*. New York: Holt, Rinehart and Winston.

———. 2010a. "The Artist's Struggle for Integrity." In *The Cross of Redemption: Uncollected Writings*, 41–47. New York: Pantheon.

———. 2010b. "The International War Crimes Tribunal: Reader's Forum, Freedomways." In *The Cross of Redemption: Uncollected Writings*, 199–202. New York: Pantheon.

———. 2010c. "The N***** We Invent." In *The Cross of Redemption: Uncollected Writings*, 108–205. New York: Pantheon.

———. 2010d. "Mass Culture and the Creative Artist: Some Personal Notes." In *The Cross of Redemption: Uncollected Writings*, 3–6. New York: Pantheon.

———. 2012 [1955]. "Stranger in the Village." In *Notes of a Native Son*. Boston: Beacon Press, 163–175.

Balibar, Etienne. 1991. "Racism and Crisis." In *Race, Nation, Class: Ambiguous Identities*, Etienne Balibar and Immanuel Wallerstein, 217–27. London: Verso.

———. 1997. "What We Owe the Sans-Papiers." Translated by Jason Francis Mc Gimsey and Erika Doucette. *Transversal Texts*. Accessed January 18, 2024. https://transversal.at/transversal/0313/balibar/en.

———. 2004. *We, the People of Europe?* Princeton, NJ: Princeton University Press.

———. 2010. "At the Borders of Citizenship: A Democracy in Translation?" *European Journal of Social Theory* 13 (3): 315–22.

Ballinger, Pamela. 2020. *The World Refugees Made: Decolonization and the Foundation of Postwar Italy*. Ithaca, NY: Cornell University Press.

Baobab Experience. 2016. "La rinascita del Baobab: Comunicato stampa." April 16, 2016. https://baobabexperience.org/2016/04/16/la-rinascita-del-baobab-comunicato-stampa/.

———. 2017. "Presìdi." *Baobab Experience* (blog). October 13, 2017. https://baobabexperience.org/presidi/.

———. 2018. "Conferenza stampa dell'associazione Baobab sul caso della nave 'Diciotti.'" Italy: Radio Radicale. https://www.radioradicale.it/scheda/551503/conferenza-stampa-dellassociazione-baobab-sul-caso-della-nave-diciotti/.

Bassi, Serena. 2018. "Whose Comatose Girlfriend? Figures of Crisis in Neoliberal Italy." *Modern Languages Open* 1:9.

Baudry, Sarah Lilia. 2017. "Rome: A Cultural Capital with a Poor Working-Class Heritage: Strategies of Touristification and Artification." In *Tourism and Gentrification in Contemporary Metropolises*, edited by Maria Gravari-Barbas and Sandra Guinand, 134–52. Abingdon: Routledge.

Beaman, Jean. 2017. *Citizen Outsider: Children of North African Immigrants in France.* Oakland: University of California Press.

———. 2021. "Towards a Reading of Black Lives Matter in Europe." *Journal of Common Market Studies* 59 (S1): 103–14.

Belloni, Milena. 2016. "Learning How to Squat: Cooperation and Conflict between Refugees and Natives in Rome." *Journal of Refugee Studies* 29 (4): 506–27.

———. 2019. *The Big Gamble: The Migration of Eritreans to Europe.* Oakland: University of California Press.

Belloni, Milena, Enrico Fravega, and Daniela Giudici. 2020. "Fuori dall'accoglienza: Insediamenti informali di rifugiati tra marginalità e autonomia." *Politiche Sociali*, no. 2 (September): 225–44.

Ben-Ghiat, Ruth, and Mia Fuller, eds. 2005. *Italian Colonialism.* New York: Palgrave Macmillan.

Beni, Paolo (relatore). 2017. "Il sistema italiano di accoglienza: Dalle prime esperienze degli anni '90 al modello attuale." Commissione Parlamentare Doc. XXII-bis n. 21. Roma: Camera dei Deputati. http://documenti.camera.it/_dati/leg17/lavori/documentiparla mentari/IndiceETesti/022bis/021/INTERO.pdf.

Benjamin, Walter. 2019 [1940]. "Theses on the Philosophy of History." In *Illuminations*, edited by Hannah Arendt, 196–209. New York: First Mariner Books.

Besteman, Catherine. 2020. *Militarized Global Apartheid.* Durham, NC: Duke University Press.

Beverley, John. 2008. "Testimonio, Subalternity, and Narrative Authority." In *A Companion to Latin American Literature and Culture*, edited by Sara Castro-Klaren, 571–83. London: Blackwell.

Bhabha, Homi. 1986. "Foreword to the 1986 Edition." In *Black Skin, White Mask*, xxi–xxxvii. London: Grove Press.

———. 1990. "DissemiNation: Time, Narrative, and the Margins of the Modern Nation." In *Nation and Narration*, edited by Homi Bhabha, 291–322. New York: Routledge.

Bhoola, Urmila. 2018. "OHCHR Country Visit to Italy (3–12 October 2018)." OHCHR. https://www.ohchr.org/EN/NewsEvents/Pages/DisplayNews.aspx?NewsID=23708&LangID=E.

Bianchi, Rino, and Igiaba Scego. 2014. *Roma negata: Percorsi postcoloniali nella città.* Roma: Ediesse.

Bigo, Didier. 2002. "Security and Immigration: Toward a Critique of the Governmentality of Unease." *Alternatives* 27:63–92.

———. 2009. "Immigration Controls and Free Movement in Europe." *International Journal of the Red Cross* 91 (875): 579–91.

Blasco, Andrea, Rossella Icardi, Nina Kajander, Michal Krawczyk, Jan Loeschner, Fabiana Scapolo, Fiona Seiger, Francesco Sermi, and Dario Tarchi. 2023. "Atlas of Migration 2023." Publications Office of the European Union. Luxembourg: European Commission. https://publications.jrc.ec.europa.eu/repository/handle/JRC135949/.

Bock, Jan-Jonathan. 2018. "Grassroots Solidarity and Political Protest in Rome's Migrant Camps." In *Camps Revisited: Multifaceted Spatialities of a Modern Political Technology*, edited by Irit Katz, Diana Martin, and Claudio Minca, 159–76. London: Rowman & Littlefield.

Bohmer, Carol, and Amy Shuman. 2008. *Rejecting Refugees: Political Asylum in the 21st Century*. New York: Routledge.

———. 2018. *Political Asylum Deceptions: The Culture of Suspicion*. London: Palgrave Macmillan.

Boochani, Behrouz. 2019. *No Friend but the Mountains: Writing from Manus Prison*. Translated by Omid Tofighian. Toronto: Anansi International.

Brah, Avtar. 1996. *Cartographies of Diaspora: Contesting Identities*. New York: Routledge.

Brand, Dionne. 2018. *The Blue Clerk: Ars Poetica in 59 Versos*. Durham, NC: Duke University Press.

Brandzel, Amy. 2016. *Against Citizenship*. Champaign: University of Illinois Press.

Brickell, Katherine, and Ayona Datta, eds. 2011. *Translocal Geographies: Spaces, Places, Connections*. Surrey, UK: Ashgate.

Brodzki, Bella. 2001. "Testimony." In *The Encyclopedia of Life Writing*, 870–71. London: Fitzroy Dearborn.

Butler, Judith. 2009. *Frames of War: When Is Life Grievable?* London: Verso.

Butler, Toby. 2006. "A Walk of Art: The Potential of the Sound Walk as Practice in Cultural Geography." *Social & Cultural Geography* 7 (6): 889–908.

Byrd, Jodi A. 2011. *The Transit of Empire: Indigenous Critiques of Colonialism*. Minneapolis: University of Minnesota Press.

Calabrò, Paolo. 2015. "Intervista a Igiaba Scego." Mangialibri. 2015.

Calhoun, Craig. 2010. "The Idea of Emergency: Humanitarian Action and Global (Dis)Order." In *Contemporary States of Emergency: The Politics of Military and Humanitarian Interventions*, 29–58. New York: Zone Books.

Camilli, Annalisa. 2017. "Un ragazzo si è ucciso, era somalo, aveva 19 anni." *Internazionale*, March 23, 2017. https://www.internazionale.it/notizie/annalisa-camilli/2017/03/23/maslax-moxamed-somalo/.

———. 2018. "La moglie dell'uomo ucciso a Firenze spiega cos'è il razzismo." *Internazionale*, March 13, 2018. https://www.internazionale.it/reportage/annalisa-camilli/2018/03/13/moglie-idy-diene-firenze/.

———. 2022. "Aboubakar Soumahoro, anatomia di una caduta." *Internazionale*, December 1, 2022. https://www.internazionale.it/essenziale/notizie/annalisa-camilli/2022/12/01/aboubakar-soumahoro-inchiesta/.

Camilli, Eleonora. 2017a. "Rome: The Only European Capital with No Official Plan for Migrants." *Open Migration*, September 6, 2017. https://openmigration.org/en/analyses/rome-the-only-european-capital-with-no-official-plan-for-migrants/.

———. 2017b. "There is No Home for Refugees in Rome: Tales from the Refugees Who Used to Live on Via Curtatone." *Open Migration*, September 21, 2017. https://openmigration.org/en/analyses/there-is-no-home-tales-from-the-refugees-who-used-to-live-on-via-curtatone/.

Campbell, Timothy C. 2011. *Improper Life: Technology and Biopolitics from Heidegger to Agamben*. Minneapolis: University of Minnesota Press.

Campbell, Timothy C., and Adam Sitze, eds. 2013. *Biopolitics: A Reader*. Durham, NC: Duke University Press.

Campesi, Giuseppe. 2015. "Humanitarian Confinement. An Ethnography of Reception Centres for Asylum Seekers at Europe's Southern Border." *International Journal of Migration and Border Studies* 1 (4): 398–418.

———. 2018. "Between Containment, Confinement and Dispersal: The Evolution of the Italian Reception System before and after the 'Refugee Crisis.'" *Journal of Modern Italian Studies* 23 (4): 490–506.

———. 2019. "Governare le migrazioni nell'Italia contemporanea." *Il Mulino*, no. 3/2019.

Caponio, Tiziana. 2008. "(Im)Migration Research in Italy: A European Comparative Perspective." *Sociological Quarterly* 49 (3): 445–64.

Capron, Alexandre. 2015. "Beware the Fake Migrant Images Shared Online." *France 24: The Observers*, September 15, 2015. https://observers.france24.com/en/20150915-beware-fake -migrant-images-shared-online/.

Cariello, Marta. 2021. "Reconfiguring 'La Donna Del Sud': Trans-Mediterranean Narratives." In *Contemporary Italian Diversity in Critical and Fictional Narratives*, edited by Marie Orton, Graziella Parati, and Ron Kubati, 159–70. Madison, NJ: Fairleigh Dickinson University Press.

Carney, Megan A. 2021. *Island of Hope: Migration and Solidarity in the Mediterranean*. Oakland: University of California Press.

Carpignano, Jonas, dir. 2015. *Mediterranea*. Italy, IFC Films.

Carter, Donald Martin. 1997. *States of Grace: Senegalese in Italy and the New European Immigration*. Minneapolis: University of Minnesota Press.

———. 2010. *Navigating the African Diaspora*. Minneapolis: University of Minnesota Press.

Caruth, Cathy. 2014. "A Ghost in the House of Justice: A Conversation with Shoshana Felman." In *Listening to Trauma: Conversations with Leaders in the Theory and Treatment of Catastrophic Experience*, 321–54. Baltimore, MD: Johns Hopkins University Press.

Casas-Cortés, Maribel. 2021. "Precarious Writings: Reckoning the Absences and Reclaiming the Legacies in the Current Poetics / Politics of Precarity." *Current Anthropology* 62 (5): 510–38.

Castles, Stephen. 2006. "Guestworkers in Europe: A Resurrection?" *International Migration Review* 40 (4): 741–66.

Ceravolo, Flavio, and Stefano Molina. 2013. "Dieci Anni Di Seconde Generazioni in Italia." *I Quaderni Di Sociologia* 63:9–34.

Cerro, Giovanni. 2022. "Una 'razza Mediterranea'? Il dibattito antropologico sulla Questione Meridionale (1897–1907)." *Quellen und Forschungen aus Italienischen Archiven und Bibliotheken* 102 (1): 386–416.

Césaire, Aimé. 1972 [1950]. *Discourse on Colonialism*. Monthly Review Press.

Chambers, Iain. 2008. *Mediterranean Crossings: The Politics of an Interrupted Modernity*. Durham, NC: Duke University Press.

———. 2017. *Postcolonial Interruptions, Unauthorised Modernities*. London: Rowman & Littlefield.

Christedes, Giorgos, Juliane von Mittelstaedt, Peter Muller, and Maxmilian Popp. 2016. "Closing the Balkan Route: Will Greece Become a Refugee Bottleneck?" *Der Spiegel*, February 9, 2016. http://www.spiegel.de/international/europe/closing-balkan-route-means -migrant-crisis-for-greece-a-1076232.html.

Ciullo, Giacomo Massimo. 2017. "Condizioni disumane nel Centro di Accoglienza Straordinaria di Ostuni." *Brindisi Time*, October 24, 2017. http://www.brindisitime.it/condizioni

-disumane-nel-centro-di-accoglienza-straordinaria-di-ostuni-la-denuncia-dellavv
-ciullo/.

Clark, Mary Marshall. 2014. "Guantanamo: La memoria del corpo in terra di confine (Remembering Bodies in the Borderlands)." *Acoma, Rivista Internazionale Di Studi Nordamericani* 6:7–22.

Coletti, Grazia Maria. 2018. "Stazione Tiburtina, accoltellato con le forbici alla schiena." *Il Tempo*, June 25, 2018. https://www.iltempo.it/roma-capitale/2018/06/25/news/stazione -tiburtina-accoltellato-con-le-forbici-alla-schiena-1074311/.

Colucci, Michele. 2018. "Per una storia del governo dell'immigrazione straniera in Italia: Dagli anni sessanta alla crisi delle politiche." *Meridiana*, no. 91, 9–36.

———. 2022. "Braccianti stranieri nell'agricoltura italiana: un profilo storico nel periodo re-pubblicano." *Archivio Storico dell'Emigrazione Italiana* (blog). June 14, 2022. https://www .asei.eu/it/2022/06/braccianti-stranieri-nellagricoltura-italiana-un-profilo-storico-nel -periodo-repubblicano/.

———. 2023. "Immigrazione e accoglienza nell'Italia contemporanea: Profilo storico." *Fondazione Giangiacomo Feltrinelli* (blog). May 11, 2023. https://fondazionefeltrinelli.it/scopri /immigrazione-e-accoglienza-nellitalia-contemporanea-un-breve-profilo-storico/.

Corrado, Alessandra. 2011. "Clandestini in the Orange Towns: Migrations and Racisms in Calabria's Agriculture." *Race/Ethnicity: Multidisciplinary Global Contexts* 4 (2): 191–201.

Corrado, Alessandra, Carlos de Castro, and Domenico Perrotta, eds. 2017. *Migration and Agriculture: Mobility and Change in the Mediterranean Area*. New York: Routledge.

Crawley, Heaven, and Dimitris Skleparis. 2018. "Refugees, Migrants, Neither, Both: Categorical Fetishism and the Politics of Bounding in Europe's 'Migration Crisis.'" *Journal of Ethnic and Migration Studies* 44 (1): 48–64.

Crisp, Jeff. 2024. "The EU Pact on Migration and Asylum: Reducing or Reinforcing the Inhumanity at Europe's Borders?" *United Against Inhumanity* (blog). April 29, 2024. https://www.against-inhumanity.org/2024/04/29/the-eu-pact-on-migration-and -asylum-reducing-or-reinforcing-the-inhumanity-at-europes-borders-by-dr-jeff-crisp/.

Cubilié, Anne, and Carl Good. 2003. "Introduction: The Future of Testimony." *Discourse* 25 (1/2): 4–18.

Curti, Lidia. 2007. "Female Literature of Migration in Italy." *Feminist Review* 87:60–75.

Cusumano, Eugenio, and Matteo Villa. 2021. "From 'Angels' to 'Vice Smugglers': The Criminalization of Sea Rescue NGOs in Italy." *European Journal on Criminal Policy and Research* 27:23–40.

Cuttitta, Paolo. 2015. "Mare Nostrum e la retorica umanitaria." *Rivista di Storia delle Idee* 4 (1): 128–40.

"Dalla parte di Metropoliz Città Meticcia!" 2016. *L'Associazione POPICA ONLUS* (blog). April 22, 2016. https://www.popicaonlus.org/dalla-parte-di-metropoliz-citta-meticcia/.

Daly, Faïçal, and Rohit Barot. 2020. "Economic Migration and Social Exclusion: The Case of Tunisians in Italy in the 1980s and 1990s." In *Into the Margins: Migration and Exclusion in Southern Europe*, edited by Floya Anthias and Gabriella Lazaridis, 2nd ed., 35–54. London: Routledge.

Dammacco, Francesca Linda. 2018. "La regolarizzazione degli stranieri in Italia." January 26, 2018. https://www.diritto.it/la-regolarizzazione-degli-stranieri-italia/.

Danewid, Ida. 2021. "'These Walls Must Fall': The Black Mediterranean and the Politics of Abolition." In *The Black Mediterranean: Bodies, Borders and Citizenship*, edited by the Black Mediterranean Collective, 145–66. Cham: Palgrave Macmillan.

Davies, Thom, and Arshad Isakjee. 2019. "Ruins of Empire: Refugees, Race and the Postcolonial Geographies of European Migrant Camps." *Geoforum* 102 (June): 214–17.

Davies, Thom, Arshad Isakjee, and Surindar Dhesi. 2017. "Violent Inaction : The Necropolitical Experience of Refugees in Europe." *Antipode* 49 (5): 1263–84.

de Certeau, Michel. 1984. *The Practice of Everyday Life*. Oakland: University of California Press.

De Genova, Nicholas. 2011. "Spectacles of Migrant 'Illegality': The Scene of Exclusion, the Obscene of Inclusion." *Ethnic and Racial Studies* 36 (7): 1180–98.

Declich, Francesca, and Silvia Pitzalis. 2021. *Presenza migrante tra spazi urbani e non urbani: Etnografie su processi, dinamiche e modalità di accoglienza*. Milano: Meltemi.

de Haas, Hein. 2021. "A Theory of Migration: The Aspirations-Capabilities Framework." *Comparative Migration Studies* 9 (1): 8.

Del Boca, Angelo. 1986. *Gli italiani in Africa orientale*. Bari: Laterza.

Delgado, James P. 2012. "Archaeology of Titanic." *Archaeology* 65 (3): 34–41.

Demaria Harney, Nicholas. 2007. "Transnationalism and Entrepreneurial Migrancy in Naples, Italy." *Journal of Ethnic and Migration Studies* 33 (2): 219–32.

Derrida, Jacques, and Anne Douformantelle. 2000. *Of Hospitality*. Translated by Rachel Bowlby. Redwood City, CA: Stanford University Press.

di Costantini, Eleonora. 2014. "Un'emergenza lunga due anni. Considerazioni sui provvedimenti umanitari a favore dei cittadini provenienti dai Paesi del Nord Africa." *Autonomie Locali e Servizi Sociali*, no. 3.

Di Maio, Alessandra. 2012. "Il mediterraneo nero. Rotte dei migranti nel millennio globale." Translated by Claudia Gargano. In *La Città Cosmopolita. Altre narrazioni*. Edited by Giulia de Spuches, 142–163. Palermo: Palumbo Editore.

Dines, Nick, and Enrica Rigo. 2015. "Postcolonial Citizenships and the 'Refugeeization' of the Workforce: Migrant Agricultural Labor in the Italian Mezzogiorno." In *Postcolonial Transitions in Europe: Contexts, Practices and Politics*, edited by Sandra Ponzanesi and Gianmaria Colpani, 151–72. London: Rowman & Littlefield.

DiPiero, Dan. 2022. *Contingent Encounters: Improvisation in Music and Everyday Life*. Ann Arbor: University of Michigan Press.

Di Rienzo, Paolo, and Brigida Angeloni. 2021. "L'agire educativo nei contesti informali di apprendimento al tempo del Covid-19: il caso della comunità murid." *Studium Educationis—Rivista semestrale per le professioni educative*, December, 50–58.

Doctors Without Borders. 2016. "Out of Sight: Asylum Seekers and Refugees in Italy; Informal Settlements and Social Marginalization." Doctors Without Borders. https://www.aerzte-ohne-grenzen.de/sites/default/files/attachments/aerzte_ohne_grenzen_out_of_sight_report.pdf.

Donadio, Rachel. 2010. "Race Riots Grip Italian Town, and Mafia Is Suspected." *New York Times*, January 11, 2010. https://www.nytimes.com/2010/01/11/world/europe/11italy.html/.

Dotsey, Senyo, and Francesco Chiodelli. 2021. "Housing Precarity." *City* 25 (5/6): 720–39.

Düvell, Franck. 2012. "Transit Migration: A Blurred and Politicised Concept." *Population, Space and Place* 18 (4): 415–27.

"Economie regionali: L'economia di Calabria." 2018. Roma: Banca d'Italia. https://www.bancaditalia.it/pubblicazioni/economie-regionali/.

elhariry, yasser, and Edwige Tamalet Talbayev, eds. 2018. *Critically Mediterranean*. Cham: Springer.

El-Tayeb, Fatima. 2011. *European Others: Queering Ethnicity in Postnational Europe.* Minneapolis: University of Minnesota Press.

"Emergencies." 2023. UNHCR. https://www.unhcr.org/en-us/emergencies.html/.

Espiritu, Yen Le. 2014. *Body Counts: The Vietnam War and Militarized Refugees.* Oakland: University of California Press.

Ettlinger, Nancy. 2007. "Precarity Unbound." *Alternatives: Global, Local, Political* 32 (3): 319–40.

*The Economist.* "Italy's Informal Workers Fall Back on Charity." June 6, 2020. https://www .economist.com/europe/2020/06/06/italys-informal-workers-fall-back-on-charity/.

*European Commission.* 2019. "The European Agenda on Migration: EU Needs to Sustain Progress Made over the Past 4 Years," March 6, 2019. http://europa.eu/rapid/press-release _IP-19-1496_en.htm.

European Council on Refugees and Exiles. 2023. "Reception Conditions: Italy." Accessed May 27, 2024. https://asylumineurope.org/reports/country/italy/reception-conditions/.

Fanon, Frantz. 1986. *Black Skin, White Masks.* London: Pluto Press.

———. 2004 [1961]. *The Wretched of the Earth.* Translated by Richard Philcox. New York: Grove Press.

Fassin, Didier. 2012. *Humanitarian Reason: A Moral History of the Present.* Oakland: University of California Press.

Felman, Shoshana, and Dori Laub. 1991. *Testimony: Crises of Witnessing in Literature, Psychoanalysis, and History.* New York: Routledge.

Ferme, Valerio, and Norma Bouchard. 2013. *Italy and the Mediterranean: Words, Sounds, and Images of the Post-Cold War Era.* London: Palgrave Macmillan.

Ficocelli, Sara. 2017. "Sgombero di Piazza Indipendenza a Roma: 'Violenza su donne e bambini vergogna inaccettabile.'" *La Repubblica*, August 25, 2017. https://www.repubblica.it /solidarieta/diritti-umani/2017/08/25/news/sgombero_di_piazza_indipendenza_a _roma_violenza_su_donne_e_bambini_vergogna_inaccettabile_-173822427/.

Fiddian-Qasmiyeh, Elena. 2010. "'Ideal' Refugee Women and Gender Equality Mainstreaming in the Sahrawi Refugee Camps: 'Good Practice' for Whom?" *Refugee Survey Quarterly* 29 (2): 64–84.

———. 2020. "Memories and Meanings of Refugee Camps (and More-than-Camps)." In *Refugee Imaginaries: Research Across the Humanities*, edited by Emma Cox, Sam Durrant, David Farrier, Lyndsey Stonebridge, and Agnes Woolley, 289–310. Edinburgh: Edinburgh University Press.

Fiore, Teresa. 2017. *Pre-Occupied Spaces: Remapping Italy's Transnational Migrations and Colonial Legacies.* New York: Fordham University Press.

———. 2018. "From Crisis to Creative Critique: The Early Twenty-First Century Mediterranean Crossing on Stage and Screen in Works by Teatro Delle Albe and Andrea Segre." *Journal of Modern Italian Studies* 23 (4): 522–42.

———. 2020. "Italy and Italian Studies in the Transnational Space of Migration and Colonial Routes." In *Transnational Italian Studies*, edited by Charles Burdett and Loredana Polezzi, 161–76. Liverpool: Liverpool University Press.

FitzGerald, David Scott. 2019. *Refuge beyond Reach: How Rich Democracies Repel Asylum Seekers.* Oxford: Oxford University Press.

Fofana, Dalla Malé. 2020. "Senegal, the African Slave Trade, and the Door of No Return: Giving Witness to Gorée Island." *Humanities* 9 (3): 57–74.

Fogu, Claudio. 2020. *The Fishing Net and the Spider Web: Mediterranean Imaginaries and the Making of Italians*. Cham: Palgrave Macmillan.

Foot, John. 2009. *Italy's Divided Memory*. London: Palgrave Macmillan.

Forensic Architecture. 2012. "The Left-to-Die Boat." https://forensic-architecture.org/inves tigation/the-left-to-die-boat/.

Forgacs, David. 2014. *Italy's Margins: Social Exclusion and Nation Formation since 1861*. Cambridge: Cambridge University Press.

*Fortune Magazine*. 2016. "The World's 50 Greatest Leaders: Mimmo Lucano." https://fortune .com/ranking/worlds-greatest-leaders/2016/domenico-lucano/.

Foster, Christopher Ian. 2019. *Conscripts of Migration: Neoliberal Globalization, Nationalism, and the Literature of New African Diasporas*. Jackson: University of Mississippi Press.

Foucault, Michel. 1980. "The Confession of the Flesh." In *Power/Knowledge: Selected Interviews and Other Writings*, edited by Colin Gordon, 194–228. New York: Pantheon.

———. 1984. "Of Other Spaces: Utopias and Heterotopias." *Architecture /Mouvement/ Continuité*. October.

Fullerton, Maryellen. 2016. "Asylum Crisis Italian Style: The Dublin Regulation Collides with European Human Rights Law." *Harvard Human Rights Journal* 29 (1): 57–134.

Gandhi, Evyn Lê Espiritu. 2022. *Archipelago of Resettlement: Vietnamese Refugee Settlers and Decolonization across Guam and Israel-Palestine*. Oakland: University of California Press.

García Peña, Lorgia. 2022. *Translating Blackness: Latinx Colonialities in Global Perspective*. Durham, NC: Duke University Press.

Gasparetti, Fedora. 2012. "Eating Tie Bou Jenn in Turin: Negotiating Differences and Building Community among Senegalese Migrants in Italy." *Food and Foodways* 20 (3/4): 257–78.

Gaudio, Giuseppe, Franco Gaudio, Alessandra Corrado, Serena Tarangioli, Francesca Giaré, Catia Zumpano, Barbara Forcina et al. 2020. "Migrazioni, agricoltura e ruralità. Politiche e percorsi per lo sviluppo dei territori." Rete Rurale Nazionale. https://www .reterurale.it/flex/cm/pages/ServeBLOB.php/L/IT/IDPagina/21203/.

*Gazzetta del Sud*. 2019. "Lavoro, al Sud tasso di disoccupazione al 18%: È il triplo rispetto al Nord," March 13, 2019. https://gazzettadelsud.it/articoli/economia/2019/03/13/lavoro -al-sud-tasso-di-disoccupazione-al-18-e-il-triplo-rispetto-al-nord-9b43097a-578f-4eef -b3b6-08bea15c1243/.

Giliberti, Luca, and Luca Queirolo Palmas. 2020. "Sul confine interno: Pratiche informali di solidarietà ai migranti tra l'Italia e la Francia." In *Confini, mobilità e migrazioni: Una cartografia dello spazio europeo*, edited by Lorenzo Navone, 153–80. Milano: Agenzia X.

Gilmore, Leigh. 2001. *The Limits of Autobiography: Trauma and Testimony*. Ithaca, NY: Cornell University Press.

———. 2011. "'What Was I?': Literary Witness and the Testimonial Archive." *Profession*, 77–84.

———. 2017. *Tainted Witness: Why We Doubt What Women Say about Their Lives*. New York: Columbia University Press.

Gilmore, Ruth Wilson. 2007. *Golden Gulag: Prisons, Surplus, Crisis, and Opposition in Globalizing California*. Oakland: University of California Press.

Gilroy, Paul. 1993. *The Black Atlantic*. Cambridge: Harvard University Press.

Giordano, Cristiana. 2014. *Migrants in Translation Caring and the Logics of Difference in Contemporary Italy*. Oakland: University of California Press.

Giuffrida, Angela. 2018. "Pro-Refugee Italian Mayor Arrested for 'Aiding Illegal Migration.'" *The Guardian*, October 2, 2018. https://www.theguardian.com/world/2018/oct/02/pro-refugee-italian-mayor-arrested-suspicion-aiding-illegal-migration-domenico-lucano-riace/.

Gladstone, Rick. 2016. "Stepping Over the Dead on a Migrant Boat." *New York Times*, October 5, 2016. https://www.nytimes.com/2016/10/06/world/europe/migrants-mediterranean.html/.

Glissant, Edoard. 1990. *The Poetics of Relation*. Translated by Betsy Wing. Ann Arbor: University of Michigan Press.

Global Slavery Index. 2022. "Europe and Central Asia." Walk Free. Accessed January 22, 2024. https://www.walkfree.org/global-slavery-index/findings/regional-findings/europe-and-central-asia/.

Goldberg, David Theo. 2001. *The Racial State*. Malden, MA: Wiley-Blackwell.

———. 2006. "Racial Europeanization." *Ethnic and Racial Studies* 29 (2): 331–64.

González Ortega, Nelson, and Ana Belén Martínez García, eds. 2022. *Representing 21st Century Migration in Europe: Performing Borders, Identities and Texts*. New York: Berghahn Books.

Gordon, Lewis R., T. Denean Sharpley-Whiting, and Renée T. White, eds. 1996. *Fanon: A Critical Reader*. Oxford: Blackwell Publishers.

Grande, Gabriele del. 2006. "La Fortezza." Fortress Europe. 2006. http://fortresseurope.blogspot.com/p/la-fortezza.html.

Grazioli, Margherita. 2017. "From Citizens to Citadins? Rethinking Right to the City inside Housing Squats in Rome, Italy." *Citizenship Studies* 21 (4): 393–408.

———. 2021. *Housing, Urban Commons and the Right to the City in Post-Crisis Rome: Metropoliz, The Squatted Città Meticcia*. Cham: Palgrave Macmillan.

Gregory, Derek. 2004. *The Colonial Present*. Oxford: Blackwell.

Gregson, Sarah. 2008. "Titanic 'Down Under': Ideology, Myth and Memorialization." *Social History* 33 (3): 268–83.

Gueguen-Teil, Cannelle, and Irit Katz. 2018. "On the Meaning of Shelter: Living in Calis's Camps de La Lande." In *Camps Revisited: Multifaceted Spatialities of a Modern Political Technology*, edited by Irit Katz, Diana Martin, and Claudio Minca, 83–100. London: Rowman & Littlefield.

Guglielmo, Jennifer. 2012. "Are Italians White?" In *Are Italians White? How Race Is Made in America*, edited by Jennifer Guglielmo and Salvatore Salerno, 1–16. New York: Routledge.

Hall, Stuart. 1993. "Cultural Identity and Diaspora." In *Identity: Community, Culture, Difference*, edited by Jonathan Rutherford, 222–37. London: Lawrence & Wishart.

———. 2021a [2003]. "'In But Not of Europe': Europe and its Myths." In *Selected Writings on Race and Difference*, edited by Paul Gilroy and Ruth Wilson Gilmore, 374–85. Durham, NC: Duke University Press.

———. 2021b [1981]. "Summer in the City." In *Selected Writings on Race and Difference*, edited by Paul Gilroy and Ruth Wilson Gilmore, 71–77. Durham, NC: Duke University Press.

Hall, Stuart, Chas Critcher, Tony Jefferson, John Clarke, and Brian Roberts. 1978. *Policing the Crisis: Mugging, the State, and Law and Order*. London: Palgrave.

Hamilakis, Yannis. 2016. "Introduction: Archaeologies of Forced and Undocumented Migration." In *The New Nomadic Age: Archaeologies of Forced and Undocumented Migration*, edited by Yannis Hamilakis. Sheffield: Equinox.

Hamlin, Rebecca. 2021. *Crossing: How We Label and React to People on the Move*. Redwood City, CA: Stanford University Press.

Handal, Alexis J., Lisbeth Iglesias-Ríos, Paul J. Fleming, Mislael A. Valentín-Cortés, and Marie S. O'Neill. 2020. "'Essential' but Expendable: Farmworkers During the COVID-19 Pandemic—The Michigan Farmworker Project." *American Journal of Public Health* 110 (12): 1760–62.

Harney, Nicholas. 2004. "Migrant Productivities: Street Vendors and the Informal Knowledge Work in Naples." *International Journal of Economic Development* 6 (January): 303–27.

Harney, Stefano, and Fred Moten. 2013. *The Undercommons: Fugitive Planning and Black Study*. Brooklyn: Autonomedia.

Hartman, Saidiya. 1997. *Scenes of Subjection: Terror, Slavery, and Self-Making in Nineteenth-Century America*. Oxford: Oxford University Press.

———. 2006. *Lose Your Mother: A Journey along the Transatlantic Slave Route*. New York: Farrar, Straus and Giroux.

———. 2019. *Wayward Lives, Beautiful Experiments: Intimate Histories of Riotous Black Girls, Troublesome Women, and Queer Radicals*. New York: W. W. Norton.

Hartman, Saidiya V., and Frank B. Wilderson. 2003. "The Position of the Unthought." *Qui Parle* 13 (2): 183–201.

Hawthorne, Camilla. 2022. *Contesting Race and Citizenship: Youth Politics in the Black Mediterranean*. Ithaca, NY: Cornell University Press.

Heller, Charles, and Lorenzo Pezzani. 2020. "Forensic Oceanography: Tracing Violence within and against the Mediterranean Frontier's Aesthetic Regime." In *Moving Images: Mediating Migration as Crisis*, 95–126. Bliefeld: transcript Verlag.

Herzfeld, Michael. 2009. *Evicted from Eternity: The Restructuring of Modern Rome*. Chicago: University of Chicago Press.

Hesford, Wendy. 2011. *Spectacular Rhetorics: Human Rights Visions, Recognitions, Feminisms*. Durham, NC: Duke University Press.

Hesse, Barnor, ed. 2000. *Un/Settled Multiculturalisms: Diasporas, Entanglements, "Transruptions."* London: Zed Books.

High, Steven. 2013. "Embodied Ways of Listening: Oral History, Genocide and the Audio Tour." *Anthropologica* 55 (1): 73–85.

Hodžić, Saida. 2017. "Refugees Write Back: Introduction." In *Maintaining Refuge: Anthropological Reflections in Uncertain Times*, edited by David Haines, Jayne Howell, and Fethi Keles, 157–58. Committee on Refugees and Immigrants Society for Urban, National, and Transnational/Global Anthropology. American Anthropological Association.

Hogarth, Christopher. 2022. *Afropean Female Selves: Migration and Language in the Life Writing of Fatou Diome and Igiaba Scego*. London: Routledge.

Holmes, Seth M., and Heide Castañeda. 2016. "Representing the 'European Refugee Crisis' in Germany and Beyond: Deservingness and Difference, Life and Death." *American Ethnologist* 43 (1): 12–24.

Hom, Stephanie Malia. 2015. *The Beautiful Country: Tourism and the Impossible State of Destination Italy*. Toronto: University of Toronto Press.

———. 2016. "Becoming Ospite: Hospitality and Mobility at the Center of Temporary Permanence." In *Italian Mobilities*, edited by Ruth Ben-Ghiat and Stephanie Malia Hom, 88–110. London: Routledge.

———. 2019. *Empire's Mobius Strip: Historical Echoes in Italy's Crisis of Migration and Detention*. Ithaca, NY: Cornell University Press.

hooks, bell. 2014. *Yearning: Race, Gender, and Cultural Politics*. 2nd ed. New York: Routledge.

Hooper, John. 2007. "UN Rebuke as Governments Squabble over Immigrants Found Clinging to Tuna Nets." *The Guardian*, May 29, 2007. https://www.theguardian.com/world/2007/may/29/libya.johnhooper/.

———. 2010. "Southern Italian Town World's 'Only White Town' after Ethnic Cleansing." *The Guardian*, January 11, 2010. https://www.theguardian.com/world/2010/jan/11/italy-rosarno-violence-immigrants/.

Horsti, Karina. 2023. *Survival and Witness at Europe's Border*. Ithaca, NY: Cornell University Press.

Human Rights Watch. 2020. "Italy: Flawed Migrant Regularization Program." December 18, 2020. https://www.hrw.org/news/2020/12/18/italy-flawed-migrant-regularization-program/.

*Il Messaggero*. 2017. "Roma, Raggi scrive al prefetto: 'Stop ai nuovi flussi di migranti,'" June 13, 2017. https://www.ilmessaggero.it/roma/cronaca/raggi_prefetto_migranti-2499778.html.

IOM (International Organization for Migration). 2019. "Libya's Migrant Report, Round 25—Flow Monitoring." Accessed April 14, 2024. https://dtm.iom.int/libya/.

Isin, Engin F., and Greg M. Nielsen, eds. 2008. *Acts of Citizenship*. London: Zed Books.

Ismail, Noora. 2017. "The Tragedy of Migration in Literature." Interview with Abu Bakr Khaal. Darf Publishers. December 18, 2017. https://darfpublishers.co.uk/the-tragedy-of-migration-in-literature/.

Itagaki, Lynn, and Jennifer Gully. 2017. "The Migrant Is Dead, Long Live the Citizen! Pro-Migrant Activism at EU Borders." *philoSOPHIA* 7 (2): 281–304.

Jackson, Michael. 2002. *The Politics of Storytelling: Variations on a Theme by Hannah Arendt*. Charlottenlund: Museum Tusculanum Press.

Jacobsen, Christine M., and Marry-Anne Karlsen. 2021. "Introduction: Unpacking the Temporalities of Irregular Migration." In *Waiting and the Temporalities of Irregular Migration*, edited by Christine M. Jacobsen, Marry-Anne Karlsen, and Sharham Khosravi, 1–20. London: Routledge.

Jacquemet, Marco. 2019. "The Digitalization of the Asylum Process (and the Digitizing of Evidence)." In *Technologies of Suspicion and the Ethics of Obligation in Political Asylum*, edited by Bridget M. Haas and Amy Shuman, 153–176. Athens: Ohio University Press.

Jones, Reece. 2016. *Violent Borders: Refugees and the Right to Move*. London: Verso.

Jones, Tobias, and Ayo Awokoya. 2019. "Are Your Tinned Tomatoes Picked by Slave Labour?" *The Guardian*, June 20, 2019. https://www.theguardian.com/world/2019/jun/20/tomatoes-italy-mafia-migrant-labour-modern-slavery/.

Kandylis, George. 2019. "Accommodation as Displacement: Notes from Refugee Camps in Greece in 2016." *Journal of Refugee Studies* 32 (1): 13–21.

Katz, Irit, Diana Martin, and Claudio Minca, eds. 2018. *Camps Revisited: Multifaceted Spatialities of a Modern Political Technology*. London: Rowman & Littlefield.

Kelley, Robin D. G. 2000. "A Poetics of Anticolonialism." In *Discourse on Colonialism*, Aimé Césaire, 7–28. New York: Monthly Review Press.

Kelly, Philip F. 2001. "The Political Economy of Local Labor Control in the Philippines." *Economic Geography* 77 (1): 1–22.

Khaal, Abu Bakr. 2014. *African Titanics*. London: Darf Publishers.

Khosravi, Shahram. 2020a. "Afterword: Waiting, a State of Consciousness." In *Waiting and the Temporalities of Irregular Migration*, edited by Christine M. Jacobsen, Marry-Anne Karlsen, and Shahram Khosravi, 202–8. London: Routledge.

———. 2020b. "Afterword. Experiences and Stories along the Way." *Geoforum* 116 (November): 292–95.

———. 2021. "The Weight of Waiting." In *Waiting: A Project in Conversation*, edited by Shahram Khosravi, 13–25. New York: Columbia University Press.

Khosravi, Shahram, and Dagmawi Yimer, dirs. 2020. *Waiting*. Wal Bet and *PARSE* Journal, University of Gothenburg. https://parsejournal.com/article/waiting/.

Khouma, Pap. 2010. *I Was an Elephant Salesman: Adventures between Dakar, Paris, and Milan*. Edited by Oreste Pivetta; translated by Rebecca Hopkins. Bloomington: Indiana University Press.

King, Russell. 1993. "Recent Immigration to Italy: Character, Causes and Consequences." *GeoJournal* 30 (3): 283–92.

———. 1996. "Migration and Development in the Mediterranean Region." *Geography* 81 (1): 3–14.

King, Russell, and Nicola Mai. 2009. "Italophilia Meets Albanophobia: Paradoxes of Asymmetric Assimilation and Identity Processes among Albanian Immigrants in Italy." *Ethnic and Racial Studies* 32 (1): 117–38.

Krämer, Sybille, and Sigrid Weigel, eds. 2017. *Testimony / Bearing Witness: Epistemology, Ethics, History and Culture*. London: Rowman & Littlefield.

Krause, Ulrike. 2022. "The Powerful (Vagueness of) Numbers? (Non)Knowledge Production about Refugee Accommodation Quantifications in UNHCR's Global Trends Reports." *Migration and Society* 5 (1): 141–51.

Labanca, Nicola. 2005. "Italian Colonial Internment." In *Italian Colonialism*, edited by Ruth Ben-Ghiat and Mia Fuller, 27–36. New York: Palgrave Macmillan.

Lacher, Wolfram. 2020. *Libya's Fragmentation*. London: Bloomsbury.

Landsberg, Alison. 2009. "Memory, Empathy, and the Politics of Identification." *International Journal of Politics, Culture, and Society* 22 (2): 221–29.

Larebo, Haile. 2005. "Empire Building and Its Limitations: Ethiopia (1935–1941)." In *Italian Colonialism*, edited by Ruth Ben-Ghiat and Mia Fuller, 83–94. New York: Palgrave Macmillan.

*La Repubblica*. 2018. "Conclusa l'operazione Spiagge Sicure in 54 comuni." September 19, 2018. https://www.repubblica.it/cronaca/2018/09/19/news/bilancio_spiagge_sicure-2068 47022/.

———. 2019. "Venezia, non ha i requisiti da profugo." May 14, 2019. https://www.repubblica .it/cronaca/2019/05/14/news/venezia_non_ha_requisiti_da_profugo_e_ben_integrato _puo_restare_in_italia_-226231083/.

———. 2020. "Il fotografo Sestini contro l'assessora leghista che usa la sua foto dei migranti per propaganda: 'Strumentalizzazione.'" October 15, 2020. https://milano.repubblica .it/cronaca/2020/10/15/news/migranti_foto_massimo_sestini_assessora_silvia_piani _lega_lombardia_polemica-270674292/.

"Larger European Orange Crop Expected." 2021. *Citrus Industry Magazine*, January 15. https://citrusindustry.net/2021/01/15/larger-european-orange-crop-expected/.

Lebron, Christopher J. 2023. *The Making of Black Lives Matter: A Brief History of an Idea*. Updated edition. Oxford: Oxford University Press.

Leogrande, Alessandro. 2011. *Il Naufragio*. Milano: Giangiacomo Feltrinelli Editore.

———. 2016. *Uomini e caporali: Viaggio tra i nuovi schiavi nelle campagne del Sud*. Milano: Feltrinelli.

———. 2019 [2015]. *La frontiera*. Milano: Feltrinelli.

Lester, Julius. 1984. "James Baldwin: Reflections of a Maverick." *New York Times*, May 27, 1984. https://archive.nytimes.com/www.nytimes.com/books/98/03/29/specials/baldwin -reflections.html?source=post_page/.

Levi, Primo. 2017 [1986]. *The Drowned and the Saved*. New York: Simon & Schuster.

Lewis, Hannah, and Louis Waite. 2015. "Asylum, Immigration Restrictions and Exploitation: Hyper-Precarity as a Lens for Understanding and Tackling Forced Labour." *Anti-Trafficking Review*, 5:49–67.

L'Hote, Leland, and Chad Gasta. 2007. "Immigration and Street Entrepreneurship in Alicante, Spain." *International Journal of Iberian Studies* 20 (June): 3–22.

Liguori, Anna. 2018. "No Cap e filiera etica, a Benevento la testimonianza del fondatore Yvan Sagnet." *Lab TV*, January 15, 2018. https://www.labtv.net/attualita/2018/01/15/no-cap -filiera-etica-benevento-la-testimonianza-del-fondatore-yvan-sagnet/.

Lipkin, Steven N. 2011. *Docudrama Performs the Past: Arenas of Argument in Films Based on True Stories*. Newcastle upon Tyne: Cambridge Scholars Publishing.

Locatelli, Jennifer, Luigi De Filippis, Mariarita Peca, Alberto Barbieri, Antonello Mangano, Giulia Crescini, Cristina Cecchini, Lucia Gennari, and Salvatore Fachile. 2018. "I dannati della terra: Rapporto sulle condizioni di vita e di lavoro dei braccianti stranieri nella Piana di Gioia Tauro." Medici per i Diritti Umani. http://www.mediciperidirittiumani .org/dannati-della-terra/.

Lombardi-Diop, Cristina. 2005. "Selling/Storytelling: African Autobiographies in Italy." In *Italian Colonialism: Legacy and Memory*, edited by Jacqueline Andall and Derek Duncan. London: Peter Lang.

———. 2012. "Postracial/Postcolonial Italy." In *Postcolonial Italy: Challenging National Homogeneity*, edited by Cristina Lombardi-Diop and Caterina Romeo. New York: Palgrave Macmillan.

———. 2021. "Preface." In *The Black Mediterranean: Borders, Bodies and Citizenship*, edited by the Black Mediterranean Collective, 1–7. New York: Palgrave Macmillan.

Lombardi-Diop, Cristina, and Caterina Romeo, eds. 2012. *Postcolonial Italy: Challenging National Homogeneity*. New York: Palgrave MacMillian.

Lowal, Shola. 2019. "For African Migrants Trying, and Dying, to Reach North America, the Darién Gap Is the 'New Mediterranean.'" Equal Times. December 9, 2019. https://www .equaltimes.org/for-migrants-trying-and-dying-to?lang=en/.

Lowe, Lisa. 2015. *The Intimacies of Four Continents*. Durham, NC: Duke University Press.

Lynes, Krista, Tyler Morgenstern, and Ian Alan Paul, eds. 2020. *Moving Images: Mediating Migration as Crisis*. Bielefeld: transcript Verlag.

Mademba, Bay. 2011. *Il mio viaggio della speranza: Dal Senegal all'Italia in cerca di fortuna*. Pontedera: Giovane Africa Edizioni.

Mainwaring, Cetta, and Daniela Debono. 2021. "Criminalizing Solidarity: Search and Rescue in a Neo-Colonial Sea." *Environment and Planning C: Politics and Space* 39 (5): 1030–48.

Malkki, Liisa. 1996. "Speechless Emissaries: Refugees, Humanitarianism, and Dehistoricization." *Cultural Anthropology* 11 (3): 377–404.

Marinari, Maddalena. 2020. *Unwanted: Italian and Jewish Mobilization against Restrictive Immigration Laws, 1882–1965*. Chapel Hill: University of North Carolina Press.

Marra, Claudio. 2012. *La casa degli immigrati: Famiglie, reti, trasformazioni sociali*. Milano: Franco Angeli Edizioni.

Masco, Joseph. 2017. "The Crisis in Crisis." *Current Anthropology* 58 (S15): 65–76.

Massey, Doreen. 2005. *For Space*. London: Sage.

Massey, Douglas S. 2020. "The Real Crisis at the Mexico-U.S. Border: A Humanitarian and Not an Immigration Emergency." *Sociological Forum* 35 (3): 787–805.

Mattone, Alberto. 2003. "Roma piange gli immigrati morti, oggi funerali in Campidoglio." *La Repubblica*, October 24, 2003. http://ricerca.repubblica.it/repubblica/archivio/repubblica/2003/10/24/roma-piange-gli-immigrati-morti-oggi-funerali.html.

Mazzara, Federica. 2016. "Spaces of Visibility for the Migrants of Lampedusa: The Counter Narrative of the Aesthetic Discourse." *Italian Studies* 70 (4): 449–64.

———. 2019. *Reframing Migration: Lampedusa, Border Spectacle, and Aesthetics of Subversion*. Oxford: Peter Lang.

Mbembe, Achille. 2001. *On the Postcolony*. Oakland: University of California Press.

———. 2003. "Necropolitics." *Public Culture* 15 (1): 11–40.

M'charek, Amade, Katharina Schramm, and David Skinner. 2014. "Topologies of Race: Doing Territory, Population and Identity in Europe." *Science, Technology, and Human Values* 39 (4): 468–87.

McKittrick, Katherine. 2006. *Demonic Grounds: Black Women and the Cartographies of Struggle*. Minneapolis: University of Minnesota Press.

Meloni, Francesca. 2014. "'Il mio futuro è scaduto'. Politiche e prassi di emergenza nelle vicende dei rifugiati in Italia." *Archivio Antropologico Mediterraneo* 12/13 (14): 87–96.

Mengiste, Maaza. 2016. "Primo Levi at the United Nations." *Primo Levi Center*, May 6, 2016. https://primolevicenter.org/printed-matter/primo-levi-at-the-un/.

Merrill, Heather. 2011. "Migration and Surplus Populations: Race and Deindustrialization in Northern Italy." *Antipode* 43 (5): 1542–72.

———. 2018. *Black Spaces: African Diaspora in Italy*. New York: Routledge.

Mezzadra, Sandro. 2006. *Diritto di fuga: Migrazioni, cittadinanza, globalizzazione*. Verona: Ombre Corte.

———. 2011. "The Gaze of Autonomy: Capitalism, Migration, and Social Struggles." In *The Contested Politics of Mobility: Borderzones and Irregularity*, edited by Vicki Squire, 121–42. London: Routledge.

Mezzadra, Sandro, and Brett Neilson. 2013. *Border as Method, or, The Multiplication of Labor*. Durham, NC: Duke University Press.

Millar, Kathleen. 2014. "The Precarious Present: Wageless Labor and Disrupted Life in Rio de Janeiro, Brazil." *Cultural Anthropology* 29 (1): 32–53.

*Ministero Dell'Interno*. 2022. "Profughi dall'Ucraina: 150.791 quelli giunti finora in Italia." July 15, 2022. https://www.interno.gov.it/it/notizie/profughi-dallucraina-150791-quelli-giunti-finora-italia/.

Mira, Toni. 2020. "Quei braccianti sfruttati e uccisi nel silenzio." *La Via Libera*, July 30, 2020. https://lavialibera.it/it-schede-205-braccianti_caporalato_coronavirus_morti_suicidi_decreti_salvini/.

"Missing Migrants." 2024. International Organization of Migration. 2024. https://missing migrants.iom.int/.

Montanari, Armando, and Antonio Cortese. 1993. "South to North Migration in a Mediterranean Perspective." In *Mass Migrations in Europe: The Legacy and the Future*, edited by Russell King, 212–33. London: Belhaven.

Monti, Aldino. 1998. *I Braccianti*. Bologna: Il Mulino.

Morlotti, Sara. 2020. "Emergenza Covid-19 e regolarizzazione degli immigrati: Aspetti giuridici." *Fondazione ISMU*, May 4, 2020. https://www.ismu.org/emergenza-covid-19-e -regolarizzazione-degli-immigrati-aspetti-giuridici/.

Morosi, Silvia. 2019. "Migranti, rogo nel ghetto di San Ferdinando: un morto." *Corriere della Sera*, February 16, 2019. https://www.corriere.it/cronache/19_febbraio_16/migranti -incendio-ghetto-tendopoli-san-ferdinando-morto-3c73efea-3195–11e9-a4dd-63e 8165b4075.shtml.

Morrison, Toni. 1993. *Playing in the Dark: Whiteness and the Literary Imagination*. Reprint edition. New York: Vintage.

Mosoetsa, Sarah, Joel Stillerman, and Chris Tilly. 2016. "Precarious Labor, South and North: An Introduction," *International Labor and Working-Class History* 89:5–19.

Moten, Fred. 2018a. *Stolen Life*. Durham, NC: Duke University Press.

———. 2018b. *The Universal Machine*. Durham, NC: Duke University Press.

Mountz, Alison. 2020. *The Death of Asylum: Hidden Geographies of the Enforcement Archipelago*. Minneapolis: University of Minnesota Press.

Mountz, Alison, and Nancy Hiemstra. 2014. "Chaos and Crisis: Dissecting the Spatiotemporal Logics of Contemporary Migrations and State Practices." *Annals of the Association of American Geographers* 104 (2): 382–90.

Musarò, Pierluigi. 2017. "Mare Nostrum: The Visual Politics of a Military-Humanitarian Operation in the Mediterranean Sea." *Media, Culture and Society* 39 (1): 11–28.

Nagle, Luz E. 2020. "Tainted Harvest: Transborder Labor Trafficking and Forced Servitude in Agribusiness." *Wisconsin International Law Journal* 37 (3): 511–68.

"Nel 2017 6.500 migranti rimpatriati." *ANSA*, May 17, 2018. https://www.ansa.it/amp/sito /notizie/cronaca/2018/05/17/nel-2017-6.500-migranti-rimpatriati_81e011a7-d5ad-4a58 -ad9e-824aef51dc5f.html.

Nyabola, Nanjala. 2019. "The End of Asylum." *Foreign Affairs*, October 10, 2019. https://www .foreignaffairs.com/world/end-asylum?check_logged_in=1/.

Nyers, Peter. 2013. *Rethinking Refugees: Beyond States of Emergency*. London: Routledge.

———. 2015. "Migrant Citizenships and Autonomous Mobilities." *Migration, Mobility, and Displacement* 1 (1): 23–39.

Olguin, B. V. 2002. "Of Truth, Secrets, and Ski Masks: Counterrevolutionary Appropriations and Zapatista Revisions of Testimonio." *Nepantla: Views from South* 3 (1): 145–78.

Oliver, Kelly. 2001. *Witnessing: Beyond Recognition*. Minneapolis: University of Minnesota Press.

Olivito, Elisa. 2017. *Gender and Migration in Italy: A Multilayered Perspective*. London: Routledge.

Open Polis. 2021. "Che cosa sono i Cas, lo Sprar e gli Hotspot." Accessed May 27, 2024. https://www.openpolis.it/parole/che-cosa-sono-i-cas-lo-sprar-e-gli-hotspot/.

O'Rawe, Catherine. 2020. "The Non-Professional Actor in the Reception of Italian Cinema Abroad." *Cinergie—Il Cinema e Le Altre Arti* 9 (18): 73–83.

Paik, A. Naomi. 2020. *Bans, Walls, Raids, Sanctuary: Understanding U.S. Immigration for the Twenty-First Century*. Oakland: University of California Press.

Palermo, Camilla. 2021. "Rome's MAAM—Museo Dell'Altro e Dell'Altrove." *Romeing* (blog). February 7, 2021. https://www.romeing.it/maam-museo-altro-altrove-rome/.

Pallister-Wilkins, Polly. 2016. "Interrogating the Mediterranean 'Migration Crisis.'" *Mediterranean Politics* 21 (2): 311–15.

Palmas, Luca Queirolo. 2017. "Transiti, connessioni e contestazioni negli accampamenti urbani dei rifugiati a Parigi." *Mondi migranti* 2:207–27.

Palmisano, Leonardo, and Yvan Sagnet. 2015. *Ghetto Italia. I braccianti stranieri tra capolarato e sfruttamento*. Roma: Fandango Libri.

Paquette, David, and Andra Mccartney. 2012. "Soundwalking and the Bodily Exploration of Places." *Canadian Journal of Communication* 37:135–45.

Parati, Graziella, ed. 1999. *Mediterranean Crossroads: Migration Literature in Italy*. Madison, NJ: Fairleigh Dickinson University Press.

———. 2010. "Introduction." In *I Was an Elephant Salesman: Adventures between Dakar, Paris, and Milan*. Bloomington: Indiana University Press.

Pasciuti, Marco. 2014. "Mafia Capitale, Buzzi: 'Con immigrati si fanno molti più soldi che con la droga.'" *Il Fatto Quotidiano*, December 2, 2014. https://www.ilfattoquotidiano .it/2014/12/02/mafia-capitale-buzzi-immigrati-si-fanno-soldi-droga/1245847/.

Past, Elena. 2013. "'Trash Is Gold': Documenting the Ecomafia and Campania's Waste Crisis." *Interdisciplinary Studies in Literature and Environment* 20 (3): 597–621.

Paul, Ian Alan. 2020. "Controlling the Crisis." In *Moving Images: Mediating Migration as Crisis*, 71–94. Bliefeld: transcript Verlag.

Paynter, Eleanor. 2017a. "Autobiographical Docudrama as Testimony: Jonas Carpignano's *Mediterranea*." *A/b: Auto/Biography Studies* 32 (3).

———. 2017b. "The Spaces of Citizenship: Mapping Personal and Colonial Histories in Contemporary Italy in Igiaba Scego's *La mia casa è dove sono* (My Home Is Where I Am)." *European Journal of Life Writing* 6 (July): 135–53.

———. 2020. "The Transits and Transactions of Migritude in Bay Mademba's *Il mio viaggio della speranza* (My Voyage of Hope)." *minnesota review* 2020 (94): 104–23.

———. 2022a. "Testimony on the Move: Navigating the Borders of (In)Visibility with Migrant -Led Soundwalks." *A/b: Auto/Biography Studies* 37 (1): 129–52.

———. 2022b. "Border Crises and Migrant Deservingness: How the Refugee/Economic Migrant Binary Racializes Asylum and Affects Migrants' Navigation of Reception." *Journal of Immigrant and Refugee Studies* 20 (2): 293–306.

———. 2023. "Gendered Asylum in the Black Mediterranean: Two Nigerian Women's Experiences of Reception in Italy." In *Migrations in the Mediterranean*, edited by Ricard Zapata-Barrero and Ibrahim Awad. Cham: Springer.

———. 2024. "Creating Crises: Risk, Racialization, and the Migration-Security Nexus in Italy and the US." In *Managing Migration in Italy and the United States*, edited by Lauren Braun-Strumfels, Maddalena Marinari, and Daniele Fiorentino, 55–76. Berlin: De Gruyter Oldenbourg.

Paynter, Eleanor, and Nicole Miller. 2019. "The White Readymade and the Black Mediterranean: Authoring 'Barca Nostra.'" *Los Angeles Review of Books*, September 22, 2019. https://lareviewofbooks.org/article/the-white-readymade-and-the-black-mediterra nean-authoring-barca-nostra/.

Paynter, Eleanor, and Katrina M. Powell. 2023. "'OutLaw Yard': Reading Traces of Displacement as Testimonial Inscription." *Migration and Society* 6 (1): 87–104.

Pesarini, Angelica. 2021. "When the Mediterranean 'Became' Black: Diasporic Hopes and (Post)Colonial Traumas." In *The Black Mediterranean: Bodies, Borders and Citizenship*, edited by the Black Mediterranean Collective, 31–56. Cham: Palgrave Macmillan.

Petralia, Peter Salvatore. 2010. "Headspace: Architectural Space in the Brain." *Contemporary Theatre Review* 20 (1): 96–108.

Pinkus, Karen. 1995. *Bodily Regimes: Italian Advertising under Fascism*. Minneapolis: University of Minneapolis Press.

Poggioli, Sylvia. 2020. "In Italy, A Migrants' Advocate Fights For The 'Invisibles.'" *NPR*, August 5, 2020. https://www.npr.org/2020/08/05/898893067/in-italy-a-migrants-advocate-fights-for-the-invisibles/.

Pompei, Daniela. n.d. "Jerry Essan Masslo." Community of Sant'Egidio. Accessed July 14, 2023. https://www.santegidio.org/pageID/30764/langID/en/Jerry-Essan-Masslo.html.

Ponzanesi, Sandra. 2004. *Paradoxes of Postcolonial Culture: Contemporary Women Writers of the Indian and Afro-Italian Diaspora*. Albany: SUNY Press.

———. 2017. "Connecting Shores: Libya's Colonial Ghost and Europe's Migrant Crisis in Colonial and Postcolonial Cinematic Representations." In *Border Lampedusa: Subjectivity, Visibility and Memory in Stories of Sea and Land*, edited by Gabriele Proglio and Laura Odasso, 119–35. Basel: Springer.

Pop, Valentina. 2013. "Italy Grants Citizenship to Lampedusa Dead." *EU Observer*, October 7, 2013. https://euobserver.com/justice/121681/.

Portelli, Alessandro. 2003. *The Order Has Been Carried Out: History, Memory and Meaning of a Nazi Massacre in Rome*. London: Palgrave Macmillan.

———. 2008. "Etiopia, la storia cancellata." *Il Manifesto*, May 4, 2008. https://archiviopubblico.ilmanifesto.it/Articolo/2003127635/.

Powell, Katrina M. 2014. "Representing Human Rights Violations in Multimedia Contexts." In *We Shall Bear Witness: Life Narratives and Human Rights*, edited by Meg Jensen and Margaretta Jolly, 196–216. Madison: University of Wisconsin Press.

———. 2015. *Identity and Power in Narratives of Displacement*. New York: Routledge.

Powell, Katrina M., Jenny Dick-Mosher, Anisa Zvonkovic, and Pamela B. Teaster. 2016. "Displacing Marginalized Bodies: How Human Rights Discourses Function in the Law and in Communities." *International Journal for the Semiotics of Law—Revue Internationale de Sémiotique Juridique* 29 (1): 67–85.

Pradella, Lucia, and Rossana Cillo. 2021. "Bordering the Surplus Population across the Mediterranean: Imperialism and Unfree Labour in Libya and the Italian Countryside." *Geoforum* 126 (November): 483–94.

Pratt, Mary Louise. 2008. *Imperial Eyes: Travel Writing and Transculturation*. New York: Routledge.

Proglio, Gabriele, Camilla Hawthorne, Ida Danewid, P. Khalil Saucier, Giuseppe Grimaldi, Angelica Pesarini, Timothy Raeymaekers, Giulia Grechi, and Vivian Gerrand, eds. 2021. *The Black Mediterranean: Bodies, Borders and Citizenship*. London: Palgrave Macmillan.

Puglia, Alessandro. 2020. "Esclusivo: i pescatori di Mazara a processo davanti al tribunale militare di Haftar." *Vita*, December 10, 2020. https://www.vita.it/it/article/2020/12/10/esclusivo-i-pescatori-di-mazara-a-processo-davanti-al-tribunale-milita/157686/.

Qasmiyeh, Yousif M. 2021. *Writing the Camp*. Talgarreg, Wales: Broken Sleep Books.

Raeymaekers, Timothy. 2021. "Impermanent Territories: The Mediterranean Crisis and the (Re)Production of the Black Subject." In *The Black Mediterranean: Borders, Bodies and Citizenship*, edited by the Black Mediterranean Collective, 117–44. London: Palgrave Macmillan.

Rannard, Georgina. 2018. "Diciotti: Rice Ball Protest in Italian Migrant Boat Row." *BBC News*, August 24, 2018. https://www.bbc.com/news/blogs-trending-45296739/.

*Redattore Sociale*. 2003. "Funerali dei migranti, associazioni critiche. 'Cerimonia tardiva e ipocrita.'" October 21, 2003. https://www.redattoresociale.it/article/notiziario/funerali _dei_migranti_associazioni_critiche_cerimonia_tardiva_e_ipocrita_/.

———. 2016. "Migranti transitanti, Raggi: 'Situazione complessa.'" October 11, 2016. https:// www.redattoresociale.it/article/notiziario/migranti_transitanti_raggi_situazione _complessa_prima_bastava_chiamare_buzzi_/.

Redazione ANSA. 2023. "Molise, Pil tra più bassi Italia, indice povertà tra più alti." *ANSA*, May 3, 2023. https://www.ansa.it/molise/notizie/2023/05/03/molise-pil-tra-piu-bassi-italia -indice-poverta-tra-piu-alti_5620305c-7913-4065-b258-b539034e029c.html#.

Renga, Dana, and Allison Cooper. 2013. "Introduction: The Banda della Magliana, The Camorra, The 'Ndrangheta, and the Sacra Corona Unita: The Mafia Onscreen beyond the Cosa Nostra." *The Italianist* 33 (2): 190–200.

Reuters. 2018. "France Offers Citizenship to Malian Immigrant Who Scaled Building to Save Child." May 28, 2018. https://www.reuters.com/article/idUSKCN1IT075.

Riccò, Giulia. 2020. "Igiaba Scego on Writing between History and Literature." *Public Books* (blog). December 8, 2020. https://www.publicbooks.org/igiaba-scego-on-writing -between-history-and-literature/.

Riedl, Rachel Beatty. 2014. *Authoritarian Origins of Democratic Party Systems in Africa*. Cambridge: Cambridge University Press.

Rigo, Enrica. 2019. "La vulnerabilità nella pratica del diritto d'asilo: Una categoria di genere?" *Etica and Politica / Ethics and Politics* 21 (3): 343–60.

Roberts, Hannah. 2020. "Italy's Coronavirus Farmworker Shortage Fuels Debate on Illegal Migration." *Politico*, April 13, 2020. https://www.politico.eu/article/italy-seasonal-migrant -farm-workers-coronavirus-covid-19/.

Robinson, Cedric. 2000. *Black Marxism: The Making of the Black Radical Tradition*. 2nd ed. Chapel Hill: University of North Carolina Press.

Roitman, Janet. 2013. *Anti-Crisis*. Durham, NC: Duke University Press.

Romeo, Caterina. 2012. "Racial Evaporations: Representing Blackness in African Italian Postcolonial Literature." In *Postcolonial Italy: Challenging National Homogeneity*, edited by Cristina Lombardi-Diop and Caterina Romeo, 221–36. New York: Palgrave Macmillan.

———. 2015. "Meccanismi di censura e rapporti di potere nelle autobiografie collaborative." *Between* 5 (9): 1–28.

Rosales, Rocío. 2020. *Fruteros: Street Vending, Illegality, and Ethnic Community in Los Angeles*. Oakland: University of California Press.

Rosi, Gianfranco, dir. 2016. *Fuocoammare*. Italy, Stemal Entertainment.

Rothberg, Michael. 2019. *The Implicated Subject: Beyond Victims and Perpetrators*. Redwood City, CA: Stanford University Press.

Rutinwa, Bonaventure. 2010. "The End of Asylum? The Changing Nature of Refugee Policies in Africa." *Refugee Survey Quarterly* 21 (1/2): 12–41.

Salerno, Daniele. 2016. "Memorializing Boat Tragedies in the Mediterranean: The Case of the Katër i Radës." In *Migration by Boat: Discourses of Trauma, Exclusion and Survival*, edited by Lynda Mannik. London: Berghahn Books.

Salvatori, Gabriele. 2021. "Metropoliz o il tempo del sogno: Discorsi, relazioni e pratiche di vita in un'occupazione abitativa romana." Thesis, Sapienza Università di Roma. http://www.editricesapienza.it/sites/default/files/6065_Salvatori_Metropoliz_interior.pdf.

Salzberg, Rosa M. 2011. "'Selling Stories and Many Other Things in and through the City': Peddling Print in Renaissance Florence and Venice." *Sixteenth Century Journal* 42 (3): 737–59.

Samaddar, Ranabir. 2020. *The Postcolonial Age of Migration*. London: Routledge.

Saucier, P. Khalil. 2021. "Carne Nera." In *The Black Mediterranean: Borders, Bodies and Citizenship*, edited by the Black Mediterranean Collective, 101–16. New York: Palgrave Macmillan.

Sbacchi, Alberto. 2005. "Poison Gas and Atrocities in the Italo-Ethiopian War (1935–1936)." In *Italian Colonialism*, edited by Ruth Ben-Ghiat and Mia Fuller, 47–56. New York: Palgrave Macmillan.

Scego, Igiaba. 2010. *La Mia Casa è Dove Sono*. Torino: Loescher Editore.

———. 2015. *Adua*. Milano: Giunti.

———. 2020. "Cosa fare con le tracce scomode del nostro passato." *Internazionale*, June 9, 2020. https://www.internazionale.it/opinione/igiaba-scego/2020/06/09/tracce-passato-colonialismo-razzismo-fascismo/.

Schultheis Moore, Alexandra. 2014. "Témoignage and Responsibility in Photo/Graphic Narratives of MSF." In *We Shall Bear Witness: Life Narratives and Human Rights*, edited by Meg Jensen and Margaretta Jolly, 175–95. Madison: University of Wisconsin Press.

Segre Andrea, dir. 2010. *Il sangue verde*. Italy.

Sellman, Johanna. 2022. *Arabic Exile Literature in Europe: Defamiliarizing Forced Migration*. Edinburgh: Edinburgh University Press.

Servizio Studi del Senato. 2015. *Immigrazione: Cenni introduttivi*. n. 210 (April). https://www.senato.it/service/PDF/PDFServer/BGT/00912705.pdf.

Shahin, Saif, Junki Nakahara, and Mariana Sánchez. 2021. "Black Lives Matter Goes Global: Connective Action Meets Cultural Hybridity in Brazil, India, and Japan." *New Media and Society* 26 (1): 216–35.

Sharma, Nandita. 2020. *Home Rule: National Sovereignty and the Separation of Natives and Migrants*. Durham, NC: Duke University Press.

Sharp, David. 2023. "What the Titanic Submersible Saga and the Greek Migrant Shipwreck Say about Our Reactions to Tragedy." *AP News*, June 23, 2023. https://apnews.com/article/submersible-titanic-titan-greek-migrant-shipwreck-7db0c63b4439de820877af272527cb83/.

Sharpe, Christina. 2016. *In the Wake: On Blackness and Being*. Durham, NC: Duke University Press.

Shenhav, Yehouda. 2012. "Imperialism, Exceptionalism and the Contemporary World." In *Agamben and Colonialism*, edited by Marcelo Svirsky and Simone Bignall, 17–31. Edinburgh: Edinburgh University Press.

Shuman, Amy. 2005. *Other People's Stories: Entitlement Claims and the Critique of Empathy.* Champaign: University of Illinois Press.

———. 2006. "Entitlement and Empathy in Personal Narrative." *Narrative Inquiry* 16 (1): 148–55.

Sigona, Nando. 2015. "Campzenship: Reimagining the Camp as a Social and Political Space." *Citizenship Studies* 19 (1): 1–15.

Sina, Ylenia. 2020. "Occupazioni, dai bambini di Metropoliz la campagna per salvare la 'città meticcia' dallo sgombero." *RomaToday,* September 1, 2020. https://www.romatoday.it /zone/centocelle/tor-sapienza/campagna-contro-sgombero-metropoliz.html/.

Slovic, Paul, Daniel Västfjälla, Arvid Erlandsson, and Robin Gregory. 2017. "Iconic Photographs and the Ebb and Flow of Empathic Response to Humanitarian Disasters." *PNAS* 114 (4): 640–44.

Smith, Sidonie, and Julia Watson. 2010. *Reading Autobiography: A Guide for Interpreting Life Narratives.* Minneapolis: University of Minnesota Press.

———. 2012. "Witness or False Witness: Metrics of Authenticity, Collective I-Formations, and the Ethic of Verification in First-Person Testimony." *Biography* 35 (4): 590–626.

Smythe, SA. 2018. "The Black Mediterranean and the Politics of Imagination." *Middle East Report* 286 (Spring): 3–9.

Soliman, Francesca. 2024. *Social Harm at the Border: The Case of Lampedusa.* London: Routledge.

Sontag, Susan. 2003. *Regarding the Pain of Others.* New York: Picador.

Soto, Gabriella. 2022. "The Time of Agony: Abjectivity Politics and the Investigation of Border Crossing Deaths along the US-Mexico Border." *Current Anthropology* 63 (3): 239–69.

Squire, Vicki. 2020. *Europe's Migration Crisis: Border Deaths and Human Dignity.* Cambridge: Cambridge University Press.

Squire, Vicki, Nina Perkowski, Dallal Stevens, and Nick Vaughan-Williams. 2021. *Reclaiming Migration: Voices from Europe's "Migrant Crisis."* Manchester: Manchester University Press.

Stewart-Steinberg, Suzanne. 2016. "Grounds for Reclamation: Fascism and Postfascism in the Pontine Marshes." *Differences* 27 (1): 94–142.

Stierl, Maurice. 2016. "Contestations in Death—the Role of Grief in Migration Struggles." *Citizenship Studies* 20 (2): 173–91.

———. 2020. "Do No Harm? The Impact of Policy on Migration Scholarship." *Environment and Planning C: Politics and Space* 40 (5): 1083–1102.

Stoler, Ann Laura. 2016. *Duress: Imperial Durabilities in Our Times.* Durham, NC: Duke University Press.

*Stranieri in Italia.* 2018. "Salvini: 'Col mio governo espulsione di tutti i migranti economici,'" March 13, 2018. https://stranieriinitalia.it/attualita/salvini-col-mio-governo-espulsione -di-tutti-i-migranti-economici/.

Tazzioli, Martina, and Glenda Garelli. 2018. "Containment beyond Detention: The Hotspot System and Disrupted Migration Movements across Europe." *Environment and Planning D: Society and Space* 38 (6): 1009–27.

*Tesfa News.* 2013a. "Italy to Hold State Funeral for Lampedusa Victims, Eritrea Objects," October 9, 2013. https://www.tesfanews.net/italy-to-hold-state-funeral-for-lampedusa -victims-eritrea-objects/.

———. 2013b. "Eritreans Held Memorial Service for Lampedusa Victims," October 24, 2013. https://tesfanews.net/eritreans-held-memorial-service-for-lampedusa-victims/.

Testore, Gala. 2019. "Italian Parliamentary Investigation on Exploitation of Migrant Workers in Agriculture." *European Website on Integration*, March 8, 2019. https://ec.europa.eu/migrant-integration/news/italian-parliamentary-investigation-on-exploitation-of-migrant-workers-in-agriculture/.

*The Dick Cavett Show.* 1969. Aired May 16 with guest James Baldwin. Accessed February 15, 2024. https://www.youtube.com/watch?v=WWwOi17WHpE/.

"The Economic Performance of Agriculture in Italy." 2017. Istituto Nazionale Di Statistica. 2017. https://www.istat.it/en/archive/200105.

Theodore, Nik. 2003. "Political Economies of Day Labour: Regulation and Restructuring of Chicago's Contingent Labour Markets." *Urban Studies* 40 (9): 1811–28.

*The Straits Times.* 2013. "Protests Mar Italy Ceremony for Shipwreck Dead," October 22, 2013. https://www.straitstimes.com/world/protests-mar-italy-ceremony-for-shipwreck-dead/.

Thomson, Alistair, and Nick Tattersall. 2007. "Worst Riots in Years Hit Senegalese Capital." *Reuters*, November 21, 2007. https://www.reuters.com/article/us-senegal-protests-idUSL211189220071121/.

Ticktin, Miriam. 2016. "Thinking beyond Humanitarian Borders." *Social Research* 83 (2): 255–71.

Tompkins, Joanne. 2011. "Site-Specific Theatre and Political Engagement across Space and Time: The Psychogeographic Mapping of British Petroleum in Platform's 'And While London Burns.'" *Theatre Journal* 63 (2): 225–43.

Torchin, Leshu. 2012. *Creating the Witness: Documenting Genocide on Film, Video, and the Internet.* Minneapolis: University of Minnesota Press.

Trentanove, Federico, Katia Cigliuti, Francesca Scarselli, Mario Venturella, Melissa Zorzi, Silvia Masciadri, and Simone Natali. 2019. "Il modello CAS di pane e rose: Pratiche di accoglienza e integrazione." In *Il monitoraggio dei Centri di Accoglienza Straordinaria: Esperienze a confronto*, edited by Paola Sacchi and Barbara Sorgoni. Torino: Celid.

Triulzi, Alessandro. 2012. "Hidden Faces, Hidden Histories: Contrasting Voices of Postcolonial Italy." In *Postcolonial Italy: Challenging National Homogeneity*, edited by Cristina Lombardi-Diop and Caterina Romeo, 103–14. New York: Palgrave Macmillan.

Tsing, Anna Lowenhaupt. 2005. *Friction: An Ethnography of Global Connection.* Princeton, NJ: Princeton University Press.

Ufficio immigrazione. 2014. "Centri convenzionati con l'Ufficio Immigrazione del Comune di Roma." Comune di Roma. http://www.programmaintegra.it/wp/wp-content/uploads/2014/01/203_Centri_convenzionati_con_ufficio_immigrazione.pdf.

UNHCR. 2024. "Mediterranean Situation." Operational Portal: Refugee Situations. https://data2.unhcr.org/en/situations/mediterranean/.

Urbina, Ian. 2021. "The Secretive Prisons That Keep Migrants Out of Europe." *New Yorker*, November 23, 2021. https://www.newyorker.com/magazine/2021/12/06/the-secretive-libyan-prisons-that-keep-migrants-out-of-europe/.

"U.S. Administration Proposes Legislation to Protect Titanic Wreck Site Source." 2006. *American Journal of International Law* 100 (4): 934–35.

Vang, Ma. 2021. *History on the Run: Secrecy, Fugitivity, and Hmong Refugee Epistemologies.* Durham, NC: Duke University Press.

Venkatesh, Vasanthi, Talia Esnard, Vladimir Bogoeski, and Tomaso Ferrando. 2023. "Migrant Farmworkers: Resisting and Organising before, during and after COVID-19." *Journal of Agrarian Change* 23 (3): 568–78.

Villa, Matteo, Elena Corradi, and Antonio Villafranca. 2018. "Fact Checking: Migrazioni 2018." *Istituto per gli Studi di Politica Internazionale.* https://www.ispionline.it/it/pubblicazione/fact-checking-migrazioni-2018-20415.

Vista Agenzia Televisiva Nazionale. 2019. *Salvini: "Con Spiagge Sicure meno vu cumprà a rompere le palle."* July 18, 2019. https://www.youtube.com/watch?v=EjTqiMp6A6M/.

Viviano, Francesco, and Alessandra Ziniti. 2018. *Non lasciamoli soli: Storie e testimonianze dall'inferno della Libia.* Milano: Chiarelettere.

Walcott, Rinaldo. 2021. "The Black Aquatic." *Liquid Blackness* 5 (1): 63–73.

Walia, Harsha. 2013. *Undoing Border Imperialism.* Chico, CA: AK Press.

———. 2021. *Border and Rule: Global Migration, Capitalism, and the Rise of Racist Nationalism.* Chicago: Haymarket.

Walters, William. 2008. "Acts of Demonstrations: Mapping the Territory of (Non-) Citizenship." In *Acts of Citizenship*, edited by Engin F. Isin and Greg M. Nielsen, 182–206. London: Zed Books.

———. 2010. "Migration and Security." In *The Handbook of New Security Studies*, edited by J. Peter Burgess, 217–28. London: Routledge.

Weheliye, Alexander G. 2014. *Habeas Viscus: Racializing Assemblages, Biopolitics, and Black Feminist Theories of the Human.* Durham, NC: Duke University Press.

Welch, Rhiannon Noel. 2016. *Vital Subjects: Race and Biopolitics in Italy, 1860–1920.* Liverpool: Liverpool University Press.

Western, Tom. 2020. "Listening with Displacement: Sound, Citizenship, and Disruptive Representations of Migration." *Migration and Society* 3 (1): 294–309.

Wheatley, Abby C. 2021. "A Politics of Survival." In *Migration and Mortality: Social Death, Dispossession, and Survival in the Americas*, edited by Jamie Longazel and Miranda Cady Hallett, 255–74. Philadelphia: Temple University Press.

Whitlock, Gillian. 2014. "Protection." In *We Shall Bear Witness*, edited by Meg Jensen, Margaretta Jolly, and Mary Robinson, 80–99. Madison: University of Wisconsin Press.

———. 2015. *Postcolonial Life Narratives: Testimonial Transactions.* Oxford: Oxford University Press.

Whitlock, Gillian, and Rosanne Kennedy. 2020. "The Messenger: Refugee Testimony and the Search for Adequate Witness." In *Refugee Imaginaries: Research Across the Humanities*, edited by Emma Cox, Sam Durrant, David Farrier, Lyndsey Stonebridge, and Agnes Woolley, 480–500. Edinburgh: Edinburgh University Press.

Williams, Jill M. 2015. "From Humanitarian Exceptionalism to Contingent Care: Care and Enforcement at the Humanitarian Border." *Political Geography* 47:11–20.

Yancy, George. 2008. *Black Bodies, White Gazes: The Continuing Significance of Race in America.* Lanham, MD: Rowman & Littlefield.

Yimer, Dagmawi, dir. 2014. *Asmat (Names).* Italy, Archivio Memorie Migranti. https://vimeo.com/114343040/.

———. 2015. "Names and Bodies: Tales from the Other Side of the Sea." Event flyer. San Diego: University of California San Diego.

"Yvan Sagnet | No cap." 2022. Accessed November 18, 2023. https://www.associazionenocap .it/yvan-sagnet/.

Zetter, Roger. 2007. "More Labels, Fewer Refugees: Remaking the Refugee Label in an Era of Globalization." *Journal of Refugee Studies* 20 (2): 172–92.

<h1 style="text-align:center">INDEX</h1>

NOTE: Page numbers in *italics* denote maps, tables, or photographs. Laws and policies discussed in the main text are indexed under the main headings for European Union and Italy. A full list of laws and policies is found in the Appendix.

abandonment of migrants: denial of asylum claim as, 71, 81–83; the EU and, 8, 34; as necropolitical governance's central impulse, 82, 89; reception as spaces of, 81, 102; by Tunisian police, 49, 107; of vessels at sea, 8, 34. See also *abbandono*

*abbandono*: as Interior Ministry term, 82; as migrant term, 71, 82

abolition: and language of "police brutality," 176; politics of Baobab Experience and emergent *accoglienza*, 88–89, 96–97, 98, 103, 107, 109–10; and reconceptualizing hospitality, 96–97, 103, 220n52; scholarship on, and reliance on "crisis" rhetoric, 19–20; witnessing for, 195. *See also* Black Mediterranean

abolitionist sanctuary, 88–89, 97, 98, 107, 109–10

Abraham, Tezeta, 153

*accoglienza. See* hospitality; informal camps— Piazzale Maslax's emergent forms of *accoglienza*; reception (*accoglienza*)

Acquaformosa: immigrant founding of, 62; SPRAR reception center, 62–63, 217–18n51

acts of citizenship. *See under* citizenship

Afghanistan, 8, 12

Africo, "Eden" mural, 56–57, *57*

Afro-European borderzone, 4, 7, 13, 21, 33, 172

Agamben, Giorgio, 6, 82, 88, 165, 207n12

agency of migrants: asylum denial as rejection of, 82; as constrained by limbo of reception, 70–71, 80, 82; and death, 52; farmworkers and, 180, 183; informal camps and, 93, 94, 102, 108; and *ospite*/guest language for migrants, 80; and precarious labor, 117, 189; *Titanic* evocations and, 52, 53; transit and recognition of, 18

agribusiness. *See* farmworkers and exploitation; farmworker representation and advocacy

Ahmed, Sara, 38, 60, 66, 107, 165, 194, 209n44, 212n5, 225n35

Aidara, Aminata, 121

Alarm Phone, 194

Albania: Acquaformosa and Arbëresche heritage, 62–63; historical migration from, 2, 14, 63, 66–67, 131, 209n55; migrant detention agreements with Italy, 19; shipwrecked vessel from (28 March 1997), and monument to, 54–56, *56*

Alfano, Angelino, 39

Ali Farah, Ubah Cristina, 26, 152; *Madre piccola (Little Mother)*, 41–42, 52, 55

Ali, Zakaria Mohamed, *A chiunque possa interessare (To Whom It May Concern)* (documentary), 31, 32, *32*, 46, 48, 51

Al Masoudi, Nasser, 177, 185

Aman (migrant narrator/interviewee, the Gambia), 71–73, *74*

Amnesty International, 36

Amsterdam, Lampedusa Cruises, 144

Andersson, Ruben, 50

anonymity: of dead migrants, 31–32, 44, 53, 213n46. *See also* (in)visibility, politics of

anti-Black racism. *See* racial logics of the colonial present; racism

anti-immigration politics: overview, 19; asylum seekers' anxiety about, 74; and Baobab Experience's activism, 86, 90, 96, 108–9, 110; budget cuts to CAS, 188, 216n14; closure of ports to rescue vessels, 36, 108–9, 141, 220n21; images of migrant boats as stoking, 50; manipulation of photographs, 193–94; Operation Safe Beaches campaign against street vendors, 115–16, 125, 126, 137; as platforms of the right wing, 60, 115; racism as legitimized by, 60, 134, 136, 223n76; real estate campaigns hawking homes to Western tourists, 141; rumors of migrants being housed in four-star hotels, 67. *See also* Australia; criminalization of migration; deservingness narratives; European Union; Salvini, Matteo; United Kingdom (Britain); United States

anti-racist activism: in analysis of police brutality in eviction of camp, 176; demonstrations in response to anti-Black violence, 40, 136, 177, 183; Palermo network, 195–97; the Rosarno demonstration (2010) as, 183; of Aboubakar Soumahoro, 187, 188

antisemitism, 13

Anzaldúa, Gloria, 161

Arab literatures of migration, 51–52, 211n107

Arab Spring uprisings: Emergenza Nord Africa migration law, *203*, 208n21, 215n1; migration in the wake of, 51, 208n27; and political turmoil in Libya, 208n27

Arbëresche culture, 62–63

asylum (legal/humanitarian protection status): as itself increasingly under threat, 7, 192; not convertible to work visa, 175; renewal of status, 173–74; Universal Declaration of Human Rights and the right to claim, 18. *See also* asylum process; asylum seekers

asylum process: asylum hearing (*commissione*), 70; policies alternately stalling or accelerating, 82, 174. *See also* asylum seekers; reception as legal and social limbo

—denial of claim: as abandonment into precarity, 71, 81–83; appeals, 76, 81–82, 217–18n51; dismissal from the CAS camp, 81, 82–83; percentage of claims denied, 174; and production of deportable subjects, 81, 82; and production of precarious workforce, 11, 82, 168, 174, 175–76. *See also* precarious labor

—legal testimony of asylum seekers: overview, 22, 59; exaggerations or falsehoods in, 130; language translation and interpretation problems in, 76, 77, 217n49; and personal experience vs. asylum officials' expectations, 71, 72–73; protectiveness of the details of, 74, 76; revisiting or preparing while waiting, 71–74; as testimonial transaction stretched across time, 59; "well-founded fear" of persecution in country of origin as burden of proof in, 22, 74

asylum seekers: appeal to history and the right to stay, 92–93, 219n24; commitment to integration and the right to stay, 74–78, 217–18n51; as legal status, 21. *See also* asylum process; integration; reception as legal and social limbo

Australia: as global north destination, 17; island detention centers, 17, 35, 194–95; migration framed as inherently a problem, 2; misciting of photograph, 183

autobiographical writing: as performance of deservingness, 75; as situating the self in history, 152; and testimonial transactions, 151. *See also* Scego, Igiaba; street vendor autobiographies; testimonial transactions

autonomy of migration approach, 212n19

available narratives: integration and, 81; as reproducing border spectacle, 23; tellability of, 22, 79, 163–64, 179; and testimony reifying crisis framings, 23, 24, 79; as underscoring suffering and vulnerability, 23

Bakary (migrant narrator/interviewee, Côte d'Ivoire), 65, 68, 69, 75–77, 81–82, 83, 86, 89

Baldwin, James: on the artist as witness, 150; on Black life, 11, 195; on the consequences of smashing the social contract, 40; as expatriate to France, 26; on history as life unfolding, 16; on integration, 66; on the racialized stranger, 66, 216n18; on witnessing and change, 24–25, 109, 195, 196

Balibar, Étienne, 79, 113, 116, 164

Balkan countries: in Eastern Mediterranean migration zone, 8; migrants from, 63

Bâ, Mariama, 120

Bangladesh, migrants from, 8, 124

Baobab Experience. *See* informal camps— Baobab Experience

Baobab reception center (Rome), closure of, 98, 219n37

BarConi (Palermo), 196–97, *196*

Barre, Siad, 37–38, 152

Bedouins, 100, 218n66

Benjamin, Walter, 6, 194

Berlin, Refugee Voices walking tours, 144

Berlusconi, Silvio, 36, 100, 209n57

Bernabucci, Sara, artwork at MAAM, 159, *160*, 215n93

Bhabha, Homi, 24, 164

Bianchi, Diego, 187, 228n45

Bianchi, Rino, and Igiaba Scego, *Roma negata*, 151, 153–55, 156–57

Biani, Mauro, "Uno a caso" ("One at random"), 135, *135*

biopolitics, 210n74. *See also* Agamben, Giorgio; Foucault, Michel; necropolitical border governance

Black Atlantic, and the Black Mediterranean, 49, 53, 54. *See also* colonial present; enslavement and slave trade

"Black," capitalization of term, 208n35

Black life: emergency conditions of, 11; and fugitivity, 11, 18, 210n79; witnessing and, 24–25

Black Mediterranean: the Black Atlantic and, 49, 53, 54; the Black radical tradition and, 13, 212n11; colonial present and influence of racial logics, 16; colonial present and liberation of the future, 48, 214n63; definition of, 4–5; precarious migration as continuation of enslavement and slave trade practices, 34–35, 49–50, 53; and racialized South/North stereotypes within Italy, 14; risk of migrant deaths as operation of capitalism, 212n19; Igiaba Scego's work in context of, 150. *See also* abolition; colonial present

blackness: in colonial iconography, 127; exclusion from Italian identity, 37–38, 41, 42, 126–27, 217n28

Black radical tradition, 13, 35, 212n11

Black studies: and capitalization of "Black," 208n35; *carne nera* (black flesh), 186; on integrationism as reifying oppression, 144. *See also* Baldwin, James; Black life; Black Mediterranean; Black radical tradition; fugitivity; racial capitalism; wake work

boats: overview, 48; anti-immigrant discourse and, 50; as archive, 51; *barconi*, 196; boat refugees, 50; as haunting, 48–49; as heterotopia, 50–51; Lampedusa cemetery for, 31, *32*, 51; as material and symbolic structures in the colonial present, 32, 49–51, 214n67; memorial artworks of, 54–56, *55–56*, 159, *160*, 215n93; slave ships and migrant boats, 35, 49–50, 53; surveillance technologies and, 50; *Titanic* invocations and, 51–52. *See also* sea crossings; shipwrecks

Bohmer, Carol, 130

Boochani, Behrouz, *No Friend but the Mountains*, 194–95

borders: constructed nature of, 4; externalization of, 19, 35–36, 40, 208n27, 212n16; weaponization of the environment and, 35. *See also* border spectacle; necropolitical border governance

borderscapes, defined, 10

border spectacle: elegy as disrupting, 46; evictions of informal camps as, 100–101, 141; as maintaining emergency imaginaries, 23; migrant "illegality" rendered as, 32–33; shipwrecks and, 8, 35

Bosnia, 10, 36, 84, 96

Brand, Dionne, *The Blue Clerk*, 11, 46, 91–92

Büchel, Christoph, *Barca Nostra* (installation), 54, *55*, 55–56

Butler, Judith, 11, 35

Buzzi, Salvatore, 98, 219n37

Byrd, Jodi, 18

Calabria: Cutro shipwreck (26 February 2023), 8, 43; migrant farmworkers in, 170, 171, 174, 176; reception centers, 56–57, *57*, 78, 171. *See also* farmworkers and exploitation; farmworker representation and advocacy; Rosarno

Calais, France, "The Jungle," 84

Calhoun, Craig, 6, 20, 210n68

Camilli, Annalisa, 188

camp (*il campo*): as term used by migrants for reception centers, 63, 80, 89. *See also* informal camps

Campidoglio Square (Rome): migrant protest (October 2016), 1–2, *3*, 4, 19, 92; state funeral for shipwreck (2003), 37–38, 40–42, 213n21

Campobasso: overview, 66; farm started by CAS staff, 188–89; immigration into, prior to 2014, 66–67; and increased arrivals of migrants (2014), 10; and reception centers (CAS), 64–66, 67–68, 74–78, 188. *See also* Molise; reception centers (*centri di accoglienza*)

Canary Islands: Senegalese sea voyages to, 51, 121, 129; in the Western Mediterranean route to Spain, 8, 10, 51, *201*

capitalism: as dependent on migration, 11; neoliberalization of agribusiness and need for precarious labor, 169–70. *See also* precarious labor; racial capitalism

Caritas (Catholic organization), 10, 144

*carne nera* (black flesh), 186

Carpignano, Jonas, *Mediterranea* (2015 docudrama), 46, 169, 179–85, *180*, *184*, 186, 228n47

Carter, Donald M., 50, 90, 124, 125, 129, 169, 172, 189

CAS. *See* reception centers—CAS

CasaPound, 136

Casas-Cortés, Maribel, 141

Cattaneo, Cristina, 54

Cecconi, Giuseppe: background of, 120; as editor of Mademba's *Il mio viaggio*, 118, 121, 132–33; on narrative ownership by migrant booksellers, 133; on the right-wing, rise of, 134. *See also* Giovane Africa Edizioni

Cennetoglŭ, Banu, Fatal Policies of Fortress Europe, *47*, *47*

Center for Political Beauty, 214n59

Central America: asylum seekers from, and US "Remain in Mexico" protocols, 36; and migration to US, 191–92, 229n3

Central Mediterranean borderzone: arrival counts, 199–200, *201*; death tallies, 36, 199–200, *201*; definition of, 8; "deterrence" policies and, 36; map of, *9*; number of women crossing, 16, 216–17n27

Césaire, Aimé, 91

Ceuta, 8, 10, *201*

Chambers, Iain, 33

Chinese Italian communities, 66

citizenship: caution against reifying the nation-state as primary frame for, 50; as collective practice among the excluded, 116, 142; defined as term, 224n11; emancipatory, 214n63; integration discourses reiterating white notions of the citizen, 80; integration used in requirements for, 218n67; *jus sanguinis* stipulation, generally, 224n10; as legal status, 142; the limits of appeals to, as imperial formation, 164; and the severe social borders of division, 189; substantive, vs. legal status, 142

—acts of citizenship: overview, 141–42; and absences, recovery of, 156–57; as changing public perceptions, 144–45, 148–50, 151, 154–56, 161–63, 225n35; "citizenship" as term in, 224n11; cultural fluency/authority established in, 142, 143, 146, 149–50, 162–63; definition of, 141–42, 224nn11–12; as disrupting or expanding normative notions of belonging, 143, 144, 145–46, 149–50, 152, 154, 156–57, 162–64, 224n16; and empathy, failures of, 148, 149, 225n35; ethical encounters enabled by, 165; Guide Invisibili (Invisible Guides) soundwalks, 142, 143–50, *147*, 163, 164, 225n35; and imperial formations, longer histories of mobility (re)inscribed onto, 141, 149, 150, 151–52, 153, 154–56, 164; the intimacy of testimony and, 143, 163, 165–66; marginalized "others" as source of, 142, 143–44, 157–58, 160, 161–63, 164–65; Metropoliz collective and MAAM (Museum of the Other and Elsewhere), 142, 157–63, 164–65, 226nn73,77; and migration as a social and political act, 224n16; narratives negotiated through, 146, 148, 224n16; and the politics of invisibility, 144, 146, 149–50, 156–57; as queering ethnicity, 151, 161–62; the right to the city, 116, 141, 142, 157–58, 160, 161–65; spatial practices of, 142–43; and substantive citizenship vs. legal status, 142, 146; testimonial transactions and, 143–44, 145, 148, 149, 151, 163–64, 165–66; transnational Italy made visible in, 141, 143, 145, 146, 150, 151, 152, 154, 162, 164–65. *See also* Scego, Igiaba

—Italian: overview, 142; awarded posthumously to shipwreck victims, 39; cultural fluency of racialized and non-Christian asylum seekers as unrecognized, 141; *jus sanguinis*, 142; *jus soli*, 224n10; language requirement for, 218n67; limits of, as strategy against systemic racism, 164, 226n89; naturalization of immigrants and G2 Italians as difficult, 142, 224n10

Città dell'Utopia (Rome), 143, 146, 167, 173

città meticcia. *See* Metropoliz collective

colonial aphasia (forgetting): definition of, 15; and deservingness narratives, 222n52; as feeding emergency imaginaries of foreignness, 150–51, 152; and the irretrievability of vocabulary, 155–56; and *italiani brava gente* ("good Italians") discourse, 15, 154; media coverage of *emergenza* as perpetuating, 15; migrant deaths and, 33, 153–54; Igiaba Scego on,

26, 41, 150–51, 152, 153–56. *See also* colonial present
—erasure and elision of longer histories: overview, 116; and the "contact zone" myth, 13, 92; "crisis" discourse as dependent on, 194; and the endless present, 2–3, 12, 16, 80, 151; the invisibilization of race and, 41; and the murder of Idy Diene, 137; and "strange grief," 37–38, 39; and strangers (constructions/perceptions of foreignness), 13, 92–93
colonial memory: "Italy's divided memory," 209n60, 213n20. *See also* colonial aphasia (forgetting)
colonial present: as age of emergency, 190, 192–93, 194–95; control of migrants' time, 70–71; definitions of, 3, 11–12, 209n44; deportation centers as structures of, 80; evictions of informal camps and, 100; and Fanon's "rule of oppression," 7; and liberation of the future, 48, 214n63; migrant consciousness of, and the right to stay, 92–93, 219n24; policing and externalization of borders, 19, 35–36, 40, 208n27, 212n16. *See also* Black Mediterranean; colonial aphasia (forgetting); emergency apparatus of migration; emergency imaginaries of foreignness; empathy, failures of; gaze, colonial; imperial formations; Italy—colonial settlements and governance in Africa; necropolitical border governance; racial logics of the colonial prese; racial logics of the colonial present; racism
Colucci, Michele, 2
construction, as precarious labor, 66–67, 227n6
contact zones, 13, 92
Conte administration, 173
Corrado, Alessandra, 185, 227n12
corruption in reception, 78–79, 93, 187–88, 216n14, 219n25; organized crime, 79, 98, 170, 218n57, 220n41
Costa, Andrea, 102–3, 108–9, 220n58
COVID-19 pandemic: and annual demonstration at 2013 shipwreck memorial, 44; domestic workers and, 172; farmworkers and, 168, 172–73, 187; informal camps and, 96; and manipulation of photographs for anti-immigrant ends, 193; Soumahoro's "Gli Invisibili" bringing PPE to farmworkers, 187; street vendors and, 223n77
Crialese, Emanuele, *Terraferma* (2011 film), 46

criminalization of migration: overview, 107; affecting the work of Giovane Africa Edizioni, 134; Baobab Experience and testimony as challenge to, 107–9; Baobab Experience charged with assisting illegal migration, 32–33; of crossing the sea to seek asylum, 32–33, 35, 39; of evicted residents of informal camps and occupied spaces, 100–101, 141, 161; and fragmentation of the figure of the refugee, 139; of freedom of movement, 108–9; informal camps framed as illegal, 94, 95, 100; of rescue and aid, 19, 78, 107, 115, 134, 161, 192, 223n76; of shipwrecked migrants, 54–55, 213n26; of street vendors (Operation Safe Beaches), 115–16, 125, 126, 137; as transforming ethical practices of care to exercises in risk, 192. *See also* culture of suspicion
crisis: conflation of migration management with, 15; and criticism-as-seeing (Moten), 184–85, 228n57; etymology of, 20; and generation of fear, 210n73; of migration, as one among many global crises, 5. *See also* emergency apparatus of migration
"crisis Italy," 21, 79
crisis racism, 79–80, 116
crisis voyeurism, 90
critical race studies, 80
critical refugee studies, 6–7, 20–21, 145, 156–57, 207n8
Cuba, "boat refugees," 50
Cufari, Franco, photo of January 2010 riots, 183–84, *184*
culture of suspicion: in deservingness narratives and the economic migrant-refugee binary, 12, 18, 66, 69, 130; farmworker advocacy and, 188, 189–90; informal camps assumed to be dangerous, 90, 91, 93, 95; locations of CAS as increasing, 64–65, 65, 67–68; of Muslim women wearing the hijab, 148; and precarious labor, 189–90; presumption that Black subjects in city centers are out of place, 64, 66, 68, 125–26, 145, 146; racialized notions of deservingness and, 66, 69, 130; reception as legal and social limbo and, 64, 65–66, 68; Aboubakar Soumahoro's persona-based activism and, 187–88; and street vendors, 125, 126, 127–28, 146, 221n10

Danewid, Ida, 96–97
Darién Gap, and migration to the US, 191–92, 229n3

deaths of migrants: anonymous death, 31–32, 44, 53, 213n46; colonial aphasia (forgetting) and, 33, 153–54; as consequence of violent bordering practices, 35–37, 212n19; and dehumaning of Black migrant workers, 154, 185–86, 190; deservingness narratives and expendability of Black lives, 137, 172, 185–86; in emergency imaginary as evidence of migrant criminality, 32–33, 35, 39; in emergency imaginary as "natural tragedy," 33, 35, 37, 39; of farmworkers, 168, 169, 170–71, 172, 177, 185, 228n41; of farmworkers, violent, 39–40, 137, 168, 173, 177, 178, 185, 194; as gap in witnessing, 8; the limits of empathy as demonstrated by the endlessness of, 22; murder of Idy Diene, 135–36, 135–37; racial logics of the colonial present revealed by risk of, 34, 36; risk of death as central to the emergency apparatus, 32–33, 34–35, 36–37, 212n19; suicide, 99, 177; tallies of, 8, 31–32, 36, 199–200, 201; *Titanic* evocations of, and agency in, 52; and "victim" as term, 212n19. *See also* anti-Black violence and the colonial present; necropolitical border governance; shipwrecks
—migrant-centered elegies: overview, 27, 34; as changing public perceptions, 42–43, 44–48; and corporeal experience, 40–41, 44; elegy as testimonial form, 45–46; "grief activism," 46–47, 47, 214n59; and humanization of dead migrants, 41–42; inscribing the shipwreck and each life lost, 44–45; names of the victims, 44–45, 47–48; on state avoidance of culpability, 42; *Titanic* references in, 52; as visibilizing race and the colonial past together, 41
—state funerals as strange grief: overview, 27, 37; control of the narrative to remove state culpability, 37, 38, 39, 213n20; criticized as farce, 39; definition of, 34, 212n5; and erasure of colonial histories and migrations, 37–38, 39; failures of empathy and, 38, 39, 194; as ongoing site of protest, 43–44; as reifying the unknowability of the deceased, 38, 39; as spanning the political spectrum, 213n21; strangerness (S. Ahmed) and, 38, 212n5; survivors remaining in reception centers, 39, 43. Funerals: 1989 refugee Jerry Essan Masslo, 39–40, 177; 2003 shipwreck, 37–38, 40–42, 213n21; 2013 shipwreck, 37, 38–39, 41, 43–48, 213nn26–27; 2017 shipwreck, 37
de Certeau, Michel, 142
de Finis, Giorgio, 162

dehumanization: by colonial propaganda, 14; "dehumaning" as term (Sharpe), 154, 186; neglect of residents in reception centers, 79; re-humaning as contrasted to, 154; through surveillance technology, 50; of workers, 154, 185–86, 190
Del Giudice, Francesca, 99
Dembele, Famakan, 177, 185
demonstrations and protests: after Soumaila Sacko murder, for migrants' rights, 137–38, 138, 187; annual protest of ongoing migrant deaths, 43–44; anti-racist, in response to anti-Black violence, 40, 136, 177, 183; Baobab Experience and, 1–2, 3, 4, 19, 90, 92, 94, 108; at the Campidoglio (October 2016), 1–2, 3, 4, 19, 92; and COVID-19 pandemic, 223n77; international support gained through, 90; for Metropoliz eviction threat, protection against, 161, 163; as street-vendor venue, and policing of, 137–39. *See also* Arab Spring uprisings; farmworker representation and advocacy— Rosarno demonstration (January 2010)
deportation: denials of asylum and production of deportable subjects, 81, 82; deportability, and anxiety in reception, 63, 81; deportability, and dehumaning of Black migrant workers, 185–86, 190; documents not given in language of migrant, 138; orders to leave (*foglio di via*), 82, 137–39; statistics on actual deportations vs. orders to leave, 82
deportation centers (CIE or CPR), 205; immediate placement in upon arrival, 61; as structures of the colonial present, 80
Derrida, Jacques, 60, 215n3
deservingness: asylum seekers' commitment to integration in hopes of achieving, 74–78, 217–18n51; Black suffering and death and, 168; Black women presumed to be sex workers or victims of sex trafficking, 16, 69; definition of, 128; the emergency apparatus and determination of, 16; and expendability of Black lives, 137, 172, 185–86; and farmworkers during COVID-19 pandemic, 172–73; humanitarian narratives of, 103, 128, 220n52; media coverage and, 16, 128, 222n52; and periodic amnesties (legalization) for workers, 186; street vendors and, 116, 137; and US invasion of Vietnam, 222n52
—economic migrant–refugee binary: overview, 12, 22, 130; and the colonial gaze, 12; "crisis" as the fault of economic migrants, 139; and the culture of suspicion, 12, 18, 66, 69, 130;

invisibilization of labor and, 125, 172; public adjudication outside of asylum courts, 18, 22; as racialized, gendered suspicion, 12, 18; the Refugee Convention (1951) establishing, 130; right-wing campaigns to expel economic migrants, 130; street vendors and, 125, 130; subversion of dominant narratives of, 119, 121–23, 128–32, 139

Diallo, Amadou, 43, 44, 195–96

Diene, Idy, 135–37

Di Maio, Luigi, 96

Dines, Nick, 168

Dodecanese Islands, Italian colonial rule of, 209n49

domestic labor sector: COVID-19 and labor amnesty, 172, *203*; legal and social limbo producing workforce, 11; in pre-2014 history of migration, 66–67; as precarious labor, 227n6; as racialized labor, 127

Doumbia, Amadou, 144

*dublinati*, 86, 99

Eastern Europe: Martelli Law as expanding asylum recognition beyond, 40; as migrant farmworkers, 168, 170; as origin of migrants, 19, 84–85, 216–17n27

Eastern Mediterranean borderzone, 8, 9, 36

economic migrant–refugee binary. *See under* deservingness narratives

economy of indifference, 172

El-Tayeb, Fatima, 151, 158, 161–62

emergency: as condition of Black life, 11; as term, 20

emergency apparatus of migration: overview, 16–20, 192; age of emergency, 28, 190, 192–93, 194–95; changes of governments and alterations of, 15; confusion and vagueness as strategic facet of, 59, 70; "crisis" presumed to be inherent attribute of migration in, 2, 6–7; definition of, 3, 116; *emergency* as term and, 20; exploitation of emergency conditions of Black life by, 11; farmworker exploitation as facilitated by, 168–69, 171, 177, 189–90; and Foucault's *dispositif*, 16, 210n74; as imperial network, 100; informal camps as fundamental site of, 88–89, 93–94; matters of real, material urgency perpetually treated as crises, 192; multiple scales of, 17; and perceived unbelonging of border crossers, 3; as perpetuating circumstances of urgency and uncertainty, 3, 59, 63, 64, 70, 141, 192; short-term funding of, 15; and the state of exception, 6, 165, 207n12; as system of relations, 16–17; unequal functioning of declarations, 19. *See also* colonial present; deaths of migrants; emergency imaginaries of foreignness; informal camps; necropolitical border governance; precarious labor; precarious migration; racial logics of the colonial present; reception (*accoglienza*)

emergency imaginaries of foreignness: acts of citizenship as disrupting, 143, 144, 161; colonial aphasia (forgetting) as feeding, 150–51, 152; the colonial gaze and, 91–92, 161; as counterrevolutionary force holding the future hostage, 17, 192, 210nn69,74; crisis racism, 79–80, 116; as crossing political administrations and exacerbated by political shifts, 60; death at sea as evidence of individual migrant criminality, 32–33, 35, 39; death at sea as "natural tragedy," 33, 35, 37, 39; definition of, 3, 116; and the endless present, 2–3, 12, 16, 80, 151; fear and, 210n73; gender stereotypes and, 16; and the humanitarian sphere, 210n68; migration as cause of dire circumstances, vs. consequence of, 93, 102, 139, 172, 190, 192; normalization of, 16; and racialization of migrants, 80; scholarship on migration and reliance on "crisis" rhetorics, 19–20; and *seconde generazioni* construed as foreign in the city of their birth, 151, 152; street vendors as cultural icon of, 116–17, 124, 125–26, 127, 137, 146; transit from global south to global north as focus of, 17. *See also* anti-immigration politics; border spectacle; colonial aphasia (forgetting); culture of suspicion; racial logics of the colonial present; strangers, constructions and perceptions of foreignness

*emergenza*: definition and uses of term, 20–21; as disregarding the histories bound up in, 21; earthquake and flooding responses, 21; *emergenza abitativa* (housing crisis), 140–41, 223nn2,5; *emergenza nomadi* (nomad emergency), 100; *emergenza rifiuti* (garbage crises), 21; intersectionality of, in neoliberal "crisis Italy," 21. See also *emergenza immigrazione*

*emergenza immigrazione* (immigration emergency): definition of, 2; invocation of, 7, 10; photographs miscited as contemporary evidence of, 14, 209n55; shift of focus to street vendors, 116. *See also* emergency apparatus of migration

Emmanuel (migrant narrator/interviewee, Côte d'Ivoire), 93–94, 101–3

empathy, failures of: overview, 194; acts of citizenship and, 148, 149, 225n35; the endless deaths of migrants as evidence of, 22; farmworker exploitation and, 189; and lack of lasting, substantive change for migrants, 8, 108; the strange grief of states as resulting from, 39, 194; testimonies that prompt new perspectives not cultivating empathy, 24; the violence of emergency as evidence of, 193–94; voyeurism as marking, 91

Enlightenment, citizenship and, 164

enslavement and slave trade: colonial economies and, 35; Global Slavery Index (2023), 227n19; memoirs by enslaved persons, as negotiated narrative, 224n28; migrant farmworker exploitation as form of, 168, 170–71, 186, 187, 227n19; sea crossings as inextricably entangled in the colonial present, 35, 49–50, 53, 132; slave, definition of, 171; and spectacle of suffering, 91

Eritrea: the *Diciotti* blocked in port with rescued migrants from (2018), 108–9; Italian colonial rule of, and erasure of history, 39, 92–93, 209n49; language of, and traces of Italian, 92; migrants from, and the 2013 shipwreck, 38–39, 43–48, 140–41, 153, 213nn26–27

Espiritu, Yến Lê, 6, 156, 217n35, 222n52

ethical encounters, 165

Ethiopia: Italian colonial conquest of, and erasure of history, 39, 153, 154, 155–56, 209n49; migrants from, and 2013 shipwreck, 38–39, 43–48, 140–41, 213n26; the Stele of Axum, return of, 155–56

European Union (EU): abandonment of migrants in transit, 8; arrival counts, 8, 199–200, *201*; border nations, significant responsibility for migration placed on, 208n21; camps at the borders of, 10, 36, 84, 96; criminalization of rescue and aid, 107, 192; death tallies, 8, 31–32, 36, 199–200, *201*; Dublin Regulation and Italy as first country of arrival, 18, 86, 208n21, 210n76; migrants as precarious workforce, 11; official migration "crisis" of (2014–2019), 7–8, 38, 85; Schengen Agreement and shift in migration trends, 139

—laws and policies: table listing, *202–4*; Dublin III, Revised Dublin Regulation, 18, 86, 99, *202*, *203*, 208n21; Pact on Migration and Asylum, 18, 210n76; Schengen Agreement, 14, 35, 139, 170, 174, *202*

European values, 18

evictions (*sgomberi*): of Baobab Experience from Via Cupa center and street, 98–99, 219–20nn38–39, 41; belongings of residents seized, 100, 101, 102; and the colonial present, 100; criminalization of the evicted, 100–101, 141, 161; and the *emergenza nomadi* (nomad emergency), 100; of farmworker camps, 126; as intentional unsettling, 85, 93, 99, 100, 141; legitimized as security measure, 161; Metropoliz collective threatened with, and campaigns to prevent, 157, 161, 162, 163; of occupied spaces, 98, 140–41, 161, 220n39; Piazza dell'Indipendenza, occupied building near, 140–41, 223n2; of Piazza Maslax, and barricade, *87*, 93, 95, 100, 103, 110–11, *111*; and trauma, 100, 101

exception, spaces of (Agamben), 6, 88, 94, 97, 165, 207n12

exclusion. *See* racial logics of the colonial present

Fall, Moustapha, 181

Fanon, Frantz, 7, 12, 24, 82

farmworkers and exploitation: overview as migrant seasonal workers, 167–69; *bracciante* as term, 167; *caporalato* "gangmaster" system, 167–68, 170–71, 172, 174, 176, 227nn17,19; *caporalato*, 2016 law criminalizing, 170, 186–87; and the colonial present, 170–71; contracts for work, strike as prompting, 186; COVID-19 pandemic and, 168, 172–73, 187; deaths, 168, 169, 170–71, 172, 177, 185, 228n41; deaths, anti-Black murders, 39–40, 137, 168, 173, 177, 178, 185, 194; diversity of workforce, 168; during reception limbo, 173–75; Eastern European migrants, 168, 170; the emergency apparatus and exploitation of labor, 168–69, 171, 177, 189–90; and empathy, failures of, 189; as form of enslavement, 168, 170–71, 186, 187, 227n19; as global issue, 169–70, 189–90; harvest labor and history of immigration to Italy, 84–85, 167; housing contract required for visa, and difficulty of obtaining, 176; housing, government or NGO provided, 171–72; housing, improvised settlements, 84–85, 126, 168, 171–72, 176, 177; intensification of labor and, 171; internal Italian migrants, historically, 85, 167, 170; invisibilization of, 168, 172–73, 185, 186, 188, 189; irregular labor, 170, 176, 177, 227n12; legal immigration status as no protection from exploitation, 170, 172, 174–75, 177; mobility of,

171, 174, 176; neoliberalization of agribusiness and "permanent temporary" workforce requirements, 169–70; numbers of people employed as, 170; orange cultivation, 167, 171, 189; physical and mental health and, 177; precarious migration and, 171; racialization of labor, 168, 169, 170–71, 172–73, 177–78; as refugeeization of labor, 168, 172, 173–78, 186–89; South Asian migrants, 84–85, 167; testimony as method and, 169; as transit laborers, 168. *See also* farmworker representation and advocacy

farmworker representation and advocacy: overview of risks of, 168–69; culture of suspicion and, 188, 189–90; demonstrations in Rome after Soumaila Sacko murder, 137–38, *138*, 187; embodied witnessing, 186–87; following Soumaila Sacko's murder, 167, 173; limits of (self-)representation, 169, 172, 185, 226–27n4; and persona-based visibility vs. movements built on invisibility, 188; *Propaganda Live* (television), 228n45; shaping viewer-consumers as witnesses, 187; Aboubakar Soumahoro and, 187–88; strike in Puglia (2011), 186–87; strike in Rosarno following worker deaths (2018), 177; unions, 137, 172, 173, 177

—Rosarno demonstration (January 2010), 178, 179, 181, 182, 183, 185; and agency of migrants, 180, 183; and anti-racist action, recognition of, 183; countering dominant narratives of precarious migration, 179, 181, 182, 183; criticism-as-seeing (as locating), 184–85, 228n57; embodied testimony, 181; extensions of testimony, 182; historicizing labor within Italy, 179; history as process of remembering, 183; *Il sangue verde (Green Blood)* (2010 documentary, dir. Andrea Segre), 178–79; intimacy, sense of, 182–83; layered forms of witnessing, 179, 181, 182, 185; media coverage and images as affirming racist associations of Black migrants with violence, 177–78, 183; "media witnessing" (recreation of famous images), 182–83, *184*; *Mediterranea* (2015 docudrama, dir. Jonas Carpignano), 46, 169, 179–85, *180*, *184*, 186, 228n47; new neorealism, 179; and the politics of (in)visibility, 169, 178, 179, 182, 184–85, 228n57; (re)inscribing public memory of specific events, 178, 181–85; shaping of viewers as witnesses, 169, 181, 183–85; tellable narratives, expansion and transformation of, 179

Fassin, Didier, 128
Fethi (migrant narrator/interviewee, Tunisia), 103–7
Fiorentini, Gianluca, 157, 158, 159, 226n73
Fiore, Teresa, 131
Florence, 133–34; as field site, 119, 120; Senegalese community rallying for support, 136, 223n77. *See also* street vendors (*venditori ambulanti*)
Floyd, George, 151, 195; mural of (Christian Picciotto), 196–97, *196*
food justice, 187, 188–89
forgetting. *See* colonial aphasia (forgetting)
Fornaro, Concetta, 67
Fortress Europe: agreements with third countries to detain EU-bound migrants, 19, 35–36, 212n16; border walls and "smart" fences, 19, 36; defiance of, as form of decolonial reparations, 4–5; Italy as gatekeeper of, 14, 63; migrant deaths and risk of death as revealing racial borders of, 34; militarization of, 19, 35; policing and externalization of borders, 19, 35–36, 40, 208n27, 212n16; prevention of disembarkation from vessels, 19. *See also* anti-immigration politics
Foucault, Michel, 3, 16, 50, 210n74
France: African migration to, 127; as colonializing power, 15, 127, 131, 209n61; and the colonial past, 150; as destination for migrants denied asylum, 82; enslaved workers in, 227n19; French translations of Senegalese-Italian cultural texts, 221n12; informal settlements of migrants, 10; Italian labor migration to, historically, 126; *jus sanguinis* citizenship, 224n10; migrant deservingness and, 78; police killings of people of North African descent, 49; Ventimiglia as transit point to, 108–9
Francis (pope), 38
Frontex, 8
*fruteros*, 117
fugitivity: Black life and, 11, 18, 210n79; fugitive witnessing, 45; of migrants, 109; and refugeeness, 18, 210n79; residents of Metropoliz and alternative version of, 161; transit as form of, 18; as unsettling, 73–74

G2. See *seconde generazioni* ("second generations" or "G2")
the Gambia, 8
Gandhi, Evyn Lê Espiritu, 50
Garrone, Matteo, *Io Capitano* (2023 film), 46, 181
Gassama, Mamoudou, 78

Gaye, Cheikh Tidiane, 121

gaze, colonial, 12, 91–92, 108, 161; disruption of, 91–92, 161, 182; the voyeur's gaze as, 91–92

gender: deservingness narratives and stereotypes of, 12, 18. *See also* deservingness; migrant women

Genoa, and the slave trade, 35

Germany: and the colonial past, 150; grief activism in, 214n59; Italian labor migration to, historically, 126; *jus sanguinis* citizenship, 224n10; Syrian migration to, 8, 208n21

Ghermandi, Gabriella, 152

Gilmore, Leigh, 107–8, 226–27n4

Gilmore, Ruth Wilson, 170

Gilroy, Paul, 50

Giovane Africa Edizioni (Young Africa Editions) (book publisher): overview and founding, 119–20; as publisher of *Il mio viaggio* (Bay Mademba), 119, 134; right-wing anti-immigrant government and temporary halt to new books, 134; social justice mission of, 120, 134; supporting migrant employment, 120, 134, 223n75; types of books published, 120. *See also* street vendor autobiographies: *Il mio viaggio della speranza* (Bay Mademba)

Gli Invisibili (The Invisibles), 187–88

Glissant, Eduoard, 49, 69

global north: agribusiness exploitation to benefit, 169–70; emergency imaginaries as focusing on migration from global south to, 17; as fraught term, 17; integration used in citizenship requirements, 218n67; Italian emigration to, 13, 66, 126, 209n43, 218n64; and post-1990 trend conflating migration and "crisis," 15; waiting period for asylum process, 10; weaponization of the environment and policing and externalization of borders, as growing practice, 35–36, 40, 212n16

global south: displacement within, 17; as fraught term, 17; migration to global north as focus of emergency imaginaries, 17

Gorée, 132

Gori, Carlo, 162–63

Gramsci, Antonio, 14

Gran Ghetto (informal settlement, Puglia), 176

Graziani, Rodolfo, 155–56

Greece: detention of migrants in camps, 10, 58; in Eastern Mediterranean migration zone, 8; enslaved workers in, 227n19; and EU agreement with Türkiye to trade migrants, 35–36; migrant deaths and, 194; migrant

pushbacks, 8; Second Tree (NGO), 194, 218n70; shipwreck (June 2023), 215n90; as transit country, 17–18, 210nn75–76; unofficial migrant camps, 84

Gregory, Derek, 11–12

guest workers, 80, 139, 218n64

Guide Invisibili (Invisible Guides) soundwalks, 142, 143–50, *147*, 163–64, 225n35. *See also* acts of citizenship; colonial aphasia (forgetting)

Hall, Stuart, 16, 20, 46, 185

Hartman, Saidiya, 33, 48, 91, 128, 144, 224n28

Hawthorne, Camilla, 150, 164, 208n35

headspace, 148

Hesse, Bernor, 123

Hodžić, Saida, 6

Holocaust survivors, testimony of, 23, 36–37

Hom, Stephanie Malia, 80, 100, 216n6

hooks, bell, 149

Horn of Africa. *See* Eritrea; Ethiopia; Italy—colonial settlements and governance in Africa; Somalia

hospitality: *accoglienza* as term and, 59; conditional welcome ("hostipitality") of reception system, 60–61, 65–66, 78, 215n3, 216n6; *ospiti* (guests), reception system's framing of migrants as, 79–80; reconceptualizing through abolition politics, 96–97, 103, 107, 220n52; Senegalese notion of *teraanga*, 97. *See also* informal camps—Piazzale Maslax's emergent forms of *accoglienza*

hotels, repurposing of, 67–68

humanitarian visas, 171

human rights: International Convention for the Safety of Life at Sea, 53; Libyan violations of detained migrants', 36; science of, as based in materiality, 54; Universal Declaration of Human Rights, 18. *See also* migrant rights

imperial formations: acts of citizenship (re)inscribing longer histories of mobility onto, 141, 149, 150, 151–52, 153, 154–56, 164; citizenship as, 164; the colonial gaze as legitimized by, 91; confederate monuments (USA), 151; Dogali monuments, 153, 154; Galleria Sciarra, 149; imperial networks, 100; language and its transmission as, 155–56; Piazza di Porta Capena / the Stele of Axum, 155–56; and racialized narratives of identity and belonging, 91, 153–56; September 11 memorial, 156. *See also* colonial present; emergency apparatus of migration

implicated subjects, 132, 154–56

informal camps: overview, 84–85; and agency of migrants, 93, 102, 108; culture of suspicion and, 90, 91, 93, 95; as emergency response strategy, 89, 103; expansion of size and number across Europe, 10, 84; of farmworkers, 84–85, 168, 171–72, 176, 177; framed as illegal, 94, 95, 100; as fundamental to the emergency apparatus, 88–89, 93–94; intentional unsettling of, 85, 93, 99, 100; Italian history of, 84–85; methodology and, 89, 219n10; proximal distance and, 94–95; as spaces of exception, 88, 94, 97. *See also* criminalization of migration; evictions (*sgomberi*); nomadism; occupied spaces; Romani people; Sinti people

—Baobab Experience (collective): overview, 1, 85; abolitionist politics of, 88–89, 96–97, 98, 103, 107, 109–10; *assistenza* (aid) and, 99; and COVID-19 pandemic, 96; criminal charges for assisting migrant freedom of movement, 108–9, 220n58; formation of, 1, 85, 98; humanitarian assistance at EU borders, 96, 220n68; international support garnered by, 85, 90, 103; occupation of old Baobab reception center, 98, 219–20nn38–39; occupation of Via Cupa, 98–99, 220n41; paying residents for labor, 95; right-wing anti-immigrant scrutiny of, 86, 90, 96, 108–9, 110; state surveillance and, 91; *transitanti* (people in transit) as term for migrants, 86; at the Verano Cemetery, *86*, 96, 110; volunteers of, 85–86, 95, 98, 103. *See also* abolitionist sanctuary

—Piazzale Maslax (Baobab Experience camp): daily life of, 87–88, *88*, 90–91, 92, 94, 95–96, 103; duration of, 85, 89; evictions bringing new arrivals to, 140; map of, *86*; named after Somali migrant, 99–100; numbers of residents, 87–88, 103; police evictions and barricade of, *87*, 93, 95, 100, 103, 110–11, *111*; police raids and document checks, 99, 100, 108–9; the politics of (in)visibility and, 85, 86, 89, 90, 103; the politics of survival and, 86, 92, 106, 219n7; support services (legal, medical), 85, 90, 108, 137–39, 173–74; visited by residents of official reception centers, 94; water supply for, 84, 100, 218n1

—Piazzale Maslax as key site of witnessing: overview, 87, 107–11; and adequate witnesses, 107–8; the camp as shaped by practices of, 87; challenging the criminalization of migration,

107–9; the colonial present recognized in, 92–93, 219n24; counter-witnessing, 108–9; demonstrations and protests, 1–2, 3, 4, 19, 90, 92, 94, 108; disrupting the colonial gaze, 91–92; and empathy, failures of, 108; media attention and, 90, 91, 95, 100–101, 106, 109, 220n52; and possibility of change, 109; press conferences, 108–9; social media, 108; solidarity and shared belonging as relying on, 92; survival of the group as dependent on, 107–9; voyeurism and the colonial gaze, 90–91, 108

—Piazzale Maslax's emergent forms of *accoglienza*: overview, 87, 88–89; abolitionist politics and, 88–89, 96–97, 98, 103, 107, 109–10; and *accoglienza* as a set of practices of survival and care, 85, 94, 106; camp assemblies, 94, *102*, 102–3, 167; community events and entertainment, 85; ethical communication, 107; humor, 96; *La vie des immigration* (collective camp diary), 103–7, *105*; as radical hospitality, 96–97, 103, 107, 220n52; residents and volunteers seen as friends and equals, 85, 97, *97*; right-wing anti-immigrant scrutiny and, 90, 96, 108–9, 110; Senagalese notion of *teraanga*, 97; shared belonging ("campzenship"), 92, 104; solidarity, 85, 92, 103, 106, 219n7; tea culture, 97, *97*

informal economy. *See* precarious labor

integration: overview of concept, 79–81; assimilation as normative expectation, 143; asylum seekers' commitment to, 74–78, 217–18n51; available narratives and, 81; citizenship requirements for, 218n67; as contentious term, 80–81; as contingent on reception conditions, 66, 79; deportability and, 63; facilitated by SPRAR other *seconda assistenza*, 61–62; housing for migrants denied, 140, 141; immigrant-founded villages and, 62; and the limbo of reception, 61, 77; migrants pursuing, 81, 218n70; as paradoxical expectation, 60–61, 66, 81, 142, 215n3, 216n6; as racialized term, 80; as reifying oppression, 144. *See also* hospitality; reception (*accoglienza*)

"intentional unsettling" of occupied spaces, 85, 93, 99, 100, 141

International Convention for the Safety of Life at Sea, 53

International Organization for Migration (IOM), 86

(in)visibility, politics of: acts of citizenship and, 144, 146, 149–50, 156–57; cultural texts and visibilizing of race and the colonial history, 41–42; farmworker advocacy and, 169, 178, 179, 182, 184–85, 188, 228n57; gender and, 68–69; informal camps and, 85, 86, 89, 90, 92, 96, 103, 110; and the limits of witnessing, 68–70; migrant demonstrations and hypervisibility, 4; processes of witnessing as linked to, 23; public witnessing, 69–70; reception as social and legal limbo and, 68–69; street vendors and, 116, 119, 124, 125–26, 189

—invisibilization: distinguished from the right to invisibility, 172; of farmworkers, 168, 172–73, 185, 186, 188, 189; of labor, and economic migrant–refugee binary, 125, 172; of precarious labor force, 82, 125, 168, 172; of race, and erasure of longer histories, 41; of undesirables, as normalizing emergency, 172

Iraq, 12

Isabella (interviewee/social worker), 63, 217–18n51

Isin, Engin, 142, 143

Italian studies: Senegalese-Italian cultural production and, 121; transnational, 7, 208n40

Italy: amnesties for undocumented migrants, 15, 130, 139, 172–73, 186; Fascist period, 12–13, 15, 153, 154–56, 290n42; internal rural-to-urban migration, 13; labor migration abroad, 13, 66, 126, 209n43, 218n64; Parliament, Soumahoro as African MP, 187–88; quotas for immigration, 15, 35, 168, 175; "Second Republic" period, 15, 209n57; shift in status from emigration to destination country, 12–13, 124, 126–27, 209n43, 216–17nn27; as transit country, 17–18, 210nn75–76; Unification as nation (1861), 12–13, 14, 126; visa limitations, 8, 14, 35, 175–76. *See also* anti-immigration politics; criminalization of migration; deaths of migrants; rescue and aid; shipwrecks

—colonial settlements and governance in Africa: Battle of Dogali, 153, 154; colonial subjects perceived as disorderly and threatening, 14; concentration camps and genocide in Libya, 14, 80, 100, 155, 213n46, 218n66; decolonization, 13, 15, 209n61; dehumanizing colonial propaganda, 14; emergency rule implemented, 14, 126–27, 209n50; iconography of blackness as buffoonery, 127; Italians sent to colonies and migration back and forth, 12, 37–38, 39, 92; Second Italo-Ethiopian War, 155–56; territories held, 209n49; violent realities of, 15. *See also* colonial aphasia (forgetting); colonial present; Eritrea; Ethiopia; Libya; racial logics of the colonial present; Somalia

—Italian identity (*italianità*): claim to, by migrants granted asylum, 146; dependence on migrants to define, 68, 185–86; exclusion of blackness from, 37–38, 41, 42, 126–27, 217n28; and uses of "Titanic" within diasporic communities, 52–53; whiteness, negotiation of, 126, 209n43, 217n28. *See also* citizenship—acts of citizenship; citizenship—Italian

—laws and policies: table listing, *202–4*; asylum right in the Constitution, 29; Bossi-Fini Law, 43, 62, 175, *202*; emergency rule impositions, 14, 209n50; Emergenza Nord Africa, *203*, 208n21, 215n1; Italy-Libya Friendship Treaty (2008), 36, *202*; Italy-Libya Memorandum of Understanding, 21, 36, *203*; Martelli Law, 14, 40, *202*; Minniti-Orlando Law, 81–82, *203*, 217–18n51; Operation Mare Nostrum ("Our Sea"), 7, 38, 107, 140, *203*; Operation Safe Beaches, 115–16, 125, 126, 137; passport requirement (1869), 209n52; Racial Law (1938), 13; Royal Decree 773 (registration of foreigners), 209n52; Schengen agreement signed, 14, 35, 170, 174, *202*; Security Decrees (2018 and 2019), 134, 161, *203*, 216n14, 218n67, 223n76; Turco-Napolitano Law, 175, *202*

—Southern Italy and Italians: colonial propaganda shaping dominant narratives of, 14; fraught relationship between internal South and position as a Southern European nation, 14, 126–27; postwar internal migration to Northern Italy, 13, 66; racist stereotypes of, 13, 14, 126, 217n28; unemployment rates in, 176, 228n36; and whiteness, 126, 217n28

Jackson, Michael, 47

Jacobs, Harriet, 224n28

Jaithe, Suruwa, 177, 185

Khaal, Abu Bakr, *African Titanics*, 51–52

Khosravi, Shahram, 63, 217n37

Khosravi, Shahram, and Dagmawi Yimer, *Waiting* (2020 film), 70–71

Khouma, Pap, 121. *See also* street vendor autobiographies: *Io, venditore di elefanti* (Pap Khouma) (1990)

King, Russell, 127

Krämer, Sybille, 22

Krause, Ulrike, 70

Kurdi, Alan, 7

Kyenge, Cecile, 39

Laboratorio 53, 143
labor unions: farmworkers, 137, 172, 173, 177; L'Unione Sindacale di Base, 137
Lamine (migrant narrator/interviewee, Senegal), 123–24, 128, 134
Lampedusa: boat cemetery on, 31, *32*, 51; shipwreck (3 October 2013), 7, 37, 38–39, 41, 43–48, 140–41, 153, 213nn26–27; shipwreck (18 April 2015), 7, 54; shipwreck (October 2003), 37–38, 40–42, 213n21
language(s): Arbëresche in Calabria, 62; asylum seekers practicing English, 74; camp assemblies and, 103; citizenship requirements for fluency in, 218n67; deportation documents not translated, 138; evidence of colonial ties in, 92; as imperial formation, 156; irretrievability of, 155–56; locals as switching, to avoid migrants, 68; methodology and translation, xvii, 26; translation and interpretation problems in asylum testimony, 76, 77, 217n49; translation in the "Second Generation condition," 156, 226n70. *See also* language classes (Italian)
language classes (Italian): asylum seekers' commitment to learning Italian, 74–78; CAS and, 64, 65, 74, *75*, 77; forms of witnessing featured in, 74–75; self-presentation requirements as triggering trauma, 74; SPRAR and, 62
Lazio: deaths of farmworkers, 177. *See also* Rome
Lega Braccianti (Farmworkers' League), 187
Lega Party: and closure of Riace SPRAR, 78; representation of migration in campaign, 193
Leogrande, Alessandro, 4, 56
Letta, Enrico, 38, 39
Levi, Primo, 8, 23, 36–37
Libya: in the Central Mediterranean borderzone, 8, *9*, *201*; coast guard, 35, 36, 212n14; debts for escape from, 170; detention, and torture of migrants, 71–73, 177; detention of migrants in, 19, 36, 63, 107, 208n27, 223n76; enslavement of migrants in, 50; human rights violations of migrants detained in, 36; Italian colonial-era concentration camps and genocide, 14, 80, 100, 213n46, 218n66; Italian colonial settlement and rule of (Cyrenaica), 12, 13, 14, 15, 209n49; Italy-Libya Memorandum of Understanding, 19, 21, 36, 107, 208n27; migrant memories of, 71–73, 74; numbers of migrants arriving from, 7; political turmoil and migration risks, 8, 208n27, 212n14; sea crossings from, 34, 36, 38; Sicilian fishermen captured in territorial waters of, 34, 212n8. *See also* al-Qaddafi, Muammar
literatures of migration: Arab, 51–52, 211n107; as connecting diasporic experiences, 152, 225n57; mainstream literary circuits and, 118, 121, 132, 152; national and international recognition of, 152–53; as shaping national memory, 42–43; by street vendors, 118–19, 152–53; work by Black Italian writers marginalized as, 152, 164
Lombardi-Diop, Cristina, 38
Lombroso, Cesare, 126
Louis (migrant narrator/interviewee, Mali), 74–75
Lucano, Domenico "Mimmo," 78
Lynes, Krista, 18

MAAM. *See* Metropoliz collective
McKittrick, Katherine, 50, 145
MACRO museum organization (Rome), 157, 162
Mademba, Bay. *See* street vendor autobiographies: *Il mio viaggio della speranza* (Bay Mademba)
Mafia Capitale investigation (Rome), 79, 98, 220n41
Malta, migration to, 8, 18, 34, *201*, 213n24
Mare Nostrum ("Our Sea"), 7, 38, 107, 140, *203*
Martelli, Claudio, 40
Massey, Doreen, 148
Masslo, Jerry Essan, 39–40, 177
Mbembe, Achille, 35, 70, 171
Mbengue, Rokhaya, 136
media and the emergency apparatus of migration: colonial aphasia perpetuated by, 15; colonial gaze of, 91; crisis as constant threat as framing in, 2; deservingness framed in, 16, 128, 222n52; image of the young Black male as ubiquitous in, 15; informal camps and fraught relationship with, 90, 91, 95, 100–101, 106, 109, 220n52; "invasion" narratives, 140; and precarious migration as afterlife of slavery, 49; shipwreck coverage, 32–33
media representations of migration: and critical refugee studies, 207n8; and farmworker precarity, violence as focus of, 169, 177–78; gender and sexualization, 16; migrant precarity, 177
Mediterranean: border crossing zones, 8, *9*; as global metonym for precarious migration, 191–92; as liquid archive, 33; map of, *9*; as rough sea, 34; as space of ongoing histories of diaspora and relations, 13. *See also* Central Mediterranean borderzone; deaths of migrants; sea crossings; shipwrecks

MEDU (Medici per i Diritti Umani, Doctors
    for Human Rights), 90, 108, 177
Melilla, 8, 10, *201*
Meloni, Giorgia, 199
Mengiste, Maaza, 36–37
methodology: overview of interdisciplinary
    approach, 4; "Black," capitalization of, 208n35;
    critical refugee studies, 6–7, 20–21, 145, 156–57,
    207n8; cultural texts as form of testimony,
    25; ethnographic research, 4, 21, 25, 26; for
    farmworkers, 169; field sites, and map of, 4, 5;
    for informal camps, 89, 219n10; oral history
    interviews, 21, 25–26, 27, 61, 71; positionality
    of the researcher, 10, 11, 26, 66, 74–75, 119–20;
    pseudonyms, 26; recorded vs. unrecorded
    interviews, 68; researcher as witness, 21; for
    street vendors, 119, 120; terminology, 20–21;
    testimonial network, 25; testimony as method,
    4, 21–27, 60, 119, 169, 192–93; translation and
    interpretation, xvii, 26
Metropoliz collective: art curation as survival
    strategy, 142, 162–63; artification processes
    and, 162, 163; citizenship and the right to
    the city, 157–58, 160, 161–65; daily life of, 161,
    226n77; eviction and activism, 157, 161, 162,
    163; founding narrative ("moon expedition"),
    157–58, *158*, 162; founding of, 157, 160–61;
    MAAM (Museum of the Other and
    Elsewhere), 157–60, *159–60*, 162–63, 215n93,
    226n73; MACRO museum organization and,
    157, 162. *See also* acts of citizenship
Mexico: migration to US, 191–92, 229n3;
    US "Remain in Mexico" protocols, 36
Mezzadra, Sandro, 11, 15, 21, 171, 212n19, 224n12
migrant(s): diversity of, 12, 13, 15; gender
    differentials in arrivals, 16, 210n66,
    216–17n27; as term, 21, 61
—terminology for: *beneficiari*, 80; *clandestini*
    as derogatory term, 95, 161, 172; *dublinati*,
    86, 99; *ospiti* (guests), 79–80; *ragazzi*, 80;
    *transitani*, 86; *vu cumprà* as derogatory term,
    115, 126
migrant rights: the 2013 shipwreck and
    discussions of, 38; advocacy for
    (*see* demonstrations and protests; right
    to the city); appeals to shared history,
    92–93, 219n24; asylum right in the Italian
    constitution, 29; Baobab Experience's uses
    of testimony to articulate, 109; construed
    as negotiable or inapplicable, 192; contracts
    and fair wages as right, 190; controlling and
    criminalizing mobility as upending notions
    of, 40; national borders as trumping, 194;

and the right to have rights, 93, 106; as
    struggle against racial capitalism and state
    violence, 97; as under threat of erasure, 93;
    white supremacy and denial of, 49.
    *See also* human rights; survival, politics of
migrant women: anti-trafficking NGO (Donne
    di Benin City, Palermo), 194; emergency
    imaginaries and presumption as sex
    worker or sex trafficking victims, 16, 69; as
    narrators of Invisible Guides soundwalks,
    148; numbers of, 16, 216–17n27; and
    politics of (in)visibility, 68–69, 148; as
    street vendors, 124; as temporary seasonal
    farmworkers, 170
migration: as creative act, 26; "deterrence"
    policies do not prevent, 36; as social and
    political act, 185, 212n19, 224n16.
    *See also* human rights; migrant rights
Millar, Kathleen, 117
Modou, Samb, 136
Moldova, Baobab Experience camps, 96
Molise: overview, 66; emigration from, 66;
    immigration into, prior to 2014 increase,
    66–67; and increased arrivals of migrants
    (2014), 10, 59, 67; monuments to the
    emigrant in, 66; poverty rate in, 66, 216n20;
    repurposed hotels as reception structures in,
    67–68. *See also* Campobasso
Molti Volti (Palermo), 188–89, 196
Morgenstern, Tyler, 18
Morocco: arrivals to EU via Spanish enclaves
    (Ceuta, Melilla) in, 8, 10, *201*; street
    vendors from, 124, 126; women as seasonal
    farmworkers, 170
Morrison, Toni, 26, 156
Moses, Becky, 177, 185
Moten, Fred, 11, 18, 165, 184–85, 210n79, 228n57
Movement for Black Lives, 48, 196–97
Mussolini, Benito, 153, 155

Napolitano, Giorgio, 38, 43
N'Diaye, Fatou: background of, 120; *Il cielo sopra
    Ibrahima* (pseud. Penda Thiam), 120;
    on racism, 134; Senagalese restaurant of, 120.
    *See also* Giovane Africa Edizioni
necropolitical border governance: abandonment
    as central impulse of, 82, 89; border
    externalization, 35–36, 40, 191, 210n75,
    212n16; closure or policing of safer routes, 35,
    36; crisis rhetorics and scholarship on, 19–20;
    definition of, 35; direct acts of violence of,
    35, 212n14; and grievability, 35, 44; informal
    camps and, 89, 107; risk of death as a product

of, 33, 35, 36, 212n19; testimony about, as critical act of visibility, 46; violent inaction, 99; visa limitations and immigration quotas, 35; weaponization of the environment and, 35; witnessing as fraught process in, 36–37, 212n19. *See also* border spectacle; deaths of migrants

Neilsen, Greg, 142, 143

Neilson, Brett, 15, 21, 171, 224n12

NGOs: active migrant engagement with integration, 81; migrant farmworker housing provided, 171–72; migrant testimony in reports by, 23. *See also* informal camps—Baobab Experience

Nicolini, Giusi, 38, 43

NoCap, 187

nomadism: *emergenza nomadi* (nomad emergency), 100; as threat to imperial aims, 218n66. *See also* Bedouins; Romani people; Sinti people

No Name Kitchen, 218n1

#NonSiamoPesci, 44

North Africa. *See* Central Mediterranean borderzone; Libya; Morocco; Tunisia

Nour, Amin, 153

occupied spaces: evictions (*sgomberi*) of, 98, 140–41, 220n39; history of practice in Italy, 220n39, 223n2. *See also* informal camps; Metropoliz collective

oral history. *See* methodology; testimony

organized crime: overview, 170; *caporalato* system in farmwork, 167–68, 170–71, 172, 174, 176, 227nn17,19; *caporalato*, law criminalizing (2016), 170, 186–87; and reception, 79, 98, 170, 218n57, 220n41

Ostuni, corruption in CAS, 79

Otranto, shipwreck monument in, 54–56, 56

Paik, A. Naomi, 98, 103

Pakistan, 8

Palermo: anti-trafficking NGO Donne di Benin City, 194; BarConi (Ballarò neighborhood), 196–97, 196; culture of welcoming in, 141; Molti Volti, 188–89, 196; NGO Porco Rosso, 188–89

Palestine, 8, 12, 86, 148, 194

paradoxes of proximity: geographical, 64–65, 67–68; proximal distance, 66, 67–68, 94–95; reception and, 27, 60–61, 62, 68, 73–74, 215n3, 216n6; street vendors and spatial politics, 125–26, 133–34, 137

Pasquini, Alice, 159

Paul, Ian Alan, 18

Petralia, Peter Salvatore, 148

photographs: of atrocities, 193–94; dehumanizing images of sea crossings, 50; and equation of precarious migration with invasion, 14; "media witnessing," 182–83; misciting of, 183, 209n55; reproducing the colonial gaze, 91. *See also* Bianchi and Scego, *Roma negata*; visual artworks

Piani, Silvia, 193

Piazza dell'Indipendenza, eviction of occupied building near, 86, 140–41, 223n2

Piazzale Maslax. *See* informal camps—Piazzale Maslax

Picciotto, Christian, mural of George Floyd, 196, 196–97

Pivetta, Oreste, 121, 132

place, 148

policing: Baobab Experience counter-witnessing against, 108–9; of borders, 19, 35–36, 40, 208n27, 212n16; of informal camps, 99, 100, 108; Rosarno demonstration (2010), 178; of street vendors, 119, 127–28, 137–39, 189. *See also* evictions (*sgomberi*)

Pontedera, 134

Porco Rosso, 188–89

Portelli, Alessandro, 42

postcolonial Italy. *See* Black Mediterranean; colonial aphasia (forgetting); colonial present

Pratt, Mary Louise, 13

precarious labor: agency of workers and, 117, 189; debts incurred in transit and need for income, 171, 227n6; definition of, 117, 227n6; the emergency apparatus and refugeeization of labor, 168, 172, 173–78, 186–89; emergency response as bolstering production of, 11, 82, 168, 174, 175–76; enslaved workers, Global Slavery Index, 227n19; exploitation of, as afterlife of slavery, 50; invisibilization of, 82, 125, 168, 172; "precarity trap," 172–73; racialization of certain sectors, 127; sea crossings as maintaining, 212n19; within Italian economy, 124. *See also* farmworkers and exploitation; street vendors (*venditori ambulanti*)

precarious migration: definition of, 2; "emergency" as producing, 11; farmworker exploitation and, 171; framed as the problem itself, 8; as "invasion," 14, 115, 140, 209n55; as resort when safer legal routes are unavailable, 8, 34, 36, 73, 168, 175–76; street vendors and risks of, 117, 119, 122, 127–28. *See also* asylum

Puglia: Albanian migrants to, 2, 131; deaths of
farmworkers, 177; farmworker strike (2011),
186–87; migrant farmworkers in, 170, 176

al-Qaddafi, Muammar, 36, 208n27
Qasmiyeh, Yousif M., 86
queering ethnicity, 151, 161–62

racial capitalism: and death as risk of migration,
212n19; the emergency apparatus in broader
web of, 169, 171, 186; and emergency as
condition of Black life, 11; migrant boats
as material and symbolic structures in, 49;
migrant justice as struggle against, 97
racial logics of the colonial present: overview,
6; anonymity of dead migrants, 44, 213n46;
colonial propaganda shaping narratives of, 14;
dehumanizing neglect, 79; disregard for, 16;
emergency rule repeatedly implemented, 14,
126–27, 209n50; enslavement and slave trade
as entangled with, 35, 49–50, 53, 132; exclusion
of blackness from Italian identity, 37–38, 41,
42, 126–27, 217n28; farmworker exploitation
and, 168, 169, 170–71, 172–73, 177–78; and
gender, 16; historical movements and notions
of race, 12–13, 14, 126–27, 208–9nn41–43,50;
Mademba's *Il mio viaggio* narrative on, 131–32;
racializing assemblages, 16, 116, 131, 161; risk
of death in sea crossings as revealing, 34, 36;
South/North dynamics within Italy, 13, 14,
126–27, 217n28; *strange grief* narratives and,
37–38; street vendors as racialized stereotypes
of all migrants, 125, 126, 127–28, 136–37;
whiteness, 38, 126, 131, 209n43, 217n28. *See
also* deservingness narratives; emergency
imaginaries of foreignness; gaze, colonial;
imperial formations; racism; strangers,
constructions and perceptions of foreignness
—anti-Black violence and: overview, 12; the
afterlife of slavery and, 49–50; anti-racist
demonstrations in response to, 40, 136, 177,
183; Baldwin on, 195; farmworkers as target
of, 39–40, 137, 168, 173, 177, 178, 185, 194;
murder of Idy Diene, *135–36*, 135–37; murder
of Jerry Essan Masslo, 39–40, 177; murder of
Soumaila Sacko, 137, 173, 177, 185, 194
racism: anti-immigration policies as
legitimizing, 60, 134, 136, 223n76; blackness
as excluded from Italian identity, 37–38, 41,
42, 126–27, 217n28; as connected to uses of
public space, 64, 66, 68, 125–26, 145, 146;
crisis racism, 79–80, 116; definition of, 170;
denial of structural and systemic fact of, 91,

154; experienced by CAS residents, 65–66,
68; experienced by street vendors, 124, 125,
128, 131–32, 134; farmworker activism as
responding to, 188; imperial formations
as inscribing, 91, 153–56; limitations of
citizenship as strategy against systemic,
164, 226n89; racialization of farmworker
labor, 168, 169, 170–71, 172–73, 177–78; as
structural to the agricultural sector, 168.
*See also* deservingness narratives; racial
logics of the colonial present; strangers,
constructions and perceptions of foreignness
Raggi, Virginia, 103, 140, 219n37
reception (*accoglienza*): overview as emergency
response strategy, 58–61, 63, 66–67; overview
of system, 61–62, *205*; *accoglienza*, as term
for hospitality, 59; as differentiating and
marginalizing migrants, 60, 63, 69; of Eastern
European migrants, 19; first aid, *205*; as
"humanitarian confinement," 216n8; initial
processing, 58, 59; lack of available data on, 70;
*prima accoglienza* (primary reception), 61–62;
*seconda accoglienza* (secondary reception),
61–62; as site of contested witnessing, 59; and
terms for migrants (*beneficiari, ospiti, ragazzi*),
79–80. *See also* asylum hearing (*commissione*);
hospitality; informal camps—Piazzale Maslax's
emergent forms of *accoglienza*; integration;
reception as legal and social limbo; reception
centers (*centri di accoglienza*)
reception as legal and social limbo: overview,
60–61; as abandonment, 81, 102; agency of
asylum seekers as constrained in, 70–71,
80, 82; anxiety, boredom, and uncertainty
for residents, 63, 64, 68, 70, 74, 76, 81; CAS
locations as feeding culture of suspicion,
64–65, *65*, 67–68; changes in the system, 15,
62, 63–64, 78, 81–82; conditional welcome
("hostipitality"), 60–61, 65–66, 78, 215n3,
216n6; culture of suspicion and, 64, 65–66,
68; as generating precarious labor force,
11, 82, 168, 174, 175–76; integration and, 61,
77; legal employment during, 64, 65, 175;
migrant witnessing possibilities as limited
by, 23, 68–69, 74, 75; as ongoing state of
transit, 61, 63, 71, 216n6; and paradoxes of
proximity, 27, 60–61, 62, 68, 73–74, 215n3,
216n6; political context and effects on,
60; precarious work during, 173–75; and
processing the past, 71–73; and proximal
distance, 66, 67–68; temporalities and, 70–71,
217n32; uncertain timeline, 10, 58–59, 64, 70,
71. *See also* precarious labor; waiting

reception centers (*centri di accoglienza*): overview, 59; adult education, 69, 77; choice of migrants to leave, 93, 102, 108; and the colonial present, 80; insufficient capacity to address need, 85; local employment created by, 62, 67, 68, 78; monthly reports by managers, 23; religious organizations as managing, 216n9; structures used for, 62, 67–68; urban, closures of, 228n34; visual art (mural) on exterior of, 56–57, 57. *See also* corruption in reception; language classes (Italian)
—CAS (*Centro di accoglienza straordinaria*): applications solicited for management of, 64, 67; arrival and assignment of residents to reception centers, 58, 59; arrival by bus to, 58, 59, 67, 216n21; asylum denial and dismissal from, 81, 82–83; belongings of migrants, 59; budget per resident, 64, 188, 216n14; as camp (*il campo*), migrant term for, 63, 80; corruption and, 78–79, 93, 98, 170, 187–88, 216n14, 218n57, 219n25, 220n41; daily life of residents in, 64, 81; dehumanizing neglect in, 79; as emergency structures, 58–60, 63, 216n6; establishment of (2014), 58, 63–64, 205, 215n1; local employment created by, 67, 68; locations of, as increasing suspicion, 64–65, 65, 67–68; management and capacity of, 59, 64, 215n2; "pocket money" for residents, 64, 93, 216n13, 219n25; psychologists' services available to residents, 217n43; racism experienced by residents, 65–66, 68; repurposed hotels as reception structures, 67–68; staff training, limits of, 67; and strangers, perception of, 68, 79–80; women and, 68–69, 69. *See also* reception as legal and social limbo
—SPRAR and related systems, 62, 205; as celebrated example of migrant reception, 62–63, 78; establishment of, 62, 63, 64; integration assistance as intention of, 61–62; local employment created by, 62, 78; Salvini and closure of, 78
Redeem (migrant narrator/interviewee, Nigeria), 49
refugees: *abbandono* (abandonment) and refugeeness, 82; critical refugee studies, 6–7, 20–21, 145, 156–57, 207n8; fragmentation of the figure of, 139; freedom of movement of, 174; as legal status, 21, 174; and resonances with fugitivity, 18, 210n79; and the state of exception, 6, 165, 207n12; status of, as no guarantee of stability, 174. *See also* asylum; deservingness narratives—economic migrant–refugee binary

religion: burials for the shipwrecked dead, 38, 42, 214n59; Islamophobia, 19; Mourid Brotherhood (Sufi), 125; perceptions of Italy as Christian, 73; Ramadan, 77, 95; representation of migrants' religious diversity, 130; women and politics of (in)visibility, 148. *See also* Francis (pope)
religious organizations: Caritas, 10, 144; reception centers run by, 216n9
rescue and aid: aerial photograph of, and anti-immigrant manipulation, 193–94; closure of ports to rescue vessels, 36, 108–9, 141, 220n21; criminalization of, 19, 78, 107, 115, 134, 161, 192, 223n76; the *Diciotti* (Italian Coast Guard ship) blocked in port, 108; end of state-sponsored, 107; International Convention for the Safety of Life at Sea and obligation to rescue, 53; migrants clinging to tuna net (2007), 182–83; Operation Mare Nostrum ("Our Sea"), 7, 38, 107, 140, 203; shipwreck of 3 October 2013 and global sympathy for, 7, 38, 140–41; Sicilian fishermen as rescuers, 34; Tunisian fishermen as rescuers, 34
residents, as term, 13
Riace, SPRAR in, 78
rights. *See* human rights; migrant rights
right to the city: acts of citizenship for, 116, 141, 142, 163–65; acts of citizenship, Metropoliz collective and, 157–58, 160, 161–65; and people's ability to document a history, 158. *See also* acts of citizenship; Guide Invisibili; (in)visibility, politics of
Rigo, Enrica, 168
Rio Grande, 194
Robinson, Cedric, 35, 212n11
Roitman, Janet, 4
Romania, migrants from, 66–67
Romani people: and the *emergenza nomadi* (nomad emergency), 100; exclusion and discrimination against, 12–13, 160; history of, 85; in the Metropoliz collective, 157, 160, 162; in Molise, 66; shared belonging among ("campzenship"), 92
Rome: Mafia Capitale investigation, 79, 98, 220n41; moratorium on migrant arrivals to, 140, 141; reception (*accoglienza*) insufficiencies in, 85; solidarity in informal camps (Baobab Experience), 85, 92, 103, 106, 219n7; water resources for migrant camps, 84, 100, 218n1. *See also* acts of citizenship; demonstrations and protests; evictions (*sgomberi*); imperial formations; informal camps; occupied spaces; tourists and tourism

Romeo, Caterina, 41

Rosales, Rocío, 117, 125

Rosarno: deaths of farmworkers, 177; legal immigration status of farmworkers in, 177; migrant-led demonstrations (January 2010), 177–78, 179, 181, 182, 185; murder of farmworker Soumaila Sacko, 137, 173, 177, 185, 194; strike following worker deaths, 177. *See also* Calabria; farmworkers and exploitation; farmworker representation and advocacy

Rosi, Gianfranco, *Fire at Sea* (*Fuocoammare*, 2016), 23, 181

Rwanda, UK attempts to send asylum seekers to, 36

Sacko, Soumaila, murder of, 137, 173, 177, 185, 194; demonstrations in the wake of, 137–38, *138*, 187

Sagnet, Yvan, 187

Saied, Kais, 199

Salvatore (interviewee/reception center manager), 64, 74

Salvini, Matteo: anti-immigrant rhetoric, 115, 126, 130; arrest of Lucano and closure of Riace SPRAR, 78; camp humor lampooning, 96; closure of urban reception centers, 228n34; criminalization of street vendors (Operation Safe Beaches), 115–16, 125, 126, 137; Italian language requirement for citizenship, 218n67; kidnapping charges, 108; and the murder of Idy Diene, *135–36*, 135–37; #PortiChiusi (Closed Ports) campaign, 108, 220n61; and racism becoming overt, 134, 136, 223n76; reduction of reception budget, 216n14; Security Decrees (2018 and 2019), 134, 161, *203*, 216n14, 218n67, 223n76. *See also* criminalization of migration; Lega Party

Samanta (migrant narrator/interviewee, Nigeria), 69

Sangare, Ousmane, 167

Sarr, Seydou, 181

Saucier, P. Khalil, 185–86

Scego, Igiaba: and acts of citizenship disrupting normative notions of belonging, 152, 154, 156–57, 163–64, 225n60; as *Afropean* writer, 225n57; on colonial aphasia (forgetting), 26, 41, 150–52, 153–56; marginalization of, 164; on potential complicity in colonial violence, 155–56; on the power of creative work, 42–43; reception of, 152–53, 164, 225n57; as "second generation" (G2) Somali-Italian writer, 41, 150, 151–52; on the shipwreck of 3 October 2013, 41, 153; on *Titanic* as name game in Somalia, 52–53; and transhistorical diasporic connections, 152, 225n57. Works: *Adua*, 52, 53, 215n85; *Cassandra a Mogadiscio* (*Cassandra in Mogadishu*), 152; "Cosa fare con le tracce scomode del nostro passato" (*Internazionale*), 151; *La linea del colore* (*The Color Line*), 225n57; *La mia casa è dove sono* (*My Home Is Where I Am*) (memoir), 40–41, 150–52, 153, 154, 155–56; *Roma negata* (collaboration with photographer Rino Bianchi), 151, 153–55, 156–57. *See also* acts of citizenship

Scorsese, Martin, 181

sea crossings: closure of Italian ports to rescue ships, 36, 108–9, 141, 220n21; death tallies, 31–32, 36, *201*; debts resulting from, 170, 171, 227n6; as haunting survivors, 48–49; hotlines for, 194; as inextricably tied to slave trade, 35, 49–50, 53, 132; as part of much longer journey, 32; as personal evidence of survival, 48; as site of contested witnessing, 33; visual art (mural) of, 56–57, *57*. *See also* boats; deaths of migrants; rescue and aid; shipwrecks

Séba, Kemi, 103

*seconde generazioni* ("second generations" or "G2"): construed as foreign in the city of their birth, 151, 152; defined as term, 223n8; naturalized citizenship as nearly impossible for, 142, 224n10; physical presence of, as reshaping Italian notions of belonging, 151; translation as condition of, 156, 226n70. *See also* citizenship; Scego, Igiaba

Second Tree (NGO, Greece), 194, 218n70

Segre, Andrea: *Come un uomo sulla terra* (*Like a Man on Earth*) (2008 documentary), 217n42; *Il sangue verde* (*Green Blood*) (2010 documentary), 178–79

Seihon, Koudous, 179, 181, 182, 183

Sellman, Johanna, 25, 211n107

Senegal: French colonial rule of, and subsequent migration, 127, 131, 222n41; migrant sea crossings from, 51; migration to Italy, history of, 124–25, 127, 129–30, 131–32, 136–37; street vendors in, 117, 124; *teraanga*, 97. *See also* street vendors (*venditori ambulanti*)

Senegalese-Italian cultural production, 120, 121, 221n12. *See also* street vendor autobiographies

Serasini, Luca, 44

Sestini, Massimo, aerial photograph of migrant boat, 193

sex work: gendered, racialized assumptions about migrants and, 16, 69; as precarious labor, 227n6

Sharpe, Christina, 45, 49, 154, 186, 214n67. *See also* wake work

shipwrecks: and the Central Mediterranean borderzone as treacherous, 8; and criminal charges, 54–55, 213n26; and declaration of emergency, 7; government abandonment of migrant vessels at sea, 8, 34; Italian coast guard boat ramming, 54–55; repeating spectacle of, 8, 32–33; *Titanic*, invocations of, 51–54; victim's names, 31–32, 44; the wreckage and bodies not recovered, 53, 54, 215n90. *See also* boats; death of migrants—migrant-centered elegies; death of migrants—state funerals as strange grief; rescue and aid; sea crossings
—incidents: 28 March 1997, 54–55; 17 October 2003, 37–38, 40–42, 213n21; 3 October 2013, 7, 37, 38–39, 41, 43–48, 140–41, 153, 213nn26–27; 11 October 2013, 38, 213n24; 18 April 2015, 7, 54; 26 February 2023 (Cutro), 8, 43; June 2023, 215n90; *Titanic* (1912; submersible visiting in 2023), 53

Shuman, Amy, 130, 163–64

Sicily: emergency rule in response to Fasci Siciliani (1890s), 14; fishermen at risk of capture by Libyan forces, 34, 212n8; fishermen rescuing migrants, 34; informal camps in, and evictions, 101–2; migrant farmworkers and, 171; reception centers in, 93, 219n25. *See also* Italy—Southern Italy and Italians; Lampedusa; Palermo

Sigona, Nando, 92

Sinti people: and the *emergenza nomadi* (nomad emergency), 100; exclusion and discrimination against, 12–13; history of, 85

Sitze, Adam, 210n74

social contract, consequences of smashing, 40

social media, 108

Somalia: Italian colonial rule of, and erasure of history, 37–38, 41, 151–52, 209n49; Italian state funeral for shipwreck (2003), 37–38, 40–42, 213n21; migrants from, 14, 37–38, 63, 151–52; "Titanic" as name game among migrants from, 52–53

Sontag, Susan, 8, 193

Sordi, Vittorio, 158–59

Soumahoro, Aboubakar, 187–88, 189

soundwalks. *See* Guide Invisibili soundwalks

South America: migrants from, 157; and migration to US, 191–92, 229n3

South Asia, migrant farmworkers from, 84–85, 167

Southern European nations, as transit countries, 17–18, 210n75

Spain: enslaved workers in, 227n19; land arrivals via colonial holdings Melilla and Ceuta, 8, 10, *201*; migrant farmworkers, 170; policing migration via colonial holdings, 10; sea arrivals via Canary Islands, 8, 10, 51, *201*; and the slave trade, 35; as transit country, 17–18, 210nn75–76; in Western Mediterranean migration zone, 8

spectacle of suffering, 90–92

spectacle. *See* border spectacle

SPRAR. *See* reception centers (*centri di accoglienza*)—SPRAR and related systems

Squire, Vicki, 18

Stefanelli, Marco, 143

Stierl, Maurice, 47

Stoler, Ann, 15, 131, 155

strange grief: definition of, 34; visual art as objects of, 55. *See also* deaths of migrants—state funerals as strange grief

strangers, constructions and perceptions of foreignness: CAS as critical to production of, 68, 79–80; claiming the right to be present despite, 92; and culture and identity as fixed vs. in flux, 141; as dominant narrative, 32; erasure of longer histories and, 13, 92–93; and European and Italian identity, 68; legal status associated with moral character, 95; migrants framed as guests (*ospiti*), 79–80; projection of, 12, 66, 216n18; and racialization of migrants, 79–80, 218nn64,66; strange encounters, 60, 95, 212n5; and strange grief, 34; and the strange grief of state funerals, 38, 39; strangerness (S. Ahmed), 38, 212n5; white sight and, 66. *See also* colonial aphasia (forgetting); racism

Stra Vox (NGO), 195–96

street vendors (*venditori ambulanti*): overview, 115–19; and adequate witnesses, 123–24, 128; Bangladeshi vendors, 124, 137–39; and Baobab Experience (Piazzale Maslax), 105, 137–39; and colloquial terms for foreignness, 126; and COVID-19 pandemic, 223n77; criminalization of (Operation Safe Beaches), 115–16, 125, 126, 137; crisis racism and, 116; as cultural icon in imaginaries of foreignness, 116–17, 124, 125–26, 127, 137, 146; and deservingness narratives, 116, 137; diversity of backgrounds and goods, 124; as figure of transit, 117; Moroccan vendors, 124, 126; murder of Idy Diene, 135–37, *135–37*;

street vendors *(continued)*
policing of, 119, 127–28, 137–39, 189; the politics of (in)visibility and, 116, 119, 124, 125–26, 189; precarious labor, 117, 125, 127–28; precarious migration and, 117, 119, 122, 127–28; as racialized stereotype conflated with migration, 126, 127–28, 136–37; racism experienced by, 124, 125, 128, 131–32, 134; Senegal–Italy migration history and, 124–25, 127, 129–30, 131–32, 136–37; spatial politics and paradoxes of proximity, 125–26, 133–34, 137; suspicion of, 125, 126, 127–28, 146, 221n10; testimonial transactions and, 117, 118–19, 122–24, 132–34; tourists, interactions with, 119–20; as transhistorical figure, 124; *vu cumprà* as slang term for, 115, 126; as witnesses of everyday life, 117–18, 119, 128

street vendor autobiographies: *Il mio viaggio della speranza* (Bay Mademba) (2011), *118*; overview, 118–19, 120–21; audience as Italian reader-consumers, 118, 121, 123, 129, 132, 134; audience as migrants, 134; authored "a quattro mani" (collaborative process), 118, 121, 132–33; collective ownership of, 133; didacticism in, 129, 132; local circulation of, 118–19, 120, 121, 133–34, 223n75; publisher of, 119, 134; racist encounters in, 125, 131–32; Senagalese identity foregrounded in, 122, 130, 152–53; as subverting dominant neoliberal narratives of citizenship and foreignness, 119, 121–23, 128–32, 139; and testimonial transactions, 118–19, 122–23, 132–34; as transruptive, 123; and trust, building of, 122–23. *See also* Giovane Africa Edizioni (Young Africa Editions) (book publisher)

street vendor autobiographies: *Io, venditore di elefanti* (Pap Khouma) (1990), 125, 129–30, 131; as collaboration with Oreste Pivetta, 121, 132; as mainstream literature, 118, 121, 132; on policing of street vendors, 119; on selling one's culture, 129

Sulayman (migrant narrator/interviewee, Guinea), 65, 68, 69, 75–77, 81, 82

surveillance: along the Eastern Mediterranean route, 36; biometric, 7; and dehumanization of sea crossing, 50; Frontex, 8; raids and inspections of informal camps, 99, 100, 108–9

survival, politics of: definition of, 86; Metropoliz collective and, 142, 162–63; Piazzale Maslax (informal camp) and, 86, 92, 106, 219n7; solidarity politics (*politica solidale*), 219n7

Sy, Alassane, 179, *180*

Syria: migration from, 7, 8, 148, 208n21; refugees in Türkiye, 35–36

Tekle, Zemede, 39

tellable narratives, 22, 79, 163–64, 179

testimonial transactions: and acts of citizenship, 143–44, 145, 148, 149, 151, 163–64, 165–66; asylum seekers' legal testimony as, 59; Baobab Experience and, 108; as relational, 23–24, 193–94; street vendors and, 118–19, 132–34

*testimonio*, 24

testimony: as countering violence and its erasure from public memory, 23; cultural texts as form of, 25; definition of, 21; emergent property of, 23–24; as evidentiary, 23–24; as intersubjective, 148; oral history, 25; as political, 24; as relational, 23–24, 193–94. *See also* testimonial transactions; testimony, migrant-authored and -centered; witnessing

testimony as method, 4, 21–27, 60, 119, 169, 192–93

testimony, migrant-authored and -centered: overview, 22; and "adequate witnesses," 23, 107–8, 123–24, 187; definition of, 22; the emergency apparatus as obscuring, 4; as enacting community, 103–7, *105*; finding new forms of testimonial narratives, 23, 211n107; and hope, 74–75; as limited by the limbo of reception, 23, 68–69, 74, 75; as political weapon, 24; rupturing emergency logics, 53–54; testimonial networks, 25, 134; *testimonio*, 24; and trauma, representations of, 22, 71, 217n35. *See also* Guide Invisibili; informal camps—Piazzale Maslax as key site of witnessing; Metropoliz collective; street vendors

—as changing public perceptions: overview, 24–25; acts of citizenship as, 144–45, 148–50, 151, 154–56, 161–63, 225n35; art curation as survival strategy, 142, 162–63; Baldwin on, 24–25, 109, 195, 196; Baobab Experience's press conferences and, 109; elegies and, 42–43, 44–46; and the failures of empathy, 24, 148, 225n35; *Titanic* invocations, 51–54; visual art and, *196*, 196–97; wordplay, 196

—as process for imagining beyond "crisis": overview, 24; acts of citizenship and, 165–66; camp residents and, 93, 104; as making change possible, 24, 194; subversion of the economic migrant-refugee binary, 119,

121–23, 128–32, 139; visual art and, 56–57; witnessing limits and possibilities, 54–57. *See also* farmworker representation and advocacy—Rosarno demonstration (January 2010); informal camps—Piazzale Maslax's emergent forms of *accoglienza*

Theodore, Nik, 127

Tianjin, China, Italian colonial possession, 209n49

Tiburtina Station, *86, 95. See also* informal camps—Piazzale Maslax

Ticktin, Miriam, 43–44, 217n32, 220n52

*Titanic* (James Cameron, 1997), 53

Toninelli, Danilo, 115

Torchin, Leshu, 181

tourists and tourism: and art curation as survival strategy (Metropoliz/MAAM), 162–63; artification and, 162, 163; migrant-led tours, 144 (*see also* Guide Invisibili); real estate campaigns hawking homes to, 141; Rome and "Destination Italy" romanticization, 144–45, 154; and street vendors, 119–20

transit: and the colonial present, 18; Europe itself as site of, 86; as form of fugitivity, 18; and migrant agency, 18; as moving concept, 18; narratives of and narratives in, 134; as political shifts, 19; of street vendor narratives, 123; *transitanti* (people in transit) as term for migrants, 86. *See also* transit migration

transit migration, IOM and EU definition of, 86, 218–19n6

transnational justice movements, naming of victims as practice in, 47–48

trauma: as affecting reception period, 71–73; asylum testimony and, 71; bodily impact of, 44; evictions of asylum seekers and, 100; and narrative, 22, 151, 181, 226n4, 228n43; as one representation of migrant-centered testimony, 22; and reception staff, lack of training, 67; self-presentation in language classes as triggering, 74; witnessing as potentially retraumatizing, 128

Tunisia: in the Central Mediterranean borderzone, *8, 9, 201*; fishermen of, rescuing migrants at sea and burying the dead, 34; numbers of migrants arriving from, 7; policing and abandoning migrants, 49, 107

Türkiye: agreements with EU to detain migrants, 19, 35–36, 212n16; in Eastern Mediterranean migration zone, 8; enslaved workers in, 227n19; migrant deaths in, 7; migration to Greece from, 10

Tuscany. *See* Florence; street vendors (*venditori ambulanti*)

Ukraine, refugees from Russian invasion, 19, 96, 220n68

unaccompanied minors, 62

undocumented migrants: denial of asylum claim resulting in dismissal from CAS as, 81, 82–83; as migrant farmworkers, 170, 171; periodic amnesty for, 15, 130, 139, 172–73, 186. *See also* precarious labor

L'Unione Sindacale di Base, 137

United Against Refugee Deaths, *47, 47*

United Kingdom (Britain): asylum deal with Rwanda, 36; asylum seekers imprisoned on barges, 36, 194; as colonializing power, 15, 209n61

United Nations, Libyan human rights violations, 36

United Nations High Commissioner for Refugees (UNHCR): and non-European asylum seekers in Italy (pre-1990), 40; protocols for determining refugee status, 22; use of testimonials, 23; and Vietnamese refugees, 50; web portal for emergencies, 17

United States: Black US citizens shot by police, 49, 195; confederate monuments, toppling of, 151; Darién Gap as site of migration to, 191–92, 229n3; the emergency imaginary and, 17, 210n73; farmworker deaths due to extreme temperatures, 228n41; farmworker visas (H-2A), 170; as global north destination, 17; governors bussing asylum seekers to distant cities, 67, 194; integration and assimilation in, 66, 80, 144; Japanese American internment, 216n21; migration in US-Mexico borderlands framed as a problem, 2; police brutality and, 49, 176, 195; "Remain in Mexico" protocols, 36; September 11 memorial in Rome, 156; the *Titanic* shipwreck site protected by, 53; Vietnam invasion by, 222n52; and the weaponization of the desert, 35

Universal Declaration of Human Rights, 18

Vang, Ma, 73–74, 145, 161, 210n79

Varotsos, Costas, *The Landing: Work Dedicated to a Migrant Humanity (L'approdo: Opera all'umanità migrante)*, 54–56, *56*

Varoufakis, Yanis, 103

Veltroni, Walter, 37–38, 213n21

Venice: legal residency granted for good character, 78; and the slave trade, 35

Venice Biennale (2019), *Barca Nostra* (Büchel), 54, *55*, 55–56
Ventimiglia, 108–9
Verano Cemetery, *86*, 96, 110
Vietnam, "boat refugees," 50; US invasion of, and deservingness narratives, 222n52
violence. *See* abandonment of migrants; farmworkers and exploitation; necropolitical border governance; racial logics of the colonial present—anti-Black violence; shipwrecks
visas: the global north and "permanent temporary" farmworkers, 169–70; Italy and limitations on, 8, 14, 35, 175–76
visual artworks: as changing public perceptions, *196*, 196–97; "image operations" shaping ideas about migration, 18; as objects of strange grief, 55; witnessing limits and possibilities, 54–57, *57*. *See also* photographs
voyeurism: as colonial gaze, 91–92; crisis voyeurism, 90; informal camps and, 90–91, 108

waiting: as active time, 71, 217n37; as key element of "crisis" urgency, 70, 217n32; reception as period of imminent encounter, 70. *See also* reception as legal and social limbo
wake work: and the Black Mediterranean, 48, 155, 214n63; definition of, 45; dehumaning violence of, 154, 185–86, 190; the farmworkers' camp and, 186; and mourning, 45–46; transit within Europe and, 214n67; and urban geographies, 196–97. *See also* Sharpe, Christina
Walcott, Rinaldo, 54, 56
Walia, Harsha, 4–5, 19
Weigel, Sigrid, 22
Weiwei, Ai, 215n93
West Africa, migration from, 1, 15, 25, 49, 71, 89, 117, 148, 179, 181, 216–17n27. *See also* Senegal
Western Mediterranean borderzone, 8, 9, 51, *201*
Wheatley, Abby, 86
whiteness, negotiation of: overview, 38; Albanian migrants and, 131; Italians in relation to global north, 209n43; and South/North split of Italy, 126, 217n28
white supremacy, 49. *See also* colonial present; gaze, colonial
Whitlock, Gillian, 25, 106, 122, 123
Wilderson, Frank, 144
witnessing: for abolition, 195; adequate witnesses, 23, 107–8, 123–24, 187; advocacy and, 178, 228n43; and audience, real or imagined, 21; autobiographical texts as, 75; contested, 4,

33, 59; as contingent, 193–94; docudrama, 179, 181; ethics of, 107, 128–29, 163, 165, 181, 182, 187, 194, 207n8; of everyday life, 90, 128; fugitive witnessing, 45; incomplete, 8; language classes and, 74–75; layered forms of, 155, 179, 181, 182, 185; and the limits of the human, 101; necropolitical border governance and fraught process of, 36–37, 212n19; public demonstrations and, 4; public witnessing, 69–70; relations of, 105, 154–55, 169, 181, 187; virtual witnesses, 44–45; visual artworks and, 54–57. *See also* autobiographical writing; Guide Invisibili soundwalks; informal camps—Piazzale Maslax as key site of witnessing; (in)visibility, politics of; media representations of migration; methodology; testimony; trauma; voyeurism
—limits on: asylum processes, 82; during reception, 23, 68–69, 74, 75; the emergency apparatus as operating through, 110–11; evictions of camps, 101; farmworker advocacy and the limits of (self-)representation, 169, 172, 185, 226–27n4; and the politics of (in)visibility, 68–70
—as reifying crisis framings: alignment with available narratives, 23, 24, 79; colonial propaganda and racial hierarchy, 14; designation of emergency, 22–23; *Fire at Sea* (film) and, 23, 181; forms of, 23; narrative tellability, 22, 79; Operation Safe Beaches and, 115. *See also* asylum process—legal testimony of asylum seekers; media and the emergency apparatus of migration
women: Italian seasonal workers (*mondine*), 85. *See also* migrant women
World War II: "boat refugees," 50; and the end of Italian colonial rule, 15; Japanese American internment, 216n21; Senegalese recruitment into French army, 127
wrecks. *See* shipwrecks

Yancy, George, 91
Yimer, Dagmawi, 153; *Asmat* (2014), 44–48, *45*, 50; *Come un uomo sulla terra (Like a Man on Earth)* (2008 documentary), 217n42
Yimer, Dagmawi and Shahram Khosravi, *Waiting* (2020 film), 70–71
Yousef (migrant narrator/interviewee, the Gambia), 26, 110, 138, 173–76, *177*, 185
Yugoslavia (former), migration to Italy from, 14

Zerihun, Eden Getachew, 44–45

Founded in 1893,
UNIVERSITY OF CALIFORNIA PRESS
publishes bold, progressive books and journals
on topics in the arts, humanities, social sciences,
and natural sciences—with a focus on social
justice issues—that inspire thought and action
among readers worldwide.

The UC PRESS FOUNDATION
raises funds to uphold the press's vital role
as an independent, nonprofit publisher, and
receives philanthropic support from a wide
range of individuals and institutions—and from
committed readers like you. To learn more, visit
ucpress.edu/supportus.